LOOKING OUTWARD

PART I

A Voice From The Grave

The Federal Prison System From The Inside

By
Robert F. Stroud

Looking Outward, LLC

A Limited Liability Company Of The

State Of Missouri, License Number: LC1323629

435 East Walnut Street

Springfield, Missouri 65806

(417) 619-4939

Copyright © 2014 by Looking Outward, LLC

ISBN: 978-0-9898137-4-7

LCCN: 2014914370

Author: Robert F. Stroud

Cover Design by: Deborah DeMan

Outline Edited by: Thomas E. Gaddis

Part I Edited by: Pam Eddings

Layout by: Harold Scherler

Prepared for Publication by: C. Dudley Martin and JE Cornwell

Table of Contents

INTRODUCTION

An interview with C. Dudley Martin, the man who interviewed

Robert F. Stroud (The Birdman of Alcatraz) for the last time.

Robert Stroud, the federal prisoner portrayed by actor Burt Lancaster in the 1962 movie "Birdman of Alcatraz," became known all over the world for his erudite treatises on how to make sick birds healthy.

What few people realize is that after Stroud wrote his bird texts, the man who had a consuming curiosity and a passion for scientific inquiry spent years writing about two other subjects dear to his heart: himself and the federal prison system.

For years, prison officials tried to suppress Stroud's secret writings, fearing public exposure of his allegations of prison guards' brutality and his graphic depictions of rampant sex behind bars. Now, two of the inmate's manuscripts may soon be headed for the public auction block.

The unpublished, handwritten manuscripts reveal Stroud's abusive upbringing, his homosexuality and his fervent criticism of the prison system. They also march somewhat in step, if not in political concert, with the tradition of powerful prison writing ranging from Alexander Solzhenitsyn's "The Gulag Archipelago" to Martin Luther King Jr.'s "Letter from a Birmingham Jail" and Eldridge Cleaver's "Soul on Ice."

This fall, Stroud's former lawyer plans to sell the inmate's final two manuscripts -- "Bobby," an autobiography of his youth, and "Looking Outward," the prison history -- through a New York literary auction house.

Prison officials say they blocked publication of the two works because the inmate's writings were lewd and they glorified criminals. Stroud sued the federal Bureau of Prisons in 1962 over the publication ban, saying his First Amendment rights were being violated, but died a year later before a court ruling could be issued.

His lawyer said Stroud's writings were hardly worthy of the government's angst.

"There's nothing salacious here. Stroud was quite clinical in his descriptions of sex," said Charles Dudley Martin of Springfield, Mo., an attorney who represented Stroud during a standoff with federal prison officials in the early 1960s over the inmate's free-speech rights.

Martin, an administrator of Stroud's estate, intends to auction legal files from Stroud's suit against the prison system as well as the late author Thomas Gaddis' notes for his best-selling book, "Birdman of Alcatraz," which the late director John Frankenheimer made into a movie.

In the "Bobby" manuscript, Stroud wrote a short autobiography about his childhood and adolescence in Metropolis, Ill., including the self-discovery that he was gay. "Looking Outward" is the inmate's five-volume history of the U.S. prison system from colonial times to the creation of the federal Bureau of Prisons in the early 1930s.

Stroud's later writing was the voice of a self-righteous, angry man who felt that he should be released because he had atoned for his misdeeds through his innovative bird experiments.

Both works are "handwritten in an accountant's hand, using the most precise writing you've ever seen, using a good ink pen on sheets of legal-size paper," Martin said. "There are some corrections where he lines through something and begins anew. There are no erasures or blackouts. He thought a lot before he wrote."

Only a handful of researchers, writers and others have read the Stroud manuscripts. Bay Area author Jolene Babyak, who wrote a biography of Robert Stroud, examined the inmate's prison history manuscript about 20 years ago.

"A big portion of it was pornographic: basically, loveless sex between prisoners," said Babyak, the daughter of a former associate warden of Alcatraz.

"A couple of hundred pages are polished. He has a lot of anecdotes about prison. He loved to shock people. . . . He had a lofty opinion of himself. He's very casual about violence, very casual about killing."

A Different Kind of Birdman

Documentary filmmaker Nina Seavey read the manuscripts in the 1990s and said, "The story of Robert Stroud is not the story of Burt Lancaster being rehabilitated by the prison system. This is basically a descent into the mind of a man who is both a genius and quite mad. In some ways, the work is impenetrable. But having said that, it's fascinating!"

Stroud went to prison in 1909 at the age of 19 for shooting to death a bartender in Alaska during a brawl over a woman. Convicted of manslaughter, he was first sent to McNeil Island Federal Penitentiary in Washington State.

He was then transferred to Leavenworth, Kan., where he stabbed a guard to death in the mess hall. Stroud was only 26. During three decades at Leavenworth, he earned the reputation as a smiling, psychopathic killer. He was convicted of murder and sentenced to be hanged, but President Woodrow Wilson commuted the sentence to life imprisonment.

Stroud bred canary birds for 22 years at Leavenworth. He described and measured their illnesses. He went on to find remedies that applied not only to canary birds but also to domestic birds, poultry and wild birds.

With only a grade school education, he taught himself to use a microscope and a microteme (a device that makes a thin slice of animal or vegetable tissue so that its matter can be examined by a microscope). He read scientific journals in German and Spanish with the help of a dictionary.

Stroud submitted his findings to scientific journals and wrote two books on birds, including his most famous work, "Stroud's Digest of the Diseases of Birds."

But his success rattled prison officials. In 1942, Leavenworth's warden took away his instruments, saying they could be used to make alcohol, and transferred him to Alcatraz.

No Birds at Alcatraz

Contrary to popular belief, Stroud was prevented from raising birds on Alcatraz. Stripped of his birds and scientific instruments, the gaunt prisoner with a hawk-like forehead spent 17 years on "the Rock" in the middle of San Francisco Bay. There, he was kept in solitary confinement -- at first in an isolation cell, and later in Alcatraz's hospital wing -- not permitted to speak unless spoken to by guards.

"Stroud was used to being alone, but not without books and scientific instruments," said Martin. "But he didn't perish or self-destruct. He put his time at Alcatraz to good use. He not only survived, he prospered."

Perhaps. But former guards at Alcatraz recall the Birdman as a ruthless killer who threatened to harm anyone who got in his way. They also say that he was depressed on Alcatraz and tried to kill himself at least once.

"Bobby," written in first person, was the nickname that Stroud's mother had given her only son. The limited autobiography covers his life as a young boy and teenager, before he went to prison. It offers a glimpse into his violent relationship with his abusive, alcoholic father. And he also relates his first intimate experiences with men as a teen.

In "Looking Outward," Stroud attempted to write a critical history of the U. S. prison system. He studied the published accounts from colonial times about federal prisoners who were kept in county jails and state prisons. He interviewed inmates who had served time at federal penitentiaries, recording their detailed descriptions of mistreatment. And he interviewed some prison guards.

In one chapter, Stroud wrote a detailed description of sex between men in prison. In another, he wrote of guards beating prisoners with whips and canes.

Another chapter details the construction of Leavenworth Penitentiary in the early 1900s. The brick prison was built by inmates, who first made sod huts on the Kansas prairie to house themselves during the winter.

Prompted New Rules

Stroud had received permission from the warden at Alcatraz to write a penal history, but bureaucrats in Washington, D.C., balked when they reviewed his manuscript. The top brass hastily created new rules for inmate authors, forbidding the publication of any inmate's work that was obscene, criticized the prison system, or glorified crime.

Stroud was transferred in 1959 to a federal prison for chronically ill inmates in Springfield, Mo., where he died in 1963. Martin, the Missouri attorney, was named administrator of Stroud's estate and gained custody of the manuscripts in lieu of compensation for his legal services. Martin tried to hawk the prison history manuscript to publishers, but they expressed little or no interest.

"Some said it was too long. Others were afraid of being sued for libel because Stroud wrote about living people -- corrupt prison officials, sadistic guards and brutalized prisoners," Martin said.

"Others said no one was interested in the prison system, or that history doesn't sell. Some of the great stories in literature are prison stories. I guess they hadn't read 'The Count of Monte Cristo' or 'The Gulag Archipelago,'" Martin said.

Martin insists that Stroud's observations on the U.S. prison system are still relevant today.

"I think it's a work of great social value. We're still trying to answer the questions that Stroud raised," he said. "The number of Americans incarcerated is greater than ever before. It costs a lot of money to incarcerate people. What do we get in return for it? Do we get a better person than what went in, or a worse person?"

PROLOGUE

"The Purpose of This Work" by Robert F. Stroud

The undertaking of this work was inspired by the following quotation:

"There is no reason for not trying to rehabilitate those who can be helped. That is the purpose of the prison. More than half of the 70,000 men and women who left prison last year will be back within five years. That is a terrible and startling fact. We must find a better way to protect the public."[1]

The above-quoted statement, coming as it does from Mr. Bennett, whom Mr. Sondem described in the article[2] as being "one of the foremost penologists of our times," and who the Writer has frequently described as being the *most vacuous and shallow-minded executive it has ever been his misfortune to meet,* is a far more amazing and startling than the mere fact that more than fifty percent of the persons released from prison today return to crime. For it is an admission of failure, a most startling admission of failure, of a terrible failure that has contributed to the ruination of many thousands of lives and the wastage of hundreds of millions of tax dollars. And the one living man most responsible for that failure, so far as Federal Prisons are concerned, is none other than Mr. James V. Bennett.

 Whenever any bureaucrat admits that his policies could ever once have been wrong, that is news of the first quality. When Mr. Bennett admits, after twenty years, that the purpose of imprisonment is the rehabilitation of the individual inmate, rather than the creation of a gigantic W.P.A. for the personal aggrandizement of its Director, Mr. Bennett, that is news that should be shouted from every housetop in America, but that is not all.

What private enterprise could admit a more than fifty-percent failure in the accomplishment of the purpose for which it was organized and still continue in business? What hospital could admit a fifty-percent failure in the treatment of its patients and still enjoy public confidence? Even institutions devoted exclusively to the treatment of such difficult and hopeless conditions as cancer, poliomyelitis, leprosy, and insanity are able to make a far less pessimistic showing.

During the same twenty-year period, with far less funds to waste per patient, the medical profession has practically completed the conquest of bacterial infections and has made remarkable strides against most other disease entities. During the Writer's lifetime it has

---

1.   James V. Bennett, as quoted by Frederic Sondem Jr., in Prison Without A Wall; Rocky Mountain Magazine, July 31, 1949. Copyright by Denver Post. Condensed in Readers Digest. September, 1949, pp.73-77.
2.   ibid. p. 75

increased the life expectancy of males born in the United States from thirty-one years to sixty-five years, and of females from thirty-three years to almost seventy years. But what most persons do not know is that for twenty years, from 1910 to 1930, the vast improvements made in public health were paralleled by equally arresting improvements in the field of penology, and it is the story of that development that the Writer proposes to tell and analyze in these pages, a development that was ruthlessly destroyed by a group of theoretical penologists who were responsible for the Federal Prison Bureau and who employed the vast powers vested in that agency to set back the cause of sane and humane prison management by at least one hundred years with an enormous destruction of the human potential entrusted to their care.

The real measure of this colossal failure in blasted hopes and ruined lives can never be tabulated, but a glance at the cost in dollars should be enlightening. The Writer does not have the data at hand, but any free person desiring to do so can obtain the Annual Reports of the Federal Prison Bureau from the Bureau of Documents, Government Printing Office, Washington, D. C.

An analysis of the figures contained therein – including appropriations and grants from other Federal Agencies – will show that during the last twenty years, every person convicted of a crime against the United States could have been pensioned at ten dollars per day for every day actually served in prison at an enormous saving to the taxpayers. Which is not to suggest that we place a premium on crime by pensioning our criminals, although that would be no more foolish than many of the other things done during the last twenty years, or some of the things being proposed today – like paying out hundreds of millions and billions of dollars to maintain prices which are higher than they should be and dumping food in the ocean while men suffer for lack of proper nourishment.

A careful study of this same material – material not available to the Writer as a Federal prison inmate, will show that during this same period, recidivism among Federal releases has increased more than one hundred percent; that the amount of money expended upon the health of Federal prisoners has increased more than twenty-fold; yet, the death rate in Federal prisons, taken as a whole, has increased three-fold, and the insanity rate has increased more than twenty-fold over what it was forty years ago.

In the light of these facts and the monumental failure of which they are indicative, a failure predicted by the Writer many years ago[3] it has been thought advisable to make a complete review and analysis of the development of the Federal Prison System from the time of the passage of the First Crime Act in 1790 to the establishment of the Federal Prison Bureau in 1930, in the hope that such a work may point the way to a better system which may at some future day be *evolved* – notice that the Writer does not say *created*. For, as John Buckle so aptly pointed out almost a century ago,[4] social advancement is always a matter of slow growth, not something that can be handed down by fiat from above.

---

3   *Kansas City Star*, Sunday, October 4, 1931, Feature Section
4   *Introduction To The History of Civilization in England.* See conclusions from the history of Spain.

Scope of Work

The original plan was to write a small volume encompassing a detailed study of the history of the Federal Prison System, including a brief analysis of that history as well as the principles that must be observed in any satisfactory penal system that hopes to create useful citizens from a substantial proportion of the persons entrusted to its care, while pointing out along the way the policies followed by various Federal Prison Administrators, and the good and bad points of each. It was realized at the start, however, that policy can never be completely divorced from personality. So it was necessary to make a study of the personalities and characters of the men responsible for the policies followed in the various Federal prisons.

Then it was realized that the character of the inmate body was also an important factor in determining the success or failure of any given policy and that considerable space had to be devoted to a study of the various elements that make up the prison population and the way these elements have changed over the years as new legislation has brought different types of criminals into our Federal prisons.

After a year of work, during which close to five million words have been written and something over one-half million words of semi-finished copy produced, (copy that is probably good enough to send to the printer just as it stands) and after many reorganizations of the material at hand, the Writer has been forced to the conclusion that the subject is far too large, and the problems presented far too complex, to be treated in a single volume.

OUTLINE

The outline created by the Writer for this work was originally divided into six parts. However, due to the death of the Writer, there were only four parts completed.

The original six parts are entitled as follows:

PART I

A Voice From The Grave

This part will deal with prison conditions in general and the lot of Federal prisoners in particular from passage of the First Crime Act until the year 1910.

PART II

The Band Wagon

Will deal with the period from 1910 to 1921 and will trace the growth of the prison reform movement and its influence upon our Federal prisons.

PART III

The Seeds Of Destruction

Will trace the degeneration of the prison reform movement up to the establishment of the Federal Prison Bureau and the putting of the bureaucratic policies into practice, and will cover the period from July 1, 1921, to January 1, 1932.

PART IV

The Mulberry Bush

Will treat the problem of sex in prison and the relationship of that problem to the building and the destruction of character, insanity, and psychosomatic illnesses, and many other complex human problems that plague Wardens, prison physicians, and disciplinarians, as well as inmates.

PART V

The Building Blocks

Will deal with the other special problems of prison administration, such as discipline; employment; recreation; education; industry; and the hundred and one other problems that make up the one vast problem of imprisonment.

PART VI

The Key To The Castle

Will outline an ideal Federal Prison System based upon the principles developed in the historical sections of the work. It is the Writer's purpose to outline a sound and workable system, which is based upon his intimate knowledge of criminal psychology and more than forty-one years of prison experience.

Throughout the work the Writer will draw heavily upon his own personal experiences and naturally, the whole work is colored by his own personality. It is written strictly from a convict's point of view, and it presents the problems of the convict in the problems of the Writer, as he saw, lived and felt them from the day he entered prison as a callow, uneducated youth to the undertaking of this work by a senile old man.

THE RIGHT TO SPEAK

Any man's right to be heard upon a given subject is dependent upon his qualifications to speak intelligently, and the reader has a right to know something of the background of the person who attempts to inform him. With that thought in mind, the Writer gives the following brief biography of himself.

He was born in Seattle, Washington, on January 28, 1890, of mentally and physically sound parents of better-than-average education.

His mother was the oldest daughter of a prominent and wealthy attorney of the State of Illinois. Her father had been a Captain in the Union Army, had served two terms in the National Congress, as a Republican during the reconstruction period, and had been one of the founders of the Prohibition Party. She had been given a good education, had married and divorced her first husband, both against her father's wishes, and for some years before meeting the Writer's father, she had maintained herself and two daughters by teaching school. At the time of the Writer's birth, she was twenty-nine years old.

The Writer's father was the wastrel scion of a once wealthy and powerful Southern family, who, through his devotion to slow horses, fast women, and red whisky, had accomplished the financial ruination of his family and reduced himself to the status of a day laborer before meeting the Writer's mother. He had started his education with a view of becoming a doctor, had dropped the study of medicine and turned to engineering, because of an attachment for a cousin who was studying that subject, but upon the death of his father, which had placed a large plantation and the family fortune in his immature hands, had abandoned all thought of completing his education in either field. He was thirty-three years of age at the time of the Writer's birth and had not been previously married.

A second boy was born of this marriage a few weeks before the Writer's eighth birthday.

The Writer's education must have begun almost before he was weaned. He could never remember having been taught his letters and numbers, and long before he was of school age, he could recognize in print any work with which he was familiar, read simple stories, perform simple arithmetical operations, count money, make change, and write a neat Spenserian script with his left hand. He loved poetry, of which *The Ancient Mariner* was his favorite. Before his first day of school, he could recite the long poem from memory, and although he has reread it but once in fifty years, with a little thought, he could still recite it.

Because of the snobbishness of his mother, who did not think the children of common clay good enough to play with her precious darling, the only early childhood playmates he had until he was old enough to attend public school, were pets. Consequently, at the time he started to school, having had no previous experience in mixing with children of his own age, the Writer was unable to join in the games of his classmates on terms of equality, and he developed an intense distaste for crowds, and a pronounced inferiority complex.

To make matters much worse, his mother had so completely dominated and filled him with so many inhibitions that he was unable to function as a normal human being. He could not have put up his hand to go to the toilet to have saved his life, or to have used it at recess in the presence of other children. The school authorities attempted to force him to write a vertical script with his right hand, and the change-over caused him to stutter, which only increased his sensitiveness and suffering, making it impossible for him to recite, with the result that at the end of six years, he had been promoted to the fourth grade, not because of his scholastic record, but in spite of it. So, as soon as he was big enough, he had rebelled.

His mother had taught him that he should never fight under any circumstance, with the result that from his sixth to his eighth year he was always wearing black eyes and puffed lips because other children were always taking pokes at him out of sheer disgust, because he was such a sissy that he would not fight back.

Then his father had taken a hand and told him that he must always fight back; that if he ever again came home whipped, he would be whipped again, and the Writer has not been whipped from that day to this. The next boy who took a poke at him received a broken arm, and it was almost a year before anyone else tried to put a hand on him. The boy who did so was five years his senior. He threw the Writer to the ground, grabbed him by the throat and drew back his other hand to strike the Writer. The next instant he was screaming with pain as the Writer's teeth ground together in the flesh of his hand. A year later his father had struck him unexpectedly from behind and had knocked him into the dust of a road. He had come up out of that dust with a rock in each hand, and his father had received two broken ribs.

When he was ten, his father had gone into business and made a phenomenal financial success, and with plenty of money, had renewed his interest in slow horses and fast women. He soon separated himself from the family and refused to make any financial provision for the support of his children.

The Writer's mother had taken employment as a seamstress, and with aid from her two daughters, who were then grown and employed, had been able to keep the family together.

At the age of twelve, the Writer had taken employment as a heater boy at Moran's Shipyard, when the battleship Nebraska was then under construction, and he had turned the bulk of his earnings over to his mother. He violently hated his father and resented the fact that his mother would not take legal action to compel his father to provide for the family or give him carte blanche to do the compelling, which he would gladly have done with a pistol. On numerous occasions he was prevented from killing his father only by his mother's influence, and after forty-eight years, he is only half convinced that it would not have been a swell idea, even though in later years he and his father became good friends. The odd thing was that his father, seeing the mess that had been made of both their lives, then agreed with him.

A year after quitting school, the Writer left home, and for the next three years, with only short visits to Seattle, he hoboed his way over most of the United States. In 1907 he went to Alaska, where he worked in various construction camps and restaurants, engaged in fishing, and in the summer of 1908, ran a peanut and popcorn stand in Cordova, Alaska.

When the season was nearing its close, he sold his business and went to Juneau, Alaska to spend the winter with a woman with whom he had been living. A former paramour of this woman, a much older man, played upon the Writer's ignorance of that relationship, arranged a party, managed to get the woman alone, and when she refused to return to him, gave her a severe beating.

The next evening, January 18, 1909, ten days before the Writer's nineteenth birthday, the Writer called upon this man and killed him.

Both the Writer and the woman were indicted for murder. The Writer entered into an agreement with the United States Attorney to enter a plea of guilty to the crime of manslaughter and receive a twelve-year sentence in return for a promise that the woman would be released. The United States Attorney also agreed to secure his release at the end of three years, providing he kept a good prison record.

The Writer was received at McNiel Island on September 1, 1909. He kept a good record for twenty-six months. At that time he was a trustee in charge of the prison laundry. Another inmate, a man serving only four years, attempted to involve the Writer in a mythical general jail delivery involving the murder of the Warden and all the guards. The story was too fantastic to be convincing, but the Warden felt impelled to investigate it. He acquitted the Writer, who then went to the prison doctor, borrowed the doctor's pocket knife to cut some meat, and proceeded to use it on the other inmate, who was the doctor's orderly, stabbing him thirteen times in the large skeletal muscles, where there was not much danger of doing him serious harm.

The other inmate was more scared than hurt.

For this offense the Writer was held ten months in solitary confinement, was sentenced to six months additional imprisonment, forfeited all the good time on twelve years, and, on September 1, 1912, was transferred to Leavenworth.

A year later, he attempted to escape.

During the winter of 1913-14, the Writer was working in the prison stone shop. It was a bitterly cold winter, and his place of work was between a large steam coil and the door. The building was kept warm enough so that the men could work stripped to the waist, but every time the door was opened, the Writer's sweating body would be struck by a blast of subzero air.

The Writer became ill. He complained to Doctor Alfred F Yoke, but the only well-defined symptoms he could report were a bad cough and the fact that he felt all in.

Of course, all men working in the stone shop coughed, and there had been a number of cases of tuberculosis, so the doctor's attention was directed to the Writer's chest, and he reported that the only thing he could find wrong was a slight effusion in the pericardium.

That condition went on for three months. The Writer's feet hurt and were often swollen, but his cellmate used to rub his legs and get the swelling out of them every night. The Writer, attributing that condition to standing on his feet all day, had not mentioned it to the doctor. But one day, being able to think of nothing else to complain about, he said:

"Say, Doc: My feet hurt!"

The doctor's response was electric.

"I want a sample of your urine! How long has this been going on? Why didn't you tell me?"

The diagnosis was chronic glomerular nephritis, Bright's Disease, and the prognosis was unfavorable.

Doctor Yoke felt very contrite about his failure to recognize the condition at once. He stated that the Writer could not possibly survive for more than two years in the rigorous Kansas climate, but that he might live as long as five years in a warm, even climate, such as that of Arizona. He suggested that the Writer apply for clemency at once.

With the delay involved in such things, it was the Fall of 1915 before the case was ready to go to the President, and by that time the Writer had gone down to one-hundred-and-eighteen pounds and was so ureic that he constantly smelled as if he had wet himself.

The United States Attorney who had handled the assault case, and the Warden, and the Doctor at McNiel Island, and the United States Attorney, who had handled the murder case, and the trial judge in both cases, and Doctor Yoke, all of which recommended clemency. The Warden of Leavenworth, Thomas W. Morgan, tried to shake the Writer down for four-hundred dollars. When the money was not forthcoming, he gave the Writer an unfavorable report.

When clemency was denied, the case went before President Wilson in December, 1915.

During the two years of his illness, the Writer had spent a great deal of time in the hospital, but he was so nervous that it was painful for him to be around people. For that reason, he had secured permission to remain in his cell whenever he wished to do so. He spent most of his time there.

The next noon after being notified that his plea for clemency had been denied, the Writer carried two steel case knives from the prison dining room. That evening, while going to supper he passed a friend who worked in the prison machine shop.

"I want a file about fourteen inches, not too coarse, and half a dozen sheets of double-emery cloth," he said.

The next day the Writer went to work. He was nominally assigned to the tailor shop. The tailor shop, shoe shop, and harness shop were in one large room. To another friend he said: "I want some wax ends, an awl, some heavy pigskin, and some strips of harness leather."

Those two knives and a great many others were turned into slim, two-edged daggers with short, ball-like leather hands, each fitted with a leather loop to be slipped over the little finger and a scabbard that could be fastened inside of the coat or sleeve and tight enough that the knife could be worn, handle down. The blades were highly polished, honed to razor sharpness, and carefully blued with apple juice. The volume of this production was predicated somewhat upon the theory of the rat and the parlor match.

If you take a rat, some parlor matches of the old phosphorus variety, and some dry hay and nail them up in a box together, you may have a dead rat, and you may have a fire. At that particular time, conditions at Leavenworth were ripe for a fire.

The Writer was dying, and he knew it. Had he followed any other course of action than the one he did follow, he would have died. For at that time, no effective treatment for his condition was known, and spontaneous recoveries were unknown.

There is something about a death sentence, whether it is delivered by a doctor or sentenced by a judge, that has a profound influence upon the personality. It converts some men into crying, sniveling cowards. In others it brings out all of their strength of character. It strikes from their minds all fear. If one is going to die, there is nothing more that can happen to him. There is no reason why he should not do anything that he pleases, or is big enough to do. If he is killed during it, or because of doing it, so what? He will be no deader than he would be anyway. For one of a realistic turn of mind, it is an interesting and exhilarating experience. If you have never enjoyed it, (if one may use that word) you have missed something!

It was so with the Writer. He had been sentenced to death in prison by a cheap, grafting, psalm-singing, hypocrite of a Warden. Well, that was fine. He would die, but he would die his way, and he had no intention of permitting that Warden to survive him.

The Writer was in no hurry to kill Morgan, for it would have been stupid to kill the man without bringing his administration into disrepute, and it would be fun to see how much mess he could make of that administration. By being of this turn of mind, the Writer would not overlook any good opportunity. He never knew when he might catch the man alone for an instant, so he made a point of keeping one of his knives within constant reach of his hand.

On Sunday, March 26, 1916, seven years after the Writer had entered prison, he entered the prison dining room for the noon meal. While the band was playing *In Paradise*, the Writer, who had not eaten anything, passed the two pork chops on his plate to a young moonshiner by the name of Floyd Collins,[5] and got to his feet, and addressed Guard Andrew Turner. Turner tried to strike the Writer with his club.

The Writer grabbed the club with both hands and tried to hold it, but Turner was a big, powerful man in perfect health, and he had no trouble wrenching the club free. The instant that the Writer realized he could not hold the club, the Writer time to draw his knife. Before the club could reach the Writer's head, his slim blade had passed through Turner's heart. The guard was dead before he reached the floor.

Fifty-eight days later the Writer was convicted of murder and also heard the unfavorable prognosis of his doctor, supplemented by the equally unfavorable and much more definite prognosis of his trial judge. This conviction was appealed. The United States Attorney was forced to go before the Eighth Circuit Court of Appeals, sitting at St. Louis in November, 1916, and to admit error on fourteen points.

The conviction of the Writer was reversed on December 2, 1916.

And here is the irony of that situation. At that time no treatment was known for glomerular nephritis. It was the generally accepted medical theory that meat, because it increased the formation of urea, was harmful to patients suffering from that condition. During the entire period of his illness, the Writer had been ordered and advised to eat no meat. While in the hospital, he had been kept on a diet of milk and eggs. Once out of the hospital, he had disregarded the order not to eat meat, but all the meat served in the

---

5   Floyd later died while trapped in a cave in Kentucky.

prison dining room was over-cooked. With the deterioration resulting from the progress of the disease, the Writer had lost most of his appetite. The sight of food often sickened him. Yet, throughout the entire course of his illness, he had craved one food, <u>red meat</u>, either raw or rare, which was the one item of food that was denied to him.

When the Writer returned to the prison, after having been sentenced to death, he addressed Mr. L. J. Fletcher, who was then the Deputy Warden:

"If you want to hang me, you are going to have to feed me. If you think that I am going to eat one mouthful of that steam-cooked slumgullian you have on the main line, you are crazy as a bedbug."

"O.K. Tell you what," said the Deputy Warden. "You give me your order for dinner right now. If what you want is available, I'll see that you get it." "When the orderly brings your dinner, you give him your order for supper. Do that at each meal! If the food you want is available in the prison, or if it can be purchased in Leavenworth, you will get it." "We think that you deserve to be hanged, and we are going to try our best to hang you, but I personally, have no desire to be needlessly cruel. Anything that you want within reason, you will get."

"Thank you, Sir! I could not ask for anything fairer than that, but I have no particular desire to be troublesome, so I will go you one better. I want a T-bone steak cut one-and-one-quarter inches thick, fried on a hot range, so that it is almost black outside, blood rare inside, and served piping hot. Tell the cook to heat two platters in the oven before cooking the steak, and to throw the steak onto one platter, spread it over with a cube of butter one-inch square; put four fried eggs on top of it; then to cover it with the other hot platter and send it over to me at once. I want milk to drink, and I want it three times per day."

"No bread, pastry, or dessert, the Warden asked? They turn out some fine pastries over there." "We have a wonderful baker." "He makes all the pastry for my own table, and it is really good." "Wouldn't you care for some French fried potatoes or canned fruit?"

"Thank you! But that is all I want, the Writer answered."

"Won't that be a monotonous diet?"

"No! I'll have fresh fruit and candy all the time."

"If there is anything else you want, let me know, the Deputy Warden said."

"Thanks! That will be all. Now, about that hanging business. I appreciate how you feel about that Warden, and that is all right with me."

"I assure you that there is nothing personal, I --- I understand. That is just what I was coming to. You don't know me, and I don't know you. You want to hang me, and I want to beat you, but that is no reason why we should not both be gentlemen about it." "You have been very considerate about the food, and I want to assure you that so long as you treat me like a gentleman, I'll treat you exactly the same way. If you succeed in hanging me, that will be my hard luck. If I beat you, that will be your hard luck. But I see no occasion for making the contest a personal one. I don't intend to pull any punches, and I don't expect you to. You would be a fool if you did."

"You are a strange person Stroud. Few men in your position would take that attitude.

I think it is very realistic." Fletcher put out his hand. "May the best man win. Is there anything else?"

"Yes! My books! Also, I would like to have a cell at the other end of the building, where I can have quiet, so I can study."

"I'll attend to that, and I will have your books sent over there." The Deputy Warden Said.

The Writer had ordered the eggs to give to men on punishment, and he would also give one steak away every day, for two meals per day was all he ever cared for, but he was going to live on meat. If it killed him, he would die happy!

The Attorney General had ordered the Writer to be given one hour in the fresh air every day. As the weather was hot, the Writer went naked. He threw away all his medicine. He wolfed his rare steaks like a dog. He went out in the yard every day and exercised as much as he could, and when he was hot, he turned a cold-water hose over his body. That is, he did everything he had been advised not to do. He did not care whether these things killed him, or not, because he was as good as dead anyway.

At first, five minutes of walking was all the Writer could stand at one time, but within sixty days he had gained forty pounds, none of which was fat, and no one would have believed that he had ever had a bad kidney. He remained on the diet of rare beef, raw fruit, milk and candy for one year. At the end of that time he was in the best health he had ever enjoyed in his entire life. He could stand on his finger tips and pick up a handkerchief off the floor twelve times. He could do a dozen push-ups on any two fingers of each hand, or on his thumbs alone. He would drag his bed across his twenty-one-foot cell, put his stool on top of his bed, and put books and blankets on top of his stool, his clothing on top of his blankets and build the pile up until it was even with the nipple on his chest, then the Writer would jump over that obstruction until he had cleared it twenty straight times. He would put one foot on his wash basin, spring up and grab his radiator, which was twelve-feet from the floor, and chin himself twelve times with either hand.

What medicine could not do, diet and good living conditions had accomplished, but the Writer had been able to obtain those things only because of the desire to hang him.

The Writer was tried again in May, 1917, before a judge who was unacquainted with the laws of Kansas, which at that time were controlling all matters of procedure in Federal Courts sitting in that state. Fred Robertson, United States District Attorney for the District of Kansas produced pardons for the convict witnesses of the Government and

argued that under the Constitution and Laws of Kansas, a convicted felon could not testify, and the Writer was thus deprived of any defense.

The jury was unwilling to hang a man without hearing his defense, so they brought in a verdict requiring a life sentence. The Writer felt however, that had he been able to put his case before that jury, the Writer might have won an acquittal. So this opinion was appealed directly to the Supreme Court of the United States on Constitutional grounds, and again, the Government was forced to go before a higher court and to admit error.

In July, 1918, the Writer was tried for the third time. At this trial, a number of convict and ex-convict witnesses appeared for the defense. Their testimony supported the theory of self-defense, which was strengthened by the fact that two guards who had previously given testimony favorable to that theory, changed their stories, and other Government witnesses were shown to be unable to tell their stories in words different from those used at the previous trial.[6]

At this trial, even though he had lost a number of good witnesses who had been available for his second trial, the Writer insisted, against the advice of his attorneys, that the jury be asked either to hang or to acquit him.

"They may accommodate you," one attorney argued.

"Well, it is my neck!" the Writer replied. "That is the way we should have played it from the first, and that is the way we are playing it now – all or nothing."

The lawyer had judged that jury correctly. Their verdict called for a death sentence. It was appealed to the United States Supreme Court on Constitutional grounds and was affirmed.[7]

The American Bar Association entertained such grave doubts concerning the fairness of this opinion that they asked the Writer's attorney, Martin J. O'Donnell from Kansas City, Missouri, to address their 1920 convention at Chicago upon the subject of this case.

On April 16, 1920, one week before the Writer was due to be hanged, President Woodrow Wilson, acting upon the advice of his personal secretary, Joseph P. Tumulty, who had made a thorough investigation of the matter, and against the advice of his Attorney General, A. Witchel Palmer, who had boasted in a speech at Topeka, Kansas that he was going to hang the Writer, regardless of whether the people of Kansas liked it or not, commuted the sentence of death to one of life imprisonment.

District Judge Robert E. Lewis, of Denver, Colorado, who had presided at the Writer's third trial, had imposed the death sentence in the manner and form required by the Statutes of his State[8] and had affixed thereto a clause requiring that the Writer be held in solitary confinement pending his execution.

President Wilson, critically ill at the time, had simply scrawled on the face of the papers:

"Commuted to life. W.W."

The situation thus created posed a rather unique problem.

The prison authorities and Attorney General Palmer wished to hold the Writer in solitary confinement, which, according to a majority of the Court in the Medley case, would constitute cruel and unusual punishment.

Under Construction of the law as it existed at that time, there is no doubt but what the Writer could have taken the matter into court and forced the prison authorities to accord him the same treatment given every other new arrival at the institution.

The four-year legal battle for the Writer's life had been a very bitterly fought one, and it

---

6   No man telling the truth ever tells the same story in exactly the same words twice. His attention is fixed on the pictures of the action he carries in his mind and not on the words which he describes that action. The attention of the man who is lying is fixed on exact words to describe the picture in his mind, for there is no picture there.
7   Stroud V United States, 251 U.S. 15
8   See *In re* Medley, 134 U. S. 160

had been only one phase of the argument. The Writer is not the kind of a person who can be taken out and slaughtered like a sheep. With recovery of his health, his almost every waking thought had been devoted to plans for escape, or to inventing headaches for his enemies.

During almost the entire four years, he had managed to keep himself armed with a knife, and the authorities had known it. He had been able to keep in constant contact with a friend in the prison population and with ex-convicts on the outside. He had introduced the use of coded communications, and he used one system of code writing that the Army Intelligence Office had not been able to break. Several of his escape plans had misfired by inches.

To keep official eyes off himself as much as possible, he had fomented all the trouble that he could. The Isolation Building had been kept in a state of constant turmoil, and he and his fellows had been able to stir up much trouble in the prison at large. Time after time he had employed his underground connections to bring about investigations and then bring relatives of other prisoners storming to the institution, threatening court action. He was never loath to involve himself in the troubles of others in not always futile attempts to throw over them the immunity from punishment that his legal status threw over him, and it is truly amazing how much trouble one or two determined and resourceful men, who have the respect of their fellow inmates, can create.

As a result of this activity, very little of which could be traced to the Writer, but for which the prison authorities blamed his influence, he was the most bitterly hated man in the prison. There had been many official plots to kill him, some of which had misfired by less than inches. On one occasion while getting out of a car in front of the courthouse, there had been an attempt to dump a revolver into his manacled hands. Instead of snatching the pistol, which he knew was empty, he had thrown his body sideways and his hands in the air. On another occasion, a drunken Warden had him taken from his cell at night with the intention of killing him. He had saved himself by turning his back and calmly challenging the Warden to go on and shoot.

"They will have to go in my back, and Pollock will want to know why I was taken from my cell at this hour."[9]

No! It had not been a game played for peanuts. Both sides had been playing for keeps, with no holds barred.[10] And, naturally, the Writer's mother and attorneys felt that once the cloak of protection thrown over him by the court was removed, his life would be of little value. They were in favor of taking the matter to court and attempting to force the Department of Justice to transfer him to another institution.

The Writer did not agree. As a small boy, during that period when his mother would not permit him to fight back, he had never run from another child. If another boy struck him, he would stand and take it, but he would not run, and now it appeared to him that going to court and forcing a transfer would be running from his troubles. His fight was at Leavenworth, and he had two good trading points. The men in charge of that institution knew him. They could give him a rough go-round, but they knew that it would not be one-sided. They knew something else; they also knew that his word was good. They wanted to keep him locked up; they did not want more court battles; more exposures;

9   John C. Pollock was Federal Judge of the District.
10   No attempt to tell the complete story of this battle has been made in this work, but many of the details are mentioned in Part II – Chapters XII to XX.

more political pressure; more investigations; or any unfavorable opinions from Judge Pollock.

The Writer would agree to drop the court action, to stay in isolation and to cause no more trouble, provided that they were willing to make concessions that would enable him to do something for himself.

It was agreed that the Writer would stay in Isolation; that he would enjoy all the privileges allowed any other first-grade prisoner, and that in addition, he would be allowed such special privileges as would enable him to keep his mind active and occupied.

"You know that I have an active and resourceful mind, and that I am going to keep it busy," the Writer said. "If I am allowed to do so legitimately, I won't be using it illegitimately. I am not going to sit back there and twiddle my thumbs until I go mad."

"I realize, the Warden said, that you must have some occupation and interest. I have authority to grant any reasonable concessions. What do you want to do?"

"I don't know. I say that we let it stand as it is until I make up my mind what I want to do, or to study. It will be up to me to convince you that any request I make will not be abused. All I want right now is your promise Warden, that any reasonable request I make that you are convinced will not be abused, will be granted."

"That is fair enough, the Warden said, and I am sure that the Attorney General will agree."

The isolation building soon became the least troublesome department of the prison. Within a year, the Writer had established the foundation of his bird business and embarked upon a program of study and research that was to keep him occupied for more than twenty-two years, and by means of which he was to become widely renowned throughout the aviculture and scientific worlds as the leading authority on the diseases of pet birds. Much of that story is told in Part III, and it need not be repeated here.

The arrangement was faithfully kept by both parties for a period of eleven years, during which period the Writer enjoyed the confidence of the prison officials to such an extent that he actually had tons of birdseed, and large quantities of chemicals and equipment shipped into the institution and delivered to him without the bags or boxes being opened. During this period, he could have, had he cared to do so, had Tommy guns and cases of

explosives shipped into the institution without risk of detection. Yet, this confidence was never violated in the minutest details.

This agreement was abrogated by Sanford Bates on August 18, 1931, when he issued orders that compelled Warden Thomas B. White, against his advice and best judgment, to order the Writer to dispose of his birds.

The Writer resisted this order with all the ingenuity and legitimate means at his disposal, but in the intervening years he had learned many valuable lessons, not the least of which is that the man who can fight his battles with a TypeWriter, Multigraph, and Printing Press does not have to use a battle ax or stiletto, and that for such a man to do so, is stupid. For the choice of weapons is really more of an intellectual and cultural matter than a moral question. It is often possible to hurt a man more by making him publicly ridiculous than by chopping his head off, and it is not nearly so messy.

So, while this battle lasted for eleven years and was fought with no less determination than those previously mentioned, not once in all that time did the Writer turn to physical force, rather than the methods of civilized political and commercial combat, though he cannot say as much for his opponents, unless the methods of a Himmler could be called civilized, but that, too, is another story and need not be discussed in this brief outline; the sole purpose of which is to provide the reader with enough information to permit him to evaluate the Writer's qualifications to discuss the subject upon which he presumes to speak.

The Writer's battle with the Federal Bureau of Prisons was, of course, a losing one. With advancing years and ill health, he was sure to fail, and on December 16, 1942, in the small hours of the morning, the Writer was seized in his sleep by a force of fifteen men armed with blackjacks, in the very best Himmler manner, was chained hand and foot, and was transported to Alcatraz, where he still remains. It was there, on May 3, 1946, that he had the interesting and enlightening experience of having more than thirty antitank grenades fired directly at him with the deliberate intention of destroying him; of hearing the firing orders for the deliberate murder of other innocent and helpless men; and through his ingenuity, resourcefulness under fire, understanding of human psychology, and utter disregard for his own life, he saved the lives of twenty-four men marked for deliberate massacre. But that, too, is another story.

Qualifications

The Writer is now sixty-one years old He has been an intense student practically all of his life. One of his most outstanding characteristics has always been an insatiable curiosity as to what makes things tick. One of his earliest memories is that of taking a clock apart to see what made it tick. Another was of watching his mother cut a chicken apart in preparation for the table with the hope of learning what made the chicken tick.

When most children have their noses in Mother Goose books, the Writer spent much of his childhood with his nose in a medical textbook on human anatomy and a high school textbook on physics. One reason was an attempt to understand what made things tick. The other was an attempt to understand what made himself tick.

This interest in the mechanics of both animate and inanimate objects has been of life-long duration and has carried him into many fields of human thought, from the structure of the atom to the structure of the universe; from the mechanics and chemistry of the living cell to the history of religious thought; from the differentiations of developing tissue to those of developing society and the growth of ideas, as these may be traced through the pages of the world's great literature. There is no subject of human interest upon which he has not read and studied as widely as his limited means and library facilities would permit.

Although he has enjoyed very little formal education, he has studied extensively in the fields of physics, chemistry, mathematics, music, art, philosophy, psychology, biology, physiology, biochemistry, hematology, anatomy, histology, pathology, and therapeutics, and he has done some original work in all of them.

He has devoted twenty-two years of his life to research in the fields of avian physiology, hematology, pathology, and therapeutics. He is the author of two books: *Diseases of Canaries*, Kansas City, Missouri, 1933, and *Stroud's Digest On The Diseases Of Birds*, Minneapolis, 1943, as well as a great many articles of various kinds, and he has, all told, seen about three million of his own words in print.

He was forty years old before he knew one rule of grammar or had ever looked into a composition book, but he has always had a flare for putting his thoughts on paper, and it is his boast that he can write anything from pornography to an epic poem; from a treatise on higher algebra to one on comparative histology; from a song to a properly drawn and phrased petition for writ of certiorari to the Supreme Court of the United States; that he can put any thought or emotion a human being can feel on paper.

During his more than forty-one years in prison he has actually lived under and experienced almost every type of prison management and witnessed the application of almost every penological theory over a sufficiently long period of time to enable him to form just evaluations of the good and bad features of each. And it is his purpose, in these pages, to show the reader exactly what makes prisons and prisoners tick. He brings to this task an amazingly accurate memory for details, since, having no security in the possession of his notes, he has made a life-long habit of storing them in the one place where they could never be taken from him, inside of his head.

On the Writer's second day in prison, as a boy of nineteen, he witnessed an occurrence, the sheer callousness of which sickened him.[11] Later as he sat alone during a period of leisure, his chin on his hand, his mind sunken deeply in bitter and brooding thoughts, an old man sat down beside him.

"How long you doing, Sonny?"

"Twelve years, and I don't give a damn whether I do any of it, or not. Do you think that S.O.B. would kill me if I went over the wire?" The Writer indicated the gun guard.

"No! He would knock you down, but he would not kill you."

"That is what I was afraid of. What will they do to the Chili?"[12]

"Oh! He will go back to the hole for about ten days."

"But the poor fellow just came out of the hole! He didn't do anything! I saw it all! He was just weak! He only stepped aside to let the man behind to pass him by."

"I know, kid! It's tough! But the Chili asked for what happened to him. Being new here, there are things you don't understand. This *screw* is not a bad guy, and in this case he was fully justified in what he did. I know that it seems hard to you, but if you ever see a hard prison, you will know the difference. I have seen men killed for stepping out of line. I am only a new man here, myself, but I just finished a thirty-five year bit in San Quentin and Folsom. I was a kid like you when I went in. I came out an old man, unable to make a go of it on the outside, but I know prison. And here is something I learned a long time ago:

"There are two types of things a man in prison should never brood or worry about: those he can help and those he can't help. Never worry or brood about a thing you can help! Do something about it! If you will keep your mind busy figuring out ways of doing something about the things you can help, then you won't have much time to worry about those things you can't help. Follow this advice and you will be surprised at the number of things you

---

11   Part I – Chapter XII
12   Chili was the nickname of a convict who had had trouble with a guard.

really can help; but cases like the Chili will not be among them. The only thing that could help him would be a new set of brains."

The old man's words burned deeply into the boy's mind and memory, for he realized that they were the fruit of long and bitter experience. They became a basic part of his own philosophy of serving time. Ignore the things you can't help! Do something about the things you can help! In forty-one years the Writer has done something about a great many situations. Many of the things he has done have not always been wise, have not always been in his own best interest, but in many cases, they have been amazingly effective. He has employed every instrumentality from persuasion to nation-wide publicity; from psychology to synthetic ink; from legal process to a battle ax, often with utter disregard for his own personal interest or safety.

Herbert Spencer[13] has defined intelligence as the capacity of the organism to exercise an influence upon its environment. On that basis the Writer can claim to be an intelligent organism, for he has always exercised an influence (sometimes good, sometimes bad; sometimes small, sometimes profound) upon every environment in which he has ever found himself and upon numerous persons in all walks of life, from reformatory punks to college professors, including practically every prison administrator with whom he has come in contact. Regardless of the outcome of his efforts, he has always been a force that had to be reckoned with and taken into consideration, and it has always been his purpose to improve the conditions under which he and his fellow inmates have had to live.

He has won more privileges, both for himself and others, than any other Federal Prison inmate. He has abolished, amended, or rewritten more rules and regulations, by the simple process of doing as he pleased and then by making his conduct legal, by the argument of *status quo*, than any man who ever wore a federal prison number on his back.

The criticism most frequently leveled against the Writer is that he is an egotist. He would not think of denying that charge. In fact, he would be ashamed to have it otherwise, although he thinks egoist would be a better word. Both are boasters. The difference is that the egotist does not deliver while the egoist boasts of things that other men consider impossible, then goes out and makes his boasts come true.

Probably the most nearly correct evaluation of the Writer's character ever printed appeared in a feature article written by William O'Grady in the *Kansas City Post*, on Saturday, April 10, 1920. The occasion for the article was the Writer's proposed execution upon April 23, 1920. Mr. O'Grady quoted L. J. Fletcher, at that time one of the Writer's bitterest enemies, as saying:

"He is the type of an industrious dreamer who dreams the impossible, then makes his dreams come true in the most spectacular manner."

This is just another way of saying that he is the kind of person who does things. Sure, he is an egotist, if you wish, but who else would have the guts and gall to attempt to write a historical work without notes, or a reference library, at his disposal, relying almost exclusively upon memory, and with the patience and driving power to hand-print five million words in the process? Of course, it is unfortunate, that the work is not as carefully documented as the Writer would like to have it, but the Reader will find ample references to source material, even if volume and page numbers cannot always be supplied.

---

13   *First Principles of Psychology*

The Legal History Of The Federal Penal System

On September 15, 1948, in the case of Stroud V. Swope, Warden No. 28295, which was on the docket of the United States District Court for the Northern District of California, on the Writer's Petition for an Injunction, an Assistant United States Attorney, in support of the Government's motion to dismiss, said:

"But, Your Honor, the man is legally dead, and he has no civil rights."

"I cannot agree," said George B. Harris, District Judge. "He may be legally dead, but the trouble is that he is not buried. To deprive any man of the fruits of his mental industry is to destroy that man."

In this volume the dead shall speak!

~~~~~~~~~~~~~

In the early days of our country, there were no Federal prisons, hence, no Federal Penal System. In fact, one of the things that contributed enormously toward making America great was the realization of the Founding Fathers that they were not omniscient, nor did they possess the last word in human wisdom.

Instead of attempting to make the world over by fiat handed down from above, they were conscious of the fact that a workable society is always the product of slow growth, the fruit of the labor of many minds, the wisdom of accumulated experience, and they were content to set up the machinery under which that growth could occur, guided only by the broad principle set out in the Constitution and Bill of Rights, which was designed to prevent the growth of tyranny by acting as a limitation on the powers of Government. They, and those who followed them took those principles seriously for more than a century.

The earliest reference to be found in the United States Code, 1935 Edition pertaining to imprisonment, is the Act of March 3, 1821, No. 2.3 Stat. 646, amended by the Act of March 2, 1833, C. 57, No. 6.4 Stat. 634, which provided that in districts where State jails and prisons were not available for the housing of Federal prisoners, the District Marshal, under the direction of the court, should procure some suitable place within the limits of the State to serve as a temporary jail. For in those days, State citizenship meant something, and it was held that the Federal Government possessed no power to remove any prisoner from one state to another.

Previously, execution of all Federal sentences for imprisonment appears to have been arranged for locally, by the United States Marshal, acting under the general authority of the Federal Courts to impose and inflict imprisonment as a punishment for crimes against the United States, authorized by the Statutes, without specific authorization from Congress as to the arrangement to be made in any particular set of circumstances. It was assumed that this power flowed directly from the right to govern. In most cases arrangements were made to house Federal prisoners in local jails of the States of Territories where convictions were given, but more than one person convicted of a Federal offense served his sentence as a servant in the Marshal's home or as an unpaid laborer on the Marshal's farm, with the Marshal's wife, son, and daughter drawing stipends from the court as special Deputy Marshals, who were assigned to guarding the prisoner, who at night, likely as not, slept with his feet chained around a stanchion in the Marshal's barn.

The prisoner and his punishment remained within the jurisdiction of the trial court, which was constrained to see that punishment did not exceed constitutional limitations. The first Crime Act, April, 30, 1790 C.9, 1 Stat., had provided flogging for a number of offenses, but by 1825 all such punishment had been repealed. The Federal Courts of that period, with few exceptions, were presided over by the best brains and characters procurable within the legal profession, who were still under the strong influence of the English Bench, and were inclined to be lenient and fair in the extreme when compared with the much lower standards of State courts. And Federal Judges often objected to the subjection of their wards to the harsh punishment then employed in many State prisons.[14]

Back in slavery days, most prison men considered the convict less worthy of humane treatment than the slave, since slaves had property value, while the convict was a public liability. They deeply resented the coddling of Federal prisoners that was demanded by the courts, and many State prisons refused to house Federal prisoners. Those institutions that did house Federal prisoners often resented the court's interference with their management, and many cases of claimed mistreatment and disputes of authority were constantly coming before the Federal courts.

It was to clarify this situation that The Congress, by Act of June 30, 1834, C. 163, 4 Stat. 739, provided that Federal prisoners housed in State and Territorial prisons should be subject to the same discipline and treatment and would enjoy all the same privileges and advantages accorded to the prisoners of the State or Territory with whom they were confined. The Act further provided for the payment of transportation and maintenance cost by the United States of America.

The following year it was provided that any person convicted of a crime against the United States could be sentenced to "any house of correction or house of reformation for juvenile delinquents within the State where such court is held, the use of which is authorized by the legislature of the State for such purpose," Act of March 3, 1835, C. 40, Stat. 777.

This is the earliest use of the word *reformation* that the Writer has found in any Federal Statute, but the idea of reformation is much older than that. It goes back to the early history of the Catholic Church. The word was often employed by the *Holy Office Of The Inquisition*, where it was argued that the repentance and reformation of a single heretic, and the saving of a single soul from the eternal fires of hell, was ample justification for all the tortures inflicted here on earth.[15]

---

14   See *In re* Birdsong 39 F 599 (1899)
15   *Introduction To The History Of Civilization In England*, John Buckle, *Scientific Outlook*, Bertrand Russell

And certain penal institutions, including the infamous solitary confinement prison in Rome, were designated *hospitals of reformation*, on the same theory that euphonious names can be made to cover shameful conditions that prompts our present-day Federal penologists to designate their dungeons and isolations as *Special Treatment Units*.[16] We still have numerous reformatories here in America that are a blot upon our civilization. Many could be named, but one in Pendleton, Indiana, and in Granite, Oklahoma, are sufficient.

It was not until the close of the Civil War that any general provision was made for caring for juvenile offenders against the laws of the United States, but by the Act of March 3, 1865, C. 121, 13 Stat. 538, it was provided that the Attorney General should have power to contract with some suitable house of refuge to which all juvenile offenders under the age of sixteen could be committed. During most of the Writer's lifetime that contract was held by the Missouri Reform School at Boonville, where conditions of vice, graft, and brutality were so horrible that a great many judges continued to send boys of fourteen and fifteen to penitentiaries, as the lesser of two evils, often at the request of the child or his parents. This situation existed up until the First World War. As bad as adult prisons were back around the turn of the century, the worst adult prison was always better than the best juvenile institution, nor is the reason hard to find.

Dr. Thorndyke estimates that two out of every five persons have some sadistic tendencies.[17] To sadistic-minded persons, helplessness is always an invitation to cruelty. That is why we still spank children. We have largely abandoned the spanking of adults, not from motives of humanity, as many persons would like to believe, but because the adult is often able to do something about it, to kill someone and then dramatize the conditions leading up to the killing into a scandal that will attract nationwide attention. The child cannot do that.

It was not until the year 1876 that the Attorney General was vested with the power to remove an adult convict from the jurisdiction of his conviction[18] This Act gave the Attorney General power to arrange for the confinement of Federal prisoners in State and Territorial prisons outside of the State or District of conviction when no suitable place of confinement existed within the State or District. The Act provided for change in the place of confinement for three reasons: one because the place was not strong enough to secure the custody of the prisoner; and two because of ill health; and three because of mistreatment. But in the latter two cases the Attorney General's power was contingent upon a request of the prisoner or someone acting in his behalf. It was at that time the generally accepted legal opinion that the prisoner had a vested right in his judgment that extended to his place of confinement and could be protected by writ of habeas corpus.[19] It is possible that there was some limited provision for moving Federal prisoners from one State to another, which was contained in the Act of May 12, 1864, C. 85, 13 Stat. 75, but the Writer has not had a chance to read this Act. During and following the Civil War,

---

16   See *In re* Medley, 134 U.S. 160, in which the Supreme Court discusses solitary confinement as punishment for crime
17   Dr. Thorndyke was a barrister and doctor of medicine in a series of fictional detective stories written by the English author, R. Austin Freeman between 1905 and 1941. Although the stories were fictional, the legal and medical facts presented in the stories were thoroughly researched by Mr. Freeman and were so accurate that they were often quoted by medical and legal experts.
18   Act of July 12, 1876, C. 183. 19 Stat 88
19   See annotation following Section 696, Volume 3, Title 18 U.S.C. Annotated, 1927 Edition, West Publishing Company, St. Paul, Minnesota

Federal prisoners from occupied territory were sent to Columbus, Ohio, though this may have been done pursuant to the War Powers of the President.

Following the War, and as a monument to the passions of that period, the United States Army employed the infamous Fort Jefferson in the Dry Tortugas as a place of imprisonment of Federal prisoners, who had been convicted of violations of the Reconstruction Act. The scandalous administration of this institution brought to light in the case of Doctor Mudd – who served nine years of a life sentence for innocently setting Booth's leg – coupled with the frightful death toll from yellow fever, forced the abandonment of this experiment in penology early in the 1870s. For the next two decades, practically all Federal prisoners served their sentences in the following State institutions: the Maryland Penitentiary at Baltimore, the Ohio Penitentiary at Columbus, the Minnesota Penitentiary at Stillwater, the West Virginia Penitentiary at Moundsville, the South Carolina Penitentiary at Columbus, and the California Penitentiary at San Quentin, which received and housed the largest numbers of Federal prisoners.

This arrangement did not work well. There were always complaints of misconduct and mistreatment, and what was even more effective, complaints of inequality and partiality, for in those days, the Equality Clause of the 14th Amendment meant something. It was the legal theory that all men convicted of crimes against the United States had to be treated alike. That did not mean absolute equality of treatment; it meant equality of opportunity, exactly the same as the political equality guaranteed by the Constitution – all men entered prison on equal footing, and their treatment from then on was supposed to depend upon just one thing, their conduct while in prison.

Legal differences were beginning to crop up, however, for many States had by this time, 1876, adopted a policy of recognizing good prison conduct by granting a uniform reduction of sentence, officially referred to as *Deduction for Good Conduct*, but popularly called *Good time*. Many States had also enacted parole laws; and some Federal Courts had held that under the Act of June 30, 1834, supra, Federal prisoners, committed to such institutions, were entitled to *Good time* and parole on the same terms as these were granted to State prisoners.

On the other hand, many State institutions farmed out the labor of their convicts to private contractors under what was known as the *contract system*. In many such institutions men were exploited for private profit under conditions far worse than any that had ever existed in the days of chattel slavery. Men were assigned to tasks that it was almost humanly impossible for them to do, then subjected to the most frightful punishments for failure to accomplish their tasks. After numerous complaints to the Attorney General and to the courts, at the suggestion of the Attorney General, Congress by Act of February 23 1887, C. 213. 24 Stat. 411, made the selling of the labor of any Federal prisoner an offense against the United States, punishable by three years of imprisonment and a fine of not less than five hundred dollars, nor more than one thousand dollars, for each offense.

At the same time, State authorities were forbidden by the Attorney General to employ Federal prisoners upon task work or to inflict upon them any form of corporal punishment, or any punishment not approved by the Attorney General. Reasons for this order will appear in a subsequent chapter, [20] but it is an ironical fact that two decades later the Superintendent of the National Training School For Boys, Washington, D. C. was publicly boasting of his electric spanking machine.

A further cause of dissatisfaction arose from the fact that a Federal prisoner was still considered to be within the jurisdiction of the Federal Court, even though he was confined in a State institution, for offenses committed during imprisonment. He could be tried and punished only under the general statutes of the United States, which covered most of the Common Law crimes, but which at that time did not make escape or attempt to escape an offense against the United States. On several occasions, the Congress had been asked to enact such legislation and had refused by arguing that every prisoner had a natural instinct to escape and that no man should be punished for following his natural instincts. The prison authorities had an obligation to retain custody of the convicted person, and they were authorized to employ any force essential to that end. But if they failed and the prisoner escaped, it was just too bad. If anyone were punished, it should be the authorities who permitted themselves to be outwitted, not the prisoner, who was only doing what any other self-respecting man would do under the same circumstances. To punish him would be poor sportsmanship, and it is only in recent years that Congress has lost its sense of humor and of fair play, that New Deal stooges have begun to think of themselves as statesmen.

This same sense of good sportsmanship was not unknown either to prison authorities or to the courts. Federal Courts not only held that Federal prisoners could not be tried for escaping from State prisons, but also in some cases, it held that State prisoners who escaped with them could not be tried either, since it would be poor sportsmanship to punish one man for an offense for which his equally guilty companion could not be punished, and that it would violate the Equality Clause of the XIV Amendment to the U.S. Constitution.

Such was the reasoning of the Ninth Circuit Court of Appeals in a case that came before it in 1908 or 1909. The case is reported in both the Federal and the Pacific Reporters for the Spring of 1909, though the title, volume, and page numbers have long since been forgotten. The circumstances however, are still clear in the Writer's memory. Three men, one Federal prisoner and two State convicts escaped from the Idaho State Penitentiary in Boise, Idaho, and were recaptured near Nampa, Idaho. The State prisoners were tried under State law for escape and sentenced to three additional years each. They took their case into the Federal Court on habeas corpus, and were ordered released by the Circuit Court in the opinion mentioned.

Previously, by Act of May 12, 1864, C. 85, 13 Stat. 75, and Act of March 5, 1872, C. 30, 17 Stat. 35, the Congress had provided for payment through the Attorney General, for the actual, reasonable subsistence of Federal prisoners in State institutions. "Such sums as it reasonably and actually cost to subsist them."

More than one State prison Warden was to learn that "actually" is an adverb of very definite meaning; that government auditors are unreasonable persons with no respect for the usual prerogatives and perquisites of public office, including all the *squeeze* on prisoners' food that the traffic will bear, and that criminal Code Section 35, not Title 18 U.S.C., Section 1003, is a law with very vicious teeth in it. The Writer knows of no case of a conviction for grafting on the food of Federal prisoners, but he does know of a number of cases where Wardens and Sheriffs, in order to avoid prosecution, have been forced to return to the Treasury, such sums as the auditors estimated had been stolen from the prisoners' food; but such is the clannishness of power that it would have been considered bad taste to force such men to subsist on prison food for a few years. There have been notable exceptions under other circumstances, however, for making things too easy for prisoners, but never an exception for making things too hard.

Between the close of the Civil War and the admission of Washington to the Union as a State in 1889, a small Territorial jail was established at McNeil Island, which was a small but well-watered island in Puget Sound, halfway between Tacoma and Olympia, under the jurisdiction of the United States Marshal for the Western District of Washington. The Writer does not know when this jail was built, but judging from the building and from the trees that had been planted shortly thereafter, it must have been erected in the 1870s.

At about the same time, a territorial jail had been built at Fort Smith, Arkansas for the purpose of handling prisoners from the then rather wild Indian Territory under the authority of the United States Court for that district, which was at that time presided over by Judge Guthery, who was one of the exceptions to the statement previously made concerning the fairness of Federal Judges of that era.

Guthery, who would easily have been mistaken for a new dealer, as far as his regard for the niceties of the law was concerned, was widely known as *the hanging judge*, and was reputed to have kept the gallows at Fort Smith well-oiled and working overtime. The Writer has talked to many men who were tried before him – and they were all sent up either for life or for two years – which was the limit for selling whisky to an Indian. All other crimes brought before him called for life or death. The average murder trial in his court was said to have required about forty minutes, and the executions were held that same afternoon. That may have been a slight exaggeration, but it was vouched for by one hundred and fifty life-timers who were in Leavenworth at the time the Writer went there.

By Act of May 17, 1889, C. 340, 30 Stat. 417, the Fort Smith jail was given the status of a National Prison, became the first United States Penitentiary, and was authorized to receive prisoners sentenced from other jurisdictions for violating the laws of the United States. It was abandoned around 1907, however, when Oklahoma became a State, and its inmates were sent to Leavenworth, but the law bringing it into being was not wiped from the Statute books until 1920, when it was superseded and made obsolete by Act of January 23, C. 51, 41 Stat. 396.

In the meantime, the United States Army had established Military prisons at Fort Jay, New York, and on Alcatraz Island in San Francisco Bay, and at a large, penitentiary-type prison at Fort Leavenworth, Kansas. The exact dates of the establishment of these prisons is not

known to the Writer, but it must have been directly following the abandonment of Fort Jefferson, for they were all growing concerns in the 1880s.

The earliest reference to the Fort Leavenworth Military Prison found in the United States Code, 1935 Edition is the Act of March 3, 1879, C. 182, 20 Stat. 389, which provided for disposal of articles fabricated by the labor of the inmates for use of the United States Army.

By Act of March 4, 1915, C. 143, 38 Stat. 1084, the name of the Fort Leavenworth Military Prison was changed to the United States Disciplinary Barracks, Fort Leavenworth, Kansas. It was made the central unit of the United States Army penal system, and all other military prisons were made branches of the Fort Leavenworth Disciplinary Barracks.

It was further provided that these institutions should be conducted along reformative lines. They were deprived of penitentiary status; confinement therein should not carry the stigma of felon or convict; and releasees from them should not be stigmatized as ex-convicts or deprived of any of their civil rights. All inmates of these institutions were made eligible for restoration to duty in the United States Army for good conduct.

Section 7 of the comprehensive penal Act of March 3, 1891, C. 529, 26 Stat. 840, made the Fort Leavenworth Military Prison available for the housing of civil prisoners, who were convicted in courts of the United States.

This same Act provided for the selection of cites, preparation of plans and estimates for the construction of two large, modern, escape-proof penitentiaries; one to be suitably located to serve the Eastern seaboard and the South, and the other to be located near the center of the United States; both were to be operated by and under the control and management of the Attorney General.[21] It was further provided that construction of these institutions, both as to the arrangement of yards and buildings was to be such as to permit the segregation of youthful offenders, under twenty years of age, from adult criminals,[22] and that the treatment and management of the former group should be, so far as possible, reformative – a provision which very fortunately for the younger offenders, was not carried out for the next four decades.

Pursuant to this Act, plans and estimates were submitted to the Congress in 1894 or 1895, and by Act of March 2, 1895, C. 189, 28 Stat. 957, the Congress provided for the regulation of such penitentiary as was to be centrally located, and set out the laws that were to govern its operation and management. It also provided for an assistant to the Attorney General to be known as the <u>Superintendent of Prisons</u>, whose duty it was to oversee the management of the proposed institutions, look after the welfare of Federal prisoners generally, visit all institutions at least once each year, grant personal interviews to inmates, listen to complaints, and report his findings to the Attorney General. The Superintendent of Prisons was entirely without managerial powers and had no authority over prison policy, which was left entirely in the hands of the Attorney General and the various Wardens who had the authority to appoint and to dismiss at the pleasure of the Attorney General.

This was a very happy arrangement. Two decades later it was the result of an enormous amount of human good. The great advantage of this setup was that the Superintendent of Prisons had no direct power or direct responsibility for prison policies. He was an impartial court to which both the inmate and the Warden could appeal. He was not bound to any one policy more than another, but it was his duty to see that whatever policy was adopted was enforced with fairness and impartiality to all prison inmates, and to point out to the Attorney General any injustices resulting from the application of the policies of the various Wardens, both State and Federal, who had Federal prisoners in their care.

The Warden, so long as he remained in charge of his institution, was the supreme authority within its walls. The Superintendent might suggest changes in management or in the treatment of individual prisoners, but he had no power to command. If he wished, he could carry the matter to the Attorney General. If he thought a Warden was unfit, he could recommend his removal from office. If he thought that a prisoner was being mistreated or had in any way been treated unfairly, he could recommend that prisoner's removal to another institution, but in all cases, he could only recommend. Final action was the function of the Attorney General, but the Attorney General always had the advice of an impartial person who was in a position to hear bother sides of every case and was not bound to uphold any policy because he had been its author.

It was not until the following year that construction of the penitentiary to be located on the Leavenworth Military Reservation was authorized (Act of June 10, 1896, C. 400, 29 Stat. 380), and it was five years before the actual beginning of construction.

---

21   ibid, Sections 1-4
22   ibid, Section 9

There may have been political factors of which the Writer has no knowledge involved in this delay, but the principal cause seems to have been an argument with the St. Louis firm of architects, who submitted the plans for both prisons, as to whether the new institutions should be built by free or by prison labor.

That was in the days when legislators had some respect for the public purse, when billion-dollar budgets and ninety-percent income taxes were unknown, when share-the-wealth advocates were treated as harmless lunatics and permitted to spout their theories from soap boxes on the street corners or in the parks instead of from the White House, and the Congress was set on having the institutions built, so far as possible, by convict labor.

On the other hand, there were construction firms with friends in Congress who thought that the new prisons should be built by contractors, and the architects argued that in the event the prisons were put up by contractors, they would be entitled to a percentage of the contract price. The Writer does not know the details, but by Act of March 3, 1901, C. 853, 31 Stat. 1185, which authorized the construction of the other institutions on land acquired for that purpose at Atlanta, Georgia, the Attorney General was authorized to transfer to the new cites whatever number of Federal convicts as could be employed and accommodated on the new project; but it was necessary to pay the architects a stipulated sum for each convict-hour of labor employed on construction. The Writer no longer remembers the exact figure, or the details, but it is possible that it would have been cheaper to have built the prisons with free labor, for the architects were still drawing that stipend on each hour of convict labor employed on construction in the late twenties, long after those portions of the original plans that had not been used had been abandoned.

One of the abandoned features was a high-walled female prison. The wall was put up separating the area for this prison from the main institution, and most of the stone for the building was cut, but the building was never started. The enclosed area was later used as a ball park, and the stone for the women's cell house was eventually broken up and used for making concrete. The high wall separating this plot of ground from the main prison yard was finally torn down.

Goodtime

The granting of time off prison sentences for good behavior has been an important feature of American penal systems for more than a century, but since it is worthy of a more detailed discussion than is possibly at this place, we will content ourselves here with mention of the important Federal legislations on the subject. It will be mentioned again in connection with a discussion of the parole law, and will be discussed in detail in Part V.

The Act of March 3, 1875, C. 145 #1, 18 Stat. 479, merely clarified the legal status of Federal prisoners in State institutions by recognizing their right to receive such deductions as were allowed to other inmates in the institutions in which they were confined – as previously recognized by the courts – and providing the machinery for making the deductions and forfeitures. This Act provided that any Federal inmate who should commit any act which was a violation of any penal statute, should forfeit his goodtime. The courts of that day, however, held that this was double jeopardy in those cases where the inmate was tried for the offense. This fact was used in 1917 to persuade Attorney General McReynolds to rule that in any case where a prisoner was tried for an offense committed in prison, previously forfeited goodtime had to be restored.

The Act of March 3, 1891, supra, authorized the Attorney General to make rules for the allowance of deductions for good conduct to be applicable to prisoners who would be confined in the institutions that would be created by that Act, and also to men confined in institutions where no goodtime was allowed, but it made no provision as to the amount of deduction to be allowed.

The first *Federal Goodtime Law* was the Act of June 21, 1902, C. 1140, #1, 32 Stat. 397, which allowed graduated deductions of from five to ten days per month, depending upon the length of the sentence. The deductions were subject to be forfeited rather arbitrarily for misconduct, but once granted, they became as much of a vested right as a pardon issued by the President or the final judgment of a court of competent jurisdiction, and could be protected by action for writ of habeas corpus.

Although this statute was very poorly drawn and was not uniformly constructed by the courts, it remained in force for twenty-eight years. It was generally a good law and in most cases accomplished exactly what the Congress intended, even if there was considerable unfairness in its administration. Because the deductions were granted by law to all prisoners whose conduct was good, it became an incentive to men to become sycophant and stoolpigeons only after they had lost their goodtime and were looking for its return.

The first change in policy was to broaden the law by allowing additional goodtime to industrially employed inmates and to men working in road camps by Act of May 27, 1930, C. 340, #8, 46 Stat. 372. Such inmates were permitted to earn not more than three days per month the first year and not more than five days per month thereafter.

This Act made it possible for a man serving a ten year sentence to complete that sentence by good conduct and industry in a little more than five years, which was a powerful incentive to good conduct and hard work, and if left that way, might have accomplished great good. But by the disgraceful Act of June 27, 1932, C. 310, #4, 47 Stat. 381, our Government sank to a moral level never exceeded by the Third Reich, the level of an *Indian Giver,* or of the appersonification of *Habit* in one of the Ancient Greek dramas.

In the Greek drama the subject, a young blacksmith, appears before his king, *Habit,* and prays for permission to make a pilgrimage to worship at the Shrine of Diana, and is told that his wish may be granted, but that he must first make a fine chain of a certain length for the king.

The young man returns to his forge, and for twenty long years he labors early and late, shaping and welding the links of the finest iron. At last the chain is completed and delivered to the king, who praises the beautiful workmanship that has gone into its fabrication.

"Now, may I make my pilgrimage to the Shrine of Diana, Sire?" pleaded the middle-aged blacksmith.

"No!" said the King. "I am so pleased with this chain that you must first make me another exactly like it."

So the blacksmith went back to his forge and he worked for twenty more years making a fine chain of the required length, and when he appeared before his King and delivered the second chain, he was a bent and broken old man.

"Now Sire, may I go to worship at the Shrine of Diana?"

"No!" snarled the King, "Seize the fool and bind him with his own chains!" he commanded his attendants.

By this Act our Government says to the convicted person:

"By good conduct you can cut a substantial portion off your sentence, by hard work you can make another substantial cut in the time you have to serve, but don't kid yourself that you are going free. After you have delivered the good conduct, and after you have delivered the years of hard and faithful labor, you are to be turned out for a while under *conditional release,* and you are going to have to serve again that time you have earned by good conduct and by hard work, on parole with one of my bright college boys looking down the back of your neck, and when you have that time all but served on parole, I am going to send you back to prison and make you serve it over for the third time."

Of course, what this piece of legislation really says to any convict who is not a complete idiot is:

"The first time anyone looks at you cross-eyed, knock his brains out and make them take your *goodtime*. Then go on and serve your sentence flat and go out free. That is, if you have anything less than ten years. If you have more than ten years, earn all the goodtime you can, but as soon as you hit the bricks, head for the first pawnshop and buy a pistol, then take off like a P 38. If you meet any probation agents on the way, drop them a slug in the belly and keep on going until you get stopped. You will probably get stopped, all right, but you haven't lost anything for you have nothing to lose."

The history of this section is as slimy as the law itself and the persons responsible for it.

The idea of compelling the ex-convict to serve his *goodtime* over again on parole was the brainchild of Otto P. Higgens, racketeering, Pendergast chief of Police of Kansas City, Missouri, whose job it was to cover up for such good boys as Charlie Gargotta, and a great many others of his ilk, and to make a police record that would fool the public. So, when he was not busy planning jobs for his own gunmen to execute, he spent his time having ex-convicts tortured into confessions of crime his own boys had committed, just to keep his blotter clean and be able to show the public an unbroken record of crimes solved.

The Writer has talked to men who were in Jefferson City at the time Higgens was Chief of Police, and has been informed that fully ninety percent of the prisoners arriving at that institution from Kansas City were suffering from such serious third-degree injuries upon arrival that they had to be hospitalized at once.

It was a fine system, but the only trouble was that you could not just grab up anyone and hang a crime on him. It had to be an ex-convict, and it had to be one who did not have friends or connections who would make trouble. Higgens' own boys were so active that the newspapers, particularly the *Kansas City Star,*[23] were on his neck so constantly that his police had a lot of trouble finding enough suitable victims to keep the blotter clean.

It was under the compulsion of this necessity that Otto the Great came up with his magnificent idea. If all convicts were released on parole for the period of their *goodtime_*

---

23   Higgens' boys had beaten up a reporter for the *Kansas City Star* for attempting to photograph a murder.

and forced to report their addresses to the police, it would be so much easier for the police to find suitable victims that could be charged with any type of crime his own boys might commit.

At this point Otto sent for a reporter on the Kansas City *Journal-Post,* and that newspaper went to town. It spread the story over its front page in big black type. The plan would even be a boon to the ex-convicts, for it would enable the police to help those who were living honestly, and the convict could have no complaint, for after all, it was only through the State's bigheartedness that he was being set free before completing his full sentence.

The point that there was nothing bighearted in the Enactment of *goodtime* laws in the first place was entirely lost sight of. They had been enacted for the very practical purpose of making prisons easier to manage. Through them the States made agreements with their convicts for good conduct, and the basic dishonestly of repudiating such agreements after the good conduct had been delivered did not seem to register on the completely criminal-minded Higgens or on the *Journal-Post.* Of course, nothing was said about how much easier the proposed system would make it for Mr. Higgen's police to find likely victims.

The proposed legislation was too slimy for even the Pendergast-dominated Missouri Legislature to swallow, but not too slimy for Sanford Bates and Company.

Notwithstanding, the fact that the basic dishonesty of this piece of legislation has been one of the most potent factors in recidivism during recent years, the law still remains on the Statute book.

The newly revised Criminal Code, Act of June 25, 1948, Title 18, U.S.C., which became effective September 1, 1948, contains two important amendments to the *goodtime* law.

Section 4162 provides that non-industrially employed inmates performing meritorious service may be allowed extra *goodtime* on the same basis as industrially employed inmates, but puts the matter of such allowance within the discretion of the Attorney General, which means the prison officials.

The application of this section over the last two years and a companion section, 4126, which provide for paying compensation for meritorious service connected with prison maintenance, has been distinctly bad, for unlike the industrially employed inmate, there has been no fixed standard of merit to be applied in such cases.

In each case, the *goodtime* and pay is left to the discretion of the prison authorities, with the result that sycophants and stoolpigeons have been the principal beneficiaries of the legislation, which has caused a distinct lowering of the moral standards of the prison population and has fostered a distinctly criminal character. For to make antisocial conduct attractive or profitable inside can never lead to anything but antisocial conduct after release,[24] as such men as O. P. Halligan and Robert McCloughry[25] so clearly understood.

Section 4165, of the 1948 Edition of Title 18, U.S.C. provides that only earned *goodtime* can be forfeited for bad conduct, and while this is an improvement over the old system of permitting the arbitrary forfeiture of any or all *goodtime* earnable on a given sentence for a single infraction of prison rules, it is still an example of the backward thinking of the Prison Bureau in such matters.

---

24   Part I – Chapter III
25   Part I – Chapter VIII

Under this provision, a newcomer to the prison may commit any offense without fear of the loss of *goodtime,* since he has not earned any; while a man with fifteen years perfect prison record could lose more than seven years earned *goodtime* for the same offense.

The only just and equitable system is one that gives the prisoner a vested right in all earned *goodtime,* but provides that no *goodtime* shall be earned during periods of bad conduct. Such a provision was attached to the original parole law, Act of June 25, 1910, and will be discussed in connection with that subject, and the whole question of *goodtime* will be discussed in Part V.

It should be added here as a matter of general information, that one of Otto's good boys, Charlie Gargotta, thoughtlessly pulled a murder right under the eyes of a Sheriff Bask, who happened to be returning from a hunting trip, and had a shotgun in his car. It also happened that there was a *Kansas City Star* cameraman on the spot, and thoughtless Charlie had used a stolen Army automatic. This unfortunate occurrence set in motion forces that landed both Otto Higgens and Charlie Gargotta in Leavenworth.

Parole

The first Federal Parole Law is the Act of June 25, 1910, C. 387, 36 Stat. 819. There have been a large number of amendments to this Act of an administrative nature, but no substantive changes in its terms. It makes the Federal prisoner serving any term other than life, eligible for parole upon completion of one-third of his sentence, and the lifetimer is eligible after serving fifteen years.

This subject will be discussed at length in Part II – Chapters II and III.

Expansion

The Acts of May 31, 1924, C. 221, 43 Stat. 248, and December 5, 1924, C. 4, 43 Stat. 687 made that part of the Leavenworth Military Reservation lying in the State of Missouri available for the establishment of a prison farm to be worked by trustee convicts from the penitentiary.

Act of June 7, 1924, C. 287, 32 Stat. 473, provided for an Industrial Reformatory for Women, later established at Alderson, Virginia.

Act of June 7, 1925, C. 32, 43 Stat. 724, provided for an Industrial Reformatory for male first offenders, later established at Chillicothe, Ohio.

The same Act provided for industrial buildings to be built at Atlanta, McNiel Island, and Leavenworth.

Industry

During the early years of the Federal Prisons, all surplus labor was devoted to construction, but, as the construction programs neared completion, employment became a serious problem.

The first Federal Prison industry was the duck mill established at Atlanta, pursuant to the Act of July 10, 1918, C. 144, 40 Stat. 896, in which provision was made for payment of a small compensation to industrially employed inmates.

The Act of February 11, 1924, C. 17, 43 Stat. 6, made provision for the establishment of industries at Leavenworth and the payment of a small compensation to industrially employed inmates.

By Act of February 26, 1929, C. 366, 45 Stat. 1318, the Attorney General was empowered to make arrangements for the employment of Federal prisoners on Government financed roads, reforestation projects, and other public works through cooperation with the Secretaries of Agriculture and Interior.

This brings our legal history up to the time of the establishment of the Federal Prison Bureau, which will be discussed in Part III of this work. The remainder of this Part I will be devoted to the discussion of prison conditions as they existed prior to 1910.

PART I – CHAPTER II

Population

It is impossible to consider the problems involved in prison management without having some knowledge of the various elements entering into the prison population, and the population of Federal prisons has always borne a distinct relationship to the peculiar nature of Federal offenses. Back at the turn of the century the principal Federal crimes were: counterfeiting; smuggling cloth, chinamen, and opium; robbery of Post Offices and the mails in different forms, such as train robbery, Post Office burglary, and various forms of pilfering from the mails; mail fraud; violation of the National Banking Laws; dereliction in office, principally of postal employees; and violations of the liquor laws.

In addition to these strictly Federal offenses, there were the Common Law crimes committed on Indian Reservations, Military Reservations, in the District of Columbia, and in the District of Alaska.

The majority of the inmates in State Prisons were petty criminals, but only a very small number of petty criminals were brought into the Federal Prisons, the reason being that there was a much higher standard of education among Federal prisoners than among the inmates of State institutions, since forgers, counterfeiters, smugglers, conmen, promoters, and Government and National Bank employees have to be men of some substance, intelligence, and education.

After the Civil War, the invention of high explosives, the building of the railroads, and the opening up of the West, caused crime in America to develop along three separate lines and produce three distinct types of professional criminals.

There were the spectacular and short-lived Western *bad men,* who have been so much glamorized in fiction and in the movies; the James, Youngers, et al, and their imitators, who were for the most part confederate veterans who had failed to put down their guns following Lee's surrender. These were horsemen and gunmen. The best of the lot specialized in train and bank robbery. They knew little or nothing of the use of explosives, and money that could not be taken at the point of a gun, they could not take. The worst were illiterate thugs and cattle thieves who hired themselves out as gunmen in the various Western range wars or as professional murderers or cattle thieves.

This group was short-lived, both as individuals and as a type, and their era virtually came to an end with the wiping out of the Dalton gang at Coffeyville, Kansas, which, if the Writer's memory serves him well, was on July 18, 1896.

There were a very few men of this type remaining in Federal Prisons at the time the Writer entered prison, and those that remained were relics of an age when the horse was the fastest means of transportation and communication, a day that had vanished with the dawn of the twentieth century.

At the same time that the *bad men* were tearing madly over the plains of the West, the hoodlum was growing up in our cities. The hoodlum was then, and still is, the product of machine politics and police corruption. He works under some political sub-boss, often a precinct Captain, for whom he pulls any kind of rough stuff required, from stuffing or stealing ballot boxes to murder, in return for the right to ply his trade, which may be anything from *canon* (pickpocket) to safe prowler, stickup man or pimp. Many of the city mobs specialized in fur, silk, and jewel robberies, and there was often a payoff to the police on a direct percentage basis of the amount taken. In some cities the fence supplied the police connection and disposed of the loot. It often worked as in a case of which the Writer has knowledge.

The fence would send for a thief.

"I want four hundred typeWriters at ten dollars apiece. Here are pass keys to open every door in three office buildings. If you are caught on the job, you are on your own. Can you can pick up a couple of good boys and get them for me?"

Or the thief might be sent out to gather up slot machines, or to wreck slot machines, at so much per machine. There are many ways of turning a dishonest dollar in a big city, and for every dollar ever taken by the Wild West *bad men,* the city hoodlum has stolen a million, but only the leaders, the fences, and the bosses have ever seen any of the big money.

Of course, there have always been ambitious hoodlums who have occasionally stepped out and pulled big jobs on their own, but the bulk of this tribe has always been composed of petty thieves, mostly kids, taking orders from someone else who took most of the profit.

The city hoodlum has never been wedded to any particular criminal technique or any particular way of earning a living. His characteristics are that he lives in the city, works under protection of the police or some political faction, and spends most of his money on clothes and women.

The Great American Bum

The growth of the railroad brought forth the hosts of men who rode the blinds, the bumpers, and the rods.[26] The hobos, the bindle-stiffs, the migratory workers who harvested our crops, built our railroads, dug our mines, and chopped down our forests – men and boys who moved from construction job to construction job in boxcars, drunks, derelicts, down-and-outers, and runaway boys from every city and village in our land, ex-convicts from every penitentiary and kids from every reform school. The beggars that followed the roads and the season with the regularity of migratory birds, and it is hardly surprising that among these hosts of homeless men and boys, who, like the Ancient Mariner, *pass like night from land to land,* there should grow up a race of thieves,

---

26   *Blinds* were the covered small area between the coal tender and the baggage car, or between two baggage cars on a moving train. Whoever could hide there and stay would arrive as quickly as the wealthy passenger. *Bumpers* are self-explanatory. The *rods* were the slanting iron underpinning of freight cars. An experienced rider could travel there for some distance with reasonable comfort, as Jack London discovered in his youth. – **Note by Tom Gaddis (Author - "Birdman of Alcatraz.")**

a criminal fraternity, the members of which traveled and lived like harmless hobos, who used the railroad in making their *getaways,* and who dominated the criminal scene for half a century.

Shortly after the Civil War such a group, called the *Lakeshore Gang,* made its appearance along the New York Central and Pennsylvania Railroads running between New York and Chicago and traversing the richest industrial sections of our land. This group was not really a gang at all; it was a fraternity of criminals, and was the nearest thing to organized banditry that this country ever had before the days of prohibition.

The police and the Pinkerton called these men yeggs.[27] They called themselves Bums or Movers. They were divided into three loosely drawn groups: the beggars; the thieves; and the Mushfakers, who were umbrella menders, scissor sharpeners, and tinkers who mended pots and pans, made and sold slum jewelry, or peddled lead pencils. Many men in this group were real cripples, and others were phony cripples who used what was called the throw out, a trick of throwing their bodies out of joint so that they looked like hopeless cripples. The thieves specialized in safe and bank burglary, usually by means of high explosives, though they were not above an occasional stickup. They preferred to work at night, when identification was difficult; and in their day, they represented organized crime in its most feared form, occupying a position in the public mind very similar to that of the kidnapper and bank bandit of a few decades later, though they were never so highly organized.

High explosives provided the thief with a quick, sure, and easy means of opening the

---

27   The *yegg* is a technical crime term for which one looks in vain in criminology indexes. Stroud's account, with several exceptions, finds astonishing verification. William B. Watts, Chief of Detectives of the Boston Police Force who studied the habits of criminals from 1876 – 1924, made a 10,000 word manuscript published after his death in the *Boston Herald* Sunday, February 8, 1925 through the courtesy of his widow. He described the origin of the term *yegg* and gave a detailed account of the methods of this railroad-based safe burglar.

Stroud's most unusual and controversial claim concerning the *yegg* – his monosexual environment and habits – is partially borne out by Watts. Since the manuscript is a newspaper account, he was indirectly revealing (when the press standards of frankness in 1925 are considered). The young graduate of the tramp camp, who is sent out by the actual burglar or *yeggman* to beg, to locate burglary sites, "is called in the *yegg* vernacular a 'gay cat.'" In another section Watts characterizes the yeggs as reckless and fearless, "but for the most part very rank morally."

This distinct criminal type created by the railroad was a feature of the crime scene in America for half a century. Techniques for extracting nitroglycerine from dynamite, the dangerous product known as "grease" became part of the *yegg* subculture. Nitroglycerine and soft yellow soap were smeared into and between the cracks of earlier band and payroll safes. The detailed method is described with analogical accuracy by both Stroud and Chief Watts.

Origin of the term *yegg* is obscure. The Oxford English Dictionary is laconic, stating that the word 'purportedly' came from the surname of an early robber. Watts, however, states that the term *yegg* and *yeggman* and *John Yegg* originated with the gypsies. Among the gypsies the cleverest thief was selected as the *yegg,* or chief. *Yegg* has always been a status term as well as a specific description in the earlier crime world after 1850.

Stroud ascribes the use of the term *yegg* to detectives and inspectors, to the outside world. The *yeggs* called each other *movers,* to distinguish their kind from *hoosiers* (of the current 'square john') and ordinary hobos. Otherwise the vernacular cited by Stroud and that by Watts are similar. Of *keister, snitch, mouthpiece, rumble,* and the like.   **Note by: Tom Gaddis (Author - "Birdman of Alcatraz.")**

strongest safes then in existence. The railroads provided an easy means of traveling from one end of the Nation to the other without ever being seen by any member or organized society. And the hordes of harmless tramps and hobos provided a way of life that was entirely beyond the reach of the law.

Opening a safe with high explosives is sometimes a noisy process, however, and citizens of that day were very apt to object to having their sleep disturbed, and would reach for that squirrel rifle or shotgun. Also, in many cases, it was necessary to prepare a series of "shots" before the money was reached. Even a single door required more than one shot on some occasions, or it might be necessary to blow a vault, blow a safe inside the vault and a chest inside the safe. Sometimes the buildings were equipped with burglar alarms. All of which meant that the mechanic, the man who actually blew the safe, and who could not work in perfect darkness, was a sitting duck for anyone who might care to fire on him from the darkness outside.

There was just one solution for that problem: the mechanic had to have enough gunmen, outside men, to protect him and keep an avenue of escape open until he could get the money. But, since the mechanic had to put his life in the hands of the men outside, he wanted to have some method of judging their character. And for that matter, each man on the job wanted to be sure that in the event any one of them was ever arrested, he would prove to be of strong enough character that he could not be forced to talk by any known torture. The only way to obtain such strength of character was by training. It was to meet this need that the Lakeshore Gang came into existence.

It was agreed by the original group of thieved rooting (stealing) along the Lakeshore that they would not go on jobs with untried hoosiers – any man not a mover was a hoosier – but only with each other or with boys trained by themselves, or other members of the group of tested and tried character. Thus grew up a loose federation of individuals and small groups propagated on the order of the Mamelukes[28] of Egypt.

In the monosexual environment of the road, all men, hobos, beggars, working-stiffs, and movers were pederasts, and there were always a sufficient number of runaway boys for their sexual gratification. It became the purpose of the movers to select from these boys those of the strongest character and train them in their profession.

They developed a sign language by which they could communicate with and locate each other; a jealously guarded slang idiom by means of which they could recognize each other and carry on extended conversations in the presence of a third party without danger of being understood. They developed a code of ethics which they enforced with ostracism and the pistol. They foreswore women, used runaway boys for their sexual gratification, and selected the most promising of these for protégés and neophytes to be introduced into the secrets and mysteries of their profession only after a rigorous apprenticeship, designed to develop strength of character, to show up character defects, to weed out weaklings, to develop a race of men who could not be compelled to talk by torture, nor to desert a companion under gunfire, carefully selected for intelligence and judgment under duress – and the only way that any person could be accepted into the profession was by means of such an apprenticeship. Those suspected of having violated the rigid ethics of the profession were ostracized. Those known to have violated them were killed, but no

---

28   A member of a military class, originally composed of slaves, that seized control of the Egyptian sultanate in 1250, ruled until 1517, and remained powerful until massacred or dispersed by Mehemet Ali in 1811.

mover could be convicted on mere suspicion, as was the case with hoodlums during the 20s and 30s.

The Writer, though never a member of the fraternity, because he had no desire to become one, has listened to more than one trial, the outcome of which was life or death, both in the jungles and in prison, and heard evidence sifted with a skill that would have done credit to many a court of law.

The beggars and *mushfakers* were not thieves, but they were often ex-thieves and they cooperated with the thieves, who often traveled as beggars or *mushfakers;* every boy was thoroughly trained in those professions before being permitted to know anything about stealing. They were taught to beg as mutes and as blind persons and tested until they could take a punch in the eye without flinching, have a pistol fired alongside their heads from behind unexpectedly without batting their eyes, or have a lighted cigar held against their flesh without crying out or uttering any sound. These same tests were commonly employed by the police.

Boys being trained as mutes were required to sit around the jungles day after day for as much as a year or more without ever uttering a sound or showing any interest in any sound or spoken word; they sat with blank faces, ignoring everything except signs addressed to them, and if you think that is easy, just try it for a single day. Remember that these were boys in their early teens, for the ideal age at which to begin a boy's training was considered to be eleven years, boys over fourteen were generally considered too old.

A common identification made of any boy who had been through this training was the *bug scars* on his arms or legs, for to inure them to pain, most *bum kids,*[29] were taught to beg with *bugs.*

A *bug* was a lye burn kept open for months and permitted to fester. A paste of wet lye was placed upon a spot about the size of a dollar on the boy's arm or leg, covered with a damp bandage and left on until the skin was destroyed and the member so badly inflamed that it really looked as if the boy had blood poison; then the boy would be sent out to beg, armed with a letter signed by a doctor in some distant town saying that to save the boy's life it would be necessary to amputate the injured arm or leg. There was only one ray of hope. There was just one doctor in America who might be able to save the member and the boy's life, too, but that doctor was always halfway across the Nation. He might be at Mayo's, John Hopkins, or in California, depending on where the boy happened to be. In any case, the boy was begging money to get to the man who could save his arm or leg. He would not go near any local doctor, because he knew the local doctor would want to cut his arm or leg off, and he wasn't going to go through life crippled. If people wanted to help him, all right. If they didn't, he would just go on bumming his way, hoping that he could get to that doctor who could help him in time. If he didn't, well he would probably die in some jungles or boxcar along the way. It was hard to resist such a plea, and a good boy with an active *bug* was sometimes good for as much as three-hundred dollars per day.

There were cases where boys did lose their arms or legs, and there were cases where the *bugs* went sour and the boys died, but those were the hazards of life, anyway, so no one paid too much attention to them. In the life these men led, there were many hazards that one could not afford to worry about, but it was a health life; even if most persons would think it a very hard one, man is a rather tough animal, so such cases were much rarer than

---

29   The term *bum kids* distinguished them from the other brats called *gazonies,* who hung around the jungles.

one would expect. The Writer has seen boys with *bugged* arms swollen to the shoulder and giving off such a stench of rotting flesh that it was impossible to stay within ten feet of

them. Any doctor would say such an arm had to come off at once. But the Writer has seen the same boy three weeks later and heard him moaning because he had not been able to keep his *bug* active. It had healed in spite of everything he had been able to do to it. Every well-trained *yegg* had several of these *bug scars,* and they were, in a way, his diploma.

For fifty years these men carried on a ceaseless warfare with the police, with the hoodlums, and with the Pinkerton Detective Agency, which had a contract to protect all member banks of the American Bankers Association, and as men engaged in this warfare, the *yeggs* found their early training of value.

When arrested, they did not talk. That does not mean that they told the police a pack of lies. They did not tell them anything, not even their names. They just dropped the blank mask over their faces that they had learned when begging as mutes and said nothing. The Writer has known *yeggs* to come to prison booked under such names as *Del Monte Bar and Casino,* because those had been the spots where they had been arrested, and the police, being unable to get one word out of them had so booked them.

Names did not mean much to the *yeggs,* anyway, since every *yegg* was known to his companions by a professional name, called a *moniker,* which could usually be represented by a symbol, like a trade-mark.

These men were very clannish, and they had to be. The Pinkertons had sworn to exterminate them, and were constantly hiring ex-convicts who had learned something of *mover* ways in prison, to go out and mix with them, and tip off their proposed jobs, so they could be shot down from ambush while in the act of committing a robbery, and many a mob was shot down by this method, but many a *Pink* was tripped by the first question he was asked in the jungle and died for it, too. That question was:

"Who was your *jocker?*" and the pseudo *yegg* had better name some well-known *yegg* and know a lot about him that the police would not know.

"Were you with him at the time he killed so and so?" and the right answer was not always Yes or No, for maybe there had been no such killing.

The first exposé of this group was written by a renegade member, Eddie Fay, *West Philadelphia Eddie,* at the behest of the Pinkerton Detective Agency, which had secured his release from a Carolina prison for that purpose, and was published by the *Saturday Evening Post* as a serial in 1914. A boy that Fay had trained, who was at that time in Leavenworth, was assigned to the task of killing Fay for it and carried out the assignment.

It was not the *Pinks,* and it was not the *Bums* who turned copper that brought about the end of this once numerous clan.

With the development of the automobile, the coming of the First World War, and the growth of the bootleg business, the techniques of the old-time *Bums* became obsolete.

For some years the Safe Companies had been making things tough by bringing out the *cannon balls* and other tool-proof and explosive-proof chests, with such perfectly fitted doors that it was almost impossible to get any grease into them. It was not that these safes could not be got – they could. The trouble was that few buildings could stand the repeated shots necessary, and more than one job had to be abandoned because the mechanic was in danger of bringing the building down around his ears before getting anywhere near the money; and the number of gunmen it took to provide protection for the mechanic, as shot after shot woke up the town, made the business unprofitable.

The Writer knew the first man to take one of the big *cannon balls*. The job had required 21 shots, and to save time, the mechanic had not left the building during the shots. When he came out with the money, he was bleeding from his nostrils and both ears, was so blind he had to be led away, and thereafter, he was deaf as a post and his hands trembled constantly. It had taken four men to protect him, and the take had been less than twenty-thousand dollars.

When in trouble, the *mover* always had one friend, and strange as it may seem, that friend was always the Postal Inspector.

Movers did not, as a rule, rob Post Offices, but they were not the only safe crackers in the country, and there were many men, not skilled mechanics, who had picked up enough of the technique in prison to open fire-proof boxes, and these men specialized in small-town general stores. In many small towns throughout the Middle West, there were no banks. The general store was also the Post Office, and having the only safe in the town, often served as a depository for money and valuables. The takes were not large, but they were substantial compared to the risks, for the only hard part about such jobs was the *getaway*. Kids were often taken out on these easy jobs. The result was that hundreds of these little Post Offices were robbed every year, and only occasionally was an arrest made.

The men who specialized in this work usually had a market for stamps at seventy-five cents on the dollar, and the average little Post Office was good for a couple hundred dollars in stamps, and "Uncle Samuel" did not like that very well.

These were one or two-man jobs, and the technique was very simple.

The men contemplating such a job would break into the powder house on some construction project and obtain dynamite, caps, and fuse. The next day they would go to some hobo jungle, get a couple of empty, five-gallon oil cans, and some Turkish towels. They would fill one of the cans two-thirds full of water, put it on the fire and bring the water to a boil. Then the *mechanic* would move the can of hot water at least ten feet from the fire, and he would unwrap the sticks of dynamite and crumble them into the water. By the time he had twenty sticks crumbled up, the water would be cool enough to put his hand in, and he would agitate the mass gently with his hand for some minutes. Then he would put a Turkish towel over the mouth of the other can and empty the water and sludge onto the towel. When the sludge had drained, the towel would be removed from the can, and the handfuls of the sludge would be transferred to another towel and rung into the can of water until nothing more could be rung from them. This would be repeated until all the sludge was wrung dry. Then the water would be poured off, and the nitroglycerin, which is a thick, oily fluid, about the same color and consistency as castor oil, that had settled to the bottom of the can, would be poured into whiskey bottles, cushioned with water, if a bottle was only partly filled, and be ready to use. The recovery by this crude process is about ten percent, and the product, because it contains many impurities, is about ten times as dangerous as pure nitroglycerin.[30]

---

30   More than one pseudo safe-blower has been trapped by bringing a spoon to skim the grease off the top of the water. The Writer has even had several Alcatraz safe-blowers tell him about doing that, but the specific gravity of nitroglycerin is still about 1.9.

The next day the man who has wrung out the grease would be helpless with a nitro headache, but his companion would secure about six bars of laundry soap, knead them into a thick, gummy mass, and wrap it in a damp towel.

A day or two later, the men would enter the town where the robbery was to be committed, then after dark they would break into a section gang tool house and obtain a crow bar, a hammer and a few feet of wire.

As soon as the town was asleep, the thieves would cover their faces with handkerchiefs, catch the night constable and tie him up with the wire.[31] Then they would break into the store. If the store contained firearms, as many of these as possible would be loaded and carried outside, while the *mechanic* loaded the safe. This was done by soaping the crack all around the door and fashioning a little soap cup at the top, into which the grease is poured, so that it would run down around the jamb of the door. It only takes about two teaspoonfuls of grease to lift the door from an ordinary fireproof box of the type of 1900.

After the box was loaded, the *mechanic* usually passed the bottle and caps outside, but many men kept them on their persons. The *mechanic* usually stayed in the store, merely stepping out of the line of the blast. If possible, he stood behind the safe and stood on his toes with his mouth wide open – to keep the concussion from bursting his eardrums.

When the safe went off, the outside man went into action. He would start shooting as rapidly as possible with everything he had in order to create the impression that he was an army engaged in a furious gun battle, to make it sound as much like the Battle of Gettysburg as possible for the few minutes it would take the *mechanic* to get the dust door open, break out the *flunk* (cash drawer) and search the safe for other valuables. Of course, everyone who made a light or opened a door or window would be shot at, but great care would be taken not to hit anyone – and any man who violated that rule would not be taken out again unless he could show good reason why it was necessary to kill.

These men had no compunction against killing, if necessary. They would kill a *Pink*, a stoolpigeon, or any member of their own group who violated their rules of professional or social conduct. They would kill any hoodlum who fooled with them, but unlike the trigger-happy punks of a few decades later, they were thieves, not killers, by profession, and they did not kill citizens or uniformed police, and very few of them would kill in order to make an escape, either from the job or from prison. It just wasn't considered smart. It was much better to surrender, take a light jolt and avoid a murder rap. They used firearms professionally to intimidate others, but they very seldom killed excepting in

protection of their own lives, and they knew that for practical purposes, a close bullet is often as effective as a fatal one.

Once they had the money and stamps, they would fire a final volley of shots into the night and take off across lots.

The first night was usually spent on foot, and sometimes it would be necessary to spend several nights on foot and several days in haystacks before getting to a spot where they could grab a train, but jobs were usually planned so that they could be on a train by daylight. Sometimes they would bury their loot and arms, walk down to the jungles and

---

31   The citizens are helpless without a leader, and the constable is their natural leader. They will not organize a pursuit until they find him.

get drunk. They would be found there the next morning, just a couple of harmless hobos, and the worst thing that could happen to them would be ten days on the rockpile.

There was little or no risk in such jobs, and it was an accident if the men were caught.

The Writer was once sitting in with a group of about a dozen safe-blowers who were talking shot. The subject of discussion was the best and quickest way to get the dust door open and to break out the *flunk* – no time was ever wasted on opening the money drawer on the job. It was broken out and carried away.

Men had been telling how they loaded the safe just right, threw a blanket over it, and did not even awaken persons sleeping upstairs, but they had trouble punching the lock off the dust door and breaking out the *flunk* without making any noise.

There was a young fellow, about twenty-seven, in the group called *Iowa Jimmy*.

As a thirteen-year-old runaway orphan who had been bound out to an Iowa farmer, Jimmy's ambition had been to become a *yegg*, but he had been unable to find a jocker who would undertake to train and teach him, so he had kept his ears open and had trained and taught himself by the hard method of trial and error. He had finally been accepted into the fraternity, but he had become a lone wolf, and he specialized on one-shot jobs. One of the men turned to Jimmy:

"How do you get the *duster* and *flunk?* It must be a problem, working alone without protection."

"Oh, I don't have much trouble. I guess I am not as good as some of you guys; I probably never shot a box without waking the town up, but I don't have any trouble in getting the money and getting away."

"But the *duster*! How do you get the *duster?*"

"Say, I been listening to you guys, but I don't think I understand. We must have been going up against different kinds of boxes. The ones I work on, the *duster* is always open, if it isn't gone. I load up the box, put on a *knocker* (cap) with a four-inch string (fuse), then I take the *grease* outside. When she goes off, I fire a few shots up and down the street. If there is a concrete sidewalk or building, I bounce the slugs off it, so they will sing. Then I run in, snatch up the *flunk* and take off. I don't fool with no silver or stamps. Too much trouble, and they ain't much good anyway, being torn and bent, so I just snatch up the *flunk* and beat it."

"Snatch up the *flunk* and beat it?" said another man questioningly. "Where in the hell do you snatch it from?"

"Why, off the floor, usually about six feet in front of the safe."

"Where in the hell is the door at?" asked another man.

"Oh! That! It's usually across the street."

"For Christ's sake! How much grease do you use?"

"I give her whatever she will drink. Usually about an ounce and a half."

There were other and bigger jobs upon which there was plenty of risk, and whenever a *Bum* was arrested cold turkey, the first, last and only thing he said to the police was:

"Send for the Postal Inspector. I will talk to him alone."

If the State rap was anything less than murder, the police would probably honor this request, and within an hour or two the *Bum* would be taken to a room for a private interview with his best and only friend in the law enforcement machinery of the Nation.

"Listen!" the Bum would say. "These mugs have me bang to rights on so and so, and they have a lot of phony raps they are trying to hang on me, and they are figuring on giving me a rough working over." (He usually had plenty of marks of his preliminary treatment on him). "I have fall dough planted in a jug. I want you to get me a mouthpiece down here right away. I want some tobacco and cigarettes. I want you to arrange to have my meals sent in from a good restaurant. And can you make these local Johns lay off? If you have any unsolved P.O. in this district, I am willing to cop for any reasonable price."

The Postal Inspector would look him over.

"O.K. Joe! I will take care of everything. No use getting a lawyer and spending your dough until I have a chance in investigate. I'll put the weed and chow on my expense account. I'll make the *flatfeet* lay off of you, too. I'll be down to see you tomorrow with a list of the jobs I have, and we will make a deal that is fair to both of us."

When the interview was over the inspector would appear before the Desk Sergeant.

"I want you to book Joe Dokes for Post Office robbery."

"Why we have him for bank burglary; we have two other charges against him and both Iowa and Minnesota want him."

"Fine! I want him, too, and I am going to get him. Now, get this! He is a Federal prisoner. I am going to have some tobacco, the newspapers, and his meals sent in to him, and I am going to be down here to see him every day. If I find one mark on his body or that he has been mistreated in any way, someone is going to do time for it."

The next day the Postal Inspector would visit Joe and tell him just what the State had on him, with all the details.

"Now it is like this Joe. They are set to bury you. I can take you away from them, and I might be able to get these State charges *nol prossed.*[32] If I can, I'll let you plead to any P.O. on this list for three years. I have a tough judge, and that is the best I can do. If the State won't drop, your best bet is to take two P.O.s from this list here. They all call for five years. That will be ten years for two of them. You do six or eight, and that will just put you over the Statute of Limitations on these raps here, I will talk to the C.A. (County Attorney) and see what I can do. I don't want to bury you, and I don't like to see anyone buried, but the State is after your scalp. You haven't a chance to beat that jug rap. The best you can get is twenty, and you might get life."

"How about that stuff in Iowa and Minnesota?" asks Joe.

---

32   A declaration that the plaintiff in a civil case or the prosecutor in a criminal case will drop prosecution of all or part of a suit or indictment.

"I can't do a thing about that – out of my district, but if you take a Federal rap and sit tight for a year or two, they might forget about you."

So Joe might plead guilty to two Post Office burglaries or to ten, and he might be sentenced from two to ten years, but in every case the deal worked out was the best one possible for the future interest of Joe Dokes or Joe Yegg, or whatever the name might be. He and the inspector were always friends. Every time the inspector visited the prison, he always called Joe out and shook hands with him, and maybe slipped him a few cigarettes.

Up until the First World War the United States Postal Inspectors had the greatest record of crimes solved of any police body in the world, and one fourth of the population of our Federal prisons was made up of *yeggs*.

These men were not liked by the prison officials, but as individuals and as a group they were the most highly respected and the closest watched men in the prison; also, so far as prison routine was concerned, they were about the best behaved group in the prison, too. Strict discipline being something they had been taught from childhood, they followed prison discipline as a matter of course, but being of superior intelligence, well grained in rough-house methods, inured to hardship and punishment, and completely loyal to their own group, they were more feared than liked by prison officials. They were the one group in the prison that could act as a body and could be just as rough as necessary if the occasion called for it, but they did not consider it smart to have trouble in prison.

Many of these men had "State hold" ordered against them on charges ranging up to first degree murder, so there were many of them who were very anxious to escape, and they would cooperate with any other prisoner, not a stoolpigeon, wanting to escape.

They hated all stoolpigeons. They hated the guards, and they hated all police, but as a group, although there were short-lived exceptions, their word was god. As bad as many of them wanted to escape, the Writer never knew of one case of a *yegg* promising not to try to escape in order to get an opportunity to do so. They were an outcast clan, but their words were good even when given to a copper, and the prison officials knew that.

The *mover* was a pederast in prison as well as on the outside. While most of them consider all women from the tribe of Delilah, and would not steal with any man who played with women, they made no secret of their interest in boys. Yet the Writer knows of not one case where one of these men were ever caught and reported for any act of perversion, for they were the most circumspect persons in the prison.

The vast majority of these men were very strict monogamists, and they forced their own strict standards upon their boy companions; most guards knowing that, probably thought it best to look the other way.

Outside, the *movers* were always searching for bright and good-looking boys with *hooky* tendencies to be trained in their profession, and they would occasionally pick up a boy in prison for that purpose, but that was not often and as a practice was frowned upon, for the majority did not consider most boys met in prison worthy of such training.

Sometimes a *yegg* would pick up a boy in prison, promise to teach him how to steal, tell him romantic lies about million dollar robberies, without any idea of giving the boy anything more than misinformation that would probably get him killed if he ever tried to put it into practice. Such men were called *romancers*, and they were not well thought of by their colleagues. In most cases, the *yeggs* absolutely refused to tell their prison boys anything about stealing, and any *yegg* who passed out professional secrets to persons of untested character was not apt to live long.

On the other hand, when one of these men saw some boy of reasonably good character who, he was convinced was bound for a life of crime, anyway, he would often teach the boy enough about the art of stealing to enable him to survive a little longer than he would otherwise. But the advice most often passed out to boys in prison by men of this group was to *get a pick and shovel* – their expression for honest work. And for every boy induced into a life of crime by these men in prison, ten were discouraged from becoming professional criminals; the fact that some were taught criminal techniques was more the fault of society than it was of this group of men. For society, by making things as hard as possible for the ex-convict, made most boys in prison feel that crime was the only field that would be open to them upon release, and even had there been no internal pressure compelling them to do so otherwise, such boys would gladly have given themselves to any man who would make an effort to teach them how to get by after release.

Yet, it was probably this situation more than any other that gave our prisons of that day the reputation of being schools of crime, and caused the false idea that this could be corrected by segregation of youthful offenders, and would decrease the percentage of recidivists. The results of this policy, over a period of one hundred years have not justified it and should have long-since convinced the public that the policy is basically wrong psychologically, as will be shown later.

Once a Yegg always a Yegg, was a common police aphorism, and in view of their vigorous early training, one would expect that to be true. Yet, it was the ambition of almost every *yegg* over thirty to obtain enough money to go into some legitimate or semi-legitimate business, settle down and live within the law, and few of them over forty were ever found on the road.

At the time the Writer came to prison, the *yeggs* made up about one-fourth of Federal Prison populations, and were dominant in setting the moral tone of the prison society, but even then, the *yegg* was on his way out, for like the Spartans of old, whom in so many respects they closely resembled, they were incapable of change, and when their techniques became outmoded and their way of life no longer possible, they passed away. A few, like the *Bugs Moran* outfit in Chicago and the *Johnny Hogan* outfit in St. Louis did try to fight the hoodlum for a place in the bootleg business, and bloody wars were fought in many of our large cities, but for the *movers* it was a losing battle. Bred in the clean, healthy air of the open road and trained to a code of honor, they could not compete with the ruthless breed of trigger-happy murderers that had climbed up out of the slums of our big cities to grasp at and obtain untold millions of bootleg wealth.

The Counterfeiters

The counterfeiters, particularly the hard-money men, were not a uniform group, like the *yeggs*. They came into crime at all ages and from all walks of life, and very few of them had any previous criminal record.

These men did not look upon themselves as criminals, nor could they be convinced that they had ever harmed any one. They were frustrated artists who were thoroughly satisfied that they could make better money at less cost than the mint. They felt that the Government actually owed them a debt of gratitude for increasing the wealth of the

Nation, for as long as their lead dollars would buy as much as any other dollars, no one was hurt by their activity, and they could not see where anyone had any complaint. It was just the bankers who complained anyway. Well, next time they would make them so good that not even a banker could detect them. Then what? They would make billions, and the country would be rolling in wealth.

These men were fanatics, actually religious fanatics, and counterfeiting was their religion. They were like other religious fanatics, too. They had seen the light, and the phony money urge had come upon them like a bolt out of the blue, like any other religious conversion, and like St. Paul, they had seen the blinding light and had fallen down, but had risen up to proclaim the glory of a new god, to become the saviors of mankind, to bring wealth and happiness to millions with their phony money.

Their fellow inmates considered them crackpots, which they actually were, but no American who has listened to the phony-money ideas that have been coming out of Washington since 1929 has any right to laugh at their reasoning, though the hard-head people back in those days would not listen, or think of electing them to public office.

While many of these men were short on formal schooling, they were, as a general rule, much better read and informed than the average person on the outside. Some had been preachers, bankers, businessmen, schoolteachers, and there were probably more college men in this group than any other, with the single exception of the bankers. This group probably contained fewer homosexuals than any other group in our Federal Prisons, too. Not one in fifty was a pederast, though many of them were four and five time losers. Practically all had been married. Many still owned their own homes, and the majority were the fathers of children.

There was nothing exclusive about the counterfeiters. They were generally of good social morality. There were very few stoolpigeons among them, and they were very well behaved as prisoners, but as animals they were much inferior to the *yeggs*, and there were very few fine physical specimens among them, since they had not lived the vigorous, outdoor life of the road. They spent practically all of their spare time studying up on methods and

materials for making better money, and as sure as they went out, they were sure to come back.

Any counterfeiter would teach any boy or anyone else how to make money. He was proud of his art and was glad to have anyone listen to him. Nothing pleases one of them so much as to get a green boy in a corner and talk him deaf, dumb, and blind, but they made few converts among the youngsters, who soon became bored to tears by so much talk of strange metals and alloys, of specific gravity figures and plating solutions. The teen-aged boy was much more interested in tales of blazing gun battles, hair-breadth escapes, of bags of gold and stacks of greenbacks so heavy they were a burden to carry away, of romances in prison, in the jungles, in haystacks, of eleven-year-old boys sleeping in their jocker's arms in haystacks while they were hunted by posses with baying hounds, coming nearer and nearer and nearer. No! The counterfeiters did not find many neophytes among the boys in prison, for actually, they were about as romantic as stuffed fish.

The *Shovers*, that is, the men who passed the phony money were usually of the same type as petty criminals everywhere, but even so, most of them were more interesting persons than their masters, and they were not as a rule, fanatics. Money *shovers* were first offenders, and one jolt was often enough to cure them. Once a man conceived the idea that he could make better money than the Government, he practically always died in prison. He would go out, spend a few months or years assembling equipment, and just about the time he was ready to start work, he would be arrested, and right back he would come. For what most of these men did not realize was that from the hour of their release, the Secret Service kept them under surveillance twenty-four hours per day and recovered every coin they spent and every coin spent by any person with whom they were seen associating, but that did not mean that the counterfeiter would be arrested as soon as they knew he was turning out money. On the contrary, they would let him go until they had learned all about his technique.

On one occasion the Writer had a chance to read an operative's notes on one of these men for one month, taken a year before the man was arrested.

The man was a college graduate. He had taught school and had held down a post as instructor while doing some post-graduate work. He was married, owned his own home, was the father of two children, was about twenty-eight or thirty years of age, and was employed as a collector for the Seattle Gas Company at the time he conceived the idea of making ten dollar gold pieces.

The daily notes went about like this:

"I picked up X when he left his home. Operative No 214 reported that X had not been out of his home all night. We rode downtown on the Yestleway cable car. He paid his fare with a nickel. It was not recovered.

"X went directly to the Gas Company Office on Jackson Street. I was there joined by Operative No. 361. At five places during the forenoon, X was observed to approach the cashier and exchange gold for silver coins. In each instance the contents of the till was examined by either No 361 or myself. No bad money was found.

"X ate his dinner at a dairy lunchroom on Third and Marion Streets. He gave the cashier a silver dollar and received fifty-five cents in change. The dollar was recovered and found to be good.

"At 3:10 P.M., in a butcher shop at 516 First Avenue, X was again observed to approach the cashier and ask for change. I inspected the contents of the cash drawer at 3:12 and found one counterfeit ten-dollar gold piece. I questioned the cashier, and she said that X had exchanged a twenty dollar gold piece and had taken all of his change in silver. There were seven twenty-dollar gold pieces in the cash drawer. All were good.

"The cashier swears that X could not possibly have given her the bad ten."

That is the way it went, and the Secret Service permitted this young man to operate for one year before they arrested him. They knew that he was making the coins in the basement of his home; that he passed one coin every day for six days each week; that he taught a class in Sunday School each Sunday and that he always put a good ten-dollar gold piece in the collection plate at each Sunday Evening church service, but every person upon whom he passed one of his phony tens was willing to swear that he could not have done it; that no ten-dollar gold piece had changed hands – and so he ran for a year without even suspecting that he was being shadowed.

Yet, this young man's technique was very simple.

"Can you break this please? I am in need of change," he would say to the cashier, pleasantly, smiling at her as he spoke. And if there was a ten dollar gold piece in the change he would shove it back.

"I would prefer to have all silver if you can spare it," he would say. He would have the phony ten in the palm of his hand, and he would make the switch as he picked up the silver and shove the phony ten back to the cashier, who, thinking it was her own ten, would sweep it into the cash drawer with a single motion of her hand, without even looking at it, and two minutes later she would have completely forgotten that part of the transaction.

This young man received a seven-year sentence, which, back in those days, was a very stiff sentence for counterfeiting. The judge castigated him from the bench and pronounced his crime, in view of his education, background, and opportunities, absolutely inexcusable. He had not needed the money, and he had not squandered it on horses, women, or fast living. As he said himself, he had just done it because it looked so easy and he was sure that he could get away with it, but he was very much surprised upon his arrival at the prison to learn that the men there had been expecting him for a year.

The way that had come about was interesting.

Two guards had had a fistfight and had been given thirty-days suspension without pay as punishment. One, an Irishman named O'Conners, had been an operative of the Secret Service before becoming a guard, and during his suspension, he had gone to Seattle and obtained temporary employment from his old boss.

When he had returned to the prison, he had sent his clothes out to the Writer, who was then laundryman, to be pressed, and he had forgotten to remove his notebook from his coat pocket.

Unfortunately, the notebook did not contain the name and address of the suspect, so it was impossible to send some discharged inmate to warn him that he *had his commitment in his pocket,* as O'Conners had expressed it when the Writer returned the suit and notebook to him.

Smugglers

The smugglers, on the other hand, were hardheaded businessmen who had balanced the chances of being caught against the profits to be made, and found the risks worth taking. A few of the younger men wore an aura of adventure about them, but these were really only the underlings, hired to do the rough physical work. The real smugglers were men well into middle age with sons and daughters in college or married and bringing up grandchildren. They were the type of men who called bank presidents by their first names, and were about as glamorous as an adding machine.

When the Writer was ten years old a piano made entirely of pressed and veneered opium had been found in a barn only one block from his home. That piano had contained one hundred and fifty thousand dollar's worth of opium, and there had been many columns about it in the newspapers, as well as about the notorious smuggler suspected of being responsible.

The Writer read every word of the lurid stories, and they stuck in his memory, for he often played in that barn with the two children of the man who owned it, and had been on hand when the father had driven in with the piano and been arrested, only to be released when he showed that his papers were in order.

He was a furniture mover and general hauler. The day before he had received a phone call asking him to pick up a piano at one of the docks and move it to a certain address. The invoice and bill of lading had been delivered to him by a messenger boy. He had picked up the piano. Shortly after noon, one of his horses had lost a shoe, so he had been forced to stop at a blacksmith shop and have the horse shod. By the time he left the blacksmith shop, it had been too late to deliver the piano that night, so he had driven to his own barn, intending to deliver the piano the next morning.

The people at the delivery address showed where they had actually ordered the piano from a firm in London. There was nothing to connect them with any dope.

There was much to cast suspicion upon the notorious smuggler, but there was no direct evidence.

Ten years later, at McNiel Island, the Writer, a boy of nineteen, was moved into a cell with a little milk-toast of a man, in his middle forties, whose face was vaguely familiar. When the Writer mentioned that he was from Seattle, the little man asked if he knew West, the mover.

"I used to visit him a lot. We have been in business together off and on for many years."

Something inside of the Writer's head clicked.

"Why, I remember you. You used to give us kids nickels and dimes for candy."

"You mean to say you were one of the kids who played with West's children?"

"Uh-huh! I saw you there a lot."

"Remember that piano they knocked off in his barn?"

"I'll say I do. It was supposed to have belonged to that famous smuggler _____." (name forgotten).

"Yes! I lost a lot of money on that deal. It cost me twenty-five thousand dollars to have that piano made in Shanghai."

"You --- You're _____, the famous smuggler?" The Writer's mouth dropped open.

The older man smiled.

"Fame in my business is hard luck, kid," he said. This is my fourth, two-year stretch here. I don't mind the time so much, but every time you are knocked over you lose a lot of money. I lost more than two hundred thousand dollars on my last deal. Of course, I'll probably make it up next time, but it put a terrible crimp in my bankroll.

And it put a terrible crimp in the Writer's childish ideas of the glamour of smuggling, to know that this meek little man who gave nickels and dimes to kids was the famous smuggler he had pictured in his childish mind so differently.

"What did they do about the piano?"

"Nothing! They knew it was mine, but they had no proof."

Another famous smuggler was Larry Kelly, a buccaneer who sailed his own windjammer and was reputed to have brought in millions of dollars worth of opium and hundreds of Chinamen.

Larry Kelly was a dumpy little man with big, bushy eyebrows and the close-knit, muscular body of an old sailor. Although he was over seventy at the time the Writer came to prison, he still worked on the excavating gang,[33] and could throw as much dirt as any of the younger men. Old Larry was just finishing up his eighteenth two-year sentence for smuggling.

One Sunday the Writer saw Larry working on a large, detailed pencil drawing of a ship.

"What you figuring, Larry? Retiring and getting a yacht?" the Writer said, looking over the old man's shoulder.

"No! This is my new schooner. As soon as I get out, I am going to Singapore and have this schooner built. Isn't she a beauty? I am going to take on a crew of two hundred Chinamen at five hundred dollars gold each, and load her with a million dollars worth of opium. I am going to land my crew and cargo on the beach and then sink the schooner. If this one pays off, I will retire."

"If you can build a ship like that just to sink after one trip and can buy a million dollars worth of opium, you have enough to retire now. Why take a chance?"

"Why! Kid! I don't have that kind of money any more, but my credit is still good. I can always get backing for a ship and cargo."

Paul, the quiet, beardless youth sitting at the next table was serving ten months, for his first dope jolt.

The Writer looked at the old man who had spent over thirty years of his life in prison and was still hoping to make one last coup, and at the beardless boy, a year younger than himself, and he made up his mind that the risks were not worth the price, even for a million dollars.

But Larry's last voyage must have paid off, for he did not come back to prison. A few years later the Writer saw an item in a newspaper that said that Larry Kelly, reputed millionaire smuggler had died at the home of one of his daughters.

Postal Employees

This was a spotty group, better educated than the average person on the outside. Some of them were men of good character, but there was a large proportion of these men who were natural stoolpigeons and did not look upon themselves as criminal. They always took the official view on every subject and were not well liked by their fellow convicts.

---

33   Part I – Chapter XVI

Bankers

Some of the young boys who had been bank messengers, Fuzzy[34] and Marcel were nice kids of good character, but the older men were more policeman than the guards. They identified themselves with the ruling class on every occasion. This was particularly true of tellers and cashiers, but when it came to bank presidents, it was the other way around. It is characteristic of every truly big man that he identifies himself with the most lowly elements in his environment. Their ways may not be his ways, but he tries to make them so, and their interests are always his interests. We have no better literary example of this than Oscar Wilde's great poem, the *Ballad of Reading Goal* in every line of which he identifies himself with his fellow inmates. It was not the Poet Laurate, who had walked with kings, but the convict, speaking.

In addition to these groups, there were still a few of the Wild West bad men serving life for murder and train robbery, and a few common men serving sentences of two years for mail fraud.

These men as a rule were not well liked. There were men of good character who were well liked in all of these groups. Few were outright stoolpigeons, as were so many of the bankers and postmasters, but some of the most dangerous stoolpigeons were to be found in these groups. It was characteristic of the Wild West bad men that they were utterly lacking in loyalty, and on a job, would often murder their companions to keep from dividing the loot. In prison, they were always planning an escape, but most of the escape plots in which they were involved were snitched off. The Writer has served time with some of the most notorious of these men and on several occasions has been instrumental in exposing them as rank stoolpigeons – one was the notorious Ben Cravins.

Conmen too, are very undependable. They are, as a rule, men of superior intelligence and fine personality, but they are lacking in sound character. The only difference between the conmen, the Wildcat promoter, the high-pressure salesman, the religious evangelist, and the political demagogy is the thin line of the law. All of them deal in lies, as their only stock-in-trade, and they come, sooner or later, naturally, to look upon all other persons as suckers, to be used for their benefit but whose rights do not have to be observed, and loyalty to such persons is looked upon as a weakness. Anything that serves their own end is justified, regardless of the affect upon others. Yet, because of their powers of expression, quick and resourceful minds, and their broad understanding of human nature and behavior, they are often an asset to the prison community of which they form a part.

The Common Law Crimes

Persons convicted of common law crimes and general criminal offenses were brought into the Federal prisons from the Federal Districts: Alaska and the District of Columbia, the Indian and Military reservations, and to a lesser extent, from the Maritime jurisdiction and the army. Of these groups, those men coming from Alaska, where crimes against property were almost completely unknown during the early days, at least ninety-five percent were convicted of three offenses: homicide, attempted rape, and selling whisky to Indians.

---

34   Part I, Chapter XIII

There were no rape cases from Alaska, for all of these charges involved white men and young Indian girls, and if the attempt was successful, there was never any complaint, for neither the girl nor her people would testify. On the other hand, men have been convicted of attempted rape for merely taking an Indian girl under eighteen in their arms and kissing her, and the offense usually brought a fifteen year sentence.

The majority of the inmates from the District of Columbia were colored, and the most common crimes were homicide and housebreaking.

Murder

Murder is unique among criminal offenses, since it is a crime that most anyone may commit, and there are few persons who have not wanted to, or actually considered plans for murdering some other human being at some time in their lives. Ervin S. Cobb, on one occasion, in an article pleading for the life of a fellow newspaperman convicted of his wife's murder, wrote:

"All married men should rally to this man's defense, for there is not a one of you who has not wanted to strangle his wife on more than one occasion, and I have long been convinced that everyone should be permitted to commit at least one murder."[35]

About one-fifth of Federal Prison populations prior to 1910 were in for murder or manslaughter, and in those days, murder, unaccompanied by rape or robbery, was not considered a crime involving any moral turpitude. Murderers come from all walks of life, are often men of good character and unusual ability, and in most prisons back in the days we are now discussing, they formed a distinct group of pronounced individualists who stayed pretty much to themselves. Not many were stoolpigeons or sycophants, but those that were, were among the worst. As a class, they are the least troublesome of any group in the prison, the best behaved, and the most apt to be made trusties. They always preferred risks, either as trusties or on parole, and in State institutions they have usually held most of the key positions in the prison, because they seldom violate any trust placed in them.

The most common criticism leveled against the murderer by his fellow inmates is that of aloofness. He has too much at stake to become involved in petty prison intrigues. Yet, while to them the prison is only a temporary residence, to him it is this home, the place where he is apt to spend the remainder of his life. So he is always deeply interested in anything that is apt to be of long-range benefit to the prison body. He is not normally apt to cause trouble, but the minute conditions become intolerable, he is the most apt to take it upon himself to straighten them out – and he will not ask others to help him.

The Hoodlum has not been discussed at length in the chapter, since he did not come in conflict with Federal Law until a much later period.

---

35   Quoted from memory.

PART I – CHAPTER III

General Discussion
Of
Prison Conditions Prior To 1910

In discussing prison conditions back in the early days of our country, we must realize that many of the conveniences we have today simply didn't exist, and that during many periods in our history, the standard of living in the free world was nothing to brag about. Even as late as the depression years of the Thirties, many persons deliberately committed crimes in order to have themselves sent to prison, where living conditions were better than they were on the outside. Society has always had to guard itself against making crime attractive to the limp, lame and lazy elements within its midst, and this fact must always be borne in mind when judging the harsh conditions of bygone days. Those conditions can be fairly just only in relationship conditions existing in the free world of that day.

Then, too, the tax-payers of the last century were not the weak and supine, thoroughly regimented variety we have today. They were hard-bitten men who labored for twelve or more hours every day, often slept on straw ticks, and on hard winters used parched corn in place of coffee -- and when they paid their hard-earned dollars into the coffers of the State, they wanted to know exactly where every dime of their money was going. They did not want it wasted in keeping pampered parasites on the Government payroll or supporting worthless criminals, who had already cost the State far too much money in slothful idleness and luxury.

The good book said: "The way of the transgressor is hard," and they really intended it to be hard. They insisted that all sentences be to hard labor, and they wanted that hard, too. They themselves, often worked from dawn to sunset, and the average working day for public servants in heavy industries was twelve hours. Naturally, such persons saw no reason why men in prison should be treated better than they, at their expense. Nor was there any reason why the convict should not be forced to earn at least a portion of his keep.

Most prison officials looked upon it as their righteous duty to make the lot of those unfortunates entrusted to them as hard as possible, consistent with life itself, and in many institutions the death rate was rather frightening. Before we go into that however, it is important that we understand just what a penitentiary is.

A Penitentiary

A prison or penitentiary is not, as many persons seem to think, a jail where prisoners remain locked in their heavily-barred cells, presided over by armed guards for twenty-four hours per day, and probably chained to the wall as an additional precautionary measure. Of course, there have been prisons of that kind, and there are cases where such conditions, or even worse, exist in American prisons today,[36] and they are the accepted mode of punishment in Spain. But it was soon discovered that this form of imprisonment is such an expensive luxury that no modern State can afford it. For where prisoners do not do the work essential to making the prison function, free men drawing State pay must do it.

You see, a prison is a community where men live and breathe and have their being, and it is subject to the very same natural laws of community living that govern the community in which you live. Men must eat and sleep and perform the functions of elimination. They must be clothed in some fashion, and those clothes must be made either by convicts or by free labor, and where men are sentenced to hard labor, there must be some kind of labor for them to do. There must be a reasonable amount of sanitation, as much for the benefit of those who work in the prison as for those who live there, for contagious diseases breed in filth, and poorly nourished bodies may easily build up a virulence that makes them a menace to all persons in the vicinity.

There must be the butcher, the baker, and the candlestick maker, so to speak. There must be men to sweep the floors, to keep the plumbing in working order, to cook the meals, dispose of the garbage, and to do the thousand and one other chores connected with good housekeeping, either in prison or on the outside. In both cases, this work consumes about twenty percent of the available labor of the community. There must either be some kind of work for the other eighty percent or they must be kept in idleness.

Since the taxpayers are not willing to support the criminal in idleness, there must be work for him to do. And work, even the simplest work, involves the use of tools. In the hands of a determined individual, every tool is a weapon. It is impossible to sweep the floor without a broom, but persons who have not seen it tried, do not realize that a broom thrown against the shoulder and used as a bayonet, even with a blunt handle, is almost as effective as a real bayonet, for no man will stand up under the force of impact of a hundred-and-fifty pound man moving thirty feet per second concentrated into an area of less than one square inch.

Failure of the press and the public to realize these basic facts has been responsible for prison officials often being subjected to unjust criticism.

A man runs amuck and kills someone, or maybe a number of persons, or over-powers guards and makes a spectacular escape, and right away there is a big hue and cry of lax administration.

"Why was a dangerous criminal allowed to obtain weapons?" screams the front-page editorial. "Why wasn't he watched more closely? What were the guards doing?"

Of course, any fool should know that there was nothing the guards could do, for guards are ordinary human beings, just like you – so are convicts, for that matter – and they cannot read the human mind. Even in Alcatraz, where men are counted every fifteen minutes of the day and night, where millions of dollars have been spent, rather foolishly, in making the place secure, where they have almost as many paid employees as convicts, there has never been a time when weapons were not available to any man determined to get and use them. There, in what is touted to the world as *the tightest prison in America;*

---

36   See *In re* Medley, 134 U.S. 160, an opinion in which the Supreme Court of the United States discusses solitary confinement as a punishment for crime.

which of course, is pure fiction, for there have been more murders in Alcatraz than in any other unit of the Federal Prison System. The public should realize, as many prison officials do, that men can always commit acts of violence, if they want to.

It is not possible to keep men who want to do so from committing acts of violence anywhere, but it is often possible to make them sorry or so over-awe them that they will not want to try anything of that kind. It is only the completely hopeless or the insane man who is apt to resort to violence where he has no chance of getting away with it. It was upon such considerations[37] that the penal theory of the last century was based.

If a convict gets out of line, kill him or make him wish that he was dead.

This public disregard for the life of a convict was called to the Writer's attention at a very early age. The Writer does not remember the names of the men involved, but it was a Pennsylvania case and occurred during the winter of 1896 and 97. It involved two brothers who had made an escape in a snowstorm through the aid of the Warden's, jailor's, or Sheriff's wife, to whom one of the brothers had made love. They attempted to get away in either a horse drawn buggy or sleigh. They were run to earth by a posse of mounted men, and although they were unarmed, they were shot down, but what stuck in the childish mind of the Writer was the boasting of one of the posse men that he had stood over one of the fallen brothers, a man who had never harmed him personally, and emptied his Winchester through the wounded man's body, just to make sure that he was dead.

The Writer's mother had a hard time trying to convince the Writer that such an action was not murder, and she did not wholly succeed, for she could not bring herself to say that shooting a fallen and unarmed man was justified, so she had to fall back upon the explanation that because the man who had done the shooting and boasting was a Deputy Sheriff, nothing would be done to him for it, which simply caused the Writer to conclude, with the direct and infallible logic of childhood, that it was perfectly all right to kill if you could get away with it, and if it were Deputy Sheriffs who were killed, the cause of justice might be better served.

The Purposes of Prison

Prisons developed along two lines, and the primary purposes of prisons of the penitentiary type seem to the Writer to have been: first, to make escape impossible by means of the high walls; and second, to hide from public view the cruelties that enlightened persons had come to consider debasing but with which society was not ready to dispense.

Before the Revolutionary War with England, prisons as we know them today did not exist, and the ordinary punishments for crime were public torture of various kinds, such as flogging, pillory, public branding, mutilations of various kinds, death, either by hanging or burning at the stake, or banishment.

In pre-Revolutionary days imprisonment seems to have been employed as a punishment for debt more often than as a punishment for crime, and one of our earliest prisons was the old Dexter prison in Boston, where men, women, and children were thrown into one big room together, with only a minimum of furniture and bedding and the crudest sanitary arrangements, and where conditions of vice, brutality and disease were said to have been something frightful.

At the same time there were two-hundred-and-fifty some felonies known to the British Common Law for which the sentence of death or banishment could be imposed.[38] Yet, before the passage of the criminal reform act during the early days of the reign of Queen Victoria, England was the most crime-ridden nation in Europe.

The oldest penitentiary in the United States was the Solitary Confinement Prison established at Philadelphia in the year 1787, which later became known as the Eastern Penitentiary.[39] In this prison, as it was originally established and operated, each inmate had a rather large cell to himself, which had a small walled court behind it to which he had access and where he could enjoy fresh air and sunshine. The only faces the inmate ever saw and the only voices he ever heard were those of his keepers and the men who brought his food.

Many other Eastern States erected prisons on this same solitary-confinement principle, but most of them were far less liberal in their conveniences, and the dungeon-type cellblock was a natural development. The Writer is under the impression that the first prison of this kind was built at Elmira, New York, in the 1790s, and the security and economy of space possible in this type of construction caused it to become standard throughout the United States, and with the innovations of open-front cells, electric lights and modern plumbing, the same type of construction is that most widely used today.

The Cell Block

The cellblock is just what the name implies. It is a solid block of cells, built like a stack of boxes with all doors opening outward upon galleries running along the face of the block. Blocks may be anything from five cells long to fifty cells long, and from three to seven galleries high, but in modern practice they are not often built over five galleries high, and where a cell house is over twenty-five cells long, the block is usually built in two sections with the stairs in the center, between the sections and the door facing the stairway, for this permits marching the men into and out of the cell house four abreast, prevents confusion, and saves time.

Usually the cellblock was surrounded by a building, and where there were a number of blocks, as at Leavenworth, they were often arranged like the spokes of a wheel, each block in a separate building, but that was not invariably the case. At San Quentin the blocks were built right out in the yard. The cell doors were of solid steel with one-inch holes for ventilation and a small wicket that the guard could look through when counting. Due to the mild climate, outer buildings and artificial heating were not thought to be necessary. At Alcatraz, on the other hand, four small blocks were originally enclosed in a single building.

This type of construction has a number of advantages. Where each block sets in its individual building, all cells face outward, toward the windows, and no inmate can see

---

38   See Masterly dissent in Weems V. United States, 217 U.S., 349, 1910, in which Chief Justice White goes into the legal history of the clause in the Bill of Rights forbidding cruel or unusual punishment, which later became a part of our National Constitution by way of the Eighth Amendment.

39   See *In re* Medley, 134 U.S. 160, 1891

into another inmate's cell. This is important, and where the converse is true, there will always be a high murder and assault rate. This design also permits one guard to keep an entire side of the building, maybe five hundred cells, under constant observation, and he can be stationed in a room beyond the end of the cell house where he can see anyone who comes out of a cell or tries to approach the windows. If there is any shooting, there is no chance of a man in his cell being hurt.

Another advantage is the fact that all cells on every gallery or all cells on one side of the cell house, can be locked and controlled from boxes at the end of the gallery or by a lever located outside on the cell house. There are many of these locking devices of varying complexity on the market, but the simplest and the hardest to beat is nothing more than a one-half by two-inch flat rod that is operated by a lever that moves it two inches and in doing so moves a similar upright strip of steel over the edge of the door. Such a lever is hard to beat. The only way that it can be done is by cutting the upright bar, which is not easy, because it is exposed. Some of the fancy systems can be beat with a piece of wire.

Our ideas of prison punishment undoubtedly developed from the monasteries of Europe, which were really papal prisons and were employed as such for centuries before the building of any frankly penal institutions. The name, *penitentiary* is of obvious religious origin and was undoubtedly intended to mean, *place of repentance* in the religious sense.

In the over-populated countries of Europe, it was considered fitting to force men to repent in solitary confinement. In Spain, that system is still in use. It is the law that the prisoner shall never be permitted to see a human face, and whenever one is taken out of his cell for any purpose, he is forced to wear a leather sack over his head.[40]

The enormous insanity rate in such prisons as well as the cost of maintaining them caused the idea to soon be abandoned in America. It was found best to put two men in a cell and give them something to do, for as previously said, America was a place where there was more work to do than hands to do it, and the taxpayers were not willing to support criminals in idleness.

Labor

When prison populations were small, those men not needed to take care of the chores of maintenance could be put to work on a rock pile or woodpile. In those days there was always a big demand for stove-length firewood and crushed stone for road building; and there was no machinery to perform such tasks. But with the growth of prison populations, it was impossible to keep them all employed at such menial tasks.

Some prisons were blessed with large farms, where the prisoners could work under gun guards or in chains and were forced to earn at least part of their keep. In some cases, they actually returned a profit to the State. This required the development of no new techniques, since the system had been well worked out on the large plantations of the South during slavery days, where generations of large slave gangs had worked under mounted gun guards and the lash. They had even developed an efficient system of running down runaways with dogs. Some of these methods are still used in some Southern States and will be discussed presently.

---

40   *Prison and Beyond*, Sanford Bates; *Life Magazine*, date forgotten.

Many years after the Writer came to prison, it was possible to stand in a prison bathroom and identify men who had served time in certain Southern prisons by the whip scars on their bodies.

The problem in many Northern States, with their denser populations, was different. Many States had built their penitentiaries on the outskirts of large cities, which had soon grown around them, and no land was available for cultivation. There were enterprising men in America who could not tolerate the idea of anything going to waste, not even the labor of convicts, and they were glad to help the States solve their problems at four-hundred percent profit on their investment by paying the State a handsome price, ranging from as low as ten cents to as high as forty cents per day for the labor of all physically fit convicts.

The Contract System

Under this system the private contractor moved factories inside of our prisons and put the convicts to work; the arguments in favor of the practice were of the very best.

Not only would the contractor pay the State a liberal price for the labor of its convicts, which would take a big load off the backs of the taxpayers, but he would teach every physically fit convict a useful trade, by which he could earn a good living after his release from prison, and teach him the habit of industry that would make him a valuable member of society.

It was a most beautiful argument, and it was not surprising that with the proper amount of *grease* massaged into the right and not overly reluctant palms, many State Legislators swelled their chest and glowed with righteous pride at what they were doing for their fallen brethren who were to be taught useful trades and have their feet set upon the path of virtue by the benevolence of the contractors. Don't Laugh! That may sound like sarcasm, but it is literal truth.

The Writer's great uncle, Robert McCartney, whose name he bears, was associated in business with Senator Marcus Hanna, of Ohio, and they owned the prison contracts at both Columbus, Ohio, and Michigan City, Indiana. The Writer's great aunt, Mrs. Emma Jane Clemens, who was the oldest person ever admitted to the bar in the District of Columbia and the sister of McCartney, has told the Writer many stories of her visits to these prisons with her brother during the years following the Civil War. She saw with her own eyes the wonderful feasts that the contractors provided for these convicts at Christmas and Thanksgiving, out of the kindness of their hearts, and heard the applause of all those convicts when her brother made his appearance. She was totally convinced that her brother was a most wonderful man, dearly beloved by all those criminals he was working so hard to assist at four-hundred percent profit on his investment.

But the good sister was not shown the dungeons, the water cure, the perforated paddle, the long benches in the idle house, where men, broken in health and no longer fit to work in the contract shops, many of them far gone with tuberculosis, sat side by side, all day long, and coughed their lungs out but dared not speak to their neighbors, since to do so was to invite more punishment. And years later, when she was a much older and much wiser woman and had read of these things in Brant Whitlock's great novel, *The Turn of The Balance* and had discussed them with Whitlock in person, she told the Writer that every time she thought of those conditions and her brother's part in them, it made her turn sick at her stomach.

But had this young woman been permitted to see the conditions under which these men were forced to work in the foundry, the bolt mill, and the cigar factory, where men were driven to perform tasks that only the strongest or the most skilled could make over any period of time, and actually worked to death, her stomach would have been turned a lot sooner.

At many prisons the task was set on a weekly basis. The new man entering the shop was given so many days or weeks in which to learn the work and develop enough skill to do the task, but once a man had done a task, the training period was over, and he had to do the task thereafter.

It was common practice for the contract foreman to bribe some stoolpigeon to help the man or give him extra work so that he would turn in a task before his training period had expired.

The Writer is more familiar with conditions in San Quentin back at the turn of the century than in any other prison using the task system, so it will serve as our example, although California had abolished the contract system some years previously and established a State-owned jute mill.

The task, if the Writer can trust his memory back as far as 1903, was four hundred and seventy-five yards of cloth for each weaver per week, which was just about what a man could get out of a five-hundred-yard warp. Each new man put in the jute mill was given thirty days in which to perform a task, and thereafter he had to turn in a full task of good cloth each week. No one drove him. He could leave the mill if he wished and go out and lie in the shade of the building when he wanted to, but by Saturday at noon he had to turn in his cloth.

The cloth was inspected and all defective cloth that was not good enough for making grain sacks was cut out and used for making potato sacks, and if there was less than four-hundred-and-seventy-five yards of good cloth, the inmate was taken to the hole, in the old sash and blind building[41] and chained to the door. There he would stand for six hours, then could sit down for two hours. This process was repeated from Saturday noon until Monday morning, during which time he was given no food and very little water. He was sent out to work Monday morning without any breakfast.

Should a man fail to make his task a second or a third time, the same punishment was repeated. Should he fail three times within one month, the fourth time he failed he was given six hours in a *straight jacket*.[42] Each additional failure brought six additional hours in the jacket.

The San Quentin straight jacket was only remotely related to the restraining jackets used in insane hospitals, and was said to have been the invention of Sam Randolf, who was Deputy Warden at Quentin for many years prior to 1911, and it consisted of a form-fitting piece of heavy canvas with eyelets set four-inches apart along the edges, and with a flap that went over the back, so that the victim was completely enclosed in heavy canvas.

The jackets came in various sizes, and for each man, a jacket was selected which would reach from his neck to his ankles and in which the eyelets in the two edges would be about

---

41   This building was a relic of the days when California had the contract system, but later it was fitted with cells and used as a place of punishment and Isolation.

42   See *My Life In Prison*, Donald Lowery; *Star Rover*, Jack London

four or five inches apart when the jacket was folded over the body.

The prisoner to be punished was stripped naked and placed on the jacket face down. The jacket was then laced down the back with sash cord by two husky, convict orderlies, who would put their feet against the man's body and use all of their strength to lace the jacket as tightly as possible. If the prisoner was thought to have inflated his lungs to steal space, he was kicked in the ribs a few times to knock the air out of him.

When the prisoner had been laced as tightly as possible from the back of his neck to his ankles, he was rolled over on his back and a quart of Epson salts was poured into him.

Two hours later, the laxative effects of the salts had caused the canvas jacket to be filled with the prisoner's body waste. Then he was rolled back over on his face, and an orderly, using a stick to twist the rope, took up all the slack caused by the laxative, and the feces, having no place else to go, was squeezed out around the prone man's neck and ankles and ran into his face. For this reason, the convicts called the jackets *shitsacks*. The prisoner was then turned on his back and left lying in that position for the remainder of his sentence.

The first time the inmate was kept in the jacket for six hours; the second time, for twelve hours; the third time, for eighteen hours; the fourth time, for twenty-four hours.

The Writer knew personally the only one of four men sentenced to ninety-six hours, who survived. He spent the next seven years in a wheelchair, but he finally recovered sufficiently to lead a criminal career for some years. Some persons might even call it a successful career, for he did not go back to prison. He specialized in single-handed stickups, and it was his fixed policy never to permit a witness to live.

Years of suffering eventually made him a drug addict with all of the addict's deterioration of character, however, so he was finally killed by other *yeggs*, who considered some of his conduct unethical, to put it mildly.

When a man had finished his sentence in the jacket, it was unlaced, and the prisoner was washed down with a garden hose. If he could be kicked to his feet, he was given his clothes and ordered to return to his cell. Otherwise, he was carried to the hospital or morgue. After the third or fourth trip to the jacket, a man would have to be taken out of the jute mill because his hands would usually be so badly crippled that it would be impossible for him to tie weaver's knots.[43]

Different prisons had different forms of torture. In Ohio, the first failure to make a task was punished by a night and day chained up in the hole; the second, by so many strokes on the bare buttocks with the perforated paddle, which was introduced in 1896 or '97, when the Writer was just beginning to read newspapers; and, while names are long since forgotten, the Writer can still remember the interview published in the *New York World* in which the Warden, who claimed to have invented it, took great pride in the paddle's effectiveness. The instrument was a heavy wooden paddle made from an oak board about five inches wide and three-quarters of an inch thick, in which a number of half-inch holes had been bored. At each stroke of the paddle, the Warden explained, each hole produced a blood-blister, and the next stroke broke the blisters produced by the previous one until the buttocks were reduced to a raw and bleeding mass that would stick to and be irritated

---

43   Note: This description of the jacket is based upon the personal stories of more than three-hundred men that Writer has known, many of them before he came to prison, who had been in the jacket. Some still carried the marks upon their bodies at the time the Writer listened to their stories.

by the rough, woolen, striped clothing the convicts wore – for in those days, no convict was permitted the luxury of underwear. The third and severest punishment employed at Columbus was a *water cure*. The prisoner was strapped in a sitting position in one end of a bathtub and a stream of water was sprayed in his face until his lungs were full of water, and he passed out. Then he was thrown over the edge of the tub where artificial respiration was applied until he was revived. Then the treatment was repeated – often as many as three times in succession. Naturally, many of the victims did not survive.[44]

In Washington Penitentiary at Walla Walla, a high-pressure *water cure* was employed. Punishment was always inflicted in the evening, after the other inmates had been locked up for the night. The prisoner was taken out in the yard and chained naked with his back to a crude timber cross set in the ground, and a half-inch stream of water at more than one hundred pounds pressure was sprayed over the body. It was the policy to avoid the face until near the end of the treatment to keep from killing the victim, and to then give him only a few short blasts in the face. The Writer once examined one of these men four months after the torture. There were still large black and blue discolorations on his chest and one of his testicles was four times its normal size. Many men were emasculated by this treatment, and of course, there were others who did not survive.

Walla Walla at that time had three cell houses, which were referred to as wings. About the second time an inmate came before the Deputy Warden, that gentleman would say:

"The next time you come over here I am going to transfer you to the fourth wing." The fourth wing was the graveyard.

The Writer does not remember the nature of the contract industry at Walla Walla. At Salem, Oregon at this time, 1900-1910, the contract industry was a foundry, and the punishment for not making a task was flogging.

The inmate was chained with his face to the cross and flogged across the back with a blacksnake.[45]

Many attempts were made to take such cases into the Federal Courts on the grounds that such treatment constituted cruel and unusual punishment, forbidden by the United States Constitution, but in most cases Federal Courts were loath to intervene in the affairs of the States. In some cases, individual Federal District Judges issued writs, held hearings, and subjected guards and officials to rigorous public examinations, but their actions served only as exposés of the institutions proceeded against. The writs granted in such cases were practically always overturned by higher courts on the grounds that the prisoner had not exhausted his State remedies, when actually, he had no means of getting into the State court. This was not so in the case of Federal prisoners in State prisons, however. In re: Birdsong, 39F599, the District court's power to punish a State court for contempt is upheld.

---

44   Note:The Writer has it on the authority of an attendant who recently worked there, that a similar treatment is still extensively employed at the Oregon Insane Hospital at Salem, with the difference that the victim is simply thrown over the edge of a bathtub, and the water permitted to drain from the lungs. No attempt is made to reestablish respiration. Deaths are reported as pneumonia. The ex-attendant, who had assisted in carrying out these murders, salved his conscience with the consolation that he had only carried out the orders of his superiors, had never acted with malice or animosity toward the victims, and had sought and found less gruesome employment just as soon as possible.

45   A long, tapering, braided rawhide or leather whip with a snapper on the end.

We had such a case in Chicago as late as 1943 or '44, when United States District Judge Barns took jurisdiction and exposed conditions then existing in Joliet on the basis of a letter smuggled out of the institution. Every Federal Judge has such power, but it is not often that one of them can be persuaded to use it in behalf of a convict.[46]

Where Federal prisoners were confined in State institutions, the situation was different, and many Federal judges issued writs on a basis of mistreatment and refused to permit Federal prisoners to be returned to the offending institutions. This was responsible for the Acts of July 12, 1876 and February 27, 1887, anti,[47] giving the Attorney General power to move prisoners from one State to another and making the employment of Federal prisoners in contract industries an offense against the United States.

The real solution to every social problem always remains in the hands of the individual, and it is fortunate that in almost every population there have always been a few individuals of courage and character who, when they dislike anything badly enough, can be depended upon to do something about it, or die trying. Had that not always been true, mankind would still be living in caves or swinging from tree to tree by its collective tails, if it had not long since vanished from the earth – and every citizen who walks into a bar and orders a beer, should remember that. He should remember that as a citizen he owes that right, and every other right he possesses, for that matter, not to the good people who made polite speeches against prohibition, but to hoodlums who were willing to do something about it, even if they died in the process. There is no case in all human history where a bad or oppressive law or condition has been corrected by the agitation of good people who obeyed it. It has always been those persons who have been willing to use an ounce of lead or a foot of steel who have brought about improvement.

Remember that while the Supreme Court was piously writing the Dred Scott opinion, John Brown was raiding plantations and putting firearms in the hands of Negroes.

Call such men criminals if you will, but remember that if the day ever comes when mankind no longer produces individuals who are willing to put their lives on the line, by killing or being killed to correct the things they do not like, humanity will be on its way out.

That principle is as true in the prison society as in any other society. In every prison there have been a few men who could be driven only so far, men who so resented cruelty and injustice that they would rather die than tolerate it – and sometimes they have died so spectacularly that they have focused public attention upon the conditions against which they rebelled. The Writer cites a few such cases from his lifetime.

There was Harry Tracy who, with his companion, Frank Merril, in the late summer of 1903, shot his way out of the Oregon State Prison at Salem, and who for sixty days cut a bloody swath across two states, killing every law-enforcement officer who fell under the sights of his rifle, even killing his own companion, and who after each killing, wrote taunting and gloating notes to the newspapers, boasting of his exploits, poking ridicule at the posses sent out to capture or kill him, and making appointments with the police for future encounters – appointments he always kept.

---

46   Changing times have produced enormous changes in Federal Court decisions during the last twenty years. **Note by: Tom Gaddis**
47   Part I – Chapter I

He was called a madman. Maybe he was mad to some extent. Maybe all of the men who do things are a little mad. The Writer can remember that in that same year many Americans were calling Marconi and the Wright Brothers mad, too. Judged by ordinary standards, Tracy was undoubtedly mad, but such men cannot be judged by ordinary standards. Let us take a closer look at the picture, for there are points that have never been emphasized.

It would have been easy for Tracy and Merril to have escaped and simply faded from the picture. What the public never knew, however, was that Tracy was not a professional criminal, and had no desire to become one, but that Merril was a *yegg*. At that time, by application of the *yegg's* technique, they could have simply vanished from sight.

Merril just wanted to escape, but Tracy wanted vengeance, and to get it, he was willing to kill anyone, even Merril, knowing full well that in the end he would have to die.

The escape from prison had been played up in the press as being particularly ruthless. Three guards had been shot, and the killing of one of them had been wholly unnecessary to the escape. Tracy had gone out of his way to kill the man. What the press never knew was that, that guard had had Tracy flogged a short time before the break.

The Writer has sat in many a jungle and heard Tracy criticized by *yeggs* as a publicity seeking madman, but that madman, even with his crude ungrammatical notes, brought conditions at Salem and the causes of his intense bitterness so forcefully to public attention that he won a large measure of admiration and respect even among law abiding persons. He never killed or injured any private citizen, although he did use a big Swede for a pack animal; he stole only to supply the barest necessities of life, and he never took more than was essential for his immediate needs. He killed only police.

That same year there were also the thirteen men who, led by Ed Marrel and Jakie Oppenhiemer, captured the Folsom Prison armory at knife-point, armed themselves, and escaped with a large group of hostages, and for a short time created a young reign of terror throughout Northern California.

In this case, it should be noted, that all but one of the hostages, including the Warden, were released just as soon as the men were clear of the prison. One man only, the day Captain, the man who inflicted punishment, was retained for special treatment. There were men in the group who wanted to kill him, but they had been voted down. It had been decided that it would be much better to humiliate him. So even this bitterly hated Captain was permitted to return to the prison under his own power and not seriously harmed, though he probably waddled like a duck after being raped thirteen times, but there is always the possibility that he did not find that too burdensome, or even may have enjoyed it.

The Writer has forgotten many of the details of this affair, although he heard them from many men who were in the prison at the time of the break, including Sheeny Bockman, the old man from whom he received his first advice on the art of serving time,[48] and he does not remember whether these men received additional sentences for this break or not. But in any case, Ed Marrel and Jakie Oppenhiemer and some of the others were transferred, after their recapture, to San Quentin, where they spent more than seven years

---

48   Prologue

in Isolation in the old Sash and Blind Building.[49] Jakie was hanged in 1911 for blacking a guard's eye, just as described in the novel. Marrel, who had been serving forty years, was released in 1911 by Governor Hiram Johnson and became a Writer. It was he who supplied London with the material for the *Star Rover*.

There have always been such men as Panny Danials of Cañon City and Joe Kretzer of Alcatraz, and whether or not we agree with their methods, whether or not we think that they were wise or that they made things better or worse for those who came after them, they have always served the very useful purpose of forcefully reminding those in power that all men are mortal, that none are born with a boiler plate between their ribs, which is the only known antidote for the virulent poison of unrestrained power.

During this early period there was some talk of reformation. As early as 1835,[50] the Congress had suggested that the treatment of juvenile offenders should be so far as possible reformative in nature, and many States have erected institutions that are euphoniously called *reformatories, houses of correction*, et cetera, but in practically all cases such institutions were, and still are, far more brutally managed than penitentiaries. In many of these institutions some pretenses of providing the inmates with education were made, though on the whole, these usually did not amount to much.

In most cases, the whole emphasis of imprisonment was punishment, and when a man's time was up, he was given a suit of shoddy, prison-made clothes, a small sum of money, usually five dollars, and in the case of Federal prisoners, a railroad ticket to his bonafide home or place of arrest, and set free.

Naturally, a great many of these men headed for the nearest pawnshop, purchased a second-hand pistol, and set out to even the score at once. The story of one such man released from a contract prison in the year 1906 was, in his own words substantially as follows:

"I went to a pawnshop and purchased an old, rusty 45 and a box of shells for five dollars. It took the last cent I had. I wanted to load the gun in the store, but I guess the Jew had been taken before. He would not stand for it. I loaded it in an alley, and I went back just before quitting time. I killed the Jew, got two good, new *rods* (pistols), some decent rags and about fifty bucks in cash. That night I elevated another guy on a bridge. He must've been a workin' stiff. I only got twenty-three bucks. I hated to do it, for it was probably his whole week's pay and he was more than likely on his way home to his wife and kids, but I could see those long rows of *tomcats*[51] waiting for me. I could not stand for a finger that close to the joint. If I could have been sure he wouldn't yap, I'd have given him his dough back and told him to beat it, but I could not take a chance. I turned him around, shot him in the back of the head and dumped him in the drink.

"I made a good score in a jewelry store a week later, and then went up to the woods to get my health back. I had only been out about ten days when I met you."

The Writer had met this man in Cedro Wooly, Washington on April 19, 1906, the day

---

49   See *Star Rover*, Jack London. This novel was based on the life of Oppenhiemer, and was first written with Oppenhiemer as the principal character, but because of objections by Oppenhiemer's family, who were orthodox Jews, London rewrote the book, making Jakie a skeptic and introducing a fictitious character who expressed Jakie's real opinions.
50   Part I – Chapter I
51   The sewing machines in the prison contract shirt factory were called *tomcats*.

following the San Francisco quake and fire, and they had spent the entire summer hiking over the timber country of Northern Washington. Living mostly on fish and game, often eaten raw, sleeping on the ground in the open.

The Writer did not know it at the time, but the man had served six years of a ten-year sentence in a prison sweatshop and had been suffering with tuberculosis at the time he met the Writer. The Writer, too had had tuberculosis, but by Fall they had both been as brown as Indians and as healthy as young seals. This man was not apprehended for the crimes mentioned or a number of others. Some years later he served a short Federal sentence in Leavenworth, where he and the Writer renewed their friendship and called together for some time. He died in the twenties in a Chicago gangwar.

A similar case was that of a member of the Dale Jones gang. This boy was sent to Boonville reformatory when he was thirteen. After getting out of the reform school, he began hanging out around Johnny Hogan's saloon and mixing with *yeggs*, but by that time the rigorous training of the earlier days was going out of use, and Tommy, as he was called, was taken out on a few jobs as an outside man, but his talent laid in another direction. He served five years in the prison sweatshop in Jefferson City, and thereafter became a trigger man for the Hogan outfit at five hundred dollars per head, and officiated at more than one-hundred-and-twenty-five murders. He tied up with the Dale Jones gang, all members of which were products of the sweatshops at Jefferson City, and was one of the few members of that gang ever taken alive. He was sent to Leavenworth for twenty-five years for train robbery, and he later died at St. Elizabeth Hospital, Washington, D. C.

The amazing thing about this case was that Tommy, and his companion in the murder business had conducted their affairs with such finesse that they had never been suspected, either by the police, their associates or rival Eagan gangsters who were their chief victims. Shortly after Tommy was in Isolation at Leavenworth, however, his associate in the murder business was killed by the Eagan gangsters, which made him think that his number was up, and that fear and worry drove him insane.

The price that society has had to pay for the contract system has been heavy in both blood and dollars.

In States like Missouri, Indiana, Ohio, and some others, dominated by strong political machines, the contract system was retained until it was finally destroyed by the *Blue Eagle*. After the N.R.A. was knocked out by the Supreme Court, The Congress, at the insistence of the labor unions, administered the final knockout punch by Act of July 4, 1935, C. 412 #1, 49 Stat 494; Title 18 U.S.C. (1948) #1761, which makes the transportation or sale of prison-made goods in interstate commerce an offense against the United States.

In many States, however, repeated scandals and exposés of political corruption connected with the operation of the contract system gave rise to the development of State-owned industries, which took two forms: one, the *State Use System*, in which the convicts are employed at manufacturing things the State would otherwise have to buy in the open market, such as shoes and clothing for the inmates of State hospitals and other institutions throughout the State; secondly, the *State Owned Industrial System,* under which the prison undertakes to manufacture some article for which there is a big demand within the State and to be sold only within the State.

An example of the *State Use System* is Lansing, Kansas, where convicts dig all the coal used by State institutions.

Examples of the *State Industrial System* are afforded by San Quentin, jute bags; Bismark, binder twine; Stillwater, farm machinery, all items in large demand by the farmers of the State.

The Writer has known many men who have served time in prisons of all three types, and, with the exception of a few terrible institutions like those of Ohio and Indiana, most inmates preferred to serve time under the *contract system* for the following reasons:

In most *contract system* prisons the contractors agreed to furnish employment to physically fit inmates. They were not obliged to employ any man not fit and capable of giving them a full day's production for every day of pay. They did not pay for the food and had no jurisdiction over it, but poorly fed men could not earn them as much profit as well fed men. So the contractors were serving themselves when they insisted that their men be well fed. Also, the contractors had a heavy investment in buildings and machinery at stake. They knew and fully appreciated the danger of riot among hungry men. So they employed their own doctor to examine all men accepted into their factories and to inspect the food of the men they employed, and in most cases, they were men of sufficient political power to make or break any State employee.

The contractors insisted upon the harshest punishment for those men who failed to make their task, but they did not want a man's health needlessly broken, and they did not want men needlessly punished otherwise, for there was a big expense involved in training new men for difficult jobs; so they did not want their men punished, so long as they did their work.

The tasks were set high for the average, untrained man, but after six months on the job, most men developed a skill that enabled them to turn out a considerable quantity of over-task work, and many contractors paid standard free rates for all over-task work, and they insisted on having a commissary where their men could spend this money earned on over-task work, because money is no inducement to the man who cannot spend it to provide himself with the pleasures and necessities of life. Some of these commissaries stocked everything but shotguns and dynamite not excepting whiskey and opium. The Writer has had many convicts tell him of being able to go to the commissary on Saturday afternoon and buy a tin cupful of while mule for a quarter or an ounce of laudanum for ten cents, but this was more often true in the Southern and Border States than in the North.

It is common for us to look upon the South, and what we call the *Bible Belt,* as the most backward and hide-bound sections of our country, but for the most hide bound and puritanical penological practices, it is necessary to go to such enlightened States as Minnesota and Wisconsin, where they still deny prison inmates tobacco, have single cells, and enforce the *Silent System.*

On the other hand, where the industries were State owned, both factory and food were often under the control of the same grafting politician, and starving convicts were often driven to impossible tasks and literally worked to death, either to supply graft, or what is far worse, for the personal aggrandizement of a politically minded Warden anxious to make a glowing report of his efficiency to the Legislature, until they revolted in flaming and bloody riot.

Privileges

There have always been wide variations in the amount of privileges allowed in different institutions. In the walled prisons of the North, particularly those having State-owned industries, like Minnesota and Wisconsin, privileges always were and still are at a minimum, and prison discipline has always been of the very strictest variety. Most of these institutions has been planned on the monastic principles of the solitary confinement prisons of Europe, but for practical and economic reasons, most of them had adopted the policy of putting two, three, or even four men in a cell, which allow the men sexual and emotional outlet, cut down on the insanity rate and largely compensated for the strictness of discipline outside the cell.

Men were forced to march in lockstep; to wear stripes; to have their head clipped once per month; and were allowed to shave only once per week. In some institutions one half of the head was clipped and the hair on the other half allowed to grow about four inches long. All of these were anti-escape measures.

The lockstep made it possible for a small number of guards to keep a large number of men under control, and in most prisons, any man who broke out of line for any reason was either knocked down or shot down at once, which usually prevented any concerted effort on the part of the inmates to over-power their guards.

The silent system and the ban on paper and lead pencils were designed to prevent men from hatching plots for escape.

The clipped head and the striped clothing were intended to make the escaped convict easily identified until he had been able to steal a change of clothing and until his hair had grown out.

In many prisons men slept on filthy, bedbug-infested, straw ticks. Such luxuries as socks, underwear, toothbrushes, tooth powder, toilet soap, newspapers, magazines, were unknown. In some institutions, men were allowed to purchase these items or to receive them from home. Again referring to Stillwater as an anomaly among prisons of this type. Men in that institution, even back around the turn of the century, were allowed to purchase clocks; shoes; floor rugs; underwear, socks, and lingerie of almost any description; and cosmetics of any brand and variety; and fancy silk neck scarves of any color desired. And what is more, it provided all inmates with a means of earning the money with which to buy.

Whether or not this was ever a contract prison, the Writer does not know, but from his earliest recollection, it has been State-owned industries, and probably the best prison industrial system in America. It manufactures all types of farm implements, from plows to tractors, and it was one of the first prisons in America to pay prisoners for their labor. As far back as 1905, no prisoner not in the hole on punishment, even if he was a cripple capable of doing no more than sweep his own floor, could earn less than twenty-five cents per day, and a good mechanic could earn as much as three dollars and eighty-five cents per day. Yet, these industries have been so profitable that it has been possible for them to support the indigent families of prison inmates from funds supplied by the industries.

To the Writer it has always seemed strange and tragic that a State so enlightened in some phases of penology should be so backward in others. Naturally, Stillwater, with all its youths dolled up like Christmas Trees, yet, with its silent system and single cells has been cursed with many of the aspects of the *Mohammedan Hell* with the results that it can boast of one of the highest insanity rates of any prison in America, being surpassed in this respect only by Federal institutions.

Tobacco, where allowed at all, was always strictly rationed. Many institutions did not allow tobacco in any form, and that is still true of many juvenile institutions, and others that did allow chewing tobacco, did not allow smoking, and the possession of smoking tobacco; cigarette papers; matches; flint and steel; or any other means of making a light were considered very serious offenses and brought down upon the offender the most violent punishment.

Of course, some of these old prisons had been constructed partially of wood, and there was a genuine fear of fire.

Most of the Northern prisons allowed inmates to write one letter per month on official stationary with half of the rules of the prison printed on the heading. But it was generally possible to obtain special letters for urgent family or business reasons, and it was not difficult, as a rule, to have letters smuggled out of these institutions. All incoming letters were delivered to the inmate, and it was in those days agreed that for the prison authorities to fail to deliver incoming letters was a violation of the Postal Laws.

Even though the prison authorities knew from a man's incoming mail that he was smuggling letters out of the institution, the inmate could not be punished on the basis of such information. He had to be caught in the act and they had to have the smuggled letter for evidence.

Visitors were allowed once per month, and a man's friends or relatives were usually allowed to bring treats of candy, fruit, or other edibles, but only in such quantities as could be consumed during the visit. In some institutions visits were allowed only on Sundays, and where an inmate could not consume all of the treat brought for him, he was allowed to call out inmate friends to meet his relatives and help him eat it (Trenton, N. J.; Jefferson City, M. O.), and more than one romance sprung up between inmates and the female relatives of men they met in prison. Wise prison authorities, who realized that such attachment might be good for their wards, did not try to discourage them.

It was an iron-clad rule in most prisons of this type that any guard who showed off his officiousness in the presence of a visitor should be fired, forthwith. Visitors were apt to be voters, and the Warden was a political appointee. To the new man, receiving his first visit, it often seemed odd to be treated like a long lost brother by one of the toughest guards in the prison during a visit, but he soon learned that that was only *company manners*. The inmate was not allowed to say anything critical of the institution, and if he violated that rule he would pay for it later. But in like manner, the institution was not permitted to say anything critical of the inmate. A prisoner might have just come out of the hole, but the guard who had put him there would assure his people that he was getting along fine and was one of the best behaved men in the prison. And the guard who violated that rule did not do so twice.

Guards were very poorly paid, worked twelve hours per day, seven days per week, and were often ignorant, brutal, and sadistic. Many of them could not read and write, and those who worked inside had a convict clerk to perform those chores for them. Many of the most brutal guards were undoubtedly driven to the use of such methods by the fact that it was the only method by which they could maintain a feeling of superiority over men who were better educated and more intelligent than they.

Cell lighting was either by candle or oil-lamp, and the number of candles or amount of oil allowed was never quite sufficient for the number of hours during which light was allowed, and in most prisons of that era, lights were usually put out at eight o'clock or eight-thirty, and in order to conserve oil or candles, all prisoners put their lights out when not needed for writing, reading or playing games.

In some prisons, offenses of a minor nature committed in the cell were often punished by depriving a man of his light for one or more weeks.

In institutions allowing two or more men to a cell, the inmates were usually allowed to have cards, checkers, chess, and dominos, and they were allowed to talk in low tones only. No talking from cell to cell was permitted, and in the old dungeon-type cells, with their narrow steel-latticed doors, and thick walls, once the men were counted and locked in for the night, each couple were in a little world of their own. There was a guard patrolling before their door it is true, but in those pre-flash-light days, he carried a lantern, and he could not see much in those deep, cavernous cells by its weak and flickering flame, and psychologically, that was good. Because of the difficulty of seeing into these old cells, the inmates were required to stand at the door with their hands on the bars during the morning and evening counts.

Naturally, pederasty was common, was expected, and was considered an offense against discipline only when there was a complaint of the employment of force, and even such cases were not taken too seriously.

Of course, modern plumbing was unknown, and the men used night buckets. The stench of one of the old-time cell houses was often enough to turn the stomach of one not accustomed to it, but even so, with all their faults these old-time prisons were in many respects superior to the Federal prisons of today.

Medical attention was of the sketchiest. Many large prisons employed no resident physician. There was usually a more or less skilled convict who could administer purgatives, narcotics, and swab and suture wounds or apply crude splints to broken bones. Aching teeth were pulled, often with forceps made in the prison blacksmith shop, and without anesthetics. In fact, any prison inmate back in those days who could not stand to have a tooth pulled or a minor operation performed without anesthetic or without crying out was looked upon as a weakling and a crybaby. On one occasion the Writer underwent a forty-five minute operation to remove a cut and frozen tendon from the palm of his hand without anesthesia or narcotics.

Where a resident physician was employed, he was often a political quack working under a two hundred fifty dollar diploma purchased in St. Louis or Kansas City,[52] and even where a competent man was employed, he was often untrained in surgery. At the time the Writer came to prison, the doctor at McNiel Island received twelve hundred dollars per year; at Leavenworth, the salary was two thousand, and neither was furnished any technical assistants.

At some prisons there were arrangements for bringing in outside surgeons for serious cases, but the red tape was so involved that the inmate usually died before the permission

---

52   There was at one time diploma mills in both St. Louis and Kansas City which for $250, supplied the would-be doctor with three months training and obtained for him his license to practice by supplying him with all of the questions that he would be asked on examination as well as the correct answers.

could be obtained. As a result, prisoners often attempted and did save the lives of their otherwise doomed companions by performing major operations upon them, following the technique from a textbook propped upon the patient's chest during the operation.

Don't laugh! The Writer has seen major operations upon the abdominal cavity performed in just that manner by a *safe blower* working without gloves and with a cigarette in his

mouth while ether was being used as an anesthetic, and he has seen the patients make uneventful recoveries – man is a very tough animal.

Rules were very strict, and they were strictly enforced. Punishments were severe. The three primary thoughts in the mind of every prison administrator were: preventing escapes; preventing riots; and making his wards work. The rigorous discipline and harsh punishment were directed toward those ends. But a fourth thought that often overshadowed the first three was that of preventing adverse publicity. It was necessary to hide many of the horrors of prison life from public view. As L. J. Fletcher once said to the Writer's mother in his presence:

"There is a somber side to all prisons, the best as well as the worst. Things occur in all of them that will not stand the light of day, which the public would not be able to understand and would never tolerate, if they knew all the facts. That will be true for as long as we use imprisonment as a punishment for crime."

Those were true words, and many a Warden's greatest worry, then and now, was and is that something will occur to show the public that somber side.

Before the boondoggling days of Hoover and Roosevelt, prisons did not employ one civilian for each three convicts[53] as is the case in the Federal prisons of today. One guard to fifteen convicts was considered sufficient, and in some walled prisons, one guard for thirty-five convicts was the rule. Since the guards worked twelve hours per day and the convicts were there for twenty-four hours per day, the effective day-time ratio was often about one to fifty; and the effective ratio at night was often as low as one to four hundred.

Under such circumstances it was considered essential to keep the convicts so closely regimented at all moments when they were out of their cells that they would have no opportunity to start trouble, and to keep them so overawed by fear of death or severe punishment that they would not dare to do so, but in most cases there was no desire to be needlessly cruel. There were sadistic keepers, of course, and there still are, who delighted in human misery, but most of them were merely weak human beings like you and me, trying to do the best they could in a very difficult situation. So long as the prisoner did his work, followed the strict routine of the prison, and attended strictly to his own business, no one bothered him.

Under the law as it existed in those days, all prisoners of equal status had to be treated alike. The guard did not know what a convict was in for unless the convict told him. He did not care. So long as a man had a number on his back, he was a convict, and that was all. A guard could be fired for pointing any convict out by name to visitors, and for telling one convict anything about another inmate's crime, sentence, or prison record.

---

53   The last figures the Writer saw were published in the *Bulletin Board* many years ago. They reported slightly more than 5,000 employees and slightly less than 16,000 inmates in the Federal Penal and Correctional institutions.

All new inmates were put on the toughest work in the prison, and all short-timers would stay there throughout their sentence. Long-timers, men serving more than five years, if they had any gumption at all, were soon taken off the hard work and put on softer jobs. Lifers in for murder were always given special preference on the soft jobs, and such men held most of the key jobs in the prison. In most State prisons, the lifers actually managed the institution. These men were always considered apart from the general run of prisoners, for it was recognized that the type of men who commit murder, barring sex criminals

and schizophrenics of course, are individualist, that they are usually more easily led than driven, and that was always taken into consideration.

In some of these Eastern and Northern prisons, the men had sewing machines in their cells and were fed in their cells (Eastern Philadelphia). There was no form of recreation, and in practically none of them were the inmates permitted to congregate en mass excepting in the dining room and Chapel. Most prisons of this type made attending Chapel compulsory and required that a Bible be kept in every cell. There were usually gun cages from which the men in the dining room or Chapel cold be kept covered. But the Writer has never known of a case where a gun guard fired on a man in either the dining room or Chapel. Only a moron would do so, for nothing could so easily convert that close packed humanity into a mob, and mobs are not nice anywhere. In prison, they are especially bad.

Inside guards, that is, those in contact with the inmates, are not usually permitted to carry firearms, because if they did, those arms would change hands, and any time the convicts wanted them, they would take them. In most prisons they were not allowed to carry any weapon of any kind excepting on special occasions.

There were no provisions for education, but the man who sincerely wanted to educate himself was usually given every encouragement. He had to supply his own books, but there were no restrictions on him getting or having any books he needed, either new or second hand. If he could not buy them, he could beg them from some University. He would be put in the cell with the man most able to help him, and he would be given a work assignment most in line with his studies, so that he would have some opportunity to apply his new knowledge.

In 1938, while the Writer was working on his second book on bird diseases, Dr. Frank, Director of Education, Federal Bureau of Prisons, visited the Writer's cell. After he had looked at some of the Writer's slides and expressed amazement at the quality of some of the Writer's pathological work, the Writer said:

"Listen Doctor: You people are always boasting about your educational programs, but actually, you have set back the cause of prison education by at least fifty years, simply by trying to do the inmate's thinking for him instead of permitting him to do it for himself."

"That can't be true. I am sure that you are prejudiced. Why we have provided greater…."

"Hold it! That is just it! *You have provided!* But you have not permitted the inmate to provide for himself."

"I think that is unfair."

"All right! For example, I entered prison as an uneducated kid of nineteen. I had only gone through the third grade in school, and I had forgotten all I had ever learned in school. I could not have written a sentence that I was sure was grammatically correct or solved a problem in long division to have saved my life. Yet, today, I am just as well educated in my field as you are in yours."

"Yes, I guess you are."

"I obtained all of my education in prison. Now, what chance do you think a youth entering a Federal Prison today has of obtaining an education in any scientific field that is as good as mine, remembering that in my field I am tops!"

"Not much, I might say, none at all. Our program is geared to the need of the average inmate. We do take every inmate through the primary grades. We have not been able to go much beyond that. Your case is an exception. I frankly don't see how you did it."

"I did it because I was permitted to do as I pleased without sixteen bureaucrats looking down the back of my neck and telling me how and what to do," and every other inmate had the same opportunity.

Hard as some of those old dungeon-type prisons were, they and the men who ran them had their good points, and one of the best things about them was the fact that no one had the time or inclination to live the inmate's life for him. He was forced to stand on his own two feet and fight for what he got, but within the narrow limits of his own little world, he enjoyed a mental and moral freedom unknown in Federal Prisons today. It is not surprising that in those institutions allowing two-man cells and permitting inmates to choose their own cellmates, prison paranoia, so prevalent in the modern Federal Prison, was unknown.

PART I – CHAPTER IV

The Deep South

Southern prisons developed along two lines, both outgrowths of slavery: the *Slave Farm* and the *Chain-gang*.

The *Chain-gang*

Most persons have heard of the scandals concerning the Georgia *chain-gangs* during the last few years, but few of them realize that prior to the Civil War there were no penitentiaries in the Deep South, that all sentences to imprisonment were sentences to hard labor on *chain-gangs*. Such sentences were executed in county jails or in temporary stockades operated by the Sheriffs of the various counties. In some States, persons convicted of crimes against the State were considered State prisoners; the State paid the Sheriffs for their keep, retained jurisdiction over them and could send them to counties where their labor was needed: on State roads, levies, or other State projects – which is still the case in Georgia and to some extent in Florida, and possibly some other States. But in the early days, some States considered each county responsible for its own prisoners, and every Sheriff had his own *chain-gang* upon which persons serving anywhere from thirty days to thirty years might be employed.

The type of shackle used on these *chain-gangs* consisted of two pieces of semi-circular strap-iron with straight ends, bent so that when the pieces were fitted around the ankle, the ends would lie flat against each other, with the three-eighth-inch holes in each end apposed. The first link of the chain was placed between the two inside ends and they were then riveted together. The outside ends were riveted, so that the leg was ringed with an iron band. In some cases, the strap-iron was bent around the leg and a single rivet held the ends together, making the chain fast.

The chain was usually ordinary trace chain, made up of welded links of one-eighth-inch bar iron, and the length between the shackles was usually from twenty-eight to thirty inches. Such lengths were necessary in order to permit the men to take ordinary marching strides and to permit them to work. The center of the chain was held up off the ground by a cord fastened to the prisoner's belt, so that he could march without entangling his feet in it, for these gangs were sometimes marched four or five miles to and from work.

The gangs were worked under a Captain, who was in charge of the men, directed the work, and was usually armed with a revolver; two or three shotgun guards took up positions from which they might cover any direction in which a man might run. The chains would not keep a man from running over level ground, but they would slow him down, and they were a great handicap on rough ground or in brush.

The systems of chaining and working men in chains was once common throughout the United States, and is still common in many Southern States.

During the Writer's childhood many Northern cities maintained *chain-gangs* upon which they worked municipal prisoners on their streets, rock piles or wood piles, and during the Civil War many deportees from Kentucky and Tennessee were marched from the Ohio River to the Canadian Border in chains.

The Writer's father was a Southerner, and his mother had been raised on the Illinois side of the Ohio, and had taught school in Kentucky. Naturally, he had heard a great deal about Southern chivalry and the great respect in which womanhood was held by all Southern gentlemen. One of the worst disillusionments of his life occurred upon his first visit to Nashville, Tennessee, in July 1905.

He and another boy his own age dropped off of a freight-train about two o'clock in the morning and were arrested by a railroad detective and taken to the city jail. On the way to jail he saw a *chain-gang* of about thirty barefoot women, clothed in single, thin cotton garments, sweeping the main street under the direction of two male guards, one of them armed with a shotgun and the other one with a revolver on one hip and a coiled blacksnake hooked to his belt, hanging over the other hip. About half of the women were white.

His second disillusionment came when he reached the jail, which consisted of a large room containing four or five rows of open steel cages. Men were housed on one side, women on the other, and neither had any privacy. There were children in the jail as young as nine years old.

Although States like Georgia and Florida and several other Southern States have now built penitentiaries, most of their convicts are still worked in *chain-gangs* on the roads. In South Carolina, they are worked in the turpentine forest, or at least, they were until a few years ago, although the Writer has not talked with anyone from there recently.

Because these *chain-gangs* often worked many miles from the jail, they were often housed in temporary stockades that consisted of several tents surrounded by a wire fence. The bunks consisted of two wooden platforms running the full length of the tent with a narrow aisle running down the center. The convicts were secured for the night by forcing them to lie down with their feet to the aisle and then running a hickory pole or a two-by-four through their chains and securing it at both ends, which made it impossible for any individual to use the night bucket without waking everyone in the squad.

Men were flogged for loafing on their work, for not treating their guards with due respect, and for attempting to escape. When a man escaped, and was later recaptured, he was flogged upon his return to the gang. Formerly, a black-snack was used, but in recent years the *bat* (to be described presently) has been employed.

These men were fed on the poorest food, usually black-eyed peas and corn pone. They were often murdered by the gun guards under which they worked. Their living conditions were, and still are, worse than one would be allowed to impose on any animal in most Northern States. But even as hard as these *chain-gangs* were, and are, the Writer has heard many Federal prisoners say that they wished they were back on the *chain-gang*. You see, bruises of the body heal quickly; those of the mind never do. Insanity, outside of paresis is practically unknown among *chain-gang* prisoners.

Even under the most harsh, brutal and degrading conditions, there were many compensations. These men were not cut off from society by high walls. On roadwork, there had to be teamsters to haul the dirt away; there had to be a water boy; there had to be a cook; there had to be a blacksmith; there had to be a camp tender; and all these men had to be trusties. There was no attempt to keep these men from striking up acquaintances, friendships, or even romances with the local populace.

Water was usually obtained from the nearest farmhouse, and teenaged girls like teenaged boys often find stripes romantic. These men were allowed to have visits every Sunday from anyone who cared to visit them, and arrangements could be made for a price, generally not over a quarter. More than one tearful little girl has gone to a Southern governor and talked him out of a pardon for the convict father of her coming baby.

As explained, all of these men slept together. They slept beside whom-so-ever they pleased. There was no guard in the tent at night, and in any case, what went on under their quilts was their own business.

Practically all of the Sheriffs sold whisky, and in the old days, laudanum for a quarter, and if he wanted to get drunk as a lord or high as a kite on Saturday night and Sunday, that too, was his business. All the *bossman*, as he was called, wanted was work.

Even the man who had no money and no sweetheart could often meet some girl who would dig up the necessary quarter or *sweet talk* the *bossman*.

Gene Talmage once cited these facts in an address defending the Georgia *chain-gang* as being more human and humane than the walled prisons of the North. And regardless of what Northerners may have thought of him, he was always a hero to the Southern convicts, and a great deal of what he said was true.

The one big attraction of the *chain-gang*, however, is and always has been the case of escape. That is still true today.

A man could saw his shackles at night so that they could be broken at a moment's notice, and then, at the first opportune moment, he could break and run. Any man who can make sixty to ninety feet on a shotgun can outrun it. Shotgun slugs travel so much slower than sound that a man has time to change his course or go down after he hears the report. The slugs will pass over him or to one side. Then he can jump up and start running at another angle. Of course, he has to outrun the dogs; yet, that is often much easier in Georgia than in Texas. That however, is the hard way.

Where armed men work convicts with tools, the arms may change hands at any moment. A man may *sweet talk* the Captain until he gets a chance to get close enough to him to snatch his pistol or knock him down with a shovel. He can use the Captain's body as a shield against the shotgun until a car comes along; then he may force the driver to drive him away, or he may use the pistol to shoot or capture the shotgun guards. Where several men are in on the play, which is relatively easy. The man who does it, however, had better not permit himself to be captured. For if he is, he will certainly never die of old age.

The correct technique as explained to the Writer by a man who has used it five times is as follows:

"It only costs you fifty dollars, but you must never be so crude as to offer the Captain a bribe.

"You send home for a fifty dollar money order drawn on some nearby Post Office. When the letter comes, the Captain will hand it to you unopened, for they never pay any attention to your mail down there. Most of them can't read and write anyway, but he will always watch you open the letter to see if you get any money in it. You might owe him a couple of dollars for tobacco or whisky. You endorse the money order and hand it to him and say:

"'Listen, Captain, when you go into town will you please cash this for me and get me a dollar's worth of *North State* and a pint of mule, and buy yourself a drink.'

"When he brings the stuff and offers you your change, you say:

"'Listen, Captain, I don't like to keep that much money on me. I might lose it or I might get into a crap game. You just keep it for me!' He will say:

"'Keep out what you want, and I will put the rest in the bank for you; then when you want it, you can make out a check,' but you say:

"'No! Captain! That is too much trouble. I don't need any money, just a little tobacco or a drink once in a while. You just keep the money, and when I want anything, you can get it for me.'

"'You wouldn't be looking for a chance to run, would you?'

"'Why, no, Captain! You know I would not do anything like that.'

"'Well, Old Thing, you had better not try to run on me.'

"In the next couple of days he will put you doing something where you have a good chance to run, and you had better be ready, and you had better take it. Otherwise, his gun might go off by accident and hit you in the back of the head. If you are caught and brought back, you had better not say one word about that money, for if you do, you will surely get shot in the head."

The Slave Farms

The other type of prison common in the South developed as a result of the Civil War and is still in use, with modifications in Texas, Louisiana, and Mississippi, but because he is more familiar with conditions in that State, most of what is said in this section is based upon conversations with hundreds of ex-convicts from Texas covering a period or more than fifty years.

Following the war, many large plantation owners found themselves with vast properties that were rapidly going to seed for lack of slaves to work them, and many of those owners who were prominent in local politics appealed to the Sheriff for prisoners to help work their land; thus grew up the contract farms which became such a prominent feature of Southern penology for many years.

In many cases the Sheriff simply went out and arrested a sufficient number of unemployed Negroes, charged them with vagrancy, and an obliging Justice of the Peace sentenced them to eleven months and twenty-nine days each. They were sent out to the farms under contract. This form of peonage was very difficult to break up, and several Southern

Sheriffs were convicted and sentenced to Federal Prisons for this practice as late as 1942. One such case is to be found in the 63rd or 64th *Supreme Court Reporter,* but the title and page number have been forgotten.

In pre-bellum days these great farms had been worked by large gangs of Negro slaves who worked under mounted gun guards and were driven under the lash; therefore, the change-over from slaves to convicts involved no new techniques.

Because of the flat country, lack of brush, and the great distances a runaway would have to travel on foot before finding shelter, it was unnecessary to use chains. The convicts were run out to the field as soon as it was light enough to see them, flanked by an armed and mounted gun guard for each side of the line. Chopping cotton (hoeing out the Johnson grass), picking cotton, or cutting cane, the men were driven across the big field, one man to a row. Many of these fields were so large that the line would not reach the turn row until noon, and a wagon would be waiting for them there with their dinner. In each squad there were squad leaders or pace-setters, who were always big Negroes, who were given special food in return for their cooperation. Always anxious to please the *bossman,* they would set as fast a pace as possible, and the other prisoners were driven to keep up with them. Stragglers were flogged at the turn row, and the big Negro pace-setters were always glad to further cooperate by holding the man to be flogged.

The men were allowed just sufficient time to gobble their dinner, and then were driven back across the field and were usually hard put to it to reach the building before dark. Often, they were driven the last couple of miles at a dog trot.

There was no doctor on the farm, and no man with a fever of less than 102° was permitted to lie in because of illness. Many convicts cut their hands off, injected coal oil into their hands, or cut their Achilles tendons to escape work.

Runaways were run down by mounted guards working with large packs of bloodhounds. Escape was possible, but it was not easy, and men who were recaptured by prison guards were often shot down on the spot. Those who were not shot were flogged, returned to the farm and placed in the No. 1 hoe squad, which was composed of the best physical specimens on the farm.

The living conditions were terrible. The men slept in wooden barracks under shotgun guards stationed in windows at the front end of the barracks. The toilets were at the back of the barracks, and any man who left his bunk after lights out, had to get permission from the guard.

The Writer has known personally hundreds of men who have served time on these farms, and some of the stories he has heard are rather amazing and occasionally, amusing.

For hundreds of years, the third grade farm in Texas was a contract farm owned by Colonel House, the confidant of Woodrow Wilson or his family, and was known as the House Farm. On one occasion, there was a sleepy guard in the *picket* (the barred window at the end of the building) and the convicts had a hole cut in the back of the building.

"Getting up, Boss!" called the first man.

"All right! Don't be long!"

"Getting up Boss!" said the second prisoner.

"All right! Don't be long!"

"San Antonio, Boss!" said the next prisoner.

"All right! Don't be long!"

"Houston, Boss!"

"All right! Don't be long!"

"San Francisco, Boss!"

"All right! Don't be long!"

On that occasion fourteen men got away, and most of them made it clean, since they had an all-night start on the dogs.

The first attempt to regulate the use of the whip by the law was back around the turn of the twentieth century, when it was provided that no prisoner could be given more than thirty lashes in any one month and that the whipping boss had to obtain a written order from the Authorities of Huntsville before whipping any convict; if granted, the order would specify the nature of the offense and the number of lashes to be applied. Men were no longer whipped on the turn row at the whim of the field boss, but there was established the office of *Dog Sergeant and Whipping Boss,* and it was this official's duty to take care of, train, and run the dogs, and to administer all punishments.

The order for punishment always came in the morning mail, which arrived after the squad was in the field, and the punishment might be for an offense two or three weeks old. One man told the Writer of his experience on the House Farm in 1906. The convicts all carried knives, some of which were actually swords, and it was the rule that no guard should ever permit any convict who was not a trusty or pacesetter, to come within ten feet of him, nor should he ever walk up on a convict unless he were covered by another guard and knew that the convict was helpless. If it was necessary to over-power a convict, trusties, building tenders, and squad leaders were used for that purpose. In the squad in which the Writer's informant was working, there was a big Negro, stoolpigeon squad leader who had one of those completely sycophantic personalities attained by no other race. Every time the whipping boss would come riding across the field with a slip of paper in his hand, this Negro would run toward him, a big, ingratiating smile on his face crying:

"Who do you want, Boss? Who do you want, Boss? I'll hold him for you! Let me hold him for you! I'll be glad to hold him for you, Boss!"

Well, one day this sycophant ran out to meet the whipping boss as usual.

"Who do you want, Boss? I'll hold him for you! I'll hold him for you!"

"I want you, you black s-o-b, and I don't think I'll have any trouble getting plenty of these things to hold you for me!"

The order called for twenty lashes. It took four men to hold the big Negro, but it would not have been difficult to get forty, had they been required.

In 1910 the State of Texas, smarting under the sting of Northern criticism, began buying the contract farms, as well as land from other sources, and establishing State farms.

Many pictures of the backs of ex-convicts had appeared in Texas newspapers as well as in Northern papers, and Texas politicos suddenly became scar conscious. So the whip was replaced with the *bat*, a thick, harness-leather strap about three inches wide and four feet long, attached to a wooden handle. The *bat* was really a worse instrument than the blacksnake, for, although it did not break the skin, it was much heavier than the blacksnake, and it produced deep bruises. Men struck over the kidneys often passed bloody urine for weeks following a flogging.

It was not long after Texas introduced the *bat* that the other States became scar conscious and turned to this form of punishment, and it is still used in most of the Southern States.

The use of the *bat* in Texas had been abolished both by executive order and by law on a number of occasions, but the next Governor to come in always had it put back.

In the 20's, Eastham became the third-grade farm, but whether this was still the old House Farm under a new name, or a new farm established by the State, the Writer does not know.

The Writer recently had a chance to talk to a man who was on *Eastham* and *Retrieve* in 1941, and he was informed that at that time Texas had abolished all punishment. The farms were graded according to the hardness of the conditions, and a man who did not behave himself at a farm where conditions were good was transferred to one where they were worse until he reached Eastham, which was the end of the line.

The practice of ordering punks and bullies as in the old days, had been discontinued, but this man said that new arrivals at these farms were met at the door by the building tender and his assistants, armed with knives as long as swords, escorted to the back of the building and raped. There were no rules outside of work. The worst punishment was that of being assigned to No. 1 hoe squad, which got all the hardest work, and the man who did not do as he was told was in danger of being shot down.

During the year this man was there, according to his statement, there were twenty-eight men murdered: fourteen by guards and fourteen by other convicts.

In one case an unarmed guard inside the compound gave a convict some order, to which the convict replied, "No! I'll by god-damned if I will."

The guard's horse was tied outside the compound. Without a word he went out to his horse, obtained a pistol from the holster on his saddle, came back in, walked up to within ten feet of the convict, then shot him four times in the body. As the convict was lying on the ground, probably mortally wounded, the guard walked over to him and shot him again through the head for good measure.

One of the convict murders occurred in a passageway going to the dining room. A building tender dropped out of line at a point where the other inmate would have to pass him, and as the other man went by, the building tender ran him through with a fourteen inch knife. The wounded man broke away and ran until he came to some steps, upon which he stumbled. The building tender ran up on him and stabbed him several more times as he was lying on the stairs.

Two shotgun guards behind barred gratings were within ten feet of where the killing occurred, yet they made no effort to interfere or save the wounded man.

In neither case nor in any of the other twenty-six cases was there any inquiry as to the cause of these murders. The building tender simply wiped the blood from his knife and went on in to supper. A killing on any other farm might cause a man to be sent to Eastham, but assaults and killings on Eastham went unpunished.

The central unit of the Texas Prison System is the penitentiary at Huntsville, called *The Walls.* This is probably the oldest penitentiary in the South, and al prisoners convicted of crimes against the State are first sent to *The Walls.*

In the old days, all prisoners were transported to *The Walls* by the pickup man who traveled from jail to jail in a buckboard[54] with a large, crate-like cage on the back in which was carried a pack of hounds. Also in the buckboard he carried several fifty foot lengths of trace-chain.

Whenever prisoners were turned over to him, he passed a loop of chain around each prisoner's neck and locked it with a padlock. These prisoners were marched down the road to the next jail, placed in the jail overnight, and any new prisoners found in that jail were added to the chain the next morning, and the chain was then marched on to the next jail. And that went on until they reached the penitentiary. But sometimes the first prisoner picked up would have to march more than a thousand miles before reaching the prison, and by that time there might be more than a hundred men on a chain.

United States Marshals from Texas brought prisoners to Leavenworth with chains around their necks as late as 1913.

At Huntsville, the new men were classified before being sent to the various farms into three groups; the Bullies, Punks, and Cripples. The latter group consisted of men who were too old or otherwise unfit for farm work, and these were kept at *The Walls.* Pending classification, all new prisoners were put on the wood gang, which was taken out several miles from the prison each day to cut wood.

Any man who had escaped from a farm and was picked up near the farm, that is, within fifty or sixty miles, would be picked up and returned to the prison by the *Dog Sergeant,* but when a man was arrested several hundred miles from the farm, he was put in the local jail and returned to Huntsville on the next chain.

What often happened in such cases was recently described to the Writer by a man who had served several sentences in Texas.

"I arrived at Huntsville, late in the afternoon as one of a long chain. We were bathed, shaved, dressed in stripes, and the next morning most of us were sent out on the wood-cutting gang. This wood-cutting gang was a process they had of hardening you up for a few weeks before sending you to a farm.

"Well, on the same chain with me there had been a fellow who had escaped from one of the farms a short time before. I was surprised to see that he was also sent out on the wood-cutting gang.

"There were quite a few fellows on the gang whom this fellow knew, and all morning I

---

54   An open, flat-bottomed, four-wheeled carriage in which a springy board fastened to the axles supplemented or served in place of actual springs. Springs, if present, were between the board and the seat and not attached to the axles.

noticed him shaking hands with these men and bidding them goodbye. He would walk up to a man and say:

"'Well, so long, Old Buddy, I probably won't be seeing you anymore. It has been nice to know you, and I sure hope you have better luck.'

"'Gee, Jack,' I heard one man say. 'You don't know how sorry I am.'

"'Well, it was just a hard break. I guess there is no use crying about it. Don't look like it would do much good, anyhow.'

"I was young and green. It was my first jolt in Texas, and the thing just did not make sense. I knew this fellow had a long sentence yet to serve, and he had just arrived the day before. I turned to a fellow I knew was a two-time loser and asked, 'What's the idea? Is this fellow going somewhere? He just arrived. What is everybody looking so glum about?'

"'Just stick around and keep your eye open, kid! You will see!'

"About three o'clock that afternoon one of the shotgun guards brought his horse in pretty close to where we were working. He called the fellow by name and told him to bring his ax.

"'Say, Old Buddy!' the guard said. 'I want you to chop a tree down for me. That big one, right over there.' The guard pointed to a tree about a hundred and fifty feet away.

"I had noticed that as soon as the guard had called this fellow's name everyone had stopped working, and they were all watching him and the guard. I watched too.

"The fellow had walked about sixty feet when the guard threw up his ten-gauge shotgun and let him have it right in the back of the head. He broke the shotgun open, blew the smoke from the barrel, and slipped another shell into the chamber.

"'Imagine that old thing,' he said, 'Trying to run off again.'

It must be admitted that these Southern prison farms were, and in some respects still are, a blot upon civilization, but outside of man-killing labor and frightful brutality, they have always had their good points as well as many advantages not possessed by the Northern prisons. There were no rules, as rules were known in the North. There was no law, either. The only crime that they ever heard of a Texas convict being tried for was the murder of a guard and an escape (Raymond Hammiton). The prisoner was, and is, a slave with no rights that his keepers or his fellows are bound to respect, not even the right to life. He lived in a primitive society and had courage to fight for and protect the things he wanted, but he was left entirely on his own. What order existed outside of work, was the order enforced by group public opinion and the steel that he always kept in easy reach of his hand. His was the lowest possible order of society, but it was still a free society in which the fittest survived.

There were no restrictions on letters. In most cases there was no censorship of incoming and outgoing mail. The most that was usually required was that the men open the letter in the presence of the guard and shake out the page so that the guard could see that there was nothing else in the envelope. Every man carried his own money, or any part of it he wished, on his person. Of course, if a man had a large sum of money, and was afraid of being robbed, he could have it put into his account in the office. He could buy anything he wanted, short of pistols and dynamite, and there were no restrictions whatsoever upon anything a man might do to help or better himself.

Not only were no obstacles thrown in the way of any creative work a man cared to do, on the contrary, all such efforts were encouraged. If a man could write anything that anyone would buy, all he had to do was write it and mail it to whomsoever he pleased. If he could find a publisher, that was fine. Of course, if he wrote anything critical of his keepers, he might get his brains blown out, but he understood that.

If a man could invent anything, he simply contacted a patent attorney in Washington, paid his fee and had his claim filed, just the same as if he were on the outside.

Many of these men gave those firms using the free-trial system of merchandising a fit, for they ordered anything they saw advertised, and once the merchandise was delivered, there was nothing the seller could do about it. If he complained to the authorities at Huntsville, he was told that he had shipped the goods to the prison at his own risk; that there was no way that he could compel the convict to pay; and that there was no method by which the article could be recovered.

The same was true in the field of entertainment. If these men desired entertainment, they had to furnish it for themselves. If a man could play an instrument or sing, he was encouraged to do so, and there was a good chance of him being put on work where he would have a chance to practice or study. Special talent in almost any line brought recognition and a chance to do something with it.

The Writer knew one man who made a nice income while at *Eastham* by writing true crime stories which were nothing more than the inside stories of the actual crimes for which his fellows had been sent to prison, obtained from their own lips. As soon as the Captain found out what he was doing, he said:

"Listen, Old Thing! You must be pretty good on slinging words around if people will buy what you write. I need someone like you to write out my reports and my business letters. How would you like to be my clerk?"

In recent years, teams of singers and entertainers from the various farms have always had before them the coveted prize of being taken to *The Walls* and allowed to appear on the institution's radio station program, and those that were good enough were kept at *The Walls* and allowed to broadcast regularly. Some even became widely known.

With such encouragement, it is not at all surprising that many skillful Writers and entertainers who have later become nationally known have been graduated from these Southern prison farms.

What kinds of men run these farms?

The guards, of course, are of the very lowest grade of Southern Cracker, for the wages paid could not attract better men. Most of them are illiterate, cruel, and sadistic slave-drivers, no better than the slaves they drive, but what of the men who have the capacity to manage such enterprises and make them return a profit to the State? They have to be men of education and ability. They fix the policies that their underlings carry out.

Let's take a look at one of these as he appeared away from his prison farm.

One evening in the fall of 1934, Guard Bammer, who was then night guard in Isolation at Leavenworth, brought two men to the Writer's cell.

"Here are some gentlemen who want to see your birds, Bob."

"I am sorry, but I am afraid they will not be able to see many of them, for they are asleep. I have a few singers in here, but I would not care to awaken those in the flight room."

One man was dressed in a rough, blue uniform, not unlike the blue Sunday uniforms worn by the convicts at Leavenworth, excepting that there were no numbers on it. He was a big, dour visaged young man in his early or middle thirties, of the typical Southern crack type. Around his waist outside of his coat was buckled a thick leather belt from which dangled a well-worn revolver holster.

The evening was warm, and the big man looked uncomfortable in his heavy woolen clothing.

The other gentleman was a much smaller man, about five-feet-eight-inches tall, weighing about one hundred and thirty pounds and although he was in his middle forties and his once-black, wavy hair was streaked with gray, he appeared to be as lithe and well-muscled as he had been at twenty. He wore no coat or hat, but his pale-yellow, silk shirt, light trousers, black string tie, and the soft shoes that encased his small feet were of the very best quality. His thin, black, soft-leather belt was never made for supporting a pistol, and there was no evidence that it or the pockets of his trousers had ever done so.

"That is perfectly all right," the small man said in a pleasant, cultured voice, smiling as he spoke and extending his hand. "I am Walter Steadman, Superintendent of Tucker Farm, Arkansas, and this is one of my guards, Harry Vauhn" (that was not the name used).

"I am pleased to know you, Mr. Steadman, and you, too, Mr. Vauhn," said the Writer, shaking hands with both men.

"I am much more interested in meeting you that in seeing your birds. I have been reading of your accomplishments for years, and I asked the Warden for permission to come over here and have a little visit with you. I have always been an admirer of men who do things, and I just had to talk to you."

"Thank you, I am always anxious to make a new friend."

The Writer uncovered some singers he had in his living room, and he and Mr. Steadman talked for about an hour. Mr. Bammer sometimes joined in the conversation, but Vauhn said nothing.

Steadman seemed deeply interested in the Writer's work, in his life, and in how he had been able to keep his sanity and accomplish so much from a solitary cell. He struck the Writer as being one of the most cultured and pleasant personalities he had ever met.

He was horrified to learn that the Writer had spent more than twenty-five years in prison, and most of it in solitary confinement.

"I don't know how in the world you have been able to stand up under it.

"Do you mean to tell me that you have not had a chance to be with a woman in twenty-five years?"

"That is right! The last time was January 17, 1909."

"How about that woman you married? Don't they ever permit you to be with her?"

"Hell, no! They stopped her from visiting me. The only reason they did not send me to The Rock (Alcatraz) was because the publicity aroused my friends, and Louis Howe stopped it."

Steadman, had taken a fancy to one of the birds that was singing, and the Writer had to step into his bird room to get a box. He had not wanted to go into the bird room, because he had a still running. (Previously, under White, he had been able to draw reagent alcohol from the hospital, but the bureau had stopped that and it had become necessary for him to make all of his own reagents.) To his consternation, Steadman followed into the darkened room, the dimly illuminated light streaming through the open door.

"Don't you get a chance to get with other inmates?"

"Very rarely. I can count them all on my fingers and have fingers left. Sometimes the opportunities have been five and even ten years apart."

"That is the cruelest thing I have ever heard of. I don't care what a man has done. There is no crime that justifies such treatment! I would not inflict that on a dog. It would be a lot kinder to kill a man than to do that."

"I fully agree with you. Had I expected it to be like this, I'd never have made the effort to make something of my life."

"How about parole?"

"I have a letter from Sanford Bates stating that I will be paroled on February 27, 1937, but I really don't think his promise is worth much."

"I wish I had you down at Tucker Farm. I could use a man of your ability, and I'd let your wife visit you every weekend and sleep with you. I'd have you on the street in thirty days. Any man who has done what you have does not belong in prison. I am going to write to President Roosevelt in your behalf. There is no excuse for such cruelty in a civilized country. Hell, for what you did in the first place you would not have had to serve over a year in my State. I want your wife's address, too. I want to write her and see if something can't be worked out for getting you out of here."

This man purchased a bird for $10 purely out of the kindness of his heart.

"I don't know what I want with it or what in the world I am going to do with it, but I want it just the same. I'll probably wind up by giving it to some woman, though I don't get to see many of them down there on the farm."

Then noticing the still, he said, "I see that you are not doing too badly, otherwise."

"Not up until now."

"You needn't worry. I'm not a stoolpigeon, and I don't like them."

There was one thing that Mr. Steadman could not understand.

"What kind of work do you do?"

"Why, just what I have been showing you."

"That is for yourself. I mean for the State."

"Why, I don't do any. I have worked only three and a half years out of all the time I've been in prison."

"Is that right?" Steadman turned towards Mr. Bammer, his face reflecting his disbelief.

"So far as I know, I've been here for twelve years and he has not done any work for the prison since I've been here."

Steadman's face showed that he still could not comprehend a prison system that did not require the convict to do some work for the State.

There was just one sour note in the whole visit. When the Writer had transferred the bird to the carrying cage, he started to hand it to Mr. Steadman. That gentleman snarled out of the corner of his mouth at the guard.

"Well, take the damn thing! Don't stand their like a numbskull!"

When they were gone, Bammer said, "If that is the way he treats his guards, I don't think I would like to work down there."

"I don't know! He seems like a swell fellow, but if that is the way he treats his guards, I wonder how he treats his convicts."

Whether or not Steadman ever wrote to Roosevelt, the Writer does not know, but he did exchange a number of letters with the Writer's wife concerning plans for using his influence in the Writer's behalf, but nothing ever came of the matter, for a short time later, Steadman found himself in trouble and was removed from office, and the case was fully reported in the *Kansas City Star*.

Also, an escaped convict who had been at Tucker Farm at the time, Rube McCann,[55] was brought to Leavenworth and placed in Isolation. So the Writer had the benefit of both sides of the story.

Walter Steadman, Superintendent of Tucker Farm, single-handedly ran one of the largest and cruelest slave farms in the South, with only convict help. He was the only free man on the farm. He used convict bosses and convict gun guards. The man the Writer had called Vauhn, was a three-time murderer serving life. Walter Steadman ran that farm and had never been known to carry a pistol, though his convict whipping boss always rode about the farm with him and was always armed with a revolver. He worked convicts under the lash, and he actually had them hitched to plows and driven like mules. During the last three months of his administration, fourteen men had been murdered by his gun guards. The blow-off came when he sent them out to hunt down a girl escapee from the women's reformatory, and one of them found the girl on a street and ruthlessly murdered her in the presence of free witnesses.

---

55   He was eventually sent to Alcatraz and was killed by a fellow convict.

McCann said of him:

"He wasn't a bad fellow at heart. I took care of his saddle horses and had one of the best jobs in the joint. I ran off as soon as he was fired, because I knew things were going to be a lot worse. One thing I can say of him, he would not permit his guards to have a man beaten to death. Time and again I have heard convict guards asked to have some man whipped and heard him say: 'No! If he continues to get out of line, shoot him in the head.'

"But he kept his guards in line too. More than once I have seen him ride up to that fellow Vauhn, who was one of the worst of them, and say, 'Give me your guns!' Then when he had the guns, he'd say, 'Strip them down and lay down!'

"Then he would turn to his whipping boss and say, 'Lay twenty on his ass, and if you don't lay them on good, I'll make him lay twenty on yours!'

"When the whipping was over, he would hand the guns back to Vauhn and turn around and ride away, without once looking over his shoulder."

The Writer then said, "I can't understand that. I can't imagine a man doing that to me, then handing me a loaded pistol. I would not shoot him in the back, but he would not live to turn around, or at least, I don't think he would."

"I don't know. Those crackers are funny people. The more you whip them, the better they like it. There is something funny about it. I don't know what it is. I have life and fifty-two years. I know that I am going to the rock. I know that I will probably never get out, yet I would not serve one more year down there for a full pardon.

"On the other hand, the Steadman had me whipped more than a hundred times in three years, but I could never bring myself to hate him."

The Writer told McCann what Steadman had said about permitting his wife to sleep with him.

"Oh! He would do that all right. He wasn't bad that way at all. There were a lot of colored families living along the edge of the farm, and I was always getting whipped for giving them State property. Then lots of times he would give me four bits for the purpose. The last time he whipped me was for giving a little colored girl about fourteen cents a bushel for corn. He gave me ten strokes with the *bat*."

"How come? I thought that you just said that he did not care about that."

"Oh! He did not whip me over the girl. It was for stealing the State's corn. He said, 'Dammit! If you'd asked me for half a dollar, I'd have given it to you.'

"'Sir, I would not have minded it so much, but when she saw you coming across the field, she jumped up, grabbed a sack of corn and ran, so I didn't get anything.'

"'Well, why in the hell didn't you say so?' He then threw me a four-bit piece and said, 'You'd better be back at the barn in time to rub Dick down or I'll lay ten more on you.' He turned around and rode off. That is just the way he was."

This case has been treated in some detail for several good reasons. It illustrates the fact that even among cultured persons we have no fixed standards of what is and what is not cruel. This man habitually inflicted the harshest physical punishment, and he was not above ordering men murdered when they were not brought rapidly into line by such punishment, simply because he thought that was the kindest thing he could do under the circumstances. He did not look upon himself as a mean or cruel person. He considered himself a generous, fair-minded, and kind-hearted man, and so he was according to his lights.

On the other hand, he looked upon the years of mental and emotional suppression to which the Writer had been subjected as the most frightful and inhuman treatment that had ever come to his attention.

Of course, it is natural for each man to rationalize his own conduct, by justifying what he does, while the same conduct by another man is considered to be needlessly cruel. But the Writer, who in all his years in prison has never been struck once, and who is so mentally and emotionally constituted that he could never have tolerated it, who for forty years has fought physical cruelty with all the resources of his mind and character, is not prepared to say that Steadman was wrong.

Bruises of the body heal quickly while those of the mind never do.

PART I – CHAPTER V

The Far West

While the prisons of the West have many features that have always been common to all of them, they must be further divided into two groups. Those of the Rocky Mountain States: Montana, Colorado, Wyoming, New Mexico, Idaho, Utah, Nevada and Arizona are to a large extent endogenous to that region and have been subject to very little influence from the East and South. While those of the Pacific Coast States, Washington, Oregon and California were in the beginning largely a product of Eastern penological thinking, they have always been subjected to the strong influence of their sister states, however, and have developed along rather hybrid lines, combining many of the most terrible features of Eastern prisons with some of the most liberal features of the Rocky Mountain prisons.

In turn, these Western prisons have exerted a strong influence upon the prisons of many Eastern states.

The Rocky Mountain States

While these states and the thinking of their people have always had much in common, there have always been differences that not only set them apart from their more populous sisters of the Pacific Coast, but also from each other.

The crime rates and prison populations of these states have always been small. In the whole area there are only two cities of over one hundred thousand population; Denver and Salt Lake City. So the prisons of this area have never contained a high percentage of petty criminals. The crimes endogenous to the area have always been murder, armed robbery and the various kinds of livestock theft. Better than half of the crimes have been committed by nonresidents passing through the state, rather than by residents.

Inmates serving life for murder have always made up a large proportion of the population of these prisons.

Another factor that must be taken into consideration is the fact that these states have always been very rich in proportion to their prison populations, so that the individual tax payers have never felt that support of their prisons placed an undue tax burden upon them, which is in distinct contrast to the feelings of the taxpayers of the predominantly agricultural states.

Of the oldest of these prisons, the old Spanish Prison at Santa Fe, New Mexico, the Writer knows nothing, and the same is true of the Wyoming prison. The populations of these institutions have always been very small, and the Writer has had a chance to meet and talk to very few men who have either worked in or served time in them, nor has he seen much about them in the news.

Of the others, only two prisons have ever had the reputation of being hard: Deer Lodge and Cañon City.

Deer Lodge is the only prison in this whole group that ever had the Silent System, or a contract factory, and even there the Silent System was never complete, for they always had two-man cells and cell mates were allowed to talk in low tones.

Back at the turn of the century, both of these prisons were widely known for the brutality of their punishment. Deer Lodge used a whipping post and Cañon City used what was called a "horse." The prisoner was bent over a structure something like a carpenter's horse and was flogged upon the bare buttocks with a strap, something like the *bat* used in the South, but not nearly so heavy.

Montana finally abolished the whipping post, but Colorado still uses corporal punishment.

The employment at Cañon City during the early days was a stone quarry, and in later years, a great many men have been employed in road work.

Idaho has some farm land that is cultivated by convicts, and Deer Lodge, in addition to a contract furniture factory in the early days, has a large sheep ranch.

So far as the Writer knows, Idaho, Utah, Nevada and Arizona have never used corporal punishment and have never maintained any industries. The only work has been that connected with prison maintenance and the making of their own clothes, and at Carson City, there was no work at all. The prisoners did not even make their own clothing. They were purchased by the State, ready-made.

There was just the one cell house, and a small wing used as a death house. There was no wall, and most prisoners never left the cell house. Doors were all thrown open in the morning, and the inmates were permitted the run of the cell house all day long. Meals were served on long tables in the corridors of the cell house, and the principal pastime of the inmates has always been gambling. All kinds of gambling games ran all day long, and this is probably still true, for this prison has always been conducted on the principles of a liberal jail rather than a penitentiary, all necessary work was done by volunteers who wanted the exercise, much as was the case at McNiel Island when it was a territorial jail,[56] and the structures were very similar, but Carson, unlike the Island, has never had an escape problem. Carved out of the side of a barren mountain and surrounded by deserts, it has never offered the escapee any place to go. Before the development of the motor car and the hard-surfaced road, any prisoner could be given a twenty-four hour start from Carson, and the Warden could still locate him with a pair of binoculars or have him intercepted simply by making two phone calls. There were no rules excepting that the man must keep the peace.

For those who did not, there was a very tough dungeon dug out of the solid rock beneath the floor.

---

56   Part I – Chapter XI

The one characteristic of all of these prisons was that there was never enough work to absorb more than a small fraction of the energies of the inmates. In Idaho, Utah, and Arizona, there was little work and the most liberal privileges of any prisons in America. About the only thing required of the prison inmate in any of these states, was that he stay there. There are large Mormon populations in these three states, and the Mormon people have always taken their religion seriously.

It was the practice for Mormon Elders to visit the prison every Sunday, and any prisoner, either Mormon or Gentile, could complain to them of any mistreatment, and they would go to the Warden and demand an immediate correction. If it were not forthcoming, that Warden might find himself on the way out, for the Mormon Church has always been a political power to be reckoned with.

Pacific Coast States

The populations of Washington, Oregon, and California were always made up of two distinct groups: the roving, hard-bitten, Western pioneer, and the representatives of the big-moneyed corporations of the East who were there to exploit the riches of the wilderness, and this latter group for many years held most of the political power. Also, unlike the Rocky Mountain States, the Pacific Coast States contained large areas of rich arable land which were very attractive to the farmers of the East, and the agriculturalist of that era was a narrow-minded, Bible-back conservative of conservatives, in direct contrast to the well-educated, often college-bred, scientific farms of the present day, who have given us some of our most extreme liberals, both in prison and National affairs.

This conflict of ideas and ideals caused prisons of the Pacific Coast States to contain some of the best and worst features of American penology of the nineteenth century.

The farmers and the big corporations, which often represented the strongest political factors in the State and paid the great bulk of its taxes, felt that the convict should be forced to support himself, and if possible, forced to pay a profit to the State in expiation for his crimes. The pioneer element possessed a strong sense of fair play however, and wanted to see every man given a chance.

At one time all of these states had the contract system: San Quentin had its sash and blind factory; Salem had its foundry. The Writer no longer remembers what was manufactured under the contract system at Walla Walla, but during his own childhood he often heard the boast that all convicts were taught useful trades.

Naturally, the contract system brought with it the task system, enforced by the most brutal punishments. Washington had the high-pressure water cure; Oregon had the whipping post; and California had the jacket, all of which have been previously described.[57]

On the other hand, on general discipline and privileges these prisons, like those of the Rocky Mountain States, were generally the most liberal in America. There was no lockstep, no silent system, no locking in the cells over Saturday and Sunday. Open air recreation and theatricals were common features at San Quentin long before the turn of the century, and at that time this institution was famous for the outstanding quality of its home talent shows, put on every Thanksgiving and Christmas.

For more than sixty years these plays have been written and staged by convicts. In the old days they were usually of the burlesque or musical variety, and the songs and musical scores were original. The female parts were played by the best looking and most talented boys in the prison. Sometimes, when funds were low, the wigs they wore were made from combed out rope, and their dresses, all designed and made by convicts, were often of the flimsiest cotton material, but they trained for months, and there was nothing shoddy about their performances, which often won extravagant praise from the dramatic critics on the San Francisco newspapers.

The outstanding features of the performances were the songs and the double-edged jokes. If you analyze the best jokes coming over your radio, or heard from the stage or screen, you may be amazed to discover that those that bring the most instantaneous response are always of a homosexual flavor. There is a reason for this. To put such jokes over at all they have to be good, and many of the best of these that you are listening to today were first told on the old stage at San Quentin.

One of the best jokes ever put over by Jack Benny was one the Writer first heard in a hobo jungle in 1903, and which had been used in a prison play several years before. It is as follows:

A male character addressing a female character says:

"Have you seen Bill's new baby?" referring to an infant recently born by the wife of Bill, another male character.

The female character says:

"Bill's new baby?" with an incredulous inflection of her voice.

"Why yes! Didn't you know that Bill had a new baby?"

"Why George," gasps the astonished female. "I would have never believed it possible."

Many of the songs used in these plays attained some popularity on the outside. The only one that sticks in the Writer's memory was one that he had the pleasure of hearing from the lips of the boy who sang it in the show of 1903. Years later, he met in Leavenworth the man who had composed it.

When the Cons Have a Prison of Their Own

It was a bright, warm evening in the early Fall of 1900. There were a dozen or more hobos lolling around on the depot platform at San Beuna, Venture. Most of the men were ex-convicts, and most of the conversation was about crime and prison.

As the round-faced, full moon sank slowly toward the broad Pacific, an equally round and smooth faced Indian boy lounging beside the Writer began to sing softly in a clear soprano voice the Spanish song Estraita. All conversation stopped. When the boy, a youth about eighteen who, the Writer later learned, had been out of Quentin only a few weeks, finished the song, several voices demanded:

"Give us the one you sang in the show last Christmas, Danny! Give us the one you sang up in the stir!"

"You should have seen him sing that song up in the stir, kid! – All dolled up like a girl. Black curls clear down to his shoulders. He let his hair grow for the occasion. He was about the sweetest thing in the prison, and Christ, how he can sing!" The man beside the Writer whispered in his ear, "You would go over pretty big up in the stir yourself. Guys would be committing murder over you."

The versatile young Indian, who must have looked like something with black curls to his shoulders and wearing a ballet skirt, dropped his voice to a deep, rich baritone.

"He wore stripes and a ball and chain for this one, kid," the older man whispered, as the boy started to sing, and the Writer tried to picture the scene in his mind and to fathom the longings and aspirations that went into that song.

"The screws will bring us booze; they will also shine our shoes,
When the cons have a prison of their own.
We will have no need for dough; we'll make our own, you know,
When the cons have a prison of their own.
We'll feed the screws on beans; we'll make them press our jeans,
When the cons have a prison of their own.
Every day we'll play handball, up against the cell house wall,
When the cons have a prison of their own.

Verse after verse the boy sang, expressing all the legitimate and illegitimate longings and aspirations of men cut off from the world by high, gray walls. And the Writer, who was then fourteen, tried t picture to himself how it must be.

"We'll dress our boy in silk and we'll make them bathe in milk,

When the cons have a prison of their own.[58]

This cooperative activity was of such great value that the practice of putting on these home talent shows is still retained at San Quentin. But there were many good features about these Western prisons, even when they were at their worst. In most of them there were no restrictions on writing. An inmate could correspond with anyone he pleased. He had to buy his own paper and stamps, but there was no restriction on the number of letters he could write and many a convict made lasting friendships through correspondence that enabled him to get on his feet after his release. The great value of such opportunities to make new friends is discussed in detail in another place.

In like manner, most of these prisons have never placed any restriction on writing for publication except that the story or article was not supposed to criticize the prison or mention the fact that the Writer was a convict, and even these rules were not always enforced. When Donald Lowry was in San Quentin, he and many other inmates of that institution sold articles and stories, which were published under their own name and

---

58   This last couplet referred to a press agent story then current, which had been put out by Flo Zigfeld, to the effect that his beautiful wife, Anna Held, acquired her lovely complexion, not from make-up pots, but from bathing every morning in sweet milk. To give veracity to the story, he had twenty gallons of milk delivered to their apartment every morning, which he dumped down the sink, while Anna bathed in soap and water, the same as anyone else. But the story swept the county, and many cities suffered a milk shortage, because every cutie who could afford it was giving the milk bath a trial.

prison address, to the *Old Pacific Monthly*. This was during the period of 1906 to 1910.

Such privileges were not unique to California prisons. They were common to the whole area, and a lot of worthwhile writing came out of these prisons.

A few years later two outstanding works originated in Salem. The first was *The American Prison System* by Webb. The second was a treatise on philosophy by Jack Giles, later an inmate of Alcatraz and the only man to ever escape from that prison, although he was promptly recaptured. Giles also published two hundred fifty-two Western stories while he was an inmate of Salem, but did not think much of this accomplishment.

He once told the Writer of some of the fan mail he had received. One woman wrote a gushing letter about how wonderful his stories were and how he just had to read the stories of some other Western Writer she named, who had thrilled her so much. Old Jack, who was a very serious-minded man, replied:

"Madam, I write such trash only because there are fools who will buy it. That is bad enough. I don't read it."

In this respect, too, San Quentin has always stood head and shoulders above its neighbors, since it is by far the largest of the Western prisons. Because its inmates have been drawn from a population that has always maintained the highest educational standards in the country, and it has always drawn brains and ability from other states, it is not at all surprising that the quantity and quality of its literary work has always been outstanding. But undoubtedly the best known piece of writing to come out of that institution is the poetic story of a rather sordid love affair. *The Blue Velvet Band* – author forgotten – which for forty years has been known to practically every crook and underworld character in America. This poem has a great appeal for crooks and convicts, because it tells of the sordid life that they understand.

What is to be emphasized here, however, is not the quality or lack of it in any particular work but the fact that in all these prisons, bad as some of them were back in those days, every man was encouraged to develop and give expression to the best that he had in him.

The same was true in the field of education. There was no state money available for the education of inmates, but in California the extension divisions of the State University were open to the convict without charge; books were available from any source whatsoever, and there were always well-educated men from whom the convict desiring to improve himself could obtain assistance. And once an inmate showed a desire to improve himself, he was given every encouragement to continue.

Junk Work

In all of these Western prisons, what is called Junk Work was not only permitted, but also encouraged. From the very first it was realized by the men in charge of the Rocky Mountain prisons that the inmates must have something to do to keep them out of mischief, and the name Junk Work is derived from the propensity of prison inmates to create useful or beautiful articles from scraps of junk found around the prison.

In Idaho, Utah, Nevada, and Arizona, there was little or no work for the prison inmate to do, but even in Washington, Oregon, California, Montana and Colorado, where there were well-developed work programs, and in the first four of them, a task system, there was always time and energy for hobby work of some kind.

The amount of painstaking labor that the convict will devote to any project that will enable him to earn money for tobacco and the other little luxuries he craves is almost beyond the belief of any person who has not been in prison, and it is not only the money, either. The prison inmate's desire to create springs from an inner urge that is analyzed and explained in a later chapter, and the amount of ingenuity he will display in converting worthless junk into objects of beauty is often positively amazing.

The inmates of these Western prisons have always produced a large variety of novelty items to be sold to visitors or to persons on the outside by mail. In Boise and Salt Lake, and this may have been true in Florence, though the Writer is not certain on that point, the visitors were allowed to deal directly with the inmates. This was also true in Carson City to a lesser extent. There the visitors were not permitted to enter the cell house, but they could stand in the offices and deal directly with inmates through the barred windows at the end of the cell house. But there were also showcases in which objects of inmate handicraft were displayed for sale.

In large prisons like San Quentin and Walla Walla, show cases, or actual stores for the sale of prison-made novelties were set up near the main gate. This was also true at Cañon City and Deer Lodge, but there were none of these institutions in which the visitors could absorb more than a small fraction of the work turned out, and the rest had to be handled by mail.

These prison stores were usually run as a concession granted to some life-timer, and he was allowed to charge a commission on all items sold. In other cases they were run by the institution and were presided over by a guard; the State took a fixed percentage on each sale which provided money enough to more than pay the guard's salary and the other expenses of operating the store.

Some men made fancy, carved toothpicks from bone or ivory; others made picture frames of various materials ranging from colored paper to inlaid ivory and pearl. Still other men worked with horse hair, beads, silk, or precious metals, and a large number made belts, watch chains and bridles from horse hair.

One of the ways of selling these items by mail was not very fair to the buyer, but its big virtue was that it worked.

The prisoner would take the name and address of some public personage from the newspaper. Then he would write a nice selling letter to that person, explaining that he was a convict trying to raise some money for some worthy purpose, maybe to support a blind mother or put a young brother through school. Some convicts were not too particular about the truth in such matters, but others were and would frankly admit that they needed the money for tobacco or the other creature comforts they were permitted to have.

The prisoner might suggest that if the person did not care to buy the item, he could show it to some of his friends or raffle it off at his lodge, church, or club. But naturally, the letter would be so constructed as to make the person to whom the article was mailed feel like a heel if he did not buy or dispose of the article at the price asked.

Once a person bought anything, he would be importuned time and again. Jack London's most prized possession was a collection of two hundred hair bridles that convicts had sent to him for his inspection and which he had purchased at an average price of seventy-five dollars each purely out of the kindness or softness of his heart. He had purchased every bridle sent to him, even though he had as much use for them as a dog has for two tails. He simply could not bring himself to blast the hopes of a man who under the handicap of imprisonment had devoted so much time and effort to the creation of a thing of beauty.[59]

Some prisons leaned to one type of work, some to another. Often, the type of work was influenced by the materials and tools the inmate was allowed to buy.

Deer Lodge became famous for the quality of the tooled-leather belts that it turned out. Carson City was known for such items as ivory cribbage boards, jewel boxes and face powder boxes, inlaid with Mother of Pearl, silver, and gold, as well as for its beaten silver and gold jewelry and lodge emblems. Of course, this was only possible because the inmates were allowed to have small hammers, Chinese drills, files, hacksaws, and engraving tools. San Quentin and Florence were famous for their braided horsehair and braided leather work; Cañon City, for the great variety of strictly novelty items designed to appeal to women – silk pillow tops, table covers, and beaded handbags.

Selling was always a big problem, and it was in that respect that the unlimited writing privilege was important, for without it, these men would not have been able to carry on, and a man who in the beginning did not know one rule of grammar or the first principle of salesmanship, under the spur of necessity, taught himself to write selling letters that were masterpieces.

Some inmates who were good workmen induced the better-educated of their fellows to write their business letters for them, and in almost every prison there were men who specialized in this work. For a small commission on sales, they would attempt to find a market for anything, and such men soon became masters of business-letter writing and salesmanship. One man who started out that way was a lifer in Florence by the name of Etting, or something like that. (The Writer is not sure of his memory of this man's name).

During the period between 1910 and 1920 he was rated the best business-letter Writer in America. He numbered among his clients such concerns as the Pullman Company, Armour Packing Company and many other large concerns, as well as hundreds of individuals, and in addition to the business letters he wrote, both for business concerns and his fellow inmates, he carried on one of the largest personal correspondences in America.

This man was pardoned by Governor Hunt about 1920, after he had served somewhere between sixteen and twenty years on a life sentence. He went to Pittsburg, Pennsylvania, married and established a business correspondence and mail-advertising business based upon the skill he had developed in prison. The last time the Writer heard of him, he was earning about thirty-thousand dollars per year, and was highly respected throughout the business world.

Another interesting case that came to the Writer's attention was that of a cripple, a three-time-loser in Cañon City, who, shortly after being sent up for a long stretch learned that his mother was dying of cancer and that his two younger brothers and younger sister were running wild and rapidly going to the dogs.

---

59   In his book, *Burning Daylight*, Jack London told of his hurt over the loss of his bridle collection when his dream home was burned by the leaches he had been supporting for years, simply because they feared its completion would mean an end to their free meal ticket.

This man blamed his bad example for the ruination of the lives of the younger children. He blamed himself for not doing more for his mother. The family was destitute. He needed money badly, money that he had always obtained at the point of a gun, and now he was in prison, helpless. He was so overwhelmed by his feeling of remorse that he attempted to destroy himself.

While he was in the hospital, his nurse, a convict who was making a fair income in his spare time by tying trout flies, gave the cripple a few flies to tie for him, more to take the man's mind off his troubles than for any other reason.

During his previous sentences, the cripple had not taken any interest in Junk Work, but now he began asking his nurse a thousand questions. He wanted to know all about it. How did a man go about buying materials, providing he had the money? How did he go about selling stuff that did not sell in the prison store? What kind of ties sold best in the store?

The nurse had a pattern for a cute little stuffed dog. Several convicts had tried making it, but it did not sell well at one dollar. It was decided to cut the pattern down so that the little dog would not be over six inches long and to have the same little dog in several poses. The nurse donated a piece of sheepskin, needles, thread, and shoe buttons for eyes, and the cripple went to work.

The small models, designed to sell for twenty-five cents, went over with a bang. They paid a good profit when made by hand, but it was not long until the cripple could not make enough to supply the demand of the prison store, for every girl visitor to the prison wanted one, and when she got home, each of her friends wanted one. Finally, the cripple obtained permission to salvage an old, worn out sewing machine, which greatly increased the number of these toys he could turn out, but still, he could not keep up with the demand.

It was not too long before this man had five other convicts working for him on new machines, was selling his little stuffed dogs to Denver department stores in gross lots, and was earning about five thousand dollars per year.

He was able to see to it that his mother's last days were free from worry if not from pain, and to provide for the education of the younger children. The success he had made, filled his younger siblings with pride. They no longer thought of themselves as social outcasts because their big brother was in prison, and this gave him an influence over them that he would not otherwise have had.

All three of the young children grew up to be normal and useful members of society, and the last time the Writer heard of the older brother, he was running a novelty business in Denver, employing about sixty persons, mostly ex-convicts who without his aid, might have returned to crime.

Hundreds of other cases could be cited. In the vast majority the success was not as spectacular as in the two cases described, but it was no less real or substantial. This junk work and the business experience obtained in connection therewith has always been one of the finest features of Western prisons, and many a convict has gone out and rebuilt his life on the basis of skills acquired in prison.

Those Rocky Mountain prisons that have always allowed their inmates the broadest latitude in that respect have never had any serious trouble and have probably had the lowest rate of recidivism in America.

In prisons like Deer Lodge, Cañon City, and those of the West Coast, this influence has reached to only a minority of the inmates, but there have been few repeaters among that minority, in sharp contrast to the number among men who did not devote their spare time to something of that kind.

There are definite psychological reasons why this must always be true, and these will be fully discussed in another place, but it may be pointed out at this place that the man in prison has reached the lowest point in our social system, and on his way to that point, his ego has taken a lot of punishment. His greatest need is to regain his self-respect, and that need is responsible for his desire to create. His second greatest need is an opportunity to make new friends who will accept him on the basis of the new values he is developing or hopes to develop through the exercise of his creative instinct, and there is no better way of finding such friends than through the correspondence connected with the sale of things of beauty.

It must be pointed out here that hobby work was not permitted in the prisons of fifty and sixty years ago with any idea of reforming the inmate. Those old-time prison men did not look upon that as any part of their functions. Some of the men sent to them were considered hopelessly criminal; others they considered casually or accidentally criminal. They expected the entire first group to return to crime as soon as they were released, and they expected a substantial proportion of the second group to do so, but that was something for the police to worry about. It was not their business. Their function was to keep their wards from going over the fence and to maintain peace and harmony in their institutions, and they were not interested in anything else. They had learned by experience that the man who is busy at some work of creation is not very apt to go over the fence or create trouble, but the man who is denied the opportunity to create anything else can often create a lot of hell. Or to put it in other words, "The devil finds work for idle hands to do."

They encouraged junk work for the very practical reason that it made their jobs easier.

PART I – CHAPTER VI

The Early History of Federal Prisons

Leavenworth

As previously mentioned,[60] by Act of March 3, 1901, Attorney General Bonaparte was given authority to transfer to the sites of the proposed penitentiaries at Atlanta and Leavenworth such Federal prisoners as could be conveniently accommodated upon the new sites and employed on the construction of the new prisons.

The Long March

Early in the Summer of 1901, the four hundred odd Federal prisoners then confined at Moundsville, West Virginia, were routed out of bed one morning before daybreak and assembled in the prison yard. Each man, as he was awakened and ordered to dress had been told by the guard to bring all his personal property with him. He and his belongings were carefully searched; he was advised to keep such items as pipes, tobacco, matches, handkerchiefs, and socks, if he had any on his person.[61] His other personal property was placed in a burlap bag, marked with his number, and thrown into a wagon.

In the middle of the yard the prison blacksmith had set up his anvil, and beside it was an enormous heap of *chain-gang* shackles with extra-long chains, about thirty-two inches, between them.

Each man was led to the anvil, and a pair of the shackles was riveted on his ankles. He was given a piece of heavy cord with which to suspend the center of the chain from his belt, so that it would not drag on the ground and trip him; he was given a pair of new cowhide army marching shoes, but no socks. Then he was served a breakfast consisting of a tin cupful of black coffee without sugar, a big chunk of boiled, fat salt pork and a big chunk of soggy cornpone, which were eaten out of hand, standing on their feet or squatting on the ground.

When all of the men had been searched, shackled, shod, and fed, guards staggered into the yard under the weight of their burdens and dropped heavy canvas bags that gave forth a clanking sound upon the ground. These bags contained more than two hundred

---

60   Part I – Chapter I
61   No prison inmates back in those days were furnished with socks, underwear, toilet soap, toothpowder, toothbrushes, combs, or tobacco, but at Moundsville, all of these items could be purchased from the prison commissary or received from home.

pairs of handcuffs and a number of chains about fifty feet long, each of which contained a long, flat link at each end and a similar link every two feet throughout its length. These big links were made so that handcuffs could be slipped through them, and the men were handcuffed to the long chains, two abreast in groups of fifty or sixty.

When all was ready, the big gate was swung open and an ex-drill sergeant barked, "Forward! March!"

As this clanking centipede of zebra-like figures filed four abreast through the big gate and turned down the dusty and badly rutted dirt road, mounted gun guards took up positions and rode through the fields on both sides of the road. An army chuck wagon and other wagons carrying blankets and supplies, driven by convict mule skinners wearing Oregon boots,[62] and the rear of this strange caravan of stripe-clad men was made up of more mounted gun guards, for this was a prison transfer of the vintage of 1901, and these men were headed for Leavenworth, about thirteen-hundred miles and more than sixty days away.

At about the same time this first group left Moundsville, bound for Leavenworth, a smaller but similar group left Columbus, South Carolina bound for the new prison site at Atlanta.[63]

Through mud and rain, through choking dust and blistering heat, this clanking, creeping zebra-like centipede with more than eight hundred blistered feet from the rough, army marching shoes worn without socks, crawled slowly across the face of the Nation; with wrists and ankles chafed raw, bruised and swollen from their shackles; with bodies chafed and raw from the rubbing of their heavy, woolen striped suits and coarse ticking shirts made stiff and sticky with perspiration, caked with mud and dust until they were as harsh and rough as sand paper, worn without underwear, these men plodded wearily on and on, day after day, all through the hot and humid months of July and August, twenty miles every day. They slept on the ground in all weather with only one army blanket per man for bedding. They ate only such foods as could be purchased on the way or conveniently prepared in the open. There was never any chance to shave, to bathe, to wash their feet or

---

62   For the benefit of those who are not familiar with manacles, an Oregon boot, is an iron ring two to three inches wide and from two to three inches thick – large enough to fit around the leg above the ankle bones and weighing from twenty-five to one hundred pounds. A special steel brace is screwed onto the heel of the wearer's shoe and fits inside of the boot on each side of his leg. There are flanges on this brace that keep the boot from slipping down and crushing the wearer's foot or ankle. The boot is made in two halves which are fastened around the leg by bolting them together by means of counter-sunken bolts that can be turned only by the use of a special wrench. With the brace, a man can walk fairly well for short distances. Without it, his foot would be crushed before he had taken ten steps. It is no great handicap in climbing into or out of a wagon or in mounting a horse, as chains would be, but it is an effective means of preventing escape.

63   Recently, in personal conversation with the Writer, James V. Bennett, Director of Federal Bureau of Prisons, stated that he had studied all the official records and newspaper files of the period and that he had never heard of Federal prisoners being marched from Moundsville to Leavenworth and from Columbus, South Carolina, to Atlanta, in chains. He poohood the idea and wound up with the fatuous remark: "Why, that would be crueler than the Nazis."

Which only goes to show how small an understanding and sense of history Mr. Bennett possesses. But for Mr. Bennett's information, there is very probably a living survivor of each of these groups. J. S. "Heck" Wallace (Part II – Chapter XII) was on the long march from Moundsville to Leavenworth. He was still alive and in reasonably good health at the time the Writer came to Alcatraz in 1942. Tommy Nelson, released from Leavenworth in 1947 or 1948 and who, less than a year ago, was living in St. Paul, Minnesota, was on the march from Columbus to Atlanta.

faces, or to change their clothing. They had no canteens, and there was no dropping out of line for a cool drink.

As they plodded down the Ohio Valley they reeked to high heaven with the odor of unwashed humanity and were set upon by swarms of flies and flying ants by day and swarms of mosquitoes by night. Many of them developed the ague (malaria). They were dosed with teaspoonfuls of powdered quinine and forced to march on. Those who complained were taken from the chain at stops, flogged and returned to it. The Writer himself saw the blacksnake scars on many of these men's buttocks and the shackle scars on their ankles, more than ten years later.

One man who claimed that he could march no more was shot five times through the body, the cuff removed from his dead hand, and his chain mates forced to march on without him. What became of the corpse or what report was made of the affair, the other prisoners never knew.

These men, with more than two month's growth of beards on their faces, reached Leavenworth in the latter part of August or the first part of September, 1901, and were marched to the Military Prison at Fort Leavenworth where they were to be confined during the building of the stockade and the throw-up of the first buildings upon the new prison site. (See Diagram).

The Building of Leavenworth

Work on the new prison commenced almost at once, and the four hundred men from Moundsville, supplemented by such other civil prisoners as happened to be in the Military Prison at that time, were marched the two and one half miles to the new site each morning under armed guard, served a cold lunch at noon, and marched the two and one half miles back to the Military Prison at night, where they were often forced to stand in line for several hours in biting Kansas blizzards, while they were counted and recounted, to make sure that none were missing, before they were marched into the prison dining room and fed a warm supper, then marched directly to their cells.

The first job was building a barbed wire stockade surrounding the twenty-three-and-one-half acre plot that was to comprise the prison proper.

Posts twelve feet high were set in the ground around the whole plot at distances of from six to ten feet apart, and these were strung with miles and miles of barbed wire, with strands from four to five inches apart.

While some men were putting up the first fence under the eyes of mounted gun guards and soldier sentries, others were putting up wooden guard towers, raised ten to fifteen feet off the ground, each of which contained a little cast-iron stove, so the guards would have protection from the weather. Still other men were engaged in building a long wooden shed in which stone for the new buildings could be cut; laying track for hauling materials into the new site; putting up a brick plant; opening up a shale pit from which material for brick making could be obtained, and the many other tasks associated with new construction.

This work went on all through the bitter winter of 1901-02. There were many cases of frost-bite and many deaths from pneumonia during that first winter, but as a result, for the first time in Federal penal history, convicts were supplied with underwear, heavy woolen socks that came up to or even above the knees,[64] woolen gloves made on the same knitting machines, and woolen caps with flaps to cover the ears. But even with this added protection, the death rate was very high.

It was not until the Spring of 1902 that the first permanent building was completed with stones cut and bricks made by the convicts. This was the one and a half story building on the West side of the grounds (#41 on Diagram) which housed the first fifty men kept at the new prison. Its companion building (#42) on the East side of the prison, was completed shortly thereafter.

The third building, the two-story Isolation Building[65] about twenty feet south of Building #41 (#38 Diagram), and a large, three-story building fifty feet south of the Isolation Building were also completed that same summer. The prison was then dedicated and all civil prisoners at the Military Prison were moved to the new institution; many of their soldier guards were discharged from the Army, so that they could move with the convicts.

From reports of men who took part in the long march and the building of the new prison, conditions during the first four years through the throwing up of the first two cell houses and the high wall, the power house, kitchen, dining room, Chapel and Administration Building, were a burning hell. The Isolation Building served as the Administration building; the big Laundry Building (#37) served as dormitory, dining room and kitchen; and Building #42 served as hospital during that period.

Bricklayers worked when it was so cold that wood fires had to be maintained to keep their cement mortar from freezing and their fingers from being frostbitten. After working out in the weather for eight hours, these men were often forced to stand at attention with folded arms in cold, snow, and even sleet storms, while they were counted and recounted. Those long periods of standing at attention out in the weather while they were counted and the count checked, sapped the vitality of the men, and they died like flies of pneumonia and meningitis.

In the summer, men pushed wheelbarrows of brick, cement, and stone up the long ramps of the high wall, while guards armed with canes drove them at almost a dogtrot, and any prisoner who let go of the handles of his wheelbarrow was certain to have his head split. Men were worked until they fell out from heat exhaustion or died of sunstroke.

During the first winter, the first four hundred men who had come from Moundsville were soon depleted by death and discharge, but the population of the new institution was built up by new arrivals directly from the courts and by large contingents from Fort Smith and California.

About two hundred and fifty men were marched up from Fort Smith in the Spring or Summer of 1902, and a big shipment of about seventy men were transferred from San

---

64   At that time these socks were knitted on hand-powered knitting machines set up in the tailor shop at the Military Prison, and it was possible to get a friend to knit one stocking that came up to the hips. These machines were later moved to Leavenworth, where as late as 1919, many other men, including the Writer, were doing the same thing.
65   Part I – Chapter VIII

Quentin to Leavenworth in 1903, which was the first large transfer of Federal prisoners by rail to occur in the United States.[66]

Of the first four thousand men to arrive at Leavenworth, approximately fifty percent died there. The Writer was never able to obtain the exact figures, but in 1913 it was ordered that tombstones be cut for all men buried in the prison graveyard. The Writer's cellmate, a fellow named Amus Hays, serving twenty-five years from Oklahoma for train robbery, had the job of cutting numbers on those stones. He did not have the full list, but he used to receive a hundred numbers at a time, and the proximity of these numbers to each other indicated a death rate of at least fifty percent. This project was never carried to completion. Only a small number of the stones cut and numbered were ever taken to the prison cemetery. Several hundred of them stood in the prison yard for some years and were finally broken up and the crushed stone was used in making concrete.

The Mutiny of 1902

The contingent of prisoners from Fort Smith was composed largely of Western bad men from the then Indian Territory: murderers, train robbers, and horse thieves serving life sentences; and booze runners, serving two years each, which was the maximum sentence for that crime back in those days.

There were some pretty rough characters in this group, more than half of whom were serving life sentences. They did not like the new home they were being required to build for themselves, and they planned to do something about it; in some manner, they secured a loaded 45 thumb buster (single action) Colt pistol.

A man named Tim Mullins worked his way as close to one of the tower guards as possible, threw the pistol on him, and ordered him to throw out his rifle and pistol and to be sure that he threw them inside the wire.

As the covered guard was complying with Mullins' orders, another guard opened up on Mullins with a rifle from a distance of one hundred yards. Mullins swung around and threw one shot at that guard, which was said to have hit him squarely between the eyes, which of course, if that is the way it happened, was pure accident. The old Colt thumb buster was a good gun, and Mullins, who had grown up with one of them in his hand, was a good shot. But at that distance, no man could make such a shot twice in a thousand tries. Yet, men familiar with gun fighting have an instinct to survive which in such circumstances often enables them to make shots that would normally be impossible.

In any case, the guard was killed instantly, and when Mullins leveled his pistol at the next guard, a man named Leonard, both guards and convicts said he jumped out of his tower and broke both legs. Leonard's own story stated that he had not been in a tower; instead, he was on the ground inside the wire and unarmed; and when the shooting started, he started running toward the gate in order to obtain a gun, but in his excitement, forgot about the excavation for C-cell house and ran right into it, breaking both legs over a timber on which he landed. The rest of the guards did not like the looks of Mullins' pistol <u>much better, after</u> seeing that first shot.

66   In this connection it should be remembered that during the Spanish American War, trains were used for the first time to move troops to embarkation centers, but even in that war, many troops were moved thousands of miles on foot, and the Congress in those days was not in favor of providing convicts with luxuries not accorded the Nation's defenders. But of course, no money-happy bureaucrat of the present day could be expected to understand that.

Mullins told the Writer, "I was afraid to fire again, afraid a miss would spoil the impression I had created, but a couple of the other boys had the screws rifles, and it did not take long to discourage the rest of them."

The prisoners took the armory, and those that could, armed themselves, fanning out over the countryside and raiding farms for horses upon which to get away. It should be noted here that this affair has always been referred to as a mutiny instead of a break. A mutiny is exactly what it was. A protest against intolerable conditions. McCloughry recognized it as such and so designated it. But many convicts did escape.

Robinson, who described this phase of the affair to the Writer, said:

"They accused me of being one of the leaders. Actually, I wasn't even in on the know, and I had not been able to get a gun at the armory. I set out on foot alone. I came to a field where a farmer was plowing. Two convicts were unhitching the horses from the plow. The farmer was running toward me, but evidently did not see me. He reached down in the grass, almost at the point where I was jumping over the fence, and snatched up a 25-20 Winchester he probably had there for shooting rabbits. I simply reached over and took the rifle out of his hand. He was so surprised that he just stood there with this mouth half open. We had no tobacco in those days. I asked him if he had any, but he was evidently too scared to answer. I pulled his lips apart with my thumb, saw that he had a chew in his mouth, reached into his pocket and found a plug of *Star chewing* tobacco and some extra shells for the rifle. I made one of the other fellows take me up on the horse with him. We rode that horse double clear down Indian Territory. I don't know what became of the other fellow. He has never been recaptured. I was not caught until 1906."[67]

The only convict injured in the escape was one who had his arm shot off by the accidental discharge of a ten-gauge shotgun as the men were arming themselves at the armory.

All of the men involved were indicted for murder, and as they were recaptured they were tried and sentenced to life imprisonment, that is, all except three who were acquitted.

These three men had picked up Guard Leonard and carried him to the prison hospital. At their trial, Leonard had testified that he was sure that they had no part in the original plot. He stated that when the shooting started, they had been as surprised as he was, and when they had seen that he was injured, they had taken him to the hospital before taking advantage of the opportunity to escape provided by the disarming of the guards.

How many men were involved in the escape, the Writer does not know. The indictment will give the names of the men the Government accused, but even that figure was probably inaccurate. Some were captured almost at once, and others were never captured. Since that was before the day of fingerprinting, it was rather difficult to identify a man after a lapse of a few years.

Of the mutineers remaining in Leavenworth on July 1, 1913, there were only four: Hewitt; Mullins; Keeting; and Robinson. Three of these men: Hewit, Mullins, and Keeting had been in the big break of 1910 in which convicts armed with wooded guns had overpowered the crew of a locomotive and run the engine through the West gate. But less

---

67   Robinson was out four years. The other fellow was not recaptured until turned in by his wife in 1930, twenty-eight years after the escape. The case was too old to convict him of murder. Whether he was brought back to finish the un-expired portion of the two-year sentence he had been serving at the time of the escape, the Writer does not know.

than three years later, on the basis of having served ten years flat and of having made one year's good conduct records, Robert W. McCloughry had recommended their release.

This was the result of a promise made to these men when they were in the hole following the escape attempt of 1910. In that attempt, six men had been involved. They had run through the gate all right, but at a switch they had taken the wrong track to reach the main line, and had run into a derail several miles from the prison. One kid in the bunch who had only been in the prison a few weeks on a life sentence took the fireman's overalls, cap, and lunch bucket. He smeared his face with coal dust, and instead of taking off into the brush, walked right back down the track toward the prisons. As he met guards and soldiers going out to search for the missing men, he greeted them and spurred them on. To the suggestion that he report to the prison, he said:

"I'll be glad to do that, but I must go the depot first and report that engine to the master mechanic. Otherwise, I'll lose my job."

That kid, named Gordon, was one of the gang who had robbed a train at Omaha a few months before. That night he walked right around the prison, through the city of Leavenworth, right down to the depot, out into the railroad yards, and caught a train which he held down all the way to Chicago. From there he made his way into Canada, where he married, became a schoolteacher, and took out Canadian citizenship. He raised a family of three children and became a highly respected member of the community.

In 1927, he was trapped through fingerprints. There was no way in the world by which he could legally be returned to the United States. But a lot of people on both sides of the line did not know that. The case received reams of publicity, and President Coolidge, as a noble gesture, gave Gordon a full pardon.

The other five men were captured within a few hours. When McCloughry interviewed Mulling, Keeting and Hewit following their recapture, they argued in substance as follows:

"What in the hell do you expect? Just because we tried to beat you once a screw got killed, you have every screw in this joint riding us to death."

"That is not true! I have never told any of my guards to ride you!"

"Well, they are doing it, anyway. What chance have we got? Why shouldn't we try anything? We haven't anything to lose but our lives, and with nothing to look forward to, they don't amount to much."

"I tell you that is not true!" the old man was quoted as snapping angrily, his chin whiskers quivering. "I don't blame you for attempting to escape. I don't blame any man for attempting to escape. I understand exactly how you feel, but I am trying to tell you that you have only hurt yourselves, that your situation is far from hopeless."

"Malarkey!"

"It is no such a thing! We were not able to prove who fired that shot. Under those circumstances, I have never felt that any of you should have been convicted of anything more serious than manslaughter, and the maximum sentence for manslaughter is ten years. By this new escape attempt you would have lost any goodtime you had on those ten years. So here is what I will do. Give me ten years with one year's good prison record, and I will use all of my influence to get you out."

"Malarkey! Every screw in this joint will try to ride us to death, so we don't have a chance."

"Hereafter, I shall investigate every one of your reports myself. If I find that any guard is riding any one of you, I shall fire him for it. You all know that my word is good. You will wear stripes for ninety days, the same as anyone else, but if you try to get along, you can. Just give me that one year's good prison record. I have to have that in order to help you. That is all."

What kind of a man was this who would hold out such hope to men serving double life, men who were as notorious and considered as hard and dangerous in their day as Dillinger was in his and who had just been involved in a most desperate and spectacular attempt to escape which had made National headlines?

He was the same man who, following the Mutiny of 1902, had posted the following order on the prison bulletin board:

"No officer of this institution is ever justified in risking his own life or in taking the life of another human being merely to prevent an escape. Escaped convicts can always be recaptured. We cannot give back a human life."

Before we can answer our question, however, we must take a closer look at the man himself and at the system of penology of which he was such a prominent exponent.

(See Diagrams Pages 282 - 285)

Key To Diagram Of Leavenworth

1. South gate and armory. The gate was close by a one-inch steel plate let down from the armory which was directly above the gate. This is the gate through which all persons entered the prison.

2. Partly finished rotunda, showing steps leading up to level of main hall and the guard cage, represented by box, which consisted of two steel doors about six or eight feet apart with a guard holding the keys to both gates between them.

3. Main hall of administration build.

4. Lavatory and toilet.

5. Guard's locker room.

6. Storeroom for medical supplies.

7. Superintendent of Construction's office.

8. Captain's office which housed prison telephone switchboard. The nerve center of the prison.

9. Dispensary.

10. Doctor's private office. It was in this office in February 1914 that Dr. Yoke told the Writer he had Bright's Disease and was going to die.

11. Warden's office, indicating location of desk at which McCloughry and Morgan held interviews. (Part I – Chapter VII)

12. Print shop.

13. Warden's anteroom, indicating desk of convict secretary before door to private office, guard's chair by window, and benches upon which the convicts on Warden's call sat. (Part I – Chapter VII)

14. Concrete platforms on the level of the main hall, dining room and Chapel which were about five feet above the level of the yard and street. Line indicates steps. Men were knocked down these steps. Brick paved, flower-bordered streets leading to East and West yards.

15. Chapel and auditorium.

16. Small Catholic Chapel back of the main Chapel. The two other small rooms indicated were sometimes used by other small religious groups.

17. Dining room. The small square at East end of room indicates Captain's dais. The seat sections are numbered 1 to 5, which is the manner in which they were officially designated. The small cross between sections 3 and 4 indicates the spot where the Writer killed Turner. The broken lines back of the Captain dais indicate a wall six feet thick in which there were left openings as indicated. The inmates entered and left the dining room through the two openings on the South end. Those toward the North end entered the kitchen. The one behind the Captain's dais opened directly into an area between the dining room and Chapel, from which stairways, not indicated, led up to a small balcony overlooking dining room, and to balcony of auditorium. There was a phone there.

18. Kitchen. The circles indicate large copper pots, behind which was a row of steam roasters. The large rectangle on the West side of the room indicates the location of the steam dishwashing machine. The small rectangle at corner of kitchen and dining room indicates the location of Bull Leonard's chair.

19. Bakery.

20. Ice plant and milk-room. The small projection at the East side of this building indicates the lower cooling of the compressor plant located directly below the ice plant.

21. Butcher shop, which was refrigerated.

22. Large cold room. The indicated steps between this room and butcher shop lead to kitchen basement, which, besides the compressor plant, contained a large number of cold rooms, running clear back under the dining room, in which six-months of food for the prison could be stored, if necessary. There was an iron door at the entrance of dining room, indicated by line, iron doors leading out to East and West yards, and an iron door opening off Railroad Avenue into kitchen basement. There were no other iron doors within this building. The only locked doors were those of some of the cold rooms containing things the convicts might steal.

The second floor of the Administration Building (#3 to 13), was occupied by the Chief Clerk's office over the Warden's office; the Chaplain's office and library over the print shop (#12). These were reached by a stairway, not shown, just outside the door to the Warden's anteroom. The South end of the second floor consisted of one large room used as a dormitory and known as No. 2 Parole Room.

Above the Chief Clerk's office and mail room, which were right together, was the Record Clerk's office. Across the hall was Dummy McCoughry's Bureau of Identification. On the third floor directly over No. 2 Parole Room, was an identical room used as the hospital and containing about 48 cots, three toilets, one bathtub, a desk and medicine cabinet, a kitchen range and one long table. At the front of the room, directly in front of the toilets was the operating table. Contagious cases were kept on one side of the room; non-contagious cases on the other. There was an eight-foot aisle down the center of the room, which separated them. They ate, if able, at the same table and from the same dishes. The only iron doors inside this building were those of the hospital and Parole Room, which were reached by stairways at the South end of the building, not shown in drawing but leading off of the passageways leading into the cell houses.

A.   A-cell house, of which only the inner wall was completed in 1912. The door, indicated at the end of the street, and the windows were bricked up so as to form a solid wall.

B.   B-cell house, under construction was completed in the Fall of 1915. It was from this cell house that Honolulu tried to escape.

C.   C-cell house. The first one completed, about 1904.

D.   D-cell house. Completed in 1905 or '06.

There were iron doors at the entrance of each cell house and at the entrance of the walks, indicated by broken lines, along the side of each cell house, but these doors were never locked in the day time. They were unlocked before breakfast in the morning and locked after the completion of the count at night.

S.   S-East yard street, brick paved and bordered with flowerbeds.

S'.	West yard street. It was on these streets that the occupants of D and C cell houses lined up and were counted before being marched into the dining room at noon and night. The X near #15 marks the spot where on January 19, 1916, the D-cell house lines lapped over, so that men on the second and third galleries became abreast of each other, and Luke Jones killed Dutch Schmidt.
L.	All spots marked L were lawn.
F.	All spots marked F were flowerbeds.
	The X on S, just between back of Chapel and hospital marks the spot where Manuel killed Guard Barr.
H.	New hospital, completed and put into use on January 28, 1915.
T.	Trees.
RR.	Railroad Avenue. X marks the spot where Pedro killed Bull Leonard. X' marks the spot where Pedro was shot by E. N. Smith.

Women's Prison: There was provision for a women's prison and for a juvenile prison in the Act of March 3, 1891. The walls for these prisons were constructed, but the rest of the plan was never carried out.

23.	Out East Gate. Put into use in 1912. The Writer put the phones in the towers indicated.
24.	East Gate Sally-port, showing derail. An afterthought following the break of 1910.
25.	Inner East Gate.
26.	Brick plant. K indicates the kilns.
27.	Old Wall. This area was used as a brickyard at the time the Writer went to Leavenworth; it had originally been set aside for a juvenile prison, but the plan was abandoned and the inner wall torn down in 1908.
28.	Cement shed.
29.	Lumber shed.
30.	Steel shed. These three frame sheds were for some years favorite trysting spots. It was in the back of the lumber shed that Manuel bored the holes which enabled a number of fellators to ply their avocation in complete safety for many months.
31.	Carpenter shop.

32. Boiler house, entered from door opening on Railroad Avenue, was thirty feet underground. The tin shop and paint shop were on the floor above and were on a level some ten feet above Railroad Avenue, and were entered from the indicated Alley.

33. Powerhouse.

34. Machine shop. All doors in this group of buildings were iron barred gates. The door entering the powerhouse from Railroad Avenue was never used and was kept locked. The others, like the iron doors entering the main building and cell houses were locked only at night.

35. Rabbit Park. This was a round steel cage probably thirty feet high and twenty-five or thirty feet in diameter. It contained a good-sized tree and a number of squirrels, rabbits, and pigeons.

It should be observed that the barbarians of the prison world of 1891 thought that green lawns, flowers, trees, and the sight of living creatures were essential to mental health. Every shop and building had its cats – and ever under the silent system, there was no rule against petting, talking-to, or playing with the cats within reason.

36. This is a large, three-story building. The upper floor, entered by a stairway from the outside was originally used as a dormitory and the second floor as a dining room while the Administration Building and dining room were being put up. This was the fourth building completed. At the time the Writer went to Leavenworth and for many years thereafter, the basement of this building, which was about five feet below the yard level, was used as a laundry, bathroom, and convict barbershop. The second floor housed the clothing department and clothing storeroom. The top floor was the tailor shop and shoe shop, where all convict shoes and clothing were made.

37.   The Isolation Building. (For detailed description and drawing see Part I – Chapter VIII). This was the third building put up and originally served as the Administration Building while the Administration Building was being put up. In the original plans this building was intended to be used for the Deputy Warden's office and place of punishment until the rotunda cell houses and adjoining offices were completed. It was then planned that the Warden's office would be on the B-cell house side of the rotunda and the Deputy Warden's office on the A-cell house side; that dungeons beneath the cell houses would be used for punishment, but that part of the plan was never carried out.

The Isolation yard. This was a walled court forty feet wide and one hundred and twenty-five feet long. At the time the Writer went to Leavenworth, the yard was separated from the main prison by an arched wall eighteen feet high at each end. The arches were closed by a light, open grillwork of small bars. A small area of the yard around the back porch of the Isolation building was paved with brick as was a walk around the whole yard, and a roadway running down to a large, barred gate, indicated, wide enough to permit a mule-drawn dump cart to draw up to the back porch to bring stone to be broken for punishment and to haul the broken stone away. The X marks the spot where Brewer built the Writer's gallows: X' the spot where Panzeran, Applegate and Suey were hanged.

38.   In 1916 Fletcher had the arches bricked up because he thought the Writer was making connections with his friends. In 1917, after failure to find a hacksaw he knew the Writer had, he accepted a stoolpigeon's story that the saw was buried in the ground, had the whole yard dug up, eighteen inches of dirt removed and replaced with concrete.

39.   West Gate through which convicts drive a locomotive in July, 1910. (Part I – Chapter VI) This gate was bricked up in 1912, and the armory, which had previously been above the gate, was moved to the site indicated (#1), and the windows were bricked over. Fletcher had the brick removed from the windows in 1917 so he could have a gun guard in there overlooking the Isolation yard.

40.   This building and its companion (#42) near the other end of Railroad Avenue were the first permanent buildings erected upon the new site. In 1912 the upper floor, that was level with the street, was used as the guard's mess. Railroad Avenue made a sharp dip after crossing the street, and the back half of the building was entered from the porch indicated and contained the band room. The basement, entered by a door a little further down the hill, was used as an oil house and a storage room for pipe.

41.   Hospital Annex for tubercular patients.

42.   Stonesaw.

43.   Blacksmith shop for general work.

44.   Stone shop. 45-0 Stone shop office. Inside of shop adjoining office was the guard's stand, about fifteen feet above the floor. There was a secondary guard stand at the back of the shop. 45-B. Stone shop blacksmith shop.

45.   A traveling hand crane by which stones were loaded on small trucks to be brought into the shop, where there was a row of tool boxes down the center and a row against each wall. The stones to be cut were placed between these and the rails. There was space enough, not indicated, for a man to step between two tool boxes in order to pass from one side of shop to the other. The shop was heated by large steam coils running the full length of the shop on both sides.

Prologue.

Note: This drawing has been made from memory. Using as a fixed scale the length of the Isolation yard (#39), which was one hundred and twenty-five feet. The distance from RR to (#46) should be 150 feet or 50 MM, and the north wall should be 50 MM beyond the stone traveler. That would put the north wall 32 MM beyond the edge of the paper.

The south end of the stone shop was actually ten feet, about 3 MM north of the end of traveler, and shop was one hundred feet long.

The outer east wall should be placed 40 MM to the east of the line indicating it, making the ball park not quite, but more nearly square.

The hospital building, which is in substantial proportion, should be shifted about one CM to the south.

In other respects the diagram is in substantial proportion.

PART I - CHAPTER VII

Leavenworth, Continued

Major Robert W. McCloughry

Warden McCloughry was a prison man of the old school. He was born about 1840 of Scotch parents, but whether or not that birth had taken place in America or Scotland, the Writer never knew.

In any case, young Robert's parents had settled in the State of Illinois, and his education for the bar had been interrupted by the outbreak of the Civil War.

He had joined the Illinois Volunteers, and being a young man of considerable capacity for details, he had risen to the rank of Major in the Commissary Department.

Following the war, young McCloughry became interested in Illinois politics, served several terms in the Illinois legislature with a number of his fellow officers from the Illinois Volunteers, one of whom was named Joseph Cannon and another J. F. McCartney, both of whom went on to the National Congress, where the former served a great many terms, the Writer believes twenty-six and was for some years Speaker of the House of Representatives.

The latter, a fellow Scot and a Captain in the Illinois Volunteers, served only two terms in Congress as a Republican, then quit that party to become one of the founders of the Prohibition Party.

After a term or two in the legislature, McCloughry was made Warden of the Illinois Penitentiary at Joliet, a job he held for more than thirty years, until in 1901, when at the insistence of his good friend, Joseph Cannon, he was appointed Warden of the new prison to be established at Leavenworth at a salary of four thousand dollars per year.

McCloughry was the father of three sons whom he brought up and trained in the prisons business. At the time he became Warden at Leavenworth, two of those sons were holding down Wardenships at State institutions. One was at Anamosa, Iowa, and the other was at Waupun, Wisconsin. Wardenships then, as now, were political plums, but the McCloughry's were prison men, rather than politicians, so with changing political fortunes, they often moved from state to state. In this manner they became known as the McCloughry Prison Dynasty, and exercised a great influence over the prisons of the Middle West, and often when a prison would get out of hand or have a riot under the management of local politicians, one of the McCloughry's was called in to reestablish order and discipline.

The son, first name forgotten, who was Warden at Waupun also held Wardenships at Chester, Illinois; Stillwater, Minnesota; and Marquette, Michigan.

Son Robert A, known as R. A. was considered the best member of the family by men who had served time under him. He was said to be a very fair man, even if a stern one, and he served as Superintendent of a number of juvenile institutions: Anamosa, Pontiac, and Boonville, Missouri.

The third son, William McCloughry, was known as The Dummy. It was said that he had been born a halfwit. He was a dour-visaged individual with the benign disposition of a mongoose. The Writer never knew this man to smile or to speak one pleasant word to anyone. He was so obviously unfitted to handle human beings that his father had him trained as a fingerprint expert, and he became the first Director of the Bureau of Identification, then located at Leavenworth, but later transferred to Washington, and still later made a part of the F.B.I.

It was said of The Dummy, that he never forgot a human face. It was also said of him that the bureau had been created just to provide a sinecure for a hopeless idiot, and that without convicts to do his work, he would never have been able to hold it. At the time that he was eventually fired, it was charged that the Congress had provided for a Director and two clerks, the latter at a salary of one hundred twenty-five dollars per month, and that The Dummy had used convict clerks and put the extra two hundred fifty dollars per month in his pocket.

Leavenworth was intended to be and probably was the first completely modern penitentiary in America.

The cells were of the open-front type, which permitted plenty of light and air, but also the eyes of the guards. Those in "C" and "D" cell houses were four feet wide by nine feet long. Each cell contained a toilet, wash basin, running water, an electric light in the middle of the ceiling, and was furnished with straw ticks, two camp stools and a double-deck bunk made in the prison steel shop from scrap and angle iron.

The large cell houses were provided with forced ventilation, which it was predicted, would remove all trace of prison odor. The giant fans that supplied the cell houses with warm air in winter and fresh, if not cool, air in summer, were said to be capable of completely changing the air in those large building every two minutes and of maintaining an even temperature of seventy-two degrees in the teeth of a Kansas blizzard and subzero temperatures outside. The prison engineer, Matt Graham, had even suggested turning ammonia into the steam coils in summer. Had this been done, Leavenworth would have had the first completely air-conditioned buildings in America. It was not done because of the fear that gaskets and valve packings designed to hold steam would not hold ammonia.

For the first time in American penal history, prisoners in a big penitentiary were furnished with sheets, pillowcases, face towels, cotton socks in summer, woolen socks in winter, cotton nightgowns (more of these later), toilet paper, toilet soap, toothbrushes, eye shades, tooth powder, and bath towels.

Every man was given a warm shower, a complete change of clothing and a shave once per week. If his work was such that he became dirty, he was given a bath and a complete change of clothing everyday if necessary, and to get these, all he had to do was to point out to his guard that he was dirty. Under McCloughry, once the cell houses were up and the new dining room in use, no man was permitted to wear soiled clothing to his cell.

Convict barbers visited the shops and shaved the men during working hours. Every man was required to be shaved or have his beard trimmed once per week and his hair trimmed once per month, but there was no regulation concerning how a man wore his hair. McCloughry, who wore a beard, recognized every other man's right to wear his hair as he pleased. Upon entering the prison, every new man was given a moderately close haircut and a clean shave, then photographed, but thereafter, he could wear his hair and beard as he pleased. Some boys and men too, for that matter, wore their hair in curls clear down to their shoulders.

Any person who wanted to be clean shaven could, upon request, obtain a card allowing him to be shaved two or three times per week. No reason had to be given. He simply stated that he wished to be shaved two or three times per week, and the permission was granted. He was issued a card showing upon what days of the week he was permitted to be shaved, and upon those days, by showing the card to his guard, he could get permission to have his hair trimmed every two weeks.

During the building of the high wall, the inmates of Leavenworth had had their heads clipped and had worn stripes, but as soon as the wall had been completed, McCloughry had abolished stripes and the clipped heads, excepting as a means of punishment for men who escaped or attempted to escape, which was a common practice in most of the prisons of that day.

These changes in the accepted mode of treating convicts were so revolutionary at that time that it was necessary for Warden McCloughry and Speaker Cannon to assure the country, the majority of the homes of which did not enjoy such conveniences, that prisons were still to be places of punishment and that the government had no intention of coddling wrongdoers at public expense. They pointed out that there was no reason why men could not be effectively punished in clean, comfortable, and even beautiful surroundings.

McCloughry said, "I have never been a believer in coddling prisoners, nor will I ever tolerate coddling in any shape, form, manner, or fashion, but I see no reason why a prison should not be clean and comfortable, contain all modern conveniences, and have beautiful lawns, trees, and flowers to lighten the drabness of prison life. Every man who enters my institution shall be made to realize that he is in prison and that loss of liberty is something not to be taken lightly. Every prisoner, no matter who he is or what he has done, shall be treated exactly alike. No laxness of discipline will be tolerated." And indeed, there was none, for Robert W. McCloughry was one of the most rigid disciplinarians among the old-time prison men.

Regulations

If they were available, it would be interesting and enlightening to reprint McCloughry's rules in full, even though they would cover about fifteen pages. But they are not available to the Writer at this time, so we will have to be content with a general outline. Every minute of the inmates' day was regimented to the minutest detail, and that regimentation was enforced by one of the strictest disciplinarians who ever drew the breath of life, yet he was probably one of the fairest. He accepted with a vengeance Kipling's line that said,

"Let all men count with you, but none too much." (Paraphrased from "If" by Rudyard Kipling.)

To McCloughry, convicts were convicts, and there were no exceptions. A man might be a millionaire or a tramp; he might be in for an ax-murder or for stealing a postage stamp; he might be serving triple life or a year and a day; it was all the same. So long as he had a number on his back, he was a convict. His own convict clerk in many respects exercised more power than most of the free officials, yet he had to follow the same rigid discipline as everyone else.

Silent System

The rule book said, "You are allowed to talk to your cellmate in low tones only." Outside of the cell there was an absolute silent system. Talking from cell to cell, talking in line, talking in the dining room or Chapel, and talking at work were absolutely prohibited, excepting where talk was necessary in connection with the work. In such cases, the rule book outlined the procedure the inmate was required to follow.

He must put up his hand and gain the attention of his guard. When the guard recognized him with a nod of the head, he must approach to within ten feet of the guard, remove his cap, fold his arms, stand at attention, state his request in a clear voice and concise manner; then he must be governed by the guard's instruction. The talk had to be confined to the work, conducted in low tones, and made as brief as possible.

It will be noted that the inmate was required to stand ten feet from the guard and state his request in clear tones. No confidential conversation between a guard and convict was tolerated, unless the convict was a trusty, for one of the things that McCloughry did not like was a stoolpigeon. A cell house guard could stop in front of a convict's cell and hold a general conversation, but he had to speak loud enough for the man in the vicinity to hear. Otherwise, he was apt to find himself in a tower.

On the other hand, the rule that conversations between cellmates must be in low tones only, meant exactly what it said, and any time that their conversation was so loud that the passing guard could hear what they were talking about, they were subject to be reported for making a disturbance in the cell house and could spend about ten days in the dungeon.

The Line

McCloughry did not believe in the lockstep, but a semi-lockstep was employed. In the original lockstep, the first man in the line was required to march with arms folded. The man behind him placed his right arm over the shoulder of the man in front of him and his left arm under the arm of the man in front of him and locked his hand over the prisoner's breast. The man behind did the same thing all the way down the line. In a later version, the first man in the line walked with arms folded, and each man behind him was required to march with both hands on the shoulders of the man in front of him. In still another version a man was required to place only one hand, usually the right, upon the shoulder of the man in front of him.

At Leavenworth, so long as the line was moving, the hands were carried at the sides, and there were no pockets to put them in. In cold weather the men were provided with cloth gloves, however. As soon as the line stopped moving, the arms were folded. To unfold the arms or to turn the head was to invite a trip to the dungeon. To step out of line without permission was to invite a split head.

It must be understood that the effective ratio of guards to convicts was usually about one to thirty-five, and in such large prisons as Leavenworth, and the other big walled prisons, these guards were not covered by gun guards. Naturally, the one thing they feared above all others was riot. If such a large mass of men got out of hand, the guards would be helpless. So it was their policy to stop trouble before it started; to knock down any man who stepped out of line in order to prevent any concerted action. This was the purpose of the Silent System, too. Of course, it was impossible to keep men from whispering out of the sides of their mouths, but when a man was caught, he might go to the hole, and he might get his head split, though most guards would warn a prisoner at least once before reporting him.

If any prisoner, even the Warden's Secretary, met a guard or visitors in one of the corridors, he was required to remove his cap if he had one on, fold his arms, face the wall, and stand at attention. He remained facing the wall until the guard or visitors passed him, and he had better not turn his head to stare after them either, for if he did not get his head split, he was sure to spend a couple of weeks standing at the door.

Dining Room

The dining room and kitchen were show places of the institution. The food was all prepared in large, steam cookers. Such dishes as stew and beans were cooked in four hundred gallon copper pots. Coffee and tea were made in pots of equal size; there was a long row of steam roasters for cooking meats, potatoes, etc. and dishes were washed by a machine and sterilized by live steam.

There was no provision for frying foods, and such items of the diet as were put on the menu as fried were actually cooked in the steam roasters.[68]

Bread and pastries were mixed and kneaded by machine and cooked in a large rotary oven.

The food was mostly good, but it had the fault of all steam-cooked food and most prison diets, even today, of being over-cooked, and men who had been living on it for a few years showed evidence of premature senility as a result of an accumulated vitamin deficiency. But the word vitamin was not coined until 1911, and it was not until about 1920 that McCollum discovered Vitamin A, and its existence became accepted in America. As late as 1915 so-called government-Scientists (the expression is a misnomer, since no man can be a bureaucrat and a scientist at the same time), took the witness stand in a Washington Courtroom and *poohooed* the whole vitamin theory (case title is forgotten, but it can be found in any good book on the history of vitamins).

This only goes to show once more that in judging historical events we must not forget that even a few years ago men did not enjoy the knowledge and conveniences of today. There may have been some excuse for over-cooked foods in McCloughry's day, but there can be

---

68   See Diagram. Part I – Chapter VI

no excuse for the same deficiencies existing in Federal Prisons today.

In the morning the men left their galleries in single file. The men from the two sides of each gallery met at the foot of the steps, and they marched out of the cell house two abreast. The lines from "C" and "D" cell houses came together in the main hall, and the men marched down the hall four abreast. After passing through the big door to the dining room, the lines split, and the men from each cell house passed through the two openings into the dining room separately, marching two abreast. Those from "C" cell house turned toward Section 5, and those from "D" cell house turned toward Section 1.[69] As the men approached the sections, the line split again, so that the men from the two sides of each gallery marched single file down along the sides of the sections, which were always filled from the back.

The tables were of the school-desk variety, all facing the front of the room. Each seated six men, and they were filled with three men from each side. A waiter led each line down the room and directed the filling of the seats. There was an eight-foot aisle between each of the sections.

As the men seated themselves, they were required to sit erect with arms folded and eyes to the front until the Captain gave the signal to start eating. There was no food on the tables, but the waiters were lined up like soldiers standing at attention, ready to start serving, and they moved down the sections rapidly.

Each man had his own place in the line and at noon and night he was required to line up on the East or West side of the prison yard,[70] each in his own place, so that when he marched out of the dining room and into the cell houses, each man would stop before his own cell. Being out of place in line was a reportable offense.

The rule book set out a system of hand signals by which a man at the table could make his wants known to the waiters, and every man was allowed all he wanted to eat of any item on the menu. A few items, like pie, cake, cookies and fresh fruit were rationed, but a man could often get seconds even on such things. Of everything else on the menu, a man was allowed all he could eat, even pork chops, or steak, when they had them. The waiters kept bringing the food around as long as anyone would take any, and the Captain held the men in their seats as long as anyone was eating. On one occasion, when he was very hungry, the Writer ate thirty-seven pork sausages at one meal, and he never ate less than three steaks or six mutton chops at a meal.

Another time, a man's wife wrote the Warden that her husband was not getting enough to eat. It developed that the man was a very big eater and that he had false teeth and could not eat fast. It was ordered that this man be permitted to enter the dining room ahead of the line and remain seated until he had finished eating.

The only restrictions on food were that what a man took, he had to eat, and no food could be carried from the dining room. These however, were not usually reportable offenses. A man who left too much food on his plate was called back and given an opportunity to eat it. The same rule applied to a man caught with stolen food. If the man would eat the food or give a sound excuse why he could not eat it, there was no report. But if he refused to eat the food, he went to the hole for wasting or stealing food as the case might be. On one occasion a friend of the Writer ate seven pies to keep from going to the hole. On another

---

69   See Diagram.
70   Diagram S-S

occasion, a guard, seeing a man steal a hot pie, made the man stand at attention for thirty minutes before shaking him down. The man had slipped the pie inside of his shirt, and the rim of the pan branded a perfect circle on his belly, and the man, who did not like pie and had stolen it for his boy cellmate, said that eating the pie was worse than playing Spartan.

At no time in the line or dining room was a man allowed to turn his head and look behind him. The eyes had to be kept to the front at all times. Failure to observe this rule would usually bring a sharp command reinforced by a thrust of a cane.

During the meal, two or three guards stood in each aisle, facing the men, so that every prisoner was under several sets of eyes at all times.

Privileges

Prisoners were allowed to receive all the letters that came for them, provided of course, that the letters were not obscene or otherwise violated of the postal laws, for the courts of that day held that for a Warden to hold up and refuse to deliver any man's mail was itself a violation of the postal laws, but the prisoner, before he was allowed to receive mail, had to sign a waiver allowing the Warden to open his mail. In many State prisons of that day the authorities were compelled to deliver all letters unopened, but the prisoner was compelled to open the letter in the presence of the guard and shake out the pages so the guard could see that the letter contained no contraband.

Each prisoner was allowed to write two regular letters per month, but special letters could be obtained for good business, family or legal reasons, and as a gift from the Warden, all prisoners were allowed to write special letters on specially printed stationary on holidays. The appropriate greeting would usually be printed in three colors, on the letterhead.

It was characteristic of McCloughry that these letters had to be given to everyone, even the men in the hole. That rule applied to all special treats. On one occasion the Writer was taken out of the hole to enjoy a special dinner and a musical concert. On another, he had half a watermelon and a spoon brought to him in the dungeon.

McCloughry had a very strong sense of justice. It was his theory that no man could be justly punished without forewarning. When an inmate violated the rules, he risked the loss of known privileges and incurred known punishments. He took his chance with his eyes wide open, and when he was caught, it was his hard luck. It was right that he suffer those known deprivations. But no man could be said to have knowingly risked something that he did not know about. In like manner, no one could be justly deprived of any special privilege.

Visits were allowed once per month from relatives and friends, but that time restriction could be applied only to the case of a regular visitor. If a man was receiving a regular visit from his wife or mother once per month, that did not mean that any other friend would be turned away. No visitor presenting himself during regular visiting hours, which coincided with working hours, was ever turned away.

The visitor was required to state his identity and address, but that was all. There was no formality connected with it. The visitor came up to the front gate, addressed the armory guard and said, "I wish to visit so and so."

The guard replied, "Have you a camera or any firearms on you? If you have, you must leave them with me."

If the visitor had a camera or pistol, the guard would let down a basket for it, then open the gate and let the visitor enter.

At the cage[71] he would be required to sign the visitor's book and state his address. The guard between the double gates would phone the inmate's place of work, and the inmate's guard would give him a pass to the place where the visit was to be held.

Visits were held wherever there was a guard available – Captain's office, Deputy Warden's office, Cell house, or even in the shops. The guard was supposed to listen in on the conversation, but no guard ever did. Visitors were permitted to bring fruit, candy, and other treats, but only in such quantities as could be consumed during the visit. Yet, no guard ever saw an inmate loading his shirt or pockets. Nor would any guard ever act officious in front of a visitor or give the visitor a bad report on a prisoner's conduct, nor do anything to humiliate the prisoner in the presence of his friend or relative. Any guard guilty of such conduct would have been fired forthwith.

All men who had not lost their privileges were given two bags of plug-out smoking tobacco, one bag of smoking tobacco and one plug of chewing tobacco, or two plugs of chewing tobacco per week. Any prisoner who did any extra work was always given an extra ration of tobacco.

One afternoon while the Writer was working in the powerhouse, a steam line burst. The Writer, listed as an electrician, volunteered to work on repairing the break, and he worked two hours overtime, until about six o'clock. It was a mean and dirty job, as such jobs usually are.

After completing the job, he was given a shower, clean clothing, then taken to the kitchen and given a special supper of sirloin steak, and he was put on the list for extra tobacco that week. He did not have to ask for any of these things. He had not expected them. He had volunteered for the job because it would enable him to look certain parts of the prison over with a view to escaping.

On another occasion, one of the most miserable guards in the prison, brought some pipe to the shop to be cut and threaded. The foreman called the Writer over.

"Just tell him what you want Graham," the Engineer said.

It took the Writer less than ten minutes to do the job. When he had finished, the guard, a fellow called "Eat 'm up Sam," asked, "Do you chew?"

"Sure!" In a prison where opportunities to smoke are restricted, all prisoners chew tobacco.

"Thanks for doing such a good job," said Sam, smiling. It was the first time the Writer had ever seen him smile. "Here! My appreciation!" And he handed the Writer a ten-cent plug of Star Chewing Tobacco.

"Well, what do you know about that?" the Writer said to another prisoner. "That sourpuss is the last person in the world I would ever expect to give me anything."

---

71   Diagram 2

"Hell!" the older prisoner said, "He had to do that. Any time you do anything special, they have to show their appreciation. McCloughry will fire a guard for bringing in anything contraband excepting for special occasions, but any time you do any private work, the guard has to give you something. If he didn't and McCloughry learned of it, he would have him up on the carpet."

Under such circumstances, and in a large population, where there will always be men who do not use tobacco, it was never a serious problem. The prison-issue tobacco was not very good, but a man could always get all that he wanted of it.

Matches were contraband, and smoking outside of the cell was prohibited as was smoking cigarettes. So for the cigarette smoker, getting a light was often a problem.

In the cell house, during the hours when smoking was permitted, the guard was required to carry a torch with him at all times and give the men lights for their pipes. As a matter of convenience, the prisoners made tapers of rolled strips of newspaper and stuck them under the edge of the name-card holders on their doors, so that the guard could light them from the torch as fast as he walked by. Most men stuck their tapers in their doors before going to bed, so the guard would light them on the first round in the morning. He was required to make three rounds between the wake-up bell and the breakfast bell. He was required to make two trips at noon, and a trip every half hour during the evening.

There was no way that a guard could shirk this duty. He had to ring call boxes located at the ends of each gallery every half hour and in such order that they would show that he had walked the galleries.

These call boxes registered the time when they were rung on paper disks, and any time a guard was off more than one minute either way on the time he was supposed to ring the box, he had to write a letter to McCloughry explaining why. His reason for missing the ring had better be good, too.

Many of the men, particularly the cigarette smokers, used flint, steel and tinder boxes for making a light. These were contraband, but their possession was not a serious offense, and the only punishment was usually the loss of the outfit. Some of the men used steel buttons, which they spun on a string, just as a child spins a button. When the button was spinning well, it was brought in contact with a chunk of emery or carborundum about as big as a hazelnut, and the sparks caught on the tinder. The Writer cut up many shovels and broke many emery wheels to make these outfits.

No guard was allowed to smoke at any time or place where an inmate was not allowed to smoke, and neither were allowed to smoke cigarettes, which were at that time prohibited by Kansas law. Those guards who chewed Piper Heidsick could usually be prevailed upon to give the inmates the empty tin boxes. These made ideal tinder boxes.

The tinder was made by tearing up a sheet, folding a thick pad of sufficient size to fit the box, then setting the cloth afire, letting it burn until there was no more smoke, then smothering it by closing the box. Shaving stick cans were also in big demand for tinder boxes. The inmate would obtain a roll of bandage from the Doctor of sufficient width to just fit snugly into the box, then he would char the outer end and smother it by putting the lid on the box.

For efficiency, either type lighter had it all over the cigarette lighters of today. A good button and chunk of carborundum would last for ten years, and a single filling of a tinder box would last a year or more.

There was no mention in the rule book of cigarettes, but as they were a violation of Kansas law, and the Deputy Wardens, Big Jim and Mackey, treated smoking a cigarette as a very serious offense. The stain of a cigarette on the fingers might bring a sentence of ten days in the dungeon. To convict a man of smoking a cigarette required something more than a guard's unsupported word. He had to have the cigarette, stains on the inmate's fingers, or the word of another guard to establish the offense. Of course, no prisoner who was not a complete fool, would surrender any contraband article he could dispose of, and a guard who turned in a report without being able to prove his "corpus delicti" was subject to reprimand.

The Cell

During those early years there were two cell houses with a capacity of 420 men in each. In addition, there were a number of dormitories which could house another 600 men. At the time the Writer went to Leavenworth, September 5, 1912, the total population was 1000 men. So it was possible to cell alone, if one wished to, but most of the cells had two men in them.

There was no segregation of the races. White and colored men celled together and next door to each other, but it was the general rule that no man would be placed with a man of another race unless it was agreeable to both parties. Within limits, men were permitted to choose their own cellmates, and cell changes, which could be had upon request, were laughingly called divorces. Almost fifteen hours of every day and at least nineteen hours of every Sunday were spent in the cell, so it was important that the two men cooped up together in a box four feet wide, nine feet long, and seven-and-one-half feet high were congenial and considerate of each other's rights and feelings. It was only by going to mass, going on sick call, going to regular Chapel services, and going to Sunday School that a man could avoid spending twenty-two hours of each Sunday in the cell.

The bunks were twenty-six inches wide, and the straw ticks lapped over the edges for several inches, so it was just possible for two thin men to squeeze past each other in the space beside the bed. When one man moved around the cell, the other had to lie on his bunk.

There was a forty-five minute church service every Sunday morning, and all inmates not specifically excused were compelled to attend. This was not done because of any hope of turning a man's heart to God, but as a security measure. All available guards were needed in the Chapel and in taking the men to and from Chapel. If men could remain in their cells at will, there was a chance of them overpowering the cell house guard and making an escape while the bulk of the guards were in the Chapel. There will be occasion to discuss these services in some detail later on.[72] There was no regular supper on Sundays. The Sunday dinner was always good, but the supper was brought to the cell and consisted of a tin cup of black coffee and a big chunk of coffee cake, raisin bread, or gingerbread, which the colored population called "gingerhorse," and of which most of them were very fond.

When the prisoners entered their cells after dinner on Sundays and after supper on weekdays, they were required to remove all of their clothing and put on nightgowns and bedroom slippers. Their regular clothing had to be neatly folded in regulation order and placed by the bars at the front of the cell, so that the guard could see at a glance whether or not any item was missing. This was an anti-escape measure, but it was of profound social and psychological significance. No man attempting to escape could get far without clothing. He might make a dummy that would fool the guard and put it in his bed, but if he did not have a complete second outfit, or at least, pants, coat and shoes, he could hardly hope to get very far, but if he took any of his regular clothing with him, he would be missed in thirty minutes. For this one reason alone, there was not a single escape from "C" or "D" cell houses while McCloughry was Warden. As soon as this clothing regulation was relaxed, there were several escapes, and escape attempts.

The simple act of removing all the clothing and putting on a fresh cool nightgown did a great deal to relieve the mind of the strains and worries of the day. When one preceded the putting on of the gown, as most men did, by rubbing the body down with a wet towel to remove the perspiration and odors of one's toil, it gave a big lift to the spirit. If one were young, his skin smooth, and he dusted himself with delicately scented talc – one of the few things that could be purchased – it made him feel that it was good to be alive, even in one of the toughest prisons in America. If the primping and posing that went with this simple process brought admiring glances from one's cellmate, a flush to the cheeks, a quickening of the breathing, who was to care? That guard had to ring his boxes every half hour. And even if he was one of those nosey characters who doubled back after passing the cell, the law of gravity and the nature of nightgowns being what they are, there was not much chance of him seeing anything not intended for his eyes, and most guards being human beings themselves, would just smile and keep on walking, anyway.

Time not devoted to each other could be spent in reading, study, playing chess, checkers, or dominos, or in conversing in low tones only.

Warden's Call

There were guards whose duty it was to pick up men from all over the institution for certain specific purposes. These pickups were referred to as "calls."

In the morning, as the men came out of the dining room, men who had been notified to do so the night before, fell out of line and lined up between the big door and the Chapel openings. This was "court call," and it contained men who had been reported as well as those who were called over for interviews, work changes, cell changes, or for many other reasons.

As soon as the men were at work, a guard went from shop to shop and gang to gang and at each stop cried, "Sick Call." Any man who wanted to see the doctor for any reason whatsoever could fall into that line and be marched to the dispensary.

There was "clothing call," at which a man could have any worn-out clothing exchanged or repaired. There was "Chief Clerks Call," at which a man could arrange for any allowed purchase. At "Chaplain's Call," a man could unburden his soul or arrange for books or special studies. There was also "Mail Clerk's Call," "Shoe Call," and a dozen others.

The procedure on all of these "calls" was the same. The guard went from department to department picking up men, which were marched all over the prison until all shops and gangs had been covered and were then marched to the particular office for which they were bound.

When the men reached their destination, they were lined up facing the wall and required to stand at attention with arms folded until they were called before the official they had come to see. They were not allowed to turn their heads or to whisper, and the guard was behind them to see that they did not.

Every Wednesday was "Warden's Call," and any prisoner who had any business with him had an absolute right to a private interview with the Warden at least once per week.

This "call" was conducted a little differently than the others. The men were marched into the Warden's anteroom[73] where there were sufficient benches to seat one hundred men. If there were more than one hundred men, some had to remain standing until others had been heard, but here there were no folded arms, no facing the wall, and whispering was permitted. It was permissible to step out to the toilet, and if a man had a lighter on him, it was usually possible to steal a couple of smokes in the toilet while waiting to be heard.

On "Warden's Call" the function of the guard was simply that of keeping order. It was the Warden's convict secretary who was the real functioning official. He passed among the men, conversing with each in low tones, sometimes advising a man as to the best manner in which to state his request. It was he who wrote the passes that sent the men back to their work, and it was he who accompanied each man into the Warden's Office and introduced him to the Warden as he placed the man's record on the Warden's desk.

This is so and so, Warden, Number so and so. He works in such and such a shop, and the secretary might add some good words for the other prisoner, then he would step outside and close the door.

"I am pleased to know you, young man, though I am not pleased to see you in a place of this kind. Step right over here. Now, what do you wish to see me about? You may feel free to discuss your problem in any manner you wish. All of my interviews are strictly confidential."

That is the way it went. Every interview was private. The Warden was seventy years of age and unarmed, but the toughest man in the prison could talk to him face to face and be fully heard. On several occasions he was knocked out of his chair, but he never permitted that to change him. The interviews continued until every man had been fully heard. Those who had not been heard by noon were sent into dinner and instructed to fall out as the line went out to work. Those that had not been heard by suppertime were sent into the dining room and ordered to fall out as the line came out. The last interview might not be held until late at night, but no man was ever turned away, nor was any other business permitted to intrude. If the President had visited the institution on Wednesday, McCloughry would probably have said, "Tell him to come back tomorrow. I am busy interviewing prisoners today."

The inmate talked without interruption until he had fully stated his problem. Then McCloughry questioned him while glancing over his record. At the conclusion of the interview, he rang for his secretary and addressed his opinion to the secretary, in case he had granted the request, so that the secretary could see that his decision was enforced. A denial was addressed to the inmate himself in the secretary's presence. There were two classes of prisoners that received short shift at the Old Man's hands.

---

73   Diagram 3

He hated stool pigeons. Any time an inmate came before him with a tip about the conduct of some other prisoner, he would snap, "Young man! I have seventy guards who are responsible for the discipline of this institution. Any time they are incapable of running it, I will fire them and get some who are capable. They do not need any help from you. That is all."

In every prison there are craven individuals who, probably from a desire to attract attention or win sympathy, are always running to the officials, asking that they or someone else be locked up for their protection while citing the mortal danger they fear as a reason. Many, if not all of the persons who do this are either schizophrenic or border-line mental cases, but such a request is often the first evidence of their flight from reality. To honor it is the surest method of encouraging their mental and emotional crackup. Such parties received short shift from McCoughry.

"You say that you fear number ____ is planning to kill you?"

"Yes sir!"

"What did you do to him?"

"Nothing, sir! I only ____"

"Poppycock! Young man, do you think inmate Number ____ is crazy?"

"No sir!"

"Well, only a crazy man kills without good reason. A man in prison, where he has no chance of escaping, will stand a lot more provocation before resorting to violence than will the average man on the outside. If you have given inmate Number ____ cause for wanting to kill you, I would suggest that you mend your own conduct instead of coming and crying to me. To be on the safe side, I shall have this man examined by the doctor. If he is crazy, appropriate steps will be taken to restrain him. In the meantime, I am confident that my guards are capable of affording you all the protection required. You may take this consolation, however; be assured that if he kills you, we will hang him for it, and should you injure him in any way, you will be properly punished. That is all."

It should be noted at this point that a criminal psychology is merely the desire to benefit or aggrandize oneself at the expense of someone else. That is the essence of all antisocial conduct. The stoolpigeon and sycophant trying to curry favor and the weakling looking for sympathy are both members of this group. Pampering such persons is the surest method of encouraging their criminal tendencies, and in the latter group, is sure to lead to the development of a persecution complex, which is the certain forerunner of paranoia. Usually, one interview with McCloughry was actually of more value to such an individual than a dozen interviews with a modern penal psychiatrist would have been; for he forced men to stand on their own two feet as men and to face reality, which is always the kindest course in the long run.

On the other hand, the prisoner with a serious problem or constructive request was given every consideration.

The boy who placed before him a wife from the head of a Denver hospital stating that his mother could not live over forty-eight hours and who had no money in the office to pay the expenses of the trip did not state his case in vain.

"I am sure, Sir, that there is property enough to pay for the trip many times over. Then too, I own my own home in St. Joseph, Missouri, but there is simply no way of getting the money here in time."

"Hmm! I shall check on the authenticity of this wire by long-distance telephone. Will you put up your right hand and swear by all that you hold most sacred that you will not try to escape?"

"Yes, Sir! I solemnly swear upon the memory of my dying mother that I will not try to escape."

"Very well! That is good enough for me! If the wire proves to be authentic, you will be on the train tonight. I will send only one guard with you. He will be unarmed and he will have orders to use no chains, not to put you in jail, and not to embarrass you in any way in the presence of your friends or family. I think I will send Mr. McGrath. He knows how to conduct himself as a perfect gentleman.

"If the expenses of this trip are not paid or if you violate the trust I am placing in you, you will put me in an embarrassing position, but by no means a fatal one. The only real danger is that you may be responsible for the curtailment of my power to show to others the same kindness I am showing you. Really, the only persons injured will be yourself and your fellow inmates."

"I understand, Sir! I will never let you down."

"For your sake and the sake of your fellows, I sincerely hope that you don't, and I do not think that you will. The guard will have orders to hold you in Denver until after the funeral. That is all."

When McCloughry trusted any man, he trusted him all the way, and very few of the convicts he trusted ever let him down. This one did, however.

His mother lingered for almost two weeks. He was permitted to spend as much time with her as the doctors would allow. No one at the hospital outside of the head doctor knew that the tall, good-looking, polite young man who was with him was anything more than a friend.

For two weeks, he lived at his mother's home. Every night he slept with his wife while McGrath went to a hotel. Every day he went wherever and did whatever he pleased, but this touch of liberty was too much for him.

While he and McGrath were waiting to get on the train to return to Leavenworth, he slipped into a crowd and vanished. The Denver police arrested him four hours later. Sobbing, he told reporters that he was afraid to return to Leavenworth for his life would not be worth a nickel. But it was not the old man whose trust he had violated that he feared, or the guard he had caused embarrassment; it was his fellow inmates. What he feared was not for his life. He knew that no one would hurt him. It was the look of contempt that he knew he would find on the faces all around him.

McCloughry did not even punish this boy, for he considered his jurisdiction to inflict punishment to extend only to offenses committed within the prison, but for the rest of his sentence the boy was almost completely ostracized. He had to spend most of his time celling alone, because no one would cell with him. The only persons who would give him a smile were a few Negroes interested in what he sat on, with which he was not the least bit stingy, but even they would not cell with him.

Another rather shy boy who had just been transferred from McNiel Island stepped up in front of the desk.

"What can I do for you, young man?"

"Listen! If you please, Sir, I am serving a long sentence. I've not had the advantage of much schooling, but the day I came to prison, I resolved to do everything possible to correct that situation."

"A good resolution. It is a shame that more men in prison do not try to improve themselves."

"That is what I have been doing. I have spent at least one hour in serious study every day since I've been in prison."

"That is fine! You want to see me about your studies?"

"Yes! I am studying engineering and mathematics. I hope to so educate myself that I will be able to make something of my life after I leave here. I had a number of books at McNeil Island and some drawing instruments. They were taken from me when I arrived here, and I was told I would be permitted to have only two books in my cell and that my other property would be put in storage. I am sure that you know that one can't get very far in such a complex subject with only two books.

"That is not all. I wish permission to have pencils, drawing paper and drawing ink. I have listed my need on these requests. I know that I am asking a lot, but all I can do is to assure you that if you grant me these privileges, I will not abuse them. I will try to use them to the best of my ability to make myself a better and more competent person. When I came here, I asked to be put in the powerhouse, hoping that I would be able to supplement my book studies with practical experience. I have been working for Mr. Graham for one month. I think that he will tell you that I have mechanical ability and learn quickly."

"Hmm! I think I had a letter from the Warden at McNiel Island about you." McCloughry flipped open the Writer's records. "Hmm! I remember now."

The Writer's heart sank. There on the top of his record sheet in bright red ink were the words:

November 1, 1911	Attempted to kill fellow inmate.
	Reduced to Third Grade.
February 1, 1912	Restored to Second Grade
March 1, 1912	Restored to first Grade

"Hmm! They actually use the grade system at McNiel?"

"Yes, Sir!"

"You were convicted of manslaughter in Alaska."

"Yes, Sir!"

"Care to tell me about it?"

"Not much to tell. I was living with a woman. A man she had lived with years before I met her beat her up. My mother had always taught me that a woman who is good enough to sleep with is good enough to protect. I took a pistol and blew his brains out."

"Where is your home? Where were you raised?"

"I was born in Seattle, but my family is from Illinois."

"Illinois! That is interesting. What part?"

"The Southern part. Metropolis."

"Well! Well! Down around little Egypt. Some mighty fine people down there."

"So I have heard. I was only down there once to visit my grandfather."

"What is his name?"

"MacCartney."

"Not Captain J. F. MacCartney who was in the Illinois Legislature after the War?"

"You know him? I don't know about Legislature. He was a lawyer and in politics. He was in Congress a couple of times, and he was a Captain in the Illinois Volunteers, but all that was so long before I was born."

"So it was. Well! Well! J. F.'s grandson. You were convicted of manslaughter. What happened to the woman?"

"I don't know. We were both indicted for murder. I pleaded guilty and turned her loose."

McCloughry glance down at the record. "You were at McNiel Island for three years."

"Yes, Sir!"

"I see here only one report."

"Yes, Sir!"

"What did the man do to you?"

"He told some lies on me, Sir. He tried to involve me in an escape plot that was a product of his own imagination in the hope of getting a parole. I had been trying very hard to make a good record because the United States Attorney had promised that if I made three years without a report, he would get me out. This fellow was the doctor's orderly. I borrowed the doctor's pocket knife to cut some meat with, then I worked him over."

"Hmm! Rather resourceful!" McCloughry pressed the button on his desk. "Three years and only one report! Three years and only one report!"

When the secretary entered, he said, "This boy has made a most unusual request. He had some drawing instruments and books at McNiel Island. He has requested permission to have them in his cell. He has also requested permission to purchase some additional drawing instruments, paper, pencils, drawing paper, and drawing ink and have them in his cell. A most unusual request, but I am granting it on the basis of his record. Three years and only one report. We will furnish him with what paper, pencils and ink he needs from the Office of the Superintendent of Construction. See that he obtains his property from storage, that he is permitted to purchase the drawing instruments he needs, and that no one molests him in the possession of them."

"Thank you Sir. A thousand thanks."

"Just continue trying to improve yourself and give me as good a record as you gave Mr. Halligan, and you will be all right, young man. J. F's grandson. Well! Well!"

"Say!" whispered the secretary, awe in his voice. "Why didn't you ask him for a pardon?"

"Why?"

"Well, I've seen a lot of fellows ask him for a pardon and get it, but you are the first person who ever asked him for all that stuff and got it. You must have put up a good talk."

"I don't know. Maybe it's because I was born on the right side of the tracks."

"Well, whatever it is, you should ask him for a pardon. You would probably get it. Take this slip to the Chief Clerk's office. Right up those stairs. The way it is made out, you can order any drawing instruments you want on it. I'll have the other stuff delivered to your cell."

Whether or not it was the Writer's good record of cutting up a stoolpigeon, or because the Writer's grandfather had served in the Illinois volunteers and in the Illinois Legislature with him that was responsible for McCloughry granting the Writer privileges never before allowed any inmate of Leavenworth, is hard to say. McCloughry chose to base it on the Writer's record of three years in prison and only one report, and once granted to the Writer on that basis, any other prisoner who could show the same qualifications could claim the same privileges. That is the way things were done in those days.

It is possible that McCloughry was really impressed by the Writer's record and his efforts to improve his education. It was characteristic of the old-time prison men that they had a lot of respect for any man who would try to help himself, but none at all for a crybaby. It was also characteristic of McCloughry that he could excuse an occasional act of violence much more readily than a series of petty reports for minor breaches of discipline. To him, killing one stoolpigeon would have been considered much less serious than three reports for talking in the dining room.

There was never a single case of one convict murdering another during his administration; but if there should have been, and the murderer gave him three years of good prison record, he would have probably used all of his influence to get that man out. The Writer was probably a fool for not appreciating that fact.

McCloughry was a hard-minded old Scotchman. His discipline was often heartbreaking, but he was never accused of not being on the square. When he opened his mouth, what came out was the absolute law, and you could gamble your life on it with complete safety.

With all their hardness and roughness, the Federal Prison Administrations of that day were in the hands of men of strong character, who had firm principles of right and wrong, and it was pervaded by a sense of fair play and sportsmanship that today is entirely lacking.

PART I – CHAPTER VIII

Leavenworth – Continued

Big Jim

Not having known Big Jim personally, the Writer finds it rather difficult to discuss this man with any degree of authenticity. Yet, from all the stories heard of him, he must have been a rather colorful character.

Big Jim Lammin was the first Deputy Warden at Leavenworth. He was an ex-Captain of detectives of the City of Chicago. He had been Captain of the Guards under McCloughry at Joliet, and had been brought to Leavenworth by McCloughry.

As the name suggests, Big Jim was a big, powerful, rip-roaring Irishman who had blackjacked his way up in the Chicago Police Department – a bluff, hearty, profane, hard-drinking, loud-mouth man with a strain of cruelty and a strain of kindness in him. It was he who had taught the guards to use those terrible canes, to be described presently; it was he who enforced the rigid rules; it was he who issued the orders to knock any man's brains out who let go of the handles of his wheelbarrow to wipe his brow during the building of the high wall. But it was he that the convicts always turned to when they wanted favors. So Big Jim must have had his good points, too.

All the convicts who served time under him claimed to have hated his guts, but they all admitted that he was a complete realist – no convict likes or respects a moralist – and like McCloughry, Halligan[74] and many other old-time prison men, his word was good. It was also said of him that he never held a grudge.

It was his theory that if the prisoner got out of line the least bit, the thing to do was to knock his brains out or hang him up to the door until he cried for mercy, but then, forget it. He was fond of declaring in a loud voice:

"I know that this place is hell, and I am the chief devil, but, god damn it, you were sent here to be punished for your sins, and I am just the guy who can make you repent of them."

When one man complained about compulsory church attendance, he was reported to have said:

"Personally, I think this place is hell enough without that, but it is part of the punishment. By God, I have to go, and you are no better than I am."

---

74   Part I Chapter XIII

When some younger inmate asked to be moved into a cell with some old *yegg*, he would roar:

"If I put you in the cell with that guy, you are going to stay there. Don't you dare come running over here tomorrow morning crying to me that he tried to _____ _____. You know god damn well that is what he wants you for! Or if you don't, I am telling you! Now, if you want the move, I will make it. If you want me to put you in with some mamby pamby who will never put a hand on you or with some kid your own age you can swap out with, I'll do that too. But god damn it, you've got to make up your own mind what you want, and after you do that, don't come crying to me if you get hurt."

Yes, Big Jim must have been an interesting character. All the convicts hated him, and the stories they told of his cruelties were often sickening; yet, the Writer never talked to any convict who did not respect Big Jim. After he was gone, whenever some incident involving bad faith, double-dealing, or injustice came up for discussion, he often heard these men exclaim:

"By god, Big Jim would never have done that!" or "Big Jim wouldn't have stood for that!"

The story of Big Jim's downfall is reserved for Part II – Chapter I where it fits in with other related events that were then of considerable public interest.

The Deputy Warden

It is the function of the guards to enforce discipline. It is the function of the Captain to see that the guards enforce discipline. It is the function of the Deputy Warden to try all inmates accused of breaches of discipline, find the accused prisoner guilty or not guilty, and fix his punishment. Normally, he has no such authority over the guards. In their case, he or the Captain has to report the guard to the Warden for any misconduct, and the Warden tries the guard and fixes his punishment, which in those days could be either a suspension without pay or a dismissal.

The Deputy Warden had much wider latitude in the fixing of punishment. He could take a man's privileges or any specific privilege away from him for any particular length of time; he could take any part of the man's *goodtime* away from him; he could sentence the man to so many days in the dungeon on bread and water, chained to the door during working hours, or if the man was one who, for medical reasons, could not be sentenced to the dungeon, he could be put in Isolation on full diet and forced to break so many boxes of rock for each meal.

Procedure

If a prisoner committed some serious offense, the guard would take him before the Deputy Warden at once. Such offenses usually involved fighting, striking a guard, attempting to assault a guard, attempting to escape, or refusing to work, but it should not be imagined that such offenses were equally serious so far as punishment was concerned. Fist-fighting, attempting to assault a guard or attempting to escape were considered relatively minor offenses, whereas striking a guard or refusing to work were the most serious offenses.

The difference between attempting to assault a guard and striking a guard does not seem to make sense, but the former charge was purely technical. For more than one hundred years the employment of corporal punishment to persons convicted of crimes against the United States has been prohibited by law.[75] The rule provides that a guard shall strike an inmate only in defense of his own person or in the protection of some other person from an assault. So, whenever a prisoner had his head split, no matter what the circumstances, he was always charged with attempting to assault an officer.

It was always up to the guard to use his own judgment as to whether he would write a report or take a man over to Isolation at once, but he was supposed to take a man over only in those cases where not doing so might lead to further trouble.

If the Deputy was not available at the moment, the man was put in Isolation and held in one of the Isolation cells until the Deputy had a chance to see him.[76]

(See Diagrams Pages 282 - 285)

Ordinarily, however, the guard wrote a report, and that night the reported prisoner received a slip which read:

You are ordered to report on Court Call directly after breakfast tomorrow morning.

The next morning the inmate fell out of line as he came out of the dining room and fell into a line that formed in the area between the dining room and the Chapel.[77] As soon as the last man was out of the dining room, the Court Call line was marched out through door #14, down street #15, around the stone at the corner of the dining room where mail was unloaded, down and across the street #S and into the front door of the building #38, through that door, and then lined up facing the long wall directly across the hall from the Deputy Warden's office. He was required to stand facing the wall with his arms folded until his number was called.

The Deputy Warden's head convict clerk would open the door and call each man's number as the Deputy directed.

The furnishings of the Deputy Warden's office are shown, as they existed in 1919. In 1912 there were two desks in the center of the office. The Captain used one for hearing requests for cell and work changes while the Deputy used the other one to try offenses. Sometimes both the Captain and Deputy would take part in the trial of an offense.

As the inmate stepped into the office, he was directed to stand before the Deputy's desk with his hands at his side.

"7974," the Deputy would say (the inmate was always addressed by his number, instead of his name), "You are charged with talking in line," or whatever the charge might be. Then he would pick up the report and read it.

"While on duty on the West side of the main hall as the line was going in to breakfast on the morning of March 27, 1908, I saw #7974, John Smith, speaking to #4873, Jack Daw, in violation of rule No. 17. I did not see #4873 make any reply. I have previously warned #7974 several times about talking in line. Signed, Guard S. B. Patterson. What have you to say for yourself?" the Deputy would add. It will be noted that the guard was required to

75   Part I – Chapter I
76   See Diagram of ground floor of Isolation building
77   See Diagram of Prison

state sufficient facts to enable the inmate to formulate a defense.

There were several good defenses the prisoner could put up to this charge. He could say:

"I think that the guard must be mistaken for these reasons: He was not on my side of the line that morning. I am in cell #D-322. That puts me on the East side of the line. With three men between us, he could not have seen me talking, nor could he have seen my number. There were ten other guards who could have seen me had I been talking;" or,

"#4873 does not cell near me. Had either of us been out of place, our own guards or the Captain would have jerked us out of line;" or maybe,

"The man stepped on my foot, and I only asked him to be careful;" or perhaps,

"That may be right. I do not recollect talking to anyone that morning, but I will not say that I did not. I do not know this Guard Patterson, and so far as I know he has never spoken to me. What does he look like?"

"He is a short fellow with red hair, about medium build."

"Yes! He did speak to me once. But he could not have seen me the other morning, for he went into the dining room ahead of me. I don't think he has eyes in the back of his head, so he could have seen someone else, got a glimpse of his number, and thought it was me."

All of these would have been good defenses, and the prisoner using any one of them, if his facts would stand up, would probably be excused.

The poorest defenses a man could use, even if innocent, were:

"That is not true. I want to be confronted with the guard. I want you to ask him what line I was in and what line #4873 was in, then look at our cell locations," or,

"It's not true. That fellow is just riding me."

A man had a right to be confronted with the reporting guard and to specify questions he wanted the Deputy to ask the guard, but in such a case, he had better have his facts straight or he was apt to increase rather than decrease his punishment. For a prisoner to accuse a guard of riding him, unless he could prove it, was equally bad.

After questioning, the Deputy would find the accused inmate guilty, not guilty or guilty but excusable.

When a convicted man who was sentenced to the hole came out of the door, the guard would say, "Turn to your left."

If he was not convicted, the guard would hand him a pass to take him back to his place of work; he would then turn to his right and go out the front door.

The left turn took the inmate back to the door that led to the Isolation proper. Both the wooden and the iron doors indicated on the drawing were kept closed during Court Call.

The Court Call guard would swing the wooden door open. Then the Isolation guard, who would be sitting at his desk, would get up and open the iron door. The Court Call guard would say, "Solitary!"

The Isolation guard would then say, "Stand over there!" indicating the steel trap door in the corner leading to the service tunnel. Next he would tell the man to remove his clothes and give him his name and number.

A Negro convict orderly would take the inmate's clothes and put them in the cabinet marked "C." He would give the prisoner a suit of dirty, cotton-flannel underwear and a pair of badly worn cloth slippers.

The guard would get up, open the utility safe with a big, iron key, take out a pair of handcuffs, and say, "Come on!"

He would unlock the iron door leading to the inner stairway to the floor above, turn right for five feet and open the door leading into the dungeons, known as the triangular dark holes.

It will be noticed that throughout the construction of this prison every place where there is a barred door, there is also a wooden door. One opened outward and the other opened inward. On all buildings, the outside door was made of bars, and the inside door was wood. In the dungeons and Isolation cells, this order was reversed.

The Isolation cells had ordinary wooden panel doors with a peep hole, 4 by 6 inches, indicated on the door to cell #5, about five feet, four inches from the floor.

The solid wooden doors to the dungeons were about two-inches thick, were made of several thicknesses of flooring, and closed like the door of an icebox. There was a heavy iron hasp at one side of the door, and a heavy steel strap built into the door, that fitted over it. The door was locked with a big padlock.

The inner door, which swung inward, was secured by a hinged and slotted strap that hooked over the same hasp as the strap of the outer door.

The bars of these doors were small, and the cross-strap that held them was about stomach high to a tall man. The only items in the cell were a covered night bucket and a rectangular tin cup that sat on the bars.

The prisoner was instructed to put his night bucket close to the door, place his tin cup within easy reach, then put his hands through the bars. The orderly filled the tin cup with fresh water and the guard placed the cuffs on the punished man's wrists, locked them, and closed and locked the door. The prisoner on punishment found himself in darkness, but not total darkness. There was a heavy wire screened transom above the door through which trickled a little air and light.

The man on punishment was required to stand chained to the door during working hours. At noon he was let down and given a chunk of bread that would just slip between the bars – about two-and-one-half-ounces.

At one o'clock he was hung up again, and when the quitting whistle blew at four-thirty, he was let down for the night and given his bed: a board two feet wide and six feet long and two blankets.

The man in the hole for the first time would sigh with relief as the guard unlocked the cuffs and let him down for the night. But we would soon discover that his troubles were a long way from being over.

About two feet had been torn from the end of each blanket. If he used one to lie upon, there was no way that he could cover his whole body with the other one. If he covered his chest, his feet would be out in the cold; if he covered his feet, his chest would be out in the cold. There was just room in the cell to lay the board flat at an angle. All four corners of the board touched the wall, but the shape of the cell was such that there was no way of sitting on the board and leaning back into a corner of the cell.

The Writer solved this problem by standing the board up against the wall, folding up one of the blankets, and putting it in the corner to sit on, then draping the other blanket over his shoulders and sitting in the corner in the intrauterine position, with his head on his knees and his hands locked around them. Years before, as a kid riding box cars, he had learned that in that position the body presents less surface to the air and loses heat more slowly than in any other position.

But the worst was yet to come. Every half hour all night long the guard came around, and with much clanging of steel, opened each wooden door, flashed a light in the cell occupant's face, then slammed the heavy wooden door and locked it with more loud clanging of steel. This was not done as a security measure; it was part of the punishment.

That is the way it went when things were normal.

In the top of each cell there was a six-inch tube that provided ventilation, and the men on punishment could talk to each other through these tubes, since they were all connected. Some guards would not say anything about this, but others would try to stop it. If the men refused to stop, the guard had another weapon. If it was summer, he went around and closed the windows and turned on the four big radiators (See Diagram). If it was winter, he turned off the radiators and opened the windows, and he would refuse to give the man making the disturbance any water.

This hot and cold treatment punished everyone who happened to be in the hole. The Writer was unfortunate enough to step into both of these situations. The first time he went to the hole there was a fellow in there who was going out on flat time[78] in ten days, and he was using those days to tell all the guards and officials what he thought of them.

For seven of those ten days, the Writer stood at the door with perspiration running off his chin.

The next time he went to the hole, Heck happened to be on a singing spree, and the Writer shivered until he thought that he would knock all his teeth out.

It is hard to say which is the worst, hot or cold. The cold is more painful, but the heat is very weakening.

The Seriousness of Offenses

The way offenses were graded for seriousness back in those days would seem rather strange to a person without prison experience or even to most present-day penologists, for ideas have changed considerably during the half century of Federal Prison existence.

---

78   The expression, flat time means that the man had lost all of his *goodtime* and had completed his full sentence.

Minor Offenses

These were offenses for which a man might be let off with a reprimand the first time or two or punished by the loss of a few weeks' privileges.

Some of the common minor offenses were: whispering in line; failure to remove cap and fold arms while addressing a guard or official; being caught in bed with one's cellmate, but without legal proof of sodomy; being seen kissing one's cellmate; possession of opium or morphine in small quantities; talking too loudly in cell; having flint and steel or button outfit (usual punishment, confiscation); entering dining room without having shirt properly buttoned at the throat; not keeping buttons on clothing; stealing almost any item excepting files, from the institution; having lead pencil or paper in cell without permission; sleeping nude in hot weather; not placing clothing in proper order at the door; scuffling or playing while at work; being out of place in line; turning to stare at a visitor; not keeping cell clean; having small knife; or speaking back to a guard on a matter where the guard was wrong or exceeding his authority – in such cases the prisoner was supposed to follow the guard's instructions but call the matter to the attention of the Captain, his foreman, or other proper authority.

Most of these offenses were usually handled by the guard on the spot. He would take the contraband article away from the prisoner. In cases of disorder he would give a sharp command the first time, and the next time he might punctuate that command with his cane. There were a few guards who would report every minor infraction they saw, but most guards would use their *shot boots*[79] only after repeated offenses of failure to obey their commands.

Moderately Serious Offenses

These were offenses for which a prisoner always went to the hole. For any minor offense, a man might go to the hole, depending on circumstances, but for the offenses listed in this group, there were no excuses; however, the term of punishment was usually short.

Escape or attempt to escape from inside the walls where no assault upon a guard was made or contemplated – these carried additional punishment of loss of all *goodtime* and the wearing of stripes for ninety days. Very few prison officials considered sodomy by mutual consent as an offense, and most guards would look the other way unless the act was committed in a very brazen manner. Proof sufficient to convict for this offense consisted of the statement of two guards that they could positively swear to entrance. One of the guard's sworn statements to entrance had to be supported by the Doctor's statement that the act had indeed been completed.[80] The second proof sufficient for conviction was the testimony of one guard supported by an admission of guilt by one of the men. Other moderately serious offenses included: fist fighting; smoking in the hospital or having smoking tobacco or papers in the hospital;[81] smoking at work; being drunk; talking in the

---

79   A report was called a shot.
80   The rub was that the Doctor would examine only with the inmate's consent. If a guard came on a couple in the act and they jumped apart before act was completed, they might then demand examination to beat the report. Or, if act occurred in the cell in middle of night, evidence could be removed by defecation before the guard could get the key.
81   Under Dr. Yoke, the offender would not be tried until released from hospital because the Doctor would not permit a sick man to be punished. This was not the case prior to 1908. The first Doctor at Leavenworth would permit men to die in the hole.

dining room; or insolence or cursing a guard – for the later offense an inmate was apt to be pretty badly worked over with the canes before going before the Deputy Warden.

The punishment for escape from inside the walls was three days in the hole. For the rest of the offenses on this list the punishment might vary from three to seven days in the hole.

More Serious Offenses

These offenses brought punishment of seven to ten days in the hole.

Stepping out of line without permission – this usually brought a split head; making a disturbance in the cell house before 9:30 P.M.; assaulting a fellow prisoner with a weapon; salacious conduct, playing or lovemaking at work – this offense, because it tended to break down discipline was more serious than pederasty, which of course was committed in moments of privacy; loafing during work; sodomy by force, reported by a guard;[82] possession of contraband in commercial quantities – this was usually tobacco, cigarette papers, or morphine and such cases often brought prolonged punishment in an attempt to force the owner to tell where he got the contraband; large amounts of money, because with enough money, it might be possible to talk many seventy-dollar-per-month guards into bringing in a pistol; smoking cigarettes – proof required was testimony of two guards, testimony of one guard supported by cigarette or material for making cigarettes found in prisoner's cell or on his person, or cigarette stain on the fingers.

Very Serious Offenses

These offenses usually brought sentences of fifteen days in the hole or more.

Escape or attempt to escape from outside the walls, which involved the breaking of a promise not to try to escape which had to be given in order to get a job outside of the walls. It was the breaking of the promise that brought the added punishment. In addition to stripes, the inmate who attempted to escape or did escape from outside the walls was forced to wear an Oregon boot for ninety days, and under McCloughry, he was usually dressed in stripes and the Oregon boot and put right back to work on the same job from which he escaped, but this time he worked under a gun guard. It is noteworthy that the man who attempted to escape from the outside received little sympathy from his fellows.

Possession of matches, making a disturbance after 9:30 P.M., and repeated violations of less serious rules also brought severe punishment. Another very serious offense was stealing from a guard or from another prisoner's cell; any man who did that was not popular.

Grace Offenses

The penalty for these offenses was thirty days in the dungeon, chained to the door.

---

82   Complaint of sodomy by a convict was no offense unless he claimed a weapon was used. If the weapon was found and the Doctor substantiated the claim that the act had been committed, the offense was allowed, for otherwise the convict could have screamed, which would have brought the guard.

Of these offenses there were only three: Striking a guard or official; refusing to work; attempting to incite a riot. It should be noted here that over-powering a guard, in an attempt to escape, even knocking him out, so long as he was not seriously or needlessly injured, was much less serious than striking a guard in a fit of anger, or even accidentally while in a fight.

The latter was serious because of the danger of it leading to a riot. The one thing the prison official in charge of the walled prisons of the old days feared above all others was a riot for it was only during a riot that the prisoner learned his real power. Any time a large prison population became angry and ran amuck, the badly out-numbered guards were helpless. Guns are of little value, for they hold only so many shells and can only be used from behind bars. Any time enough excited and determined men fan-out and charge a gun, even a machine-gun, they can take it. Some will die, but so will the gunner, and he knows that. Steel doors may hold one or a few men helpless, but enough angry and determined hands can easily tear them from the wall. Prison authorities fear that mass of strength, and anyone who has ever been through a prison riot knows that they have a right to fear it. For what angry men can accomplish with nothing but their hands, once they throw fear and restraint to the winds, is truly amazing. The Writer has seen heavy, steel doors torn from their moorings and used for battering rams. The strongest building falls apart under such treatment.

For refusing to work a man stayed in the dungeon for thirty straight days or until he said that he was willing to do what work he could. Not even the Doctor would take him out. It was reasoned that so long as he was sane and wanted to kill himself, that was his business, and there was nothing anyone could do about it. He could end his punishment any time he wished to call the guard and say the necessary words. Under McCloughry, thirty days was the limit, and at the end of that time the prisoner would be carried to the hospital.

In the case of a man sentenced to thirty days, the situation was different.

No man could spend thirty straight days in those old dungeons without serious injury to his health, so the man sentenced to thirty days was kept in the dungeon until the Doctor said that his health was in danger of permanent impairment, which was usually from fourteen to seventeen days, when his legs started to swell badly. He was then taken out of the dungeon and put in an Isolation cell[83] which contained a bed, a campstool and a stone about fourteen-inches square and three or four feet long (Cell #3).

The prisoner was given his full meals the first day, the medical attention he needed, and a pipe and tobacco. He was advised to eat lightly, but was given all he wanted to eat of any item on the menu. He was also given a shave, a hair-cut, a hot bath, and a complete outfit of clean clothing. The bed was a regulation bunk, with straw tick and pillow, sheets, pillow case, and all the good blankets he wanted.

The next morning he was given his breakfast; then the guard came down and opened his door, and orderlies carried from two to five boxes of rubble[84] into his cell. He was given a doughnut – shaped stone hammers and shown an iron ring, and he was told that he would have to work for his dinner, by breaking that stone small enough to put through the iron ring. He was usually given a couple of pieces of rubber hose about two inches long to

---

83   See Diagram of Isolation Building
84   The boxes held about three-and-a-half or four cubic feet of rubble, usually stone shop waste, and the Writer has broken four boxes in about fifty to sixty minutes, and on one occasions, he finished in forty-eight minutes.

slip over his thumb and first finger on the hand he held the stone with to keep him from mashing them.

If the man was weak and really tried to break his stone but could not get done by dinner time, the guard would give him his dinner, but if he refused to break his stone or would not try to do so, he was not fed until it was broken.

Once most men had a meal or two under their belts, they finished breaking their rock in two hours or less. Then the guard would open his door and give him a shovel to carry out the crushed rock. The first day or two, while he was still weak, the orderlies would carry the crushed rock out for him, but as soon as he was able, he was required to bring in and carry out his own rock, with some other man breaking rock to help him, or if there was no one else breaking rock, an orderly would help him carry the boxes in and out.

The rock was carried down the hallway to the back porch of the Isolation building and the boxes emptied over the edge of the porch.

The prisoner's door was left open, as was the iron door at the back of the Isolation building, and when his rock was removed and his cell swept and mopped, he was free to go out into the little court at the back of the Isolation building, where he could walk around, lie on the grass or do anything there was to do until dinner time. There was no guard over him, for there was no place he could go. If there were several men, they could talk, so long as they did not get loud. They were in plain view of both guards and convicts working in both ends of the West yard, thanks to those barred arches in the walls at both ends of the Isolation yard. They were not allowed to smoke out on the yard, but they could if they could score for a lighter. No other guard would pay any attention to them. The one thing they dared not do was be caught signaling, calling to, or waving at any man working near those arches.

There were a couple of steel pins in the ground at the lower end of the yard and some horseshoes they could pitch if they wished.

Probably one reason McCloughry's harsh system worked so well was because he knew when to relax that harshness. The idea was to build these men up in body and minds, so they were fooled with as little as possible. If they stole a smoke or some other little pleasures, what of it?

The men were called in from the yard a few minutes before dinner. They were not searched. Any one of them could have carried one of those steel pegs or a horseshoe in with him and knocked the guard's brains out, but he could have done that with his stone hammer too. It never occurred. Had any guard expressed fear of it happening to McCloughry, he would have said:

"If you are that cowardly, you have no business in prison work. Report to the Chief Clerk and get your money. That is all."

As soon as the line went out to work at one o'clock, the process was repeated, and the Isolation men broke rock for their supper, and when they were finished, they were allowed to go to the yard until supper time.

They were allowed to have all they wanted to eat of any item on the menu, and in addition they could have milk. The orderlies brought over a large surplus of food and always saved food for themselves and the night guards, and there was usually enough to give each of the men in Isolation a bowl of milk and something to go with it at nine o'clock.

The wooden doors were usually left open during the evening, but no talking from cell to cell was allowed. The night guard or one of the orderlies would usually slip these men the newspaper or something else to read. The guard would give them all the tobacco they wanted, and here, as elsewhere, he had to bring around the torch every time he rang his boxes. If a man could not sleep and wanted to smoke during the middle of the night, the guard would bring him a light. Of course, if a man made a disturbance, his door was closed, and he would not get anything.

The Writer's first night in this prison was spent in the Isolation Building, and the eerie quietness of the place stood out to him. No one spoke above a whisper. No guard working on night duty in a cell house or around sleeping men was allowed to wear shoes. The only time a guard spoke in an ordinary tone of voice was when speaking to a prisoner in the cell house, and that was so the other prisoners would know the inmate was not snitching to him and that he was not knifing with the inmate.

From week to week, as the inmate's strength returned, his task was increased until he was breaking four or five boxes of rock twice each day.

At the end of three weeks, he was taken out of his cell, stripped, weighed, and examined by the Doctor. If the Doctor reported that he was physically fit, he went back in the hole the following Monday morning to complete his sentence. If the Doctor said that he was unfit to stand more punishment, he would be retained in Isolation a couple more weeks. If still unfit, the Doctor might get him released.[85]

In the case of a man convicted of striking a guard, the last half of the sentence would be remitted only in the event that the guard went to the front for the man who had struck him and asked that the man be released. Most guards would do that, and many a guard would ask that the man be released to him and assigned to work under him. The guard who would not do it was looked down upon by his fellows as a poor sport.

The inmate would be called out to the Deputy Warden's Office, and the guard would make his plea in the prisoner's presence. The Deputy Warden would make a little speech, and the prisoner would say that he was sorry and thank the guard who had fronted for him.

This was good psychology. It placed the prison under obligation to the man he had struck. It did a lot to remove bitterness. And it often turned a man who might become bitter and dangerous into a well-behaved prisoner.

This brings us to another character of the old-time prisons and prison men. It was an unwritten law that every guard must look out for the interests of his men with just as much diligence as he devoted to their discipline. Unless the offense was one that made a report mandatory, no guard reported another guard's man without telling that other guard on the phone first, stating the case, and asking the other guard what he wanted done. Many a guard who ignored that rule was punched in the nose for it. A guard, who would not fight for his men was looked upon as a pretty poor character by both guards and convicts. This made for good discipline, too. Many a prisoner walked the straight and narrow path because he could not let down the man who had stood up for him.

Another feature of McCloughry's system of penology, was that no man should be

---

85   This was the rule under Doctor Yoke from 1908 to 1913.

permitted to feel that there was anything personal about his punishment. He was punished for violating the rules. When he had undergone the prescribed punishment, the book was closed and the offense was not mentioned against him again. All the men who served time under "Big Jim" appreciated one of his principal characteristics of never holding a grudge.

William Mackey, who became the second Deputy Warden at Leavenworth in the Spring or Summer of 1911 would call each man released from punishment out to his office and give him a little lecture, which is best illustrated by an actual case. The following interview occurred on September 25, 1913, when the Writer was released from the hole after his attempt to escape.

Mackey leaned back in his swivel-chair and smiled at the Writer.

"Well, Fifty Four (the Writer's number was 8154) you tried to beat us and you failed. You know, it is a sucker game. They all fail, for we always get them back. You made your mistake, and you have been punished. I wanted to turn you out in three days, as I have always done in such cases, but the new Warden would not stand for it. He insisted that I should keep you for full ten day limit, but I would not go for that. I do not know what you did to make him so sore at you, but seven days was the best I could do."

"He tried to make a stoolpigeon out of me, and I ate it up. I was on my way to the sewer at the time, and I had fifty pounds of tools under my clothes. He even phoned my guard and told him to give me any pass I wanted without question so I could talk to men planning to escape and report to him personally.

Mackey smiled.

"I did not know that. Anyway, I want you to know that so far as I am concerned there are no hard feelings. I am not responsible for you being here, but it is my job to punish you. That does not mean that I blame you for trying. If I were in your position and saw what I thought was a good chance, I would take it. If you had beaten us, I would not hate you for it; I would admire you for it. Any time a man is smart enough to out-think me and get away without hurting anyone, I give him all the credit in the world for it, but still, when he gets caught, and they always get caught, I am compelled to punish him. Of course the rule states that you will have to wear stripes for three months, and I have nothing to do with it. Also, I am compelled to put you in the stone shop. That is not my doing. If I had my choice, I would put you right back in the powerhouse. You could not make it when you had all the tools in the prison, the run of the joint, and all the time you wanted, and I think that you have too much sense to try again. On the other hand, you are a good mechanic, and Mr. Graham says you're one of the best men he ever had. I think you should be employed where you can do the most good, but I have been overruled.

"You violated the rules, and I had to punish you. If you violate them again, I'll have to punish you again, but I want you to feel when you walk out that door that you have paid for your mistake. I want you to know that no one is mad at you or going to ride you while I sit in this chair. If anyone tries to, don't blow up and lose your head. Come over and tell me, and I will put a stop to it quickly.[86] Any time you want a favor that is within my power to grant, don't be afraid to come over here and ask for it. I may not grant it, but I will give

---

86   In those days men with the character to commit serious offenses were never ridden by the guards, nor would their superiors permit it. Such men, if left alone, go on and follow prison routine, naturally. They cause no trouble. If not left alone or treated fairly, they may cause bloodshed. It was the constant, petty trouble-maker who was ridden to death by the guards.

your request the same consideration that I will give anyone else's, and if your request is one I can reasonably grant, I will do it. I give you my hand on that." Mackey's hand came across the desk.

"Thank you, Sir!" said the Writer, taking the proffered hand. "How about my privileges?"

"I have not touched them. You are paying a high price as it is."

"You know that I lost my shoes and my belt in the sewer?"

"Yes! You will be on your feet a lot out there in the stone shop. I'll give you an order for a pair of soft shoes and I'll tell Osborn to make you a belt." These were special favors that were hard to get.

Call this cheap psychology if you will, but it paid off. No matter how serious the offense or how severe the punishment; when that punishment was over, it was over, and the book was closed. The prisoner was made to feel that there was nothing personal in his treatment; he knew he had brought his punishment upon himself and that he had paid the debt in full. It did a great deal to prevent lasting bitterness.

The last thing Mackey said as the Writer stepped out the door was:

"Remember! If you come over here again, you will be punished on your report. This matter has been paid for, and it will never again be thrown in your face."

In one respect past bad conduct did return to plague the offenders. The first time a man went to the hole he lost one day's *goodtime* for each day spent on punishment. The next time it was two days lost for each day spent in the hole, and the third time, it was three days. This continued until all of the offender's *goodtime* was lost, and such *goodtime* was never restored. McCloughry took the view that by repeated misconduct the offender had earned no *goodtime*. *Goodtime* taken in a lump for a specific offense could be and often was restored on the basis of subsequent good conduct.

Even if a man had been in the hole for only a single day, he was given a bath, shave, haircut, and clean clothing from the skin out before being permitted to go to his cell, and he was required to do no work his first day out of the hole. If working on a gang, his guard would tell him to go over and sit in the shade. The shop guard would say:

"You can take it easy today. You don't have to do anything, if you do not feel like it."

PART I – CHAPTER IX

Leavenworth, Continued
(The Guards)

Canes

It has already been mentioned that the guards carried canes, and those canes were definitely something. Although they were designed to look like ordinary walking sticks, they were actually one of the most dangerous and deadly hand weapons ever invented.

Who invented them the Writer does not know. It may have been McCloughry or they may have been a relic from an earlier day. In any case, they were used in practically all the institutions ruled by McCloughry and his sons, and they may still be in use in Wisconsin; at least they were in use there until recently. Even if McCloughry did invent those canes, it was characteristic of him that he never carried one. He carried a light, ebony, gold-headed walking stick.

The canes were made of turned and steamed hickory rods about one inch in diameter at the thickest point, where the hand grasped the handle, which was bent in the form of a shepherd's crook. The shaft of the cane tapered slightly to a point about ten inches from the ground. That last ten inches was a heavy tapering steel ferrule that was not over three-eighths or one-half inch in diameter at the end where it struck the ground, and that end was neatly rounded.

When new, the canes were painted black, and it was impossible to see where the wood stopped and the steel began, but once in use, the paint soon wore off.

It was the theory that the guards could use the crooks to separate fighting men or to restrain an unruly prisoner without any danger of being struck, but in practice, it did not work out that way. That steel ferrule would split a man's scalp like a knife, and it was so much easier to knock a man down than to struggle with him. That there were many guards who accepted this view was evidenced by the number of white turbans always to be seen in that sea of heads in the big dining room. The guards split heads, and the Doctor sewed them up.

The Writer had it on the authority of many of the guards themselves that a good proportion of those deaths during the early years were the result of skull fractures.

The canes however, were even more dangerous when used for thrusting. The small end concentrated the force of the blow into such a small area, that even a moderately hard thrust was sure to procure deep-seated injury.

Officially, as already stated,[87] the guards were supposed to use their canes only in self-defense or in protecting some other guard or inmate from assault, but such is human nature that whenever you place a potent weapon in the hand of any man and clothe him with authority, there is strong temptation to use it. This is true of all men, but it is particularly true of "little" men, and that adjective is not used in a physical sense. You do not hire very many big men at a wage lower than that paid to ditch diggers, but even the best of men may become cruel under the influence of unrestrained power.

But it should always be remembered when reading stories of prison brutality that the average prison guard is naturally no more cruel or sadistic than you would be under the same circumstances. As one guard who has read this work pointed out:

"A man may feel compelled to do things he does not like to do. I was on a submarine during the war, and we were strafing lifeboats. I did not like to do it. It made me sick. But I was ordered to do it, and I did it. I may be ordered to do things as a guard that I don't like to do, but I will do them.

"In time of war a man in the Army or Navy is subject to the death penalty for refusing to obey orders. Yet, we have just finished hanging thousands of persons who were in the Military services of Germany and Japan who were denied the plea of Superior Orders. Every civil servant of the United States is sworn to uphold the Constitution and Laws of the United States. There is no way he can be fired for refusing to obey an unlawful order. Under those circumstances, I do not think that any man can escape moral responsibility for his actions on the plea of Superior Orders.

"Maybe he can't be fired, but they can keep him from getting a promotion or get back at him in other ways."

As it will be pointed out time and again in this work, the prison guard is only an ordinary human being, who like anyone else, tries to do the best he can in very difficult situations that are often made worse by the stupidity or conflicting orders of his superiors. A very small percentage of guards are intentionally cruel, but there is always a small number of persons in any group who delight in cruelty. At no time at Leavenworth did the active headhunter number more than ten percent of the guard force, but it was always this small minority that was involved in the cruelties that made scandals.

It was the same way with reports. Most guards preferred to enforce discipline with their voices rather than with their canes or pencils, but the same small minority kept the Court Call line full every weekday morning.

The majority of the Leavenworth guards in the beginning had previously been soldier guards at the Military Prison. A great many of them were Spanish American War Veterans, and some of these had served several enlistments in the Army before coming to the prison.

These men fell right in with the strict military discipline employed by McCloughry; yet on the whole, they were the best and the best-liked guards in the prison, for the Army had trained them to handle men. They had been buck privates themselves before they had become drill sergeants, and they knew just how the men under them felt.

There were a number of guards who had followed McCloughry down from Joliet or had come to Leavenworth from other State Institutions. Several who had been on the long march from Moundsville were still at Leavenworth at the time the Writer went there in 1912. These men were less well liked than the soldiers, but there were some good men in the group.

By far the worst group at Leavenworth during McCloughry's time was composed of men who had been hired locally. These men had grown up as farmers, proved failures in that field, became small-town policemen, and had passed from that into prison work. With such men, a little power is always more dangerous than opium for it goes to their heads. They become martinets and develop an intense personal hatred for any man who fails to kowtow to them or recognize them as superior beings, which they themselves, know that they are not.

Barring Marines, who with few exceptions, are trained sadists who actually imagine themselves to be superior beings and belong in the same class with Hitler's goose-stepping SS troops,[88] this farmer group has always supplied the most hated and poorest guards in the prison. The three most hated guards at Leavenworth at the time the Writer went there belong in this group.

One, a man name Hull, probably had a reason to hate convicts. The story around the prison, though it may or may not have been true, was that his wife had run off with a trusty convict and left him with eight small children to raise alone on a guard's pay. Another was known as "Eat-'M-Up Sam,[89] and the third one was one-eyed Alex.

These three men, when on jobs where they could do so, wrote more reports than all the rest of the guards at the prison. Hull and Sam were not big men, and at the time the Writer knew them, were not physically fit to be headhunters, but Alex, who had lost his eye and killed a man in a gun battle when he had been a small-town constable, was one of the worst headhunters in the prison. Whenever trouble started, he wanted to rush right into it, swinging his club.

The Writer was never closely associated with Hull, and what he saw of the man, he did not like, but he had many close contacts with Sam and Alex, and considerable trouble with the former, yet both men had their good points and were evidently trying to do the best they could. Their big fault was in the narrowness of their ideas.

Medical Attention

During the early years of our Federal Prison System, the medical attention given to prison inmates was not much. It was 1915 before the hospital building at Leavenworth, the plans for which were drawn in 1892, was completed. It was 1927 before they had a resident surgeon; 1928 before they had a modern dental clinic or an X-ray machine; and 1931 before it was possible for the Leavenworth inmate to obtain properly fitted glasses.

---

88 This judgment does not apply to the Marines trained during the recent war, but to those who had several enlistments in the peace-time Marine Corps.

89 Part I – Chapter VII

The medical department charged with the care of more than a thousand men consisted of three rooms on the main hall[90] and one on the third floor of Administration Building. There was no autoclave, no X-ray, and no laboratory. Urinalysis, blood counts, and sputum examinations were made by a convict in the crowded dispensary.

The staff consisted of one Doctor and such helpers as he could gather up around the prison or train himself, and he had to deal with such diseases as diphtheria, measles, smallpox, pink-eye, tuberculosis, pneumonia, influenza, and meningitis.

The name of the first Doctor at Leavenworth has long since been forgotten. It is not really important, since there is nothing good to be said of him. He was described to the Writer as being a big, powerful man in his middle forties; a drunken, incompetent, sadistic quack who laughed at human suffering and took a keen delight in inflicting pain. Not one person, either guard or convict, that the Writer ever talked to had one good word to say of him. Most of the stories told of him are too revolting to be credible, but one, which is well authenticated, will suffice to show the character of this man and explain part of the high death rate during the early years of that institution.

It is the story of Robinson, the mutineer[91] who was recaptured in 1906. He was well known to the Writer, and his story may be verified from the papers filed in his behalf at the time his life sentence was commuted from "life" to "time served," effective July 1, 1914.

A few days after Robinson, one of the men accused of leadership in the Mutiny of 1902, was returned to Leavenworth with a life sentence, he went on sick call one morning and asked for a physical. He was not sick.

The Doctor looked at him closely.

"Hmm! You are a sick man. I am checking you into the hospital. I want to give you a thorough examination."

Robinson attempted to protest that there was nothing wrong with him.

"Take him to the hospital and put him to bed," the Doctor ordered, and there was nothing Robinson could do but go.

Robinson was taken to the dormitory on the third floor, stripped of his clothing, and put to bed. Shortly thereafter the Doctor came up to the hospital and went through the motions of examining Robinson's chest and abdomen. Suddenly, he placed his knee against Robinson's hip, grabbed his ankle, and broke his leg between the hip and knee.

"Wow, you _____, you will never run again!" he said, laughing at the helpless man's agony.

Robinson was carried to the Isolation Building, dumped on the floor of one of the Isolation cells, and left there for two years. He was given a straw tick and some blankets, and he was fed on the floor, like a dog. His wooden door was kept closed, and the only persons he saw were the guard and orderly who brought his food. His leg was not set, so the bones failed to knit, and the inflammation gradually subsided. The broken ends of the bones became rounded, and the acute agony eventually passed away, but there was always

---

90   See Diagram of Prison, Part I – Chapter VI, and Key to drawing, paragraph describing the third floor of Administration Building.
91   Part I – Chapter VI

the nerve-racking sensation produced by those bones rubbing together every time he tried to move.

Robinson told me, "No one ever spoke to me. I don't know how I kept from going mad. Maybe I did go a little mad. I learned later that that was the story that had been circulated throughout the prison. I lived and dreamed of the day when I would get within striking distance of that Doctor with six inches of steel in my hand. Only that hope kept me from ending my misery. I lost all track of time. My hair was way down past my shoulders, and my beard was almost down to my navel. I had just about given up hope when one morning, a strange man stepped up in front of the door and said, 'How are you?'

"I don't know what I said, but he turned to the guard and said, 'Open the door!'

"'Oh no! You can't go in there,' the guard protested. 'He is hopelessly insane, and he is dangerous.'

"'Open that door!' the stranger snapped. 'That is an order!'

"'All right, Doctor, but you should not go in there. He might bite you,' the guard said.

"That was the first time I knew he was a Doctor. I had not spoken to anyone for two years, so it was hard for me to speak, but I managed to tell him that my leg was broken, and he looked at it and ordered me taken to the hospital."

The sadist had finally been fired for drunkenness, and a few months later he blew his own brains out.

Doctor Yoke

The new Doctor was Alfred F. Yoke, brother-in-law of Judge Hoop, then Senior Judge of the Eighth Circuit Court of Appeals. He had received his appointment through the political influence of Judge Hoop, which gave him a measure of independence he might not otherwise have enjoyed.

Doctor Yoke was a competent, sincere, and conscientious physician. He was a master of the art of sight diagnosis. He could judge a man's temperature at a distance of twenty feet, and he was so sure of his judgment that it took two thermometers to convince him that he was wrong. He held the job for a few months less than twenty years, and during that time he fought and pleaded constantly for better medical facilities; for X-ray equipment; for the assistance of a resident surgeon; for a modern dental clinic; none of which he ever obtained. But even without them, he established one of the most outstanding medical records in America.

It did not take Yoke long to let everyone know that he was the Doctor. Concerning medical questions, he made it known that his word was the law, and he would tolerate no interference from anyone.

He took Robinson to the hospital and had him bathed, shaved, and his hair cut. He examined the leg and told Robinson that he was sorry, but being no surgeon, there was nothing he could do about it. He got Robinson some crutches, and as soon as Robinson had learned to use them, he had him given a permanent cell in the Isolation Building, all the privileges of any other prisoner and an opportunity to walk on the yard every day when the weather was good.[92]

As already stated, Doctor Yoke was a physician, but not a surgeon. The sight of blood and of pain sickened him. He could not set a broken finger, and lancing a boil turned his stomach. The suffering he saw around him made him sick at heart and cut him to his very soul. He was eventually fired for being incompetent, too liberal with narcotics, and permitting convicts without medical training to perform major operations.

During his tenure he had to fight smallpox, diphtheria, influenza, pneumonia, and meningitis. There were times when he had to trace down and isolate spreaders of syphilis and gonorrhea without the aid of modern laboratory techniques. Tuberculosis was a very common prison disease in those days, especially so among young boys placed to work in the stone shop, and he had to fight to get these victims out into the fresh air. There was no medical center to which he could send his dying patients. There was no insulin, no sulfa drugs, and no antibiotics. Yet with all these handicaps, this remarkable man fought sickness and suffering with a skill that was truly amazing.

He employed such medically trained or intelligent convicts as he could get, and those without training, he trained himself. Where it was a case of life and death, he permitted safe blowers with steady hands and dexterous fingers to perform major operations. The Writer has seen such operations on the abdominal cavity, performed by a convict working without gloves or masks, a cigarette in the corner of his mouth, working from a description of the operation in a book or journal propped open upon the patient's chest, and he has seen those patients made uneventful recoveries.

During those three terrible winters, 1917-18; 1918-19; and 1919-20, when the influenza pandemic was striking down people on the outside like flies under a flit gun, this man, in a prison which then had a population of almost four thousand men, with cell accommodations for only eighteen hundred, with men sleeping in bunks stacked up three high in the corridors, lost only seven men from respiratory conditions. On one occasion he had five hundred cases of influenza and more than fifty of pneumonia at once, and while oxygen was then available for cutting and welding, there was none available for saving convict lives; yet Yoke weathered this storm without a single death. He also had two hundred fifty-some cases of diphtheria that same winter without losing a case either.[93]

At the same time he had to administer treatments to thousands of drug addicts at a rate of thirty to fifty per month, yet the Writer never heard of a fatality from this treatment in Doctor Yoke's hands, and he could not have had more than five or six in the whole twenty years.

A book could be written about the accomplishments and struggles of this man, and he will be mentioned time and again throughout later Sections of this work. Like all men, he was a human being and sometimes made terrible mistakes that excited the wrath of the very men he was trying so hard to serve.

The irony of the situation was that it was only after his removal that all the conveniences he had been crying for, for so many years were provided. Yet, from that day to this, in not

---

92   When this case was investigated by Joseph Fishman, McCloughry contended that he had not known that Robinson's leg had been broken; both his Doctor and Deputy assured him that the man was hopelessly insane, and he had taken their word for it. The man was considered too dangerous to be sent to St. Elizabeth. This was before the building of Howard Hall.
93   See annual report for fiscal year 1919

a single instance have his mortality records ever been equaled. In the year 1940, in the same institution, but with cell accommodations for a thousand more men than he had and a population of only two thousand men, with seven Doctors constantly employed and with specialists available in all emergencies, with the power to ship all hopeless cases to the Medical Center at Springfield, Missouri, more men died in that single month than Doctor Yoke ever lost in any single year. The Writer was in the hospital for an appendectomy from September 2-9, and during the early morning of the latter day, the eleventh death for that month occurred.

Spiritual Guidance

As this is written a young man suffering from that very common complaint among Federal prison inmates of the present day, "prison psychosis," is in the adjoining ward of the prison hospital at Alcatraz and is bemoaning his lack of spiritual guidance.

The Writer cannot help smiling as he thinks back to the days of McCloughry, of Big Jim, of William Mackey and of the guidance this young man would have received under the McCloughry Administration. Yet, it is not funny to see a fine specimen of young manhood undergoing mental and moral disintegration, and he cannot help but wonder whether or not in the long run McCloughry's system, with all its faults was not preferable, for bruises of the body heal quickly while those of the mind never do.

Holy Joe

That part of the spiritual guidance of the inmates of Leavenworth during the days of McCloughry which was not handled by that gentleman himself, was entrusted to the long, bony, fumbling hands of old Joseph – Holy Joe Levett.

Old Joe had been fourteen years old when the first Confederate shell had whistled and burst over Fort Sumter. He was a tall, gangling youngster, already over six feet, who had grown up behind a plow on a stony, upland, Indiana farm, and as he had trodden the hard, dry furrows, he had dreamed of faraway places and glorious and romantic deeds, as most farm boys do. With the flames of war sweeping over the nation, Joe ran away from home and joined the Army in time to get into the first *Battle of Bullrun,* and from then on, for almost four years, Joe was in every battle in which the Army of the Potomac was engaged, up to and including the second *Battle of the Wilderness*, where he was captured.

Joe was sent to the infamous Andersonville prison, where men ate their own feces, and lived in mud like swine. Those who had reached the end of their endurance walked across the deadline and permitted themselves to be shot down. Joe survived by trading his young body for small bits of other men's meager rations.

Joe was finally transferred to Libby Prison, where the good Christian Ladies of Richmond visited the Union prisoners in their tobacco-warehouse hospital, and several of them stopped by the cot of the tall, dying boy and wept over him, for he was by that time reduced to such a state that his shoulder blades had broken through his skin.

Some of the ladies would bring bits of food, but they had so little themselves, and there were so many dying boys in the besieged city. One of these kind ladies gave the tall, dying boy a Bible and offered to try to get a letter through the lines to his mother; she urged Joe to read the Bible and to pray to God for his deliverance.

Joe was no great shucks as a reader, and he was far too sick to read much, but he did pray to God for his deliverance. It was his last thin hope, and he grasped at it like a drowning person. He not only prayed to God; he did more than that. He made a deal with God. He promised God that if he were delivered, he would devote the remainder of his life to spreading the word of God.

It was only a few days later that Joe was exchanged. His mother had come East, and she met him as he was carried off the train in Baltimore. It was weeks before he was able to travel to his home. It was months before he completely regained his health and strength, but with youth and good food he did regain it, and he kept his promise to God, too.

Joe went back to his plow, but he read his Bible every evening, and he saved his pennies. During some of the hard years after the war, pennies were pretty difficult to find, but Joe finally had enough to put himself through some small protestant seminary and be ordained.

But Joe was no great shucks as a preacher. He was sincere enough and he tried hard, but his funeral-toned voice and hellfire and brimstone sermons just did not draw people to hear him. He managed to marry and to eke out a precarious living for his wife and family of several daughters, but never in his life was he able to hold a Church that paid him more than nine hundred dollars a year. So when he heard that Uncle Samuel was going to build some new prisons, he applied for a job as Chaplain, which paid eighteen hundred dollars per year, and on the strength of his war record, he received the appointment.

At the time he came to Leavenworth, Joe was a tall, gaunt, large-boned man of fifty-five or six, with seamed, Lincolnesque face, snow-white hair and a snow-white goatee about six inches long. If he ever had any delusions about guiding imprisoned souls to God, they were soon lost. It did not take him long to discover that the only men who make a show of religion in prison are sycophants hoping to use that method of currying favor for personal gain, and for such persons Old Joe had the sincere man's supreme contempt, which the duties of his office would not permit him to voice, but which he was not entirely able to conceal.

Joe rationalized the conditions, the sorrow, and the suffering he saw around him by consoling himself with the fact that they were not as bad as Andersonville. When inmates took him to task for tolerating things over which he had no control, and called him an old hypocrite, he patted them on the shoulder, had them sit down, and he told them his stories of Andersonville and of Libby Prison. He did not hold back anything, even told the selling of his body for a chunk of moldy and muddy bread. He assured them of his complete understanding and sympathy, but urged them to seek their deliverance in the word of God as he had done.

When the new Chapel was completed, attendance of services was made compulsory, but it was obvious to Joe that while you could lead a horse to water or drive a man to church, you could not make either of them like it.

He tried to conduct his services in accordance with the traditions of his faith: an opening hymn; a rather long prayer; several more hymns, with the congregation standing; an announcement of his text; another hymn; an hour of sermon; another short prayer; another hymn; and the benediction.

He organized a rather nice choir of fine, young voices, but it probably hurt him to discover that his singers were possessed of wanton spirits, less pious than promiscuous, not above taking advantage of choir practice and the fact that his old eyes were not too good at penetrating the cavernous gloom of the unlighted chapel, to desecrate the House of God with the sins of Sodom.

But it is entirely possible that Old Joe's eyes were not as dull as they seemed, and that he was more understanding than the prisoners realized. Maybe he thought of the Army of the Potomac, of lonely bivouacs under the summer stars, of Andersonville of which he loved to talk by the hour, and maybe he only pretended not to see things not intended for his eyes. In any case, he went to McCloughry and told him that he did not want or need the presence of a guard at choir practice because his boys could not sing with the spirit he desired under the nervous tension created by the guard's presence. And if he did feel a little disappointment that his boys could not give all their thought to things of the Spirit, it was not a new experience for him. Old Joe's life had been made up of many sorrows, disappointments and frustrations. So he learned not to peer too intently into the gloom, to lift his eyes toward the heavens and to limit his service to two short hymns, a short and snappy prayer of less than three minutes, if one could imagine anything Joe did being snappy; the sermon took less than twenty minutes for delivery and avoided all reference to acts of commission or omission that might offend either his congregation or its keepers. The service then closed with a short hymn and a really snappy benediction.

Joe had learned much of this the hard way, as so many mortals do. The architects who planned the prison were theoretical rather than practical penologists, and they had played a ghastly trick upon him. They had made every other floor in the prison of concrete, but they had made the Chapel floor of wood and used the vast empty space beneath its sloping floor for the location of the heating coils and fans that supplied hot air to both the dining room and Chapel.

When a thousand pairs of heavy brogans were dragged across that wooden floor in unison, it would vibrate like a sounding board, or the head of a giant drum, and it would fill the auditorium with the rumbling sound of distant thunder, against which no human voice could compete. This accompanied by a low moan, issuing from behind a thousand pairs of closed and immovable lips, had an unearthly effect that would have to be heard to be appreciated.

There was not a thing that the guards could do about it. Not a thing for them to see. No one could be accused of anything more than shifting in his seat, but it was a thousand men shifting together that did the trick. There grew up a tacit understanding between Joe and his congregation. So long as Joe did not tread on too many toes or bear down too heavily on the hellfire and brimstone, they would give him exactly forty-five minutes. He preached with a watch on his pulpit, but occasionally he forgot. The prisoners had no watches, but they knew when that forty-five minutes was up just as well as Joe did. Occasionally, they would be wrong too, and be a minute or two premature in their shifting.

At the first sign of a rumble, Joe would glance down at his watch and if he had run one second overtime, he would chop himself off in the middle of a word, spread his long, bony hands out over the heads of his audience and say, "God bless you all," which was the signal for the orchestra to strike up a march.

On the other hand, if the inmates were premature, Joe would shake his head slightly and keep right on talking, and the prisoners would accept that verdict.

When Joe got on a delicate subject, the prisoners would give him a slight warning, and he would drop it in the middle of a sentence or go on to something else.

The Writer will never forget the first of Joe's sermons he attended, not because of anything Joe said, but because he was to learn one of the tricks of the prison and to meet a man who was to be his friend for many years. The man was a *yegg* called Freddy. The same one who after his release killed Eddy Fay, who had trained him.[94]

The Writer had been put in the cell with Freddy's fall partner (the man convicted with him). Freddy's cell put him way ahead of his partner in the line, so when he came to the Captain, he signaled for permission to step out to speak to the Captain, spoke to him just long enough for the Writer and his cellmate to come along, and stepped into the line between them. That was one of the few ways men not celling or working close together had of meeting or talking to each other. If they were lucky and got a seat on the inside, not too close to the guard, it was fairly safe to talk if one was careful. All through this service the three men talked and Freddy, speaking out of one side of his face in careful whispers, recited for the Writer a little poem that had been written in the Ohio Penitentiary at Columbus while he was there.

The verse was so appropriate to the occasion and so perfectly expressive of the average convict's aversion to conventional religious ideas that it stuck in the Writer's memory and fixed his memory of the occasion.

"The prisoners were assembled upon the Sabbath Day

 Within the prison Chapel, to hear the parson pray

No sooner were they seated, than up rose Doctor Clocks,

And immediately, with the cons, he began to chew the socks.

He told us wondrous stories of an ancient bum named Paul,

Who drifted in Jerusalem, with religion for a stall.

And as he told these stories and other hoary lies,

My heart was filled with sadness, and tears rose to my eye.

For boxcars were not invented then, and poor Paul had to hike.

He didn't have the Kale to rush the can as often as he'd like.

And after all his weary wanderings, when his feet were tired and sore

He had no bronc to cheer his life in those sad days of yore."[95]

---

94   See part I – Chapter II
95   Written in Columbus, Ohio, in the year 1908. The word *bronc* is an abbreviation of the word bronco, and in the criminal argot of that day it was synonymous with *boy, punk, gazoony,* or *neophyte*. Of course, a careful reading of the Scripture may cast some doubt upon the poet's conclusion, but the poem is intended to be facetious rather than factual. The name of the author was once known to the Writer, but it has long since been forgotten.

Joe Levett was not much of a preacher, but he did know when to sit down, and he was not as loath to protest about injustices as most of the inmates thought. On one occasion, when he had seen a guard strike a boy needlessly from behind, he had complained to McCloughry. The convict clerk, Jimmy H., mentioned a number of times later heard the argument, and quoted McCloughry as saying, "If you do not like what goes on here, I would suggest that you resign."

"I believe that it is admitted that we both obtained our appointments and hold our posts on the strength of our war records," Old Joe snapped back. "I would suggest that you compare your war record with mine. I think our comrades would agree that, if either of us should resign, it should be you."[96]

McCloughry was said to have flushed a deep red, turned and walked away. He had seen no combat during the war, while Old Joe had an amazing combat record.

The guard was reprimanded and thrown in a tower, where he would not come in contact with the inmates.

The principal objection to Joe was not his preaching or the fact that he did not practice what he preached to the extent of making himself a human force within the prison, however. As Chaplain, he was in charge of the Library, the school, what little there was, and he had to pass upon all books purchased by or delivered to inmates. And while he had no hope of leading any great throng of wayward souls through the Pearly Gates, he was not going to stand by and see them led to perdition if he could help it by permitting them to read the new-fangled scientific theories being put out by such arch heretics as Spencer, Huxley, and Darwin, who were trying to tell the world that the story of creation was a lie, that man was nothing but a glorified ape that had come down from the trees, picked up a club and started using it to hunt meat with. Nor should they read the rantings of such infidels as Thomas Paine and Robert G. Ingersol. There was no excuse for them wanting to read the lewd and degrading stories of Poccaccio and Buy du Mauposant, but there was nothing wrong with Shakespeare. He might get a little off color and sexy once in a while, but he never leveled his sarcasm at the established Church. There was nothing wrong with them reading the Bible either, including the Book of Deuteronomy, but Havloc Ellis' discussion of the very same subject was taboo; and the prisoners did not like that.

When confronted with these inconsistencies, the only defense Joe could make was that Deuteronomy was part of the word of God, and that made it all right.

---

96   Both men were active members of the G.A.R. which was at that time a very powerful political force in America.

PART I – CHAPTER X

Leavenworth – Continued

Recreation

This subject may be treated very briefly – there wasn't any.

The Phonograph

Some time back around 1907 or '08, it was while the Writer was in Alaska, and the newspapers made a lot of it at the time, some Congressman or Senator, probably at the request of some recording company, had tacked a rider onto an appropriation bill providing that every person undergoing imprisonment for an offense against the United States should be allowed to enjoy a two-hour concert of recorded music at least once every two weeks. This law has never been repealed and is still in effect.

So all Federal prisons had to buy phonographs and records, and the inmates had to have their music every other week.

At Leavenworth, Old Joe selected the records, and because he was as opposed to popular music as he was to popular literature, he purchased only the best classical and semi-classical selections. Most of the men did not like that, but the Writer has always been thankful for Old Joe's selections, which did much to broaden his understanding and appreciation of the best in music.

The machine was played at night in the cell house and dormitories,[97] and each Sunday it was played in the hospital. Because the machine could only be heard by one side of a cell house at a time, it was played one week on one side of the cell house and the next week on the other side. Each of the dormitories had the phonograph one evening per week. And that was the extent of the official recreation allowed.

Mr. King, The Man Who's Feet Hurt

There was a guard at Leavenworth, named King, who in his youth had had great ambitions of becoming a great musician. At considerable difficulty he had given himself the foundation of a good musical education, but he had never been outstanding enough

---

97   Dormitories were called Parole Rooms because they housed trusties and semi-trusties.

to make much of a living from his music. He had met and married a young lady with ambitions very similar to his own, and they soon had a family on the way.

With bills and babies coming along in rapid succession, Mr. King was forced to look around for some more substantial method of making a living; so he became a guard at Leavenworth – a step he always regretted most bitterly. He felt that had he continued his efforts just a little longer, they would have been crowned with success.

Mr. King was a fine, big, nice-looking man with a pleasing and cultivated personality. He soon became one of the best-liked guards at the prison. Inmates were always showering him with little attentions, and wherever he went, he had one of the best behaved gangs or departments in the prison. He wrote very few reports, because he very seldom had occasion to do so, and he could not understand why other guards were always having troubles that never came to him. But for twenty years Mr. King did not have the remotest idea of why he was so well liked, and when the Writer finally told him, he almost fainted, for he had always been a little suspicious of the convicts' fondness for him.

Strange as it may seem, Mr. King was liked because his feet hurt.

He was a portly man, and he had small hands and feet. Pounding pavement all day long or running up and down steep cell house stairs was not easy on his delicate arches. With well-fitting shoes and building arch supporters, it was not so bad, but when he was on the night shift in the cell houses and had to climb those steep stairs and walk those long galleries in cloth sneakers, it was pure murder.

Being an intelligent man, it did not take Mr. King long to figure out a way of avoiding some needless steps. When he was on the first half, he had to carry that torch around the galleries every half hour up until nine-thirty, but from nine-thirty until midnight he would use the back stairs and walk only one side of the cell house at a time. That way he passed each cell every hour instead of every half hour, and of course, convicts, being egotist, naturally thought that he was doing that just to be decent and considerate to them. They noticed too, that he was never sneaking, or heeled back, even when he must have known reasons for doing so. On the last half, he used the back-stair system of ringing his boxes from midnight until morning. As he always made all of his rings on time, what was the difference?

The word went around the prison that Mr. King was one of the swellest and most understanding guards in the place, a prince, and the convicts began to treat him like one, which, naturally, swelled his ego.

A convict suggested that he need not carry that torch all the way around either, if he did not feel like it, unless someone complained and called Light. But word passed along the galleries that no one had better call Light.

"God damn it. He is willing to give us a break, so don't none of you idiots go spoiling it. If you want a light oftener than every hour, get a lighter or borrow one from someone near you."

Considerate guards are never too plentiful, and back in those days, any convict who did anything to put a good guard in the middle was apt to do a lot of hard time, for he surely would not be very popular with his fellows. So, whenever Mr. King was around, everybody was on their good behavior.

Of course, the officials noticed that and they said:

"This King is a good man. He understands convicts. He keeps down trouble." And Mr. King was always given the best work assignments. Cell houses when he was on nights; the main hall when he was on days.

Mr. King did not understand that. He thought that it was his forceful personality which kept the convicts in line. He would bark at them, and they would smile and do whatever he told them to. He might even threaten to knock their brains out, but they would still smile at him, for they knew he could not mean it, and he could not understand why other guards were always having trouble. They must be weak and soft. The way to keep convicts in line was to let them know who was boss. And Mr. King continued to accept the favors the convicts showered upon him, and he came to look upon them as his due, without ever guessing why.

Now all that hard talk on Mr. King's part was pure wind, whistling in the dark, for within his heart, Mr. King was an abject physical coward and he feared and despised all convicts, but because he was big and impressive looking, no one ever suspected his inner feelings.

Like many a fond parent who has failed to accomplish his ambition in life, Mr. King cherished rosy dreams of seeing them accomplished through his children. He began their training in music before they were out of the cradle. And being at heart a martinet, he drove them with all the rigor that he lacked the courage to apply to his convict wards. They had to study their music early and late. They had to grow up to be great singers.

He produced five very beautiful and very talented and very well trained daughters, but they probably all grew up to hate music, and several of them grew up to hate Mr. King, and they ran away and got married just as soon as they were big enough to do so. All of which made Mr. King very bitter.

But during this training process, Mr. King had a bright idea. It would be good training for his girls if he could get permission to bring them to the prison and have them sing for the convicts. The amusement-starved men would not be a critical audience, and the thunderous applause of such a large mass of men would give the girls confidence. So Mr. King went to McCloughry and obtained permission to have the two oldest of his daughters sing to the men each Christmas and Easter Morning.

Thus began an institution that lasted for more than twenty years.

Old Joe had thought it would be best to have the girls sing at a special holiday Chapel service, but Mr. King was too wise for that. He was not going to have the girls sing against the notoriously bad acoustic of that Chapel and over that wooden floor. The dining room was a much better auditorium.

So Christmas morning, just as the convicts were finishing their breakfast, the two little girls stepped out on the little balcony above the Captain's dais and broke into Silent Night, without any musical accompaniment.

They were only about six and nine at the time; the smallest girl's head just could be seen over the balcony railing; their thin, little voices were almost lost in that vast space, but never did an entertainer have a more appreciative or attentive audience. That big room became almost as quiet as the grave, and those thin little voices floated to its farthest corners. Thanks to papa's training, the girls really could sing, and when the song ended, the applause was a mighty roar that shook the steel rafters until the girls began another song.

The little girls sang encore after encore for almost an hour, and the Captain had to use his gavel to finally stop the applause.

That is the way it began, and for twenty years, each Christmas and each Easter Sunday morning the King girls sang for the convicts. As the older girls grew up and ran away from home to get married, younger girls not born at the time of that first recital, took their places.

And to all the convicts, particularly those who had been present that first Christmas morning, Mr. King was the grandest guy in the world.

After twenty years, Mr. King was old and broken with disappointment, and he could no longer walk even one side of those big cell houses. He was nearing retirement age, so they put him on the last half, over in Isolation, where he would not have anything to do but rest his feet, for the magneto boxes had long since been abandoned.

And every night Mr. King, having no one else to talk to, used to stop at the Writer's door and talk. He had reached that point in life where he had to unburden himself of his disappointments.

There was only one of the girls left, and she was almost eighteen years old, and soon she would be running away like the rest of them. He had slaved, he had risked his life a thousand times, to give them a good start in life, and they had thrown it away and hated him in the bargain.

The Writer began to ask polite questions in a sympathetic manner. How had Mr. King trained his daughters?

With the rod, of course. When other little girls had been out playing with dolls or with little boys, his had been studying their music. He would whale the hide off of them before he would stand for any such foolishness.

The Writer was profoundly shocked. He could not believe his ears. How could a man who was so understanding in his dealings with convicts be so stupid in the up bringing of his own daughters? The Writer questioned Mr. King concerning his understanding and consideration of convicts, and again he was profoundly shocked, for he could find not the slightest trace of the broadmindedness that had always been attributed to the man. Then, one night about one o'clock, he discovered that Mr. Board, the man on the evening watch, had left his door unlocked. He pulled it open and said: "Mr. King!" in a loud whisper.

Mr. King had been coming down the hall and was almost in front of the Writer's door. He almost jumped out of his skin. He threw up his arms as if to defend himself, but his whole body was shaking and his legs were starting to crumple under him.

"Take it easy, Mr. King! Take it easy!" the Writer said, smiling as he grabbed the old man to keep him from falling. "I did not mean to startle you. I just wanted to tell you about this door."

"You! You weren't going to kill me?"

"Hell! Don't make me laugh. Why should I want to hurt you?"

"I don't know. I thought you hated me and was going to jump me. All the rest of the inmates hate me."

"Hate you! Jump you! Man, don't you know that not a convict in this prison hates you? Why, I or any other old-timer in the joint would jump anyone who even looked like he wanted to jump you. For twenty years you have always been one of the best-liked guards in the institution."

"Are....Are you sure! You wouldn't fool me?"

"Why in the hell do you think everyone treated you like a prince?"

"I thought they were afraid of me."

"Hell! No! They appreciated the way you treated them. The also appreciated you bringing the girls up to give them a little amusement, but mostly the fact that you had gumption and decency enough to turn your back on their romancing and give them a chance to have a little fun."

"But I didn't! If I'd caught anyone, I'd have written him up."

"Don't you remember how you used to walk the galleries in D-Cell house one side at a time and never double back in order to give the guys a break?

"Why! Why! I never even thought of such a thing. I used to do that because my feet hurt. I brought the girls up just to give them a little practice, and once I had started, I couldn't stop it."

"Well, I'll be damned! We all thought you were doing those things for us, and there is not an old-timer in this joint who would believe anything else. Every one of them would walk through fire for you. About the door, I just wanted to tell you not to say anything, or you will get both yourself and Board in trouble. Just wait until five o'clock, and when the Captain leaves, after bringing the keys over, come down and lock it before the day man comes on."

"You won't say anything?"

"Hell, no! Why do you think I told you?"

"But what if the Captain should shake the doors? Sometimes he does."

"Don't worry! This one will have a hard wood wedge under it. He can shake until he is blue in the face."

But after that the Writer and Mr. King really became friends, and they often laughed about the double misunderstanding that had worked out so amazingly well.

One night about six months later, as Mr. King sat down to take off his shoes, he suffered a stroke and was forced to retire.

It was about a year before the Writer saw him again, but by that time, he had improved sufficiently to walk with two canes, and every time he came up to the prison, he used to come over and see the Writer and his birds.

The last time he came over he brought his youngest daughter with him. She was a beautiful girl with a beautifully trained speaking voice. She had sung for the boys many times, but the Writer had never had the pleasure of hearing her, for she had been born about the time he had gone to Isolation. She had to do most of the talking, because Mr. King was no longer able to speak or hear very well. It appeared that she too, had disappointed her father, by trading her prospects of a singing career for a husband.

"I just had to bring him up to see you and your birds. I have heard Papa speak of you so often, that ever since I was a little girl, I feel as if I have known you all my life."

"It is the same way with me. I have never known one of you girls from the other, but the King girls have always been a bright spot in my life. I hope that you have made the happiest choice and that nothing but good fortune dogs your footsteps."

"Oh! I am sure of it. He is wonderful," she said blushing.

The brand new husband, at least a foot taller than his wife, appeared to be a fine young man worth a dozen singing careers, and the Writer certainly hopes it worked out that way, for he has always had a soft spot in his heart for the King family, even if it was based upon a misunderstanding of the facts.

A few weeks after that visit, which was in the middle Thirties, Mr. King did of apoplexy.

The Drilling

There was nothing in the way of fresh-air recreation in the old days, as has been previously indicated, but every work day during good weather, every man in the prison whose work did not take him into the open air a lot, had to drill for thirty minutes. This applied to all the office workers; the laundry; the kitchen and dining room; the stone shop; the tailor and shoe shop.

With hands at their sides and eyes to the front, the men marched four abreast at a good stiff military marching pace set by the guard who was usually an ex-drill sergeant out of the army. He marched at the head of the line, carried his cane like a saber, and he really put the boys through their paces. No slouchiness, slovenliness or being out of step was tolerated. The only way that any man employed where marching was mandatory could escape it was by being excused by the Doctor.

Most of the men hated this drilling, but it was a good thing for them and for the institution in more ways than one.

The soldier guards, like drill sergeants in general, usually preferred to enforce discipline by the sound of their voices rather than with their canes or pencils, and they would usually prefer the cane to the pencil. A man who was out of step or talking while marching, might receive a gentle thrust in the ribs the first time. The next time it might be a little harder. Also, there was no other method known that more effectively established the guard's authority and control over his men than marching them. That is why the drill sergeant has always been the backbone for every fighting army from the dawn of history until the present day.

For the men, it enabled them to get the kinks out of their bodies, some air into their lungs, and some sunshine on their skin. In good weather, most men marched without caps, with their sleeves rolled up, and for men who had no other opportunity for fresh air and sunshine, this was essential to good health. For the man who was going to have to live under strict discipline, there was no less painful method of establishing the habits of discipline than by military drilling. The Writer is convinced that the elimination of military marching from modern Federal penal institutions, particularly the receiving institution, has been a serious mistake.

Trusties

It has been stated that McCloughry had no use for stoolpigeons, and that is true. Having pencil and paper without permission was a serious offense. Using it to write love notes to other convicts was an offense, but using it to write snitch notes to officials was even more serious.

McCloughry was the only official to whom a convict could send any kind of a note, and the only way the convict could do that was by calling his guard and saying, "I wish to make a private complaint."

The guard would give him paper, pencil, and envelope, and he could write and seal his complaint and it would be on McCloughry's desk the next morning. But if he had written a snitch note about some other prisoner instead of a complaint, he was sure to be in the hole before noon. If he wanted to complain about some other convict's conduct toward him, the man to complain to was the guard who had power to take both of them at once before the Deputy Warden.

This does not mean that McCloughry did not obtain information from convicts, for he sometimes did, but all other convicts were forewarned of this a long time in advance, and there were only two kinds of information that he wanted: authentic information concerning plans to escape and concerning contraband coming into the institution. The men he wanted this information from, were his trusties.

Red Number Men

The numbers on the clothing of the ordinary convict were stamped on with red paint. All men celling in the cell houses under McCloughry were Red Number Men.

All Red Number Men wore gray clothing. They were not allowed to leave their place of work without a pass and were not supposed to approach within less than ten feet of a guard without his special permission. Red Number Men doing special work might be able to get a pass to any part of the institution without question, but any time a Red Number Man was stopped on the yard, he had to show his pass. He had not pledged that he wouldn't do anything he could get away with. The guards expected him to test the limits and were there to watch him.

Yellow Number Men

Trusties were men who were trusted only inside of the wall. They wore blue clothing with bright yellow numbers stamped on them and a yellow star stamped on the left breast. The Red Number Men used to say that McCloughry at least had the decency to put stars on his stoolpigeons, so you always knew who they were.

All Yellow Number Men had to sleep in the dormitories, and there were a large number of jobs in the prison that could be held only by Yellow Number Men, such as runners, clerks in certain offices, and other jobs involving considerable trust. These men were trusted to go any place they pleased or had business without a pass at any time between seven o'clock in the morning and five o'clock at night. They were not allowed on the yard after the five o'clock count.

McCloughry was a great believer in the power of the solemn oath, and before any man could be made an inside trusty, he had to put up his right hand and swear that:

He would not attempt to escape from the parole room in which he was placed;

He would not carry any contraband article from one part of the prison to another for any other inmate;

Should he learn of any plot to escape or to harm any officer, he would inform the proper authorities;

In the event of a riot or fight between any convicts and officers, he would always go to the officer's assistance.

It will be noted that this man was not pledged to snitch on any other prisoner concerning ordinary infractions of the rules, though some of them would do that to get in good with the guards they worked for.

The ceremony of swearing in a trusty under McCloughry was as solemn and formal as swearing in a justice to the Supreme Court of the United States or a Grand Dragon of the Ku Klux Klan.

The Captain and two or three guards would be present, standing at attention. The Chief Clerk, who was a Notary Public, and the Chaplain would be standing at attention on either side of the chair of the Deputy or Warden, which ever was officiating.

The prisoner would be required to stand at attention while he was questioned at length; then the oath was read to him in a very solemn tone of voice, and he was required to hold up his right hand while he repeated it. Then he was required to sign the written oath, and the Chief Clerk affixed his seal.

Then everyone relaxed, shook hands with the prisoner and congratulated him on his new status. Call all of this hog wash if you like, but it worked. Very few of McCloughry's trusties ever let him down.

White Number Men

In addition to the pledges required of a Yellow Number Man, the White Number Man was required to swear that he would not run off and that he would not bring any contraband article into the prison.

White Number Men wore blue clothes with white numbers and a white star over their hearts.

They held jobs that required them to go outside of the walls. They were permitted to go anywhere they pleased or had business inside of the walls at any hour of the day or night without a guard, and they were permitted to go out through the main gate and anywhere on the reservation during working hours without question. They were never searched excepting upon special order, and the only offenses for which they were subject to go to the hole were those they had sworn that they would not commit. For all other offenses the most serious punishment to which they were subject was reduction to Red Numbers.

Parole Rooms

At the time the Writer went to Leavenworth there were four of these dormitories: No. 1 was located on the top floor of the Isolation building; No. 2 was located on the second floor of the Administration Building; E was located in the basement under C-cell house; and F was located in the basement under D-cell house.

No. 1 Parole Room occupied the entire top floor of the Isolation Building.[98] There were fourteen large cells similar to those on the lower floor, and four large rooms over the Deputy Warden's offices and the dungeons. There were both barred and wooden doors on the cells, the same as on the floor below, but these were never locked. There were only wooden doors on the rooms, which had formerly been used as the offices of the Warden, Chief Clerk, and Superintendent of Construction.

The cells were separated from the front part of the building by a steel grill which cut across the corridor and in which there was a steel door, but this door, like those to the cells, was never locked. Each of the cells had one, and each of the rooms had several windows four-feet wide and ten-feet long, which came down to within eighteen inches of the floor, and because of the thickness of the wall, the ledges of these windows were wide enough to sit or recline upon.

There was enough floor space to accommodate a hundred and fifty men without over-crowding, but under McCloughry there were never more than twenty-five to forty men in this dormitory. These men were always the best educated and most cultured men in the prison, and they held the top positions of trust within the institution. These positions included the Warden's Secretary and Clerk, the Deputy Warden's Secretary and two clerks, the Doctor's secretary and chief technician, and other key men around the prison. This was the choice spot in the institution, and it was sometimes referred to as the Banker's Club because it did contain a high proportion of bankers, although just being a banker could not get a man in.

He had to be a White Number Man holding a top job, which meant that he had to be serving at least five years or more. No short-timer could work up to one of those jobs

---

98   See Diagram, Part I – Chapter VIII

in a few weeks. He had to have a perfect or near perfect prison record coupled with outstanding technical or administrative ability; and he had to be personally acceptable to the men who were already there.

These men were all on their honor. To all intents and purposes, within their own quarters they governed themselves. They were looked on as stoolpigeons by the Red Number Men, but in a sense, this was not true. They were knowingly pledged to turn over to the officials only specific types of information, and so far as the Writer knows, there were very few incidents of them snitching on each other. Any man who was even suspected of discussing what he learned or saw in the dormitory was told that he could no longer stay there and must ask for a move.

These men were technically under the guard in Isolation, who could go up there any time he pleased by way of the inside stairs,[99] but such was their influence that no guard who bothered them could remain in Isolation.

The Warden's and Deputy's Secretaries and Clerks were the only men in the prison on a special diet. They ate at a special table in the back of the dining room and received milk with all of their meals, but outside of that, they ate the same food and observed the same strict dining room regulations as anyone else. When they worked overtime, which they often did, they were entitled to a special meal at night, but that order, as previously explained, applied to anyone who worked overtime.

The only other concessions allowed these men were those of playing hand ball back of the Laundry up until seven o'clock at night – this only applied to those whose work was such that they could not be spared to march at the time the other office workers marched – and they could take walks around the prison reservation on Sunday afternoons, weather permitting.

They were permitted to sit on benches on the Warden's Lawn, lie on the grass, or go down to the little store at the car-stop. They were not supposed to have money, but as most of these men had jobs where they frequently did favors for both guards and visitors, they often received money tips. When these amounted up to more than five or ten dollars, they were supposed to take the money to the Chief Clerk's Office and have it put to their account. But so long as they were not definitely accused of violating their pledge by bringing contraband into the prison, McCloughry did not object to them buying themselves occasional treats. He did not consider these privileges a violation of his pledge to treat all prisoners alike, nor was it, for these men had earned their privileges by honest service and good conduct – something every man who entered the prison had an opportunity of doing.

No. 2 Parole Room, as already explained, occupied the southern half of the second floor of the Administration Building, which had been divided by a solid brick wall from the northern half which contained offices. The room was approximately fifty feet wide and seventy feet long and was separated by an iron door from the second-floor stairway landing. This landing was on the level with and continuous with the gun galleries in C- and D-cell houses.

On one side of the door at the front of the room was a lavatory containing several washbasins; the toilets were separated from the rest of the room by a seven foot high marble screen. A bathtub was on the other side of the door.

99   Diagram, Part I – Chapter VIII

The gun guard had to pass the front door every thirty minutes, so these men were under considerably more surveillance than the men in No. 1, and they did not have influence enough to remove a guard that they did not like. The gun guards would usually report any

rule infraction they saw, and there were occasional reports out of this room for smoking cigarettes and gambling.

There were both White Number and Yellow Number Men in No. 2, and a few of the White Number Men earned the privilege of going outside of the walls on Sunday afternoon.

Like the men in No. 1, they enforced their own order. They had no power to say who was put in their room, but if any man made himself obnoxious, he was told to move. If he refused, he might be taken back behind the toilet screen and forced to fight, while other men watched for the gun guard. This room usually had about a hundred men in it, but it could hold a hundred and fifty in a pinch.

E- and F- Parole Rooms were of the lowest grade, and the men in them were subject to more surveillance than those in the other two. They were located, as previously explained, in the basements of the cell houses. Each of these basements contained forty-two cells, the same as the blocks above, but these cells had originally been intended for use as dungeons, and they were not equipped with plumbing or electric lights. These basements were about nine feet below the level of the ground, and they afforded rather dark and dreary quarters. The bunks were arranged two-high and about twenty-inches apart the full length of both walls. Most of the dark, dungeon cells also had bunks in them. These men were allowed to have small tables which they placed at the heads of their bunks, and there were several large tables at the end of the cell house at which men could write letters and play games.

Each one of these rooms normally held about one-hundred-and-seventy men, and in a pinch they could hold two hundred. But these men enjoyed much less floor space per man than did those in No. 2.

The bulk of the men in these two rooms had yellow numbers. They were the runners, orderlies, et cetera, but there were a few White Number Men, mostly colored, who preferred to cell down there because of the predominance of members of their own race. These rooms also contained a large number of Red Number Men, and any Red Number Man who had six months good record could get down there on trial, if he wished – in those days, any Red Number Man with a reasonably good record was subject to being made a trusty, providing he could take the oath.

As a matter of security, these rooms were absolutely safe, and there never was an escape or an attempt to escape from either one of them. The large number of men pledged to snitch of any such action, and the general and mixed nature of the groups made anything of that kind impossible. In fact the Writer knows of only two cases of men escaping from outside the wall. One was a White Number Man, and the other was a Yellow Number Man.

Being below the ground level, these rooms received daylight only through rows of windows that were on the ground level outside, and the yard guard patrolled these windows every half-hour. These guards could see into the lightened basement at night, while the men inside could not see them, since the yard lights were not as bright as the lights inside the building. Consequently, these men never knew when they were being watched.

Of course, there were plenty of places that were outside of the guard's possible line of vision, so these men could in some respects do just about anything they wanted to. But there were rather frequent reports out of these rooms for fighting and gambling and for creating a disturbance, for the same rules applied in the parole rooms as anywhere

else. A lot of the colored boys liked to shoot craps, and they would sometimes let their enthusiasm run away with them.

It was almost impossible for the yard guard[100] to see the numbers on the men's clothing through these windows, so he could not write a report. He would bring to the attention of the Night Captain anything he saw that was out of the way; then the Night Captain would investigate and try to catch the offenders in the act.

It should be noted here that McCloughry's system did not exempt any trusty from any part of the rigid discipline. All men were required to observe the same rules. The difference with the trusty was that in respect to some things, he was on his honor, and no one watched him. In respect to others, he was allowed to live under conditions where the chance of him being caught violating almost any rule throughout sixteen hours of every day was practically nil. If caught however, he was subject to be reported, the same as anyone else.

The greater his trust, the greater the amount of secure privacy he was permitted to enjoy.

This gives us a fairly complete picture of general conditions at Leavenworth under Warden McCloughry.

---

100   The night yard guards were two in number and were assigned to the East and West yard, respectively; it was their duty to inspect all windows of all buildings containing men every half hour. There were magnate boxes which forced them to make their rounds regularly. These men were armed with pistols. There was one other guard armed with a pistol who patrolled around the wall outside of the prison once every hour. The gun gallery guard was armed with a repeating shotgun, and he patrolled the gun galleries in both cell houses and in front of No. 2. Parole Room every half hour. The only other armed man on duty at night was the man in the armory. There were no guards in the towers at night until April, 1920. The story of that change will be told in another place (Part II – Chapter XIX)

PART I – CHAPTER XI

McNiel Island

Sometime between the early settlement of the Puget Sound area in 1850, and the admission of Washington to the Union as a State in 1889, a Federal Jail was built upon McNiel Island, located about halfway between Tacoma and Olympia, in the then Territory of Washington. This jail fell under the authority and jurisdiction of the United States Marshal for the Western District of Washington.

The exact date of the building of this jail is unknown to the Writer, but it must have been between the years 1875 and 1880, since trees planted shortly after the jail was opened and still standing at the time the Writer went there in 1909, appeared to be between thirty and thirty-five years old. This institution was operated as a jail for the confinement of persons convicted of crimes against the United States up until the year 1908.

In the year 1907, a Mr. LaDow, first name forgotten, then Superintendent of Federal Prisons, was ordered to make a complete study of all institutions in which Federal prisoners were confined, particularly the penitentiary at Fort Smith, Arkansas and the prison on McNiel Island, and to make recommendations as to whether they should be abandoned, or improved and enlarged.

Mr. LaDow, who had not previously visited Puget Sound, was very favorably impressed with what he saw. He recommended that Fort Smith Penitentiary be abandoned and the men confined there be sent to Leavenworth. He recommended that McNiel Island be retained, given the status of a penitentiary, and placed under the jurisdiction of the Attorney General. He further recommended that the Government take steps to acquire title to the whole Island and build there an institution large enough to accommodate the entire Federal Prison population of the United States.

Mr. LaDow argued that the spot was ideal for that purpose for the following reasons. 1) The danger of escape was practically nil. 2) Only a very small guard-force would be required. 3) The mild and healthful climate and beautiful surroundings would be a benefit to the men who worked there as well as to the inmates. 4) The large amount of fertile land would furnish healthful employment for many inmates and make the institution almost self-sustaining.

Had Mr. LaDow's recommendations, which were really the suggestions of the United States Marshal, been carried out in their entirety, the project would undoubtedly have proven to be one of the greatest advances ever made in Federal Penology. They were eventually carried out, many years later, under the Federal Prison Bureau, but in the intervening years much of the original idea had been lost, and results have fallen far short of what might have been attained twenty-five years earlier.

During that time, the institution consisted of one old, dungeon-type cell house, constructed of brick and sandstone, and containing one small cell block made of brick. The block was seven cells long and three tiers high, and contained forty cells and two dungeons for punishment, an Administration Building adjoining the end of the cell house; a recently built hospital, and a few outbuildings. There was a small steam boiler in the basement of the Administration Building, which supplied heat to the rooms, plus one small heating coil in the cell house, and the driers in the laundry. There was no power plant, and the amount of heat supplied to the cell house was negligible, since the coil was of one-inch pipe and not over sixteen-feet long.

A carbide-acetylene generator supplied gas to the Administration Building and to one small open burner at each end of the cell house. The only outside lights were supplied by lanterns set on poles.[101]

The dungeon-like cellblock was made of brick set in ordinary lime mortar and for this reason, the tops of the doors and the ceiling of the cells were steeply arched. The cells were six-and-one-half by ten feet,[102] and the lattice doors were made of one-and-a-half inch strips of steel strap riveted together in such a manner as to leave four-inch-square openings between the strips.

Probably the best picture of this prison can be given through the eyes of the Writer as it appeared to him the first time he saw it.

Arrival

He had been taken from the steamship Jefferson at Bellingham Washington at two o'clock in the morning on September 1, 1909, and put on a train for Seattle. As there was no chance of getting anything to eat at that hour, the Marshal promised to get breakfast in Seattle, and bought some peanuts from the new butcher on the train.

In Seattle he learned that he had just five minutes to catch the train for Tacoma.

In Tacoma he hustled the Writer onto a streetcar and said, "If we make connections, we will be at the Island within an hour. If we don't, there is a nice lunchroom at the car stop, and we will eat there."

He just missed the connection, but the lunchroom was closed, and the only things he could buy were some oranges and popcorn.

There had been a long, tiresome, hour's wait at the car stop, and the guard, who had not been to the Island for more than a year, bought the Writer half a dozen bags of Bull Durham and half a dozen books of cigarette papers and assured him that he would be allowed to take them in.

---

101   See Diagram No. 1, McNiel Island, for general layout of the prison yard. The dotted lines indicate construction which began in 1908 and was completed in 1911.
102   See Diagram No. 2, McNiel Island, which is a scale drawing of the floor plan of the cell house and Administration Building.

Another hour had been spent on the slow, bumpy car to Steilacoom.

There, the Writer had been rushed onto a launch. The Marshal said, "Don't worry! We will be there in a few moments. I'll see that you get a good dinner. They really feed good there. The guards and Warden eat the same food as the inmates, so you know, they just have to feed good."

The Writer accepted that reasoning with reservations, but said nothing. A headland was rising up out of the mist, and haze hung over the water.

First Appearance

"Is that it?"

"Yes! We will be there in a few minutes."

The Writer took a long look at the place that was to be his future home, possibly for twelve long years.

Sitting on a high bluff, at least forty feet above the water, in a notch cut out of an enormous glacier moraine[103] was a neat brick and sandstone building. On the west side of the building, there was a row of old cherry trees set amidst flower beds, and beyond the trees the hillside was neatly terraced and covered with white-clover lawn. The neatly-trimmed lawn in front of the building was cut by flower-bordered paths, each carefully marked with white-washed stones.

(See Diagrams Pages 282 - 285)

On the east side the building the beauty of the picture was marred by a wall of earth that rose, ledge upon ledge to a height of seventy to ninety feet. Behind the buildings the orchard and timber-covered hills faded away in the distance. Seen from the water, as the Writer was seeing it for the first time, the prison might easily have been mistaken for the home of some beauty-loving millionaire, the landscaping of whose estate was only partially completed, were it not for two facts:

The trim white, red roofed guard towers, and the zebra-like figures that crowded like ants along the face of the excavation.

"What kind of work do they do?" the Writer asked.

"Excavating," the Marshal replied.

"Is that mountain there what they are excavating?"

"Why, yes! Why?"

"Oh nothing," said the Writer looking at his soft white hands that had not touched a shovel

---

103   McNiel Island itself is nothing more than a gigantic moraine. During the Ice Age, the glaciers came down from the Cascade Mountains on one side and the Olympic Mountains on the other, and where they met they piled up huge masses of ice, thousands of feet thick, and that ice scooped out the channel that is Puget Sound. When the ice finally melted, hundreds of large moraines were left behind, which are now islands, and McNiel is one of them.

in years. "But I know that if they put me on that, I am going to die. I should have left you in that crowd in Tacoma. Not a way in the world you could have caught me."

"Don't feel that way. I'll say a good word for you to Halligan, the Warden. He is a fine man and a very fair one. I am sure that it will not be as bad as you think. We will be there shortly."

The launch ran in under a sheer bluff at least a hundred and fifty feet high, a few hundred yards east of the prison, and the keel scraped on the gravel bottom.

"If you step on those rocks," said the owner of the launch, "you may be able to get ashore without getting your feet wet."

"Christ! What a place. Not even a wharf," the Writer thought as he wet one foot scrambling ashore.

The three men: the Writer, the Marshal, and the guard, trudged down the rocky beach for a distance of a hundred and fifty yards or more before they came to a well kept roadway that led up the face of the bluff at an angle of about twenty degrees.

At the top of the hill the road came out on the level of the prison lawn, directly under one of the white, red-roofed guard towers, and directly in front of the prison, then it fell off and ran down the other side of the bluff at an angle of at least forty degrees.

The small rectangular plot of lawn beneath the tower was separated from the prison enclosure by a twelve-foot, barbed wire fence in which was set an iron gate.

"My. Meyers will be out presently," said the man in the tower, who was armed with both a pistol and rifle. "You can leave your guns with me."

"We haven't any on us. We left them in our suitcases, which we checked in the depot in Tacoma."

Mentally, the Writer kicked himself. He had permitted two unarmed men to escort him through a town he knew as well as the palm of his own hand.

A pleasant looking man came around the side of the building and hurried toward the gate. He unlocked it, greeted the guard and Marshal and led the way around the main prison building to the back, along a path, and into a large room filled with men,[104] several of whom were in uniform, though most of them were wearing ordinary working clothes. The best dressed man in the room was an imposing figure with iron-gray, almost-white, hair, a close-cropped mustache, fine features and fine broad shoulders.

"Pardon me," said the pleasant looking man who had met them at the gate. "We are just serving dinner." He stepped into a little room at one side (Deputy's Office), picked up some boxes of knives and forks and passed them through the bars of a window opening into the cell house.

"Oh! You permit them to use knives and forks!" exclaimed the guard.

"Oh, yes! They are picked up and counted after each meal."

---

104   Guard's dining room. See Diagram No. 2.

"How about shaving?"

"They are permitted to shave once per week, but have to turn their razors in when they have finished. Each man, if he has one, uses his own razor."

"Don't you have any trouble? Don't they ever kill each other?"

"We haven't' had any yet. Oh! We have a fist fight once in a while, but nothing more serious than that."

"Well, I'll be _____" said the guard.

Meyers rang a bell and threw a lever near his hand. The guard in the little room directly across from his also threw a similar lever. There came the sound of the banging of many doors, the clatter of many feet, and the murmur of many voices.

The Marshal had approached the nicely-dressed, imposing-looking man and handed him some paper.

The handsome but hard-faced man favored the Writer with a scowl.

"Stand over there," he barked, indicating a spot near the wall, and the Writer noticed that none of the other men, excepting Mr. Meyers, spoke in his presence.

He looked over the papers carefully, took out his fountain pen, signed one of them, and hand it back to the Marshal.

"Have a nice trip," he said in the same closed, clipped, rather harsh voice in which he'd addressed the Writer. "Any trouble?" he nodded toward the Writer.

"Not a bit. This is a pretty good boy. He just got messed up over a woman. It was a sham…."

The imposing looking man had turned his back. He pulled out a chair at the head of the table and sat down. Mr. Meyers sat down at the other end of the table, then the other men pulled out chairs and sat down. He nodded at the guard and Marshal, and they sat down too.

A waiter came in through a door at the end of the room, loaded with heavy dishes which he placed in front of the man with the iron gray hair.

Beginning with Mr. Meyers, each man passed his plate the length of the table, to the man with the iron-gray hair, and he placed on that plate the food he wanted the man to have. He did not ask any man what he desired to eat. He filled his own plate last, and when he had finished, the large serving dishes were empty, and the waiter took them away. Later the waiter served some dessert in small, individual dishes.

Most of the men got up and drifted from the room, and the guard who had helped bring the Writer down from Alaska went with them. The man with the iron-gray hair and the Marshal disappeared behind a stairway leading to the floor above.[105]

_____

105   Warden's Private Office, Diagram, No. 2.

The Writer was very tired and hungry. He had had a long wearisome trip from Alaska; he had had no sleep the night before and no substantial food since the previous evening. His feet hurt; his back ached; he wanted to smoke. Everyone seemed to have forgotten that he existed. Having nothing else to do, he studied his surroundings.

The big door that separated the offices from the cell house might have been borrowed from some medieval castle. It was a double door, six-feet wide and at least sixteen-feet high, and the upper fourth of each half curved inward to form a pointed arch in the typical, twelfth-century manner. They were almost five inches thick, and had evidently been constructed of 4" x 4"s bolted together, then faced, inside and out, with what appeared to be three-eighths or half inch boiler plate. Their faces were studded with hundreds of bolt heads. Each half must have weighted close to half a ton, and the pins in the gigantic wrought-iron hinges upon which they swung were as large as the Writer's wrists. What amazed the Writer more than anything was the fact that cut into the left half of the door was what appeared to be an ordinary wooden house door with a glass window set in it at eye level.

The locking device was equally amazing. It consisted of a medieval padlock, weighing at least ten pounds and taking a key that weighed at least a pound, and an eight by eight timber that turned on a four inch bolt set into the masonry on the right side of the door and lowered into a four-inch forged steel stirrup on the left side. This timber was lifted by a block and tackle to an upright position to permit the opening of the doors. Those doors could not have been forced from within with anything less powerful than dynamite; yet, any man with a pocket knife or a screw driver could have gone through that set-in wooden door in five minutes, but that was not the only strange contradiction to be found in this little prison.

After what seemed ages, the Marshal and guard again appeared, shook hands with the Writer, wished him luck and made him promise to write to them. A promise that he knew at the time he would not keep. They belonged to a phase of his life that had definitely ended.

The prison guards again crowded into the room.

Mr. Meyers picked up an iron rod and struck a big triangle, made from a one-inch bar of octagon high carbon tool steel, several times. Again he threw the lever on his side of the building while a guard threw the one on the other side. Again there came the sound of slamming steel doors. The levers were thrown again, and there came the sound of the clatter of many feet.

Mr. Meyers opened a little steel wicket and shouted:

"Excavating gang."

He struck the triangle once.

"Car crew Number one!"

He worked a small lever. He lifted the timber to its upright position by means of the block and tackle, unlocked the enormous padlock, and a guard swung the left half of the big door open.

Eight stripe-clad men with their hats in their hands filed out of the door, across the room to the porch and disappeared from sight.

The big door was closed, and the big lock hung in the staple but it wasn't locked.

Mr. Meyers struck the triangle twice.

"Car crew Number two!" he cried.

Eight more men filed through the dining room, and were checked off on a list. Occasionally, individual names were called.

Finally, a whole string of individual names were called, and about a dozen men filed out. About half of these men were dressed in neat gray uniforms. The other half wore stripes. They did not cross the office in such long strides. They strolled down the porch in a leisurely manner, talking, joking and laughing. Some of them with their arms hooked together.

"Frank," called Mr. Meyers, and a Japanese man who had been talking in his own language with another member of that nationality, turned and started back.

"I'll be out presently. Tell so and so to get his camera and ask Doctor _____ to come down."

"Yes, Mr. Meyers! Will do."

"Have you any clothing?"

"No, Mr. Meyers. Old stuff. No fit. I make tomorrow or next day."

"All right, Frank."

For another half hour Mr. Meyers puttered around his office, checking over papers, calling out an individual prisoner occasionally, giving him some instructions and then returning to his papers.

Finally, he got up from his desk, turned toward the Writer, smiled and said pleasantly, "Come on! Did you have a hard trip?" He led the way down a narrow board walk past a number of low, dilapidated buildings[106] toward a new building that the Writer was to learn later was the hospital, on the lower floor of which was the prison tailor shop.

"Pretty tiresome. We were five days getting here."

"A hot bath will do you good. The Marshal said something about you having had no breakfast or dinner, but it is too late to get you anything now. You will have to wait until supper time."

"What I need more than anything else is a smoke."

"If you have anything to smoke, go on and smoke. There has been nothing to prevent you from smoking."

"I did not know about your rules."

---

106   See Diagram No. 1.

"You don't come under them until you are dressed in. You should have asked me."

The Writer took a long drag from his cigarette.

"You had better make the most of those while you can. They are not permitted here, and I'll have to take them from you when I dress you in. They are prohibited by State Law, you know."

Dressing In

The Writer was led to the back, north side, of the hospital building, where a boy barely older than himself and dressed in stripes had tacked a sheet to the brick wall, placed a campstool in front of it, and set up a camera. The Writer was told to sit down before the camera, and Mr. Meyers pinned a strip of cardboard across his chest. He was then told to turn around for a side view, and Mr. Meyers shifted the cardboard to his shoulder. He was photographed in both positions, with his hat on and with it off.

"Stroud! Is that the way you pronounce your name?"

"Yes!"

Mr. Meyers turned the strip of cardboard over so the Writer could see the number stamped upon it – 1853.

"We always call a man by his name here. It is less degrading than using his number, but all of your clothing and property will be marked with your number, so you should remember it."

Mr. Meyers led the way into a large room on the ground floor of the hospital building which was obviously a tailor shop. There was a long table before the south windows, holding stacks of gray and striped clothing and several big bolts of striped cloth. Two Japs worked at machines, and the obsequious Frank came forward with a stool in one hand, a pair of clippers in the other, and a barber cloth over his arm.

"Sit here, please. I cut hair," he said.

"You may wear your hair any way you wish as soon as it grows out," explained Mr. Meyers, "but we clip the heads of all new men as a precaution against lice and to reveal scars for the Beitillon record."

The Jap brought his face close to the Writer's ear.

"You got money, tobacco, cigarette paper, opium, slip me. I save for you. No do, they take."

The Writer did not know whether or not he could trust the Jap, but thought that he had just as well take a chance, so he slipped him all but the broken bag of Bull Durham, six books of papers and about two dollars in small change. He thought it wisest not to slip the Jap a ten-dollar gold piece he had on him and the broken bag of tobacco and book of papers that Mr. Meyers had seen.

As soon as the Writer's head had been clipped, Frank stepped forward with a tape and took the Writer's measurements.

"Take everything out of your pockets," said Mr. Meyers, "the strip!"

Frank was drawing water in a bath tub located in a little alcove off the tailor shop. A strange, sour-faced, young man, dressed in civilian clothing, who wore his hat on the side of his head and talked out of the corner of his mouth, stepped into the room and engaged Mr. Meyers in conversation.

The Writer ran his hand over his clipped head.

"It won't take it long to grow out," observed Mr. Meyers.

"One kid here, we call Fuzzy, wears his hair clear down to his shoulders," said the photographer, who was standing in the doorway.

"Fuzzy runs things in the ground. I've been looking for the old man to order him to braid it or to cut it off. He might order you to make Fuzzy a dress, Frank." Meyers said, smiling.

"He order, me do!" said Frank with a broad, toothy grin.

The Writer found undressing under half a dozen pair of strange eyes extremely embarrassing, and the homosexual turn the conversation had taken made it even more so. Did these men, both officials and convicts, think that he was like the undoubtedly-notorious Fuzzy? He had never been sensitive about displaying his body in the seclusion of a room, regardless of the sex of his companion, even when that companion was a person of short acquaintance. But this was different. Then he had been free, and he had felt confident that he could always control any situation in which he found himself.

His face flamed, and he was sure that the Jap noticed it and had no difficulty in reading his thoughts. And that made him blush all the more. He became angry, and his heart began pounding so hard it shook his whole body.

The Jap's glances were frankly admiring, but he was also an understanding person. He snatched up a towel, handed it to the Writer and showed him into the bathroom.

The Writer was cold, and the piece of yellow laundry soap on the side of the tub did not look very inviting. The Jap stepped into the bathroom and handed the Writer a bar of scented toilet soap.

"So sorry about water. No can help." Indicating the soap. "You use, personal from me to you."

"Thanks, Frank!"

"How long you do?"

"Twelve years."

"Long time. Me, twenty years. You from Alaska?"

"Yes! Juneau, for manslaughter."

"Me, too! 1907, Valdez."

"You Frank Hioshedia?"

"Yes! You know?"

"In 1907 I was fishing partner with Joe Tackenuchi in Katella. He told me all about your case. I am glad to know you."

"Me, too. I wash back." The Jap grabbed up a towel, dipped it in the water, and rubbed the Writer's body vigorously.

The Writer could only guess what the others might think, but he knew from the Jap's face that the fact that he had known Tackenuchi made a vast difference.

"Thanks, Frank!"

"Very welcome." The Jap bowed and showed his teeth.

As the Writer stepped out of the bathroom, Mr. Meyers stepped forward and looked his body over for scars, then he said, "All right, Doctor!"

So the young man who looked and acted as if he might be a pimp or a racetrack tout was the Doctor. He stepped forward, poked the Writer's body here and there, examined him for inguinal hernia, noticed that he had a varicocele on the left side and remarked:

"You must have started jacking off pretty young."

The Writer's face flamed; he could feel his heart pounding like a trip hammer. He had spent his childhood with his nose in his father's medical books, and he was convinced that this Doctor was the utmost quack.

The Writer could see that Meyers did not like the remark, either. He turned his back and walked to the door.

"Do you suffer from any serious illnesses or defects?"

"Only my heart, and of course, you recognize that." The Doctor had his fingers on the Writer's pulse.

"It does seem to be beating very fast and hard. What is wrong with it? I did not bring my stethoscope."

"Oh! Nothing much! I have congenital myocardial insufficiency and am subject to attacks of fibrillation and palpitation."
"Fib - - - what? How do you spell it?"

"F-i-b-r-i-l-l-a-t-i-o-n, fibrillation. The failure of the myocardial fibers of the right auricle and ventricle to act in rhythm. The systole is incomplete and the heart starts to run away with itself trying to catch up. Sometimes I fall down and my hand and face turns blue."

The Doctor pulled out his watch. He dropped the wrist and put his hand on the Writer's chest.

"Come here!" he called to Mr. Meyers. "Feel that!"

"His heart does seem to be pounding awfully hard for a man at rest. What is wrong with it?"

"What did you call it?" the Doctor asked.

"Congenital myocardial insufficiency."

"I am going to have to look that up. There must be something on it in the books. His case is just like Mitchel's. I had not been able to figure out what was wrong with him. He has a pulse rate of one-sixteen. Yours is one-twenty-four."

"Mine sometimes goes to one-forty or better."

"I am subject to palpitation myself. Mine was caused from ptomaine poisoning. What caused yours?"

"Mine is congenital."

"How long you had it?"

Mr. Meyers smiled, shook his head, and again returned to the door, where he stood looking out over the water toward Anderson Island.

"Naturally, all my life. When a thing is congenital, you are born with it."

It was the Doctor's turn to blush.

"Think he is able to work?" asked Mr. Meyers from the doorway.

"Don't know! I'll have to look it up. It must be the same condition Mitchel has. He says that he has been that way all his life, too. It must be in the books.

"It is! Look under myocardium!"

"This is the first time I ever heard of it."

I could probably tell you a lot of other things you have never heard of. If I use my head I can probably use you, the Writer thought to himself. I must remember to look up that Mitchel.

Frank handed the Writer a hickory shirt and a ragged, patched, misfit suit of stripes. The pants were much too long for him and would go around him twice.

Frank snipped a piece from each leg and ran up new hems on his machine.

"Now, try!"

"Haven't you a belt or suspenders?" asked Mr. Meyers.

"No! With clothes that fit me, I don't need them."

"I fix." Frank threaded a big needle. He dropped to his knees and took a big tuck over each of the Writer's hips. "I make new clothes to fit this week, he whispered, as his hand slipped behind the Writer and felt of his buttocks.

"Never mind!" the Writer said. "These will be first rate. You know I came down here for killing a man who thought he could play me for a sucker." The Writer had been on his own for more than six years. He had no delusions or aversions concerning such things, but he had no intention of getting off on the wrong foot. What he would do, he did not know, but he would be damn careful about who he did it with.

"No offense, please! It was accident! I make clothes next week."

Mr. Meyers handed the Writer two pairs of cheap, cotton socks.

"Put one pair in your pocket and take care of them. You will have to wash them yourself and turn the old ones in to get more. You may keep your own shoes, if you wish. Your underwear, socks, and handkerchiefs will be washed, ironed, numbered, and returned to you. Your suit and hat will be put in storage against the day of your release."

From the tailor shop, the Writer was returned to the Administration Building and taken to a room which he afterwards learned was the Warden's outer office.

The office was cut into two parts by a boxed-in counter about a foot wide and almost chest high. On one end of the counter was a piece of heavy plate glass about an inch thick and eight inches square. Outside the counter was a desk at which a convict in a gray uniform sat before a typeWriter. Behind the counter was a filing cabinet and a safe. There was another steel filing cabinet against the opposite wall, and in a dark corner between the end of this cabinet and the door was a scale with a measuring rod attached to it.[107]

Introduction To The King

Behind the counter, only visible from the chest up, stood the man with the iron-gray hair. His face was stern, hard, expressionless as a concrete wall, and the deep-set, cool-blue eyes, looking out from beneath very heavy brows that seemed to be puckered in a perpetual frown, were steady and penetrating. There was about the man an air of distinction and authority that told the Writer that he must be the Warden.

If the Writer could have looked into the future and pictured tears rolling from those cold eyes and down that granite face, unheeded, while his own eyes were the ones that were hard and accusing, he might have felt better at that moment.

"Stroud!" said Mr. Meyers, then turned on his heels and vanished.

"Step on those scales!" The barked order and the growl in the voice that gave it reminded the Writer of a vicious Airedale.

For a moment he looked around the room, bewildered. He had just come in out of the bright sunshine and could not see into the dark corner.

"There! Are you blind?" the man growled.

The convict got up from his chair and showed the Writer the scales, weighed and measured him, and making deductions for shoes and clothing, recorded the Writer's height as six-feet, one-inch and his weight stripped as one-hundred-forty-three pounds.

"Any scars on your body?"

---

107   Diagram No. 2.

"No! Only a vaccination on the right arm."

"Say Sir when you speak to me!" the man growled.

"No Sir! Only a vaccination on the right arm, Sir!"

"Why the right arm?"

"I am left handed, Sir."

"Write with your left hand?"

"No, Sir! I can write with either hand, but usually use my right, Sir!"

"Put down ambidextrous!" This was addressed to the convict secretary.

"Step over here! Give me your hand!"

The Writer extended his left hand.

"I said right hand. Don't you know right from left?"

"Not without stopping to think, Sir. With me it makes so little difference."

The big man grabbed the hand roughly.

"Keep your comments to yourself! Just answer my questions," the man snarled. "You will learn to do as you are told here."

He bent the Writer's first finger back hard and pressed it on the piece of glass, then rolled it on a card. The Writer had not realized that this man was so big. He must stand six-feet, three-inches, the Writer thought as he looked up into those hard blue eyes.[108]

"What is your name?"

"Robert Stroud, Sir!"

"Your full name?"

"I was christened Robert Franklin Stroud, Sir."

"Your age?"

"Nineteen, Sir."

"When were you born?"

"January 28, 1890, at Seattle, Sir!"

---

108   Actually, Halligan stood five-feet, nine-inches, but he had the head and shoulders of a much larger man. He made up for his deficiencies in height and slightly protruding abdomen, by hiding the lower part of his body behind that counter and standing on a little bench that lifted him six inches off the floor. All this was a part of his system of making the proper impression on new men.

"Just answer my questions," snapped the man, as if he would like to bite the Writer's head off. "Put down age twenty."

"What is your offense?"

"I pleaded guilty to manslaughter, Sir!"

"Were you guilty or not guilty?"

"I pleaded guilty, Sir."

"Answer my question!" the man barked, pressing down hard on the finger he was then printing. "Were you guilty or not guilty?"

"I blew the man's brains out, and I pleaded guilty to manslaughter, if that is what you want to know, Sir. Manslaughter is a technical charge…"

"Shut up! Put down guilty!"

"Yes, Sir!"

"Ever been convicted of a felony before?"

"No, Sir!"

"Ever arrested before?"

"Yes, Sir! Twice!"

"Where?"

"Once in Seattle for carrying a pistol and once in Katella, Alaska, for buying food stolen from a Company Commissary, Sir!"

"Oh! Running a fence, Eh?"

"No, I was running a restaurant. I did not know the food was stolen, Sir!"

"Convicted?"

"Yes, Sir!"

"Sentence?"

"Ninety days in jail, Sir!"

"Put down ninety days in jail for running a fence and buying stolen food."

"Were you convicted of the pistol charge?"

"No, Sir! I was released."

"Were you guilty?"

"I had the pistol, if that is what you mean. The judge did not think I had committed an offense, so he turned me loose, Sir!"

"Do you drink?"

"Occasionally, Sir!"

"Use narcotics?"

"No, Sir!"

"Tobacco?"

"Yes, Sir!"

"Smoke or chew?"

"Smoke, Sir!"

"How long have you used tobacco?"

"Ten years."

"Impossible!"

"Since I was nine years old, Sir!"

"Parent's permission?"

"Certainly, Sir!"

"Well, you won't use any here. You are too young."

There was much more of the same, but finally the finger printing was completed, and the questioning came to an end.

The man handed the finger print cards to his secretary who reeled off from them what was to the Writer a meaningless jargon about loops and whirls and scars while the man studied each of the Writer's fingers in turn with a magnifying glass.

"One more question. In case of serious sickness or death, who do you wish notified?"

"My mother, Mrs. E. J. Stroud, 414 E. 22 Avenue, Seattle, Washington."

"Cell house!"

Mr. Meyers appeared, led the Writer over to the big door, lifted up the timber with the block and tackle, unlocked the ten-pound lock, and swung the left hand door open just far enough for the Writer to slip through it.[109]

---

109   Compare this "dressing in" process which actually consumed about an hour and a half with that of Leavenworth, which consumed an entire day. The present-day induction process is spread over one month and contains many features that would not have been legally or publicly tolerated in 1909.

PART I – CHAPTER XII

McNiel Island, Continued

Prison

Just how does it feel to be in prison for the first time and to realize that you are completely cut off from everything you have ever known; that you are no longer the master of your own life; that you are at the complete mercy of hostile men whose motives and intentions you're not able to even guess; and that you are apt to spend the best years of your life in a new and strange environment. That realization comes when the new prisoner hears an iron door slammed shut behind him and finds himself alone.

It is in a way like a one-way ticket to Mars or like waking up and finding yourself in a foreign land. It is true that the men he will meet will still speak the English language, but familiar words in their mouths will have strange meanings at which he can only guess – and often, he will guess wrong and be made to feel ridiculous.

For he is surrounded by strange beings who are living under standards of which he has no knowledge and react in the most unexpected manners. He will find his spirits plunged to the very depths of despair, and they will spring back with strange and unreasonable elation at the sight of a friendly smile, the clasp of a hand or at some little, unexpected kindness.

It is not a nice experience or one that a thinking man forgets easily.

Cellhouse

A dead stench, as if from the grave, struck the Writer in the face as he stepped through that door and stumbled down the four or five, steep, narrow, deeply worn, stone steps leading to the floor-level of the cell house. He found himself in a little cage from which he could see no avenue of egress. There was nothing that even looked like a door.

The stench was that of dead, cold air, the old odor of unwashed bodies, and unsanitary night buckets, of the accumulated filth of years.

"To your right," Mr. Meyer's voice came through the wicket.

The Writer turned and discovered that the end of the cage swung inward upon a bar as a hinge. He stepped through the opening.

"Don't forget to close the gate."

The Writer pulled the end back in place. There came to his ears the clank of steel striking steel. Mr. Meyers had thrown a lever which locked the cage from the outside.

So this was prison. The day was warm and sunny outside, but here it was damp and cold, and the Writer shivered in spite of the heavy woolen stripes he was wearing.

He shivered mentally as well as physically as he looked around him. The windows did not appear as if they had been washed since the building had been put up, and the heavy bars had been recently reinforced by riveting two-inch strips of steel across each section, halfway between the spreaders, with the result that they emitted so little light that the whole interior was thrown into deep and perpetual gloom. Only directly in front of the windows was there what would ordinarily be considered enough light to read by, and it was evident that on dark days, reading would be impossible.

Everything was incredibly filthy. The floor had evidently just been mopped, and was still wet, but all that the mopping had accomplished was to spread the dirt over the floor more evenly. All the cracks were filled with it.

There were deep grooves in the concrete floor in front of the cage, worn by the repeated passage of thousands of hobnailed shoes.

All of the doors to the cells were locked by a lever device. A one-half-inch by two-and-one-half-inch steel bar ran in steel brackets above the doors for the full length of each gallery. The traveling bars for all three galleries were riveted to a single upright bar at the end of the cell house, and these were connected to flat rods of similar dimensions which connected with levers located in the Deputy Warden's office and in the guard room on the other side of the building. A similar flat bar was pinned to the lower part of the doorframe of each door and was bolted to the traveling bar in such a manner that when the lever was in one extreme position, these bars were upright and just clear of the edges of the doors. In the other extreme position, these bars lapped over the doors, which swung outward, for a distance of three inches at the top. On the hasp beside each door was an old hog-eye bull lock.

This was one of the crudest of gallery control and dead locking devices, but it was also one of the best; since all of the working parts were in plain sight, there was little chance of sawing them without detection, while some of the more modern devices, enclosed in steel boxes, can almost be beat with a hairpin.

The four-inch openings in the lattice doors, which were not over sixteen inches wide – that is, the doors were no wider than the thickness of the wall at the front of the cells – admitted so little light that it was impossible to distinguish anything beyond the door's opening. These cells were black, evil-smelling caverns which seemed to the Writer to be symbolic of all the misery of the ages – of man's eternal inhumanity to man, and if anyone had told him that the day would ever come when he would feel regret at leaving that old cell house, he would have thought that person mad.

The gloom, the chill, the filth, the rutted floors, the stench of the night buckets, the silence, almost like that of the grave, fell upon the Writer's spirits and reduced them to the lowest point in his experience. The rough woolen stripes chafed his body, particularly his neck, wrists and the inside of his thighs. His legs and ankles ached from cold and from standing up for so long, but there was no place to sit down. The damp floor was impossible. He tried sitting on the iron steps, but the cold of the metal penetrated the thick woolen cloth and sent a chill through his body that forced him to his feet. He tried walking up and down in an effort to restore his circulation and his spirits, but the sound of his own footsteps echoing and re-echoing through the large silent building filled him with a nameless terror. He was frightfully lonely, frightfully miserable. He would have almost been willing to give an arm for a smoke or for someone to talk to.

There was a couple of open-type acetylene gas jets up near the front of the building. There were five toilet bowls and a large wash basin with three taps at the back end of the block, and a big, galvanized iron hopper with a faucet above it, in which, he was to learn later, the night buckets were emptied, but the purpose of which he was not able to fathom at the time.

Wheeled over against the wall on each side of the block were three tables; each was two-feet wide and sixteen feet long, and on top of each table, turned upside down, were two benches about eight-inches wide and sixteen feet long. The Writer would have given anything to have been able to take one of those benches down to sit on, but he did not know whether or not that was permissible. He wondered about the rules. He had been told to read them, but no one had given him a rule book.

He approached the window beyond which he could see Mr. Meyers busy at his desk, and tapped on the glass.

Mr. Meyers made a motion indicating that he should open the window, and he noticed that this window operated from the inside. He lifted the sash.

"What can I do for you?" Mr. Meyers asked.

That gentleman who took my fingerprints said something about rules."

"Over there." Mr. Meyers pointed. "Under the stairs."

The Writer started to turn away.

"Don't forget to close the window," Mr. Meyers admonished.

Under the stairs, framed under glass, and fastened to the soft brick with wood screws was a single sheet of long-form legal paper upon which all of the rules of the prison were printed in six-point type.[110]

At first, the Writer was unable to read them, but gradually his eyes adjusted themselves to the deep gloom.

He learned that he must always address an inmate by his last name; that he must always remove his cap from his head and his pipe from his mouth when addressing any guard or official; that he must address the guard or official as Mister followed by his surname, or use the word Sir. He must obey all orders instantly, without question or argument. If he thought any order seemed unreasonable or unfair, he should take the matter up with the Warden or Deputy Warden at the first opportunity.

Absolutely no talking was permitted during count, after the lights-out bell at eight thirty P.M., or before the rising bell at six-thirty A.M. During meals only such talking was allowed as was essential to the passing of food. No one was allowed to smoke at the table or when passing through the Guard's dining room in going to or from work. No one

---

110   Cf. Rulebook, McNeil Island Prison, 1910.

was allowed to get up from the table during meals without permission of the guard. All inmates were required to stand at the door with their hands on the bars during counts because of the impossibility of seeing back into the cell. Whistling was prohibited in all buildings at all times.

There were rules for this and rules for that. Long before he had read to the end of the list the Writer's head was in a whirl. How in the world would he ever be able to understand and remember all those rules? Since his thirteenth birthday he had been moving in a stratum of society where the only rule was that of survival. He had always considered it his absolute right to do anything he pleased, so long as he injured no one else, and those who had injured him, he had settled with in his own way.

Had he known it, he might have been grateful that he had not been sent to a rule-ridden prison like Leavenworth was at that time. There were very few of the McNiel Island rules that were of a regimental nature, but the Writer resented even those few. He made up his mind that he would never wear a hat, so that he would not have to take it off to a guard, and later he started a fad of going hatless by telling other inmates that caps caused baldness and that he owed his fine head of hair to the fact that he had never worn a hat or put any lotions on his hair.

The most important of all the rules was the last one on the list, for it expressed Halligan's idea concerning stoolpigeons.

It is the duty of each and every inmate to obey these rules at all times. No inmate should concern himself about the conduct of others until he is absolutely certain that his own conduct is above reproach.

Punishments

Reprimand - Loss of all or part of privileges for such time as the Warden may direct; loss of all or part of good conduct allowance; confinement on bread and water, chained to the door during working hours, for such periods as the Warden may specify.

Privileges

During periods of good conduct each inmate shall be allowed to draw one ration of tobacco per week; write two letters per month; write such other special letters as the Warden or Deputy Warden may approve; receive visits from relatives and friends once per month; receive from home or purchase through the prison authorities the following items: shoes, socks, shoe polish, handkerchiefs, underwear, belts, suspenders, toilet soap, shaving soap, shaving cream, talcum powder, face cream, face lotion, tooth brushes, tooth powder, tooth paste, such books as Warden may approve, subscriptions to newspapers and magazines, and such other items as the Warden may from time to time approve.

Tobacco, cigars, cigarettes, cigarette papers, candy, stationary, stamps, and food are prohibited.

Visitors may bring treats of candy, fruit, and pastries in such amounts as can conveniently be consumed during the visit.

The Writer had walked around the block several times, and he was under the impression that he was entirely alone. Then he stepped over by the hopper where the night buckets were dumped to look out one of the back windows[111] and saw an Indian sitting on a campstool reading a book.

"Hello!" said the Writer as pleasantly as he knew how, since he was as glad as a lonely puppy to see another human being.

"Ugh!" the Indian said.

"Have you any idea how long it will be before the gangs come in?"

The Indian looked out the window, studied the shadows for a moment or two before turning back to his book.

"No!" he said.

"Have you anything to smoke?"

"No!" the Indian said.

"Well, it is nice to have met you."

"Ugh!" the Indian said as the Writer turned away – he wondered if the Indian represented a fair sample of the hospitality he would encounter in his new environment.

The Writer knew that he had one good friend and a number of acquaintances in this prison – men he had known in Seattle or Alaska, but he had been able to recognize no one he knew in those lines going out at noon, but that was hardly surprising. He had had only a fleeting glimpse of each man as he filed rapidly through the guard's dining room. It was hard to believe that he could miss his friend, Big Mike, but no one who has not tried to do so has any idea how hard it is to pick out an acquaintance whom you have never seen in stripes from a large group of stripe-clad figures.

Big Mike

As the name suggests, Big Mike was a big Irishman who stood well over six feet and weighed well over two-hundred pounds without an ounce of fat on his hard, well-muscled body.

In his thirty-six years, Big Mike had been and done many things. He had been a sailor on British ships, a miner and fisherman along the Pacific Coast, a gambler and a stick-up man on many occasions. He had served time in Dublin and Reading Goals in Westminster, British Columbia. He had been in Reading at the time Oscar Wilde was there, and more than once he had seen the goalers[112] with lime on their boots.

---

111   The back of the cell block faced the front of the prison, which makes the use of the words front and back rather confusing.
112   See Ballad of Reading Goal

He had literally worn his fingers to the bone picking oakum.[113] The scars had completely obliterated his fingerprints

– and he still had the whip marks on his back from the twenty-five lashes he had receiver as part of his punishment.

Following his release from Westminster, Mike had acquired some money, probably with a gun, and he had gone to Alaska, where people did not ask questions. He went into the saloon and dance hall business, and became an honest and respected citizen. (It must be remembered that at that time fully half of the population of Alaska were either ex-convicts or persons who either wanted to forget or be forgotten. Asking questions was not considered polite. On the other hand, Alaska at that time had the lowest rate of crimes against property of any country in the world, because there was no getaway, for one reason, and because it was populated with men who would reach for a gun before calling a policeman.)

Now it happened that a kid, named Dean, who had been hanging around Mike's place rolled a drunk and was arrested for it, and Mike knew that the boy was due for a long stretch in prison if something was not done and done fast. He also knew that such a thing would give his place a bad name, if he did not do something about it, so he returned the drunk's money out of his own pocket, hired a lawyer for Dean, and tried to get his case squashed. Mike had another reason for not wanting to see the kid go to jail. You see, Mike was a wolf (pederast), something that is not uncommon in any country where there are a hundred men for every woman, and he had been sleeping with Dean.

There was a young Assistant United States Attorney who was anxious to make a reputation for himself. He had Mike called before the Grand Jury and questioned about his activity in Dean's behalf.

Now, Mike was more familiar with British law than with American law, and he simply denied everything, which under British law, he had a right to do under the rule of self-incrimination. He did not know that under American law one had to refuse to answer questions on the ground that they may be self-incriminating.

Mike was convicted of perjury and sentenced to three years. He appealed his case to the Ninth Circuit Court and lost.

The Writer had known of Mike ever since he had first gone to Alaska and had met him a number of times before his arrest. They had been in jail together, and Mike had tried to make him, both before their arrests and in the jail, without success. Having failed, he and the Writer had become good friends, for the Writer had always liked Mike, who had a colorful and interesting personality, and did not think anything amiss about him trying. In that environment, anything else would have been surprising.

After what seemed ages, the Writer heard a large triangle somewhere in the distance struck several times.

The office became a place of activity. Mr. Meyers hoisted the big timber from in front of the door and unlocked his ten-pound lock. The Writer took up a position near the cage, where every man who came in would have to walk past him. He heard Mr. Meyers throw the big levers that unlocked all the doors. There was a clanking of steel upon steel.

---

113   Loose hemp or jute fiber, sometimes treated with tar, creosote, or asphalt, used chiefly for caulking seams in wooden ships and packing pipe joints.

The East half of the big door swung outward and eight or ten men poured into the cage; another clanking of steel upon steel, and they spilled out into the cell house and raced toward their cells, calling and shouting to each other as they went.

Group after group of stripe-clad men spilled into that cage and spread out over the cell house, and with each group the Writer's spirits sank lower and lower. Several times he saw men he thought he knew, but they looked right through him, as if he were not there. He knew exactly how the Ancient Mariner had felt when his shipmates had cursed him with their eyes.

Mike! What had become of Mike? The last thing Mike had said as they had shaken hands in the jail had been, "I hope you don't have to follow me, kid, but if you do, I'll have a cell waiting for you."

"Thanks, Mike! That will be swell. I know I can make you behave. The best of luck to you!"

"Don't be sure about that. It gets pretty lonesome in the *big house*."

"I'll worry about that when I get there, but I'll be mad if you don't have that cell for me, and I don't say I won't change my mind."

"I'll have it. So long!"

"So long, Mike!" the Writer had shouted as the steel door closed between them. Now, he was in the *big house*, but where in the hell was Mike? He was so lonely it hurt, and in all these men milling around him he could not see one friendly face.

Then, in one of the last group to come in, he saw Big Mike standing head and shoulders over the men around him.

"Mike!" the Writer screamed.

"Bob!" The big Irish grin that spread over Mike's face was like a ray of sunshine. The Writer forgot how miserable he had felt. He forgot the men milling around him. He was no longer lonely.

Two long strides brought them together. They were shaking hands, clinging to each other.

"How long did you bring? Christ! I'd hoped you would get off with less than that? What happened to Kate?" The questions tumbled over one another.

"Where are you celly?"

"I don't know. I want to cell with you. Remember your promise!"

"Christ, Kid, I have a cell mate. The place is full. Not an empty bed in the house. You will have to double up with someone, for there is no place to put you."

"If I double up with anyone, it is going to be you. I am not going in with a stranger. If they try to make me, they will be a man short in the morning, for I will throw a towel around his neck and roll him under the bed."

"Christ, Kid! You can't do that here!"

"I can do it anywhere, because the way I feel right now, I don't give a damn!"

A dozen men and boys were now crowding around the Writer, shaking his hand to welcome him. Some of them had known him on the outside; some he had never seen before, but they were all welcoming him. Their strange conduct of a few moments before was easily explained. They had only a limited time to wash up and to get their water for the night, and there were only three faucets for eighty men. Those who did not hurry got left.

A boy pressed something into the Writer's hand.

"Don't look until you get in your cell. Put it in your pocket. It is the best I could do. Don't let the screw see you."

"Gee! Thanks!"

"Get the water, Tom!" Mike shouted at someone. "Come on, Bob! My cell is down here. I'll see the Little King and see if I can get you put in with me."

Mike showed the Writer to the last cell on the lower gallery on the East side of the building.

"Stay here! I will see what I can do!"

"Tell him anything! Tell him we are friends! Tell him you are my uncle! Tell him I will choke anyone else," the Writer shouted after Mike as he rushed away.

In a moment he was back, his big arms bulging with a pile of four brand new big double blankets. He carried a spoon and a tin cup in his hand.

"It's fixed for tonight, Kid, anyway, but I don't know what the King will do. I told the Little King, Mr. Meyers, that I knew you outside and that you are a quiet person who does not make acquaintances easily, and that it was hard enough on you to have to double up with anyone, not to mention a stranger. Here is your spoon and tin cup. You have to keep them yourself and take them to the table with you."

"Thanks, Mike! Christ, but I want a smoke!"

"Didn't they give you a pipe and tobacco?"

"No! I can't smoke a pipe anyway, I never could!"

"I'll see what I can do!" Again Mike rushed away. A moment later there was a stroke on the triangle. The lever on the other side of the building was thrown. All the men were in their cells. Mike came running down the corridor, slammed the door behind him, and the bar was immediately shot.

"That was close! I hope I don't get shot, but don't think I will. O'Conners is in the window. Here! I got these from Mitchel. He gave me half of what he had." Mike handed the Writer six brown papers.

"Gee! Thanks, Mike! Is this Mitchel a kid with a bad heart?"

"He has been trying to convince this quack we have here now that he has a bad heart in order to beat work."

"I must talk to him the first chance I get. I heard the quack talking to Mr. Meyers. I think we can work out something. I had the quack going, and I fed him a line of tripe."

"He don't know beans from Boston. He is a two-hundred-and-fifty-dollar, ninety-day wonder from a St. Louis diploma mill, but he would not excuse a man with a broken leg from work."

"I am going to work on him, anyway. You got any tobacco, Mike?"

"Not much. I will give you half of what I have, but you had better wait until after supper to roll up. There is no rule about cigarettes here, but the papers are contraband. If you get caught, the King will want to know where you got the papers and will punish you for refusing to tell him."

Waiters were wheeling the tables out from the wall, turning down the benches, while others were placing the plates and other dishes. Then they came along dishing out food. Two of them would carry a big pan, while a third loaded the plates. Bread was put on several big platters on each table and there were several syrup pots on each table. Bread was the only food that was not rationed.

A guard came by the cell.

"Stroud," he said.

"Yes, Sir!"

"Your place at the table is the second seat from the far end on the far side of this table right here in front of the cell. That is where you will sit until further orders. Be sure to take your spoon and cup with you." He stepped around the corner and vanished.

There was a blow on the triangle as the levers were shot, and there was a clatter of many feet as the men rushed toward their allotted places as if they were going to a fire. There was no order. There was a guard on the second gallery on each side of the cell house and a gun guard in each front window, but they were just there to enforce the rules and see that each man had his allotted amount of food.

Each man started eating as soon as he was seated. The waiters came along pouring hot black coffee in the tin cups the men held out to them. Half a dozen were reaching for bread at once, and a big, freckled-faced boy sitting beside the Writer stuffed half a dozen thick slices in his pocket and placed four others beside his plate. The Writer took two slices. The platter was empty. The guard gave a signal and a boy with reddish-blond fuzzy hair almost long enough to braid refilled it. That must be the boy the photographer mentioned, the Writer thought, and made a mental note to ask Mike about him.

The supper consisted of hash – there was a big helping on each plate, and to the Writer, who never did like hash, it tasted terrible. He remembered the rule about leaving food on the plate, and wondered how in the world he was going to eat it all. For as hungry as he was, he had no stomach for that. There was a side dish of stewed corn, which the Writer has always thought of as being excellent food for chickens with rocks in their gizzards. Having no rocks in his own gizzard, he has never eaten it. There was also a side dish of fried carrots which were not bad, and there were two big apples beside each plate.

The man across the table passed the Writer a syrup pot, and he handed it to the boy on the end of the table.

The boy looked down the table and saw that he and the Writer were the only ones who had not had syrup. He looked in the pot, dumped half of the syrup over his hash, handed the pot back to the Writer and indicated that the Writer should dump the rest on his hash.

The Writer looked down the long table. Every man on it was eating syrup on his hash, and they were all eating as if they were starving. The Writer had never heard of such a combination, but thought that he might as well try it. It was not half bad, (if you are ever good and hungry, as these men were, try it sometime. Also try syrup on beans, another popular Island dish) but the Writer found that one slice of bread, half of his hash, and one apple was all he could eat.

The freckled face boy pointed to the side dish of stewed corn. The Writer shook his head. The corn vanished in two gulps.

The freckled face boy pointed to the slice of bread beside the Writer's plate and the uneaten hash. The Writer again shook his head. The boy traded plates with the Writer, swiped the edge of the slice of bread across the Writer's plate, picked up most of the hash on the bread, took two bites, made a second swipe with what was left of the bread, took two more bites, and that plate was as clean as if it had been washed.

The boy pointed to the apple. The Writer hesitated, then shook his head. The boy reached over, picked up the apple and put it in his pocket.

The Writer looked down the table. There was not one crumb of food in sight. The guard made a motion with his hand. A moment later there came a stroke on the triangle, and again the scene was one of the wildest confusion, with men rushing madly in every direction. Everything seemed to be done on the run.

The Writer had just reached the cell when Mike came charging in.

"Did you get your apples?"

"I ate one at the table, and left the other one. The boy beside me got it."

A boy in a gray suit, the same boy who had slipped the Writer that package, came rushing up to the cell with an apple in his hand.

"Say, Bob! Here is your apple. Rider is not very bright, but it just dawned on him that you did not know that you were allowed to take your apples to your cell."

"Tell him, thanks! The rule…"

"Damn the rules!" Mike exclaimed, "don't pay any attention to the rules. Watch the other guys and do what they do, and you will be all right."

The guard was coming down the line locking the bull locks, as the waiters were cleaning up the tables. The dishes were stacked and carried away. Each table was hastily wiped with a wet cloth; the benches were thrown up on top of it, and it was rolled back against the wall. Two boys rapidly swept the corridor and another one followed behind them with a dirty mop that he had rinsed in a toilet and which he sloshed rapidly over the floor. By the time the boys were through cleaning up, the guard had all the cells locked, the levers were then released, and he went around and locked the waiters in their cells individually.

Note: The bull-nose, hog-eye, jail lock was the preferred prison lock of the last century. The correct name of this lock is unknown to the Writer, but it obtains its slang name from two of its features: bull-nose, from the shape and hog-eye from the shape of the key hole of a door lock employing the same principle of internal construction, although the key hole of the jail lock was almost rectangular in shape.

Inside of both the jail lock and the door lock was a number of steel washers, some of which were movable and some fixed. The body of the jail lock was made of cast steel and the hasp was made of case-hardened tool steel, which was file and saw proof. Inside of the lock were sixteen or more steel washers one-sixteenth of an inch thick. Part of these washers was fixed, and part of them moved. There had to be a groove in the key for each fixed washer. The movable washers were turned by the studs between the grooves. Each fixed washer had two holes in it which permitted the horns of the hasp to slip through it. Each movable washer had a half moon cut out of each side at right angles to the long axis of the key hole. When the key was inserted and turned ninety degrees in either direction, the half-moon shaped openings were brought to the position of the hasp, and the hasp was released and slipped out, leaving the lock in two pieces. But in this position the key was at a right angle to the keyhole and the holes in the fixed washer, and could not be withdrawn until the hasp was replaced and the key turned ninety more degrees, which locked the hasp in place. Sixteen washers could be arranged in more than one-thousand-billion combinations.

These locks could be picked with a toothpick by moving each movable washer individually, but it was a slow and tedious process, and once started, it had to be carried to completion to avoid detection, for once one washer was moved out of line as much as one-eighth of an inch, the key could not be inserted.

The great weakness of these locks was the ease with which keys could be made for them. A blank key was whittled from a piece of some soft wood, like white pine. It was inserted in the lock and turned both ways several times, then removed. The fixed washers would leave dents in the soft wood. Then the prisoner would simply cut the grooves with a pocket knife, razor blade, or anything he had to cut with. These locks turned so easily once the correct key was inserted, that it was usually considered safe enough to use the wooded key; yet, there was always a chance of one of the wooden studs breaking off and spoiling things, so most men preferred to cut a replica of the wooden key from a celluloid tooth brush handle or a piece of an aluminum bowl. While this lock was almost foolproof, could not inadvertently be left unlocked by a careless guard, and was practically tool proof, it was the easiest lock in the world to beat for anyone who understood its mechanism. Because of the standard thickness of the washers, a man could take the impression, memorize the order of the washers, and send the combination to someone else and have the key made for him, since anyone with a rule could make a perfect fit the first time.

There came another stroke on the triangle. The building became as quiet as a tomb. This was the evening count, and even whispering during count was a serious offense. Everyone had to stand at the door with his hands on the bars. The count was made by Mr. Meyers and the guard, and they actually counted hands rather than men, because of the difficulty of seeing into the cells. They started on the bottom tier and worked up to the top. Then they retraced their steps, walking all the galleries the second time. This was in order to give any inmate who wished to speak to Mr. Meyers an opportunity to do so. When the process was completed, and the count okayed, another stroke of the bell released the men.

The Writer heard a door open up toward the front of the cell house.

"What is that?" he asked Mike.

"They are taking the Chili down. He is in the hole for fighting."

"What do they do to you?"

"Chain you to a ring in the door about breast high."

"What do they feed you?"

"Two slices of bread every noon."

"How long do they keep you in there?"

"Usually a week or ten days. Never less than five days, and I never knew the King to keep anyone over fifteen days. Ten days is the usual jolt."

A dark skinned young man carrying a water bucket shambled up in front of the cell. He was wearing a black patch over one eye, and his other eye had a black ring around it more than an inch wide. He had evidently recently had a most beautiful black eye.

"Hello, Mike! I hear you got a fish. Is he good looking? Make a light so I can see him. You know, you have all the luck."

"Go on with you. This fish would not only black your good eye, he would pluck it out."

"Poplet! You had better go on and wash up and get your water." Mr. Meyer's voice came floating down the corridor.

"Aw, lay down and keep your shirt on, you Dutch _____ _____." The Chili shambled away.

"What did he mean about the fish?"

"They call new men fish. Don't mind him. He is crazy."

"Say, do they let him get away with that?" the Writer asked in astonishment.

"What can they do? There is nothing more they can do to him. Anyway, he is crazy, and they know it."

"Isn't there any danger of them working him over?"

"Not here! If he pulled a stunt like that in some joints, he would get his brains beat out. There has been only one man hit by a guard since I've been here. He was raising hell and keeping everyone awake. The King ordered him taken out and cuffed to the bars of a window in a new building and left him there all night. The guard hit him over the head with the cuffs and split his scalp. The King fired the guard and posted an order which read:

> "No officer shall ever strike or speak back to any inmate, no matter how violent he may be. If an inmate attempts to assault you, step out of his way and signal the gun guard. Then report the matter to me."

"Who is this King? I thought a fellow named Halligan was Warden."

"That is him. They call him the King because he is the King of this Island, and he lets everyone know it. They sometimes call Meyers, the fellow who just counted, The Little King. He is Deputy Warden, but the Warden runs the show."

"I know Meyers. He dressed me in. Who is the guy with the iron-gray hair who took my finger prints? I thought he was going to bite my head off."

"That's him! The King! That is an act he puts on to impress new men. He is not as bad as you would think from the act, but he is a rotten, penny-pinching, yellow-bellied, belly-robbing son of a bitch; but outside of that, you have to give it to him. He does have his points."

"I wouldn't give him anything, not even the sweat off my ass, the copper _____ _____, but I guess as a Warden he is as good as the most of them. I have seen worse. If he wasn't such a belly robber, he wouldn't be so bad. He is ts least square," said the other man in the cell.

"Oh, Tom! I almost forgot," said Mike. "Tom, this is Bob Stroud, the fellow I told you about knowing in Alaska; he has twelve years for manslaughter. Bob, this is Tom Allen, an old-time, black-powder box man and one of the rightest guys you will ever meet. Tom and I usually play a couple of games of crib each evening. If you wish, we will make it three handed."

"I am glad to know you Tom. If you stand with Mike, you are aces with me. You two go on and play. I would much rather get my clothes off and lie down."

"I am glad to know you too, but I am not glad to see a kid like you in a hell hole like this for the best years of his life."

"I'll put the blankets on the bed," said Mike. "These four new ones will be almost as good as a mattress. Then I'll make a light, and you can smoke. We have to save matches. We get only ninety-six Chinese matches per week."

Mike suited his actions to his words.

"Is it o.k. to strip my clothes off? I'm tired as hell, and these stripes have my skin rubbed raw. I am going to get some light underwear the first time I write to my mother."

"You can roll your pants and coat around your shoes for a pillow." Tom suggested.

The Writer sat down on the bed and took his clothes off and rolled them into a bundle for a pillow while Mike lit the little brass oil lamp. He placed the papers Mike had given him, the package the boy had given him and a handkerchief Mike had loaned him under his improvised pillow."

"You got any tobacco, Mike?"

Mike took out his pipe and bag of tobacco and filled the pipe. Then he fumbled in the drawer of the table and brought out his crib board, an old deck of cards, an old pipe, and an empty tobacco sack. He dumped half of the tobacco in the empty sack.

"You can have this pipe along with half of my tobacco. You will have to go easy on it because it has to last you until Saturday, and this is only Wednesday."

"Thanks, Mike! But I don't need the pipe. I can't smoke it."

"You will need it, all right, to stall with, if nothing else. You can't smoke cigarettes on the works, and papers are hard to get. But neither of us is going to smoke much for the rest of the week.

The Writer got into the bed, which was a standard, three-quarter width (40 inches) bed spring fastened to the wall by iron pegs driven into the brick. It was wide enough for two men, but if it sagged in the center, they would have to sleep awfully close together.

He rolled his cigarette, lit it from a taper held over the lamp. Then he lay back and drew the rank smoke into his lungs. He told Mike of the tobacco, papers and money he had slipped to the Jap.

"That is the last you will see of that," both of his cellmates said.

The Writer unwrapped the package they boy in the gray clothes had slipped him and exclaimed joyously:

"What do you know!"

"Pipe down a little! The guard may hear you!" Mike admonished.

There was an almost full sack of Bull Durham, about half a book of brown papers, and some Chinese matches. The Writer wanted to divide this windfall with his two cellmates, but they would not take it. Tom did not smoke and Mike said that he had smoked a pipe so long that he could not enjoy a cigarette.

A convict with a wooden tray of books, papers, and magazines stepped up in front of the door. He handed Mike a paper.

"You gentlemen want anything else to read?"

And when he was assured that they did not, he said, "Hello, Browny! I don't suppose you remember me, but you used to feed me in Katella.[114] I am sorry you fell so hard. I was lucky; I got a year and a day for smuggling some furs. I go out in a few weeks."

"Say! Are you the guy who went trapping up at Berkring Glacier?"

"Sure!"

"No wonder I did not know you without the beard!"

The Writer started to get up, naked as he was.

---

114   While in Katella the Writer worked for a woman known as Edna Brown. They lived on the top floor of a building she owned. He never called her or referred to her by any other name than Edna. She never called him or referred to him by any name other than Kid or The Kid. Some persons thought she was his mother; others his mistress. Both groups were wrong, but they never took the trouble to explain their relationship to anyone. The result was that the Writer had become known to many persons as Browny's Kid.)

"No don't. I know that you are tired, but I have a book here I am sure you will want to read." He fumbled in his box, swung his body close to the bars and stooped and shoved something under the door.

Tom picked up a package and threw it to the Writer.

"You know who suggested that you might like to read that book?"

"I think I do."

"I'll be seeing you." Then the librarian vanished around the corner.

There were three bags of Durham and three books of papers and a note in the package. The note read: "We go 50-50. I buy what you want. You know who."

The Writer was ready to shout for joy. He was rich. He could not give any of this new wealth to his cellmates, but he would repay Mitchel and the strange boy who had befriended him with compound interest – which he did.

"You had better go easy kid, and conserve those things all you can, and you had better arrange not to have over one book of papers or bag of tobacco at a time, for if there is a shake down, you will lose them," advised old Tom, as he bit a tiny chew of tobacco from his plug.

Old Tom

The Writer studied the older man carefully. He was the most physically repulsive member of the human race the Writer had met so far. He was not really old, probably not over forty-five, for there was little gray in his thin, stringy, muddy black hair. He could have easily posed for Frank Nast's original cartoon of a bank burglar.

He was overly fat, but it was not the fat of health and good living; it was the sickly, sallow fat of too many years on prison diet. There were rolls of it around his little pig eyes. He had three baggy chins and a sagging abdomen. His lower lip was fat and drooping, and it revealed a mouthful of stained, rotting teeth that had never seen a toothbrush or a dentist. There were only two teeth in the front of his month that matched up. The rest were snags that had rotted down to the gums and should have been removed years before.

The sight of this man looking longingly at his small plug of tobacco, and then nibbling a pea-sized chew off one corner of the plug with that one tooth he could bite with, while the saliva drooled over his loose, lower lip was one of the most revolting pictures the Writer had ever seen, and it was not until weeks later that the Writer learned something of the self-sacrificing character of the man, and then, the sight of old Tom taking one of his tiny chews was no longer revolting. But on this first night the Writer could not imagine what Mike saw in the man that justified the high praise of his introduction.

Mike

The Writer rolled and squirmed between the soft new blankets, luxuriating in the sensation they sent tingling through his soft, smooth skin, as he drew big drafts of smoke deep into his lungs. He could not waste his time thinking about old Tom, for he had another problem to think of, and that was Mike. He knew that as soon as that lights-out bell rang, Mike would be in bed with him. He knew that Mike was a wolf. He knew that he might plead that he was tired, and Mike would give him a pass that first night. But he was not tired really, and he knew that the touch of Mike's skin and the strength of Mike's powerful arms would send a thousand thrills chasing each other through his body. He knew that even if Mike gave him a pass this first night, there would be other nights, and he knew that this time he would not say No and mean it, so why say it at all. He wondered if old Tom would gossip. There would be no way of keeping him from knowing. He did not want to start a twelve year sentence with a reputation of being a punk, but the Chili's remark and Frank's pass and even Meyers' remark about Fuzzy convinced him that that was exactly what everyone suspected anyway.

The cribbage game had ended, and Mike had blown the lamp out, as he explained, to save oil, and old Tom had told a story of one of the Eastern prisons he had been in where taking a man's light away for six months was one of the punishments.

The guard came by carrying a lantern. The Writer was thankful that the guard could not see anything inside his cell.

"Does that guard always carry a lantern?" The Writer asked.

"Yes! That is the King's orders." Mike said.

"I'd think he would use a flash light. Then you couldn't see him coming a mile away."

"That is just it. The King doesn't want the guards spying on you. They are here to see that you don't fight and don't leave. Your cell is your home, and the old King feels that a man has a right to a little privacy in it."

"Say! What is this story about Fuzzy? I heard Meyers make a crack about him today."

Mike repeated the story of how the King himself had caught Fuzzy and an Indian named Columbia George.

"Didn't he punish them?"

"No! He told George to cut it out and George said, 'Go away! Can't you see I am busy?' and the King went. He put Fuzzy back in the excavating gang and kept him from getting a pardon."

"By putting that rap on him?"

"No! By not putting it on him."

"Gee! He must not be such a bad guy, after all."

"He has his points. If he was not such a belly-robbing penny pincher."

"I would not say anything about Fuzzy, if I were you," old Tom cut in. "He is a good kid, and he has suffered too much embarrassment as it is."

"I am the last person who would intentionally embarrass anyone. I don't like it myself."

"If I did not know Bob could keep his mouth shut, I wouldn't have said anything," Mike confided.

"I am new, and I am just anxious to learn all the angles."

"Just keep your eyes and ears open and your mouth shut, and it won't take you long to learn plenty. That is what the guy who taught me to blow safes used to say when I was a kid."

A horrible thought passed through the Writer's mind. Old Tom had once been a green kid serving his first bit in prison. Would the day ever come when he would look like Old Tom? God forbid. It would be better to take a dive off the top gallery.

The building had become very quiet. There had been some talking from cell to cell earlier in the evening, but that had ceased long ago.

The Writer could hear Mike taking off his shoes, and Old Tom had already climbed into the upper bunk. The sound of the triangle rang clean and clear throughout the building.

Mike pulled the covers back and got into bed. His great weight sagged the springs, and the Writer could not help rolling against him. He was wearing a malodorous undershirt, sticky with stale perspiration.

"Why don't you take that shirt off, Mike? It is always better to sleep naked. It lets your body breathe, and you rest better."

"My shoulder gets cold."

"Why don't you put on my top shirt then? It is clean."

"This is all right! Christ! I am tired! Another hard day's work tomorrow. Good night, kid! See you in the morning."

"Gee! Mike! I'm not sleepy. This is our first chance to talk to each other alone, and I got a million questions to ask you, a million things to talk about. Remember the first time you met me Mike?"

"I'll say. That was outside. This is in prison. Well, I've got to get some sleep. Eight thirty seems like an awfully early bedtime for night owls like us who did not sleep at all on the outside, but this hard work and salt air will sure make you sleep here." Mike yawned.

"O.K. Mike! With these springs we are going to have to sleep close together. If we both lie on our sides, we will be more comfortable, and there will be more room. You can throw your arm over my shoulder if you want to. Should you kick or push in your sleep, I will be like the colored girl in the story. I'll just have to push back, because there is no place to go through this wall," the Writer said with a little giggle, turning his face to the wall.

"I know. I'll try not to disturb you. I always go to sleep on my right side," and Mike turned his back to the Writer.

The Writer rolled over. He did not like the odor of that stinking undershirt. Tentatively the Writer slipped his arm over the big man's shoulders. Mike caught his wrist and gently pushed the arm away.

"Remember kid!" Mike whispered, "Twelve years is a long time. I only have three. I can do mine standing on my head. You can't. Good night and sweet dreams."

"If you are too sweet I might soil you. You know I've been in jail seven months."

"If you do! I'll spank you," Mike said drowsily.

"I wish you would!"

But Mike probably did not hear that last remark. He was already asleep.

The Writer lay awake for many hours, staring into the blackness. Trying to puzzle out the riddle of the future and the problems of his own emotions in this new environment.

The Writer celled with Tom and Mike for six weeks. He slept with Mike every night. Neither man ever put as much as a hand on him. There was never a moment of personal conversation between he and Mike either. The comradeship that had existed between them in the Juneau jail where they had spent so many hours discussing their personal problems with each other had completely vanished. And when the Writer had met up with problems in prison life that he could not solve alone, he had carried them to old Tom. Thereafter, he and Mike were acquaintances who spoke when they met, but they were no longer friends.

It is a strange quirk of human psychology, but the Writer has since that time had a strong aversion to spring beds. Even to this day, he would rather sleep on a steel cot or on a mattress thrown on the floor than on springs that sagged the least bit.

PART I – CHAPTER XIII

McNiel Island, Continued

The King And His Little Kingdom

O. P. Halligan was born in the North of Ireland in the late sixties or early seventies of the nineteenth century. He had gone through only the third grade in school, and had come to America at the age of thirteen. He had thereafter made his own way, so he had been able to avail himself of few of the educational advantages his adopted country had to offer. Of that early part of his life, the Writer knows very little.

Before coming to McNiel Island as a guard in 1905, he had worked for some years as an attendant at the Washington State Asylum at Steilacoom, just across the bay from the Island, where he had met and married a red-headed nurse.

The marriage was childless and does not seem to have been a very happy one.

There were many stories as to why Halligan had lost his job with the State, but the truth was probably that the guard's job paid more money, for seventy dollars per month, with room, board, and laundry thrown in was not to be sneezed at back in those days.

Following the report of Superintendent of Prisons, LaDow,[115] the Congress, by Act of May 27, 1908, C. 200 #1, 35 Stat. 374, empowered the Attorney General to take over the institution, operate it as a penitentiary, and directed him to have summated to the Bureau of the Budget estimates covering its maintenance and expansion.

The Attorney General asked the United States Marshal, who had previously been in charge of the operation of this institution as a jail, to recommend a suitable man for the job of Warden, which would pay the handsome salary of two-thousand-dollars per year.

Now, it must be understood at once that running this institution as a jail was one thing, but as a penitentiary, would be something else again.

The primary function of the jail was to retain custody, usually for only a very short period. The jail had few or no rules. Each guard in each case would exercise his own judgment as to what would be inimical to that end. The work of maintenance and the farm was done by trusties working under little or no supervision, who were glad to work in order to escape the confinement of the cell house. In good weather a few men worked on the excavation, purely for exercise. No one was compelled to work. The cell doors were left open all day long; the men carried their money on their persons, and most of them sat at those long tables all day long, gambling. Blackjack and poker games ran openly. The inmates were allowed to purchase practically anything they pleased, barring hacksaws, shotguns, and whisky, and many of the guards would bring in the latter for a consideration. When there was special work to be done, like unloading barges of supplies, a guard would come to the window and call for volunteers. Sometimes he would get them. If the work was of an unpleasant nature, the prisoners would tell the guards to do it themselves, and they would have to do it if they wanted it done.

The guards took turns at acting Jailor, and were of substantially equal authority. Men went to the dungeon for fighting, creating a disturbance, and little else. The Marshal took the men's purchase orders on weekends and delivered the merchandise ordered the following weekend, but any guard going to town could and would make purchases for the prisoners. To a large extent, both guards and inmates did as they pleased, and the Marshal held court, granted interviews, and listened to complaints each weekend.

On Saturday, May 30, 1908, the Marshal called all the guards together and informed them of the changes to be made and asked them to select by vote from among their number the man that they thought was best suited for the job of Warden and under whom they would rather work.

The selection was not hard to make. There was only one man on the force who could look the part or who had the personality for it. By unanimous vote the guards chose O. P. Halligan, and he was installed in office at once.

Mr. Halligan chose as his personal secretary a highly educated and very competent young man by the name of Adams.

Adams was serving either seven or ten years, the Writer had forgotten which, for embezzling a quarter of a million dollars in gold dust from the United States Assay Office at Seattle, of which he had been director. At that time, large shipments of gold dust from Alaska were constantly arriving at the office. A common impurity of gold dust is a heavy substance known as black sand (magnetic iron oxide). Adams had made a practice of extracting a very small amount of gold from each shipment and adding its exact weight of black sand. The shipment would weigh out accurately, but the assay would be a little low, hardly enough to notice, but enough to amount to something when thousands of shipments were involved.

The Marshal supplied Halligan with a copy of all the regulations in force at Leavenworth, and of all the Attorney General's orders concerning the new institution, and ordered him to formulate a practical system for running the Island prison as a penitentiary.

Halligan and Adams sat down together and worked out the necessary adaptations of the Leavenworth rules to conditions existing at the Island, and when they had finished their task, the result was approved by the Marshal, acting for the Attorney General, and the rules printed and posted.

It is safe to say that neither the guards nor the convicts liked the result.

In fact, the guards were so angry that they held a rump meeting and voted unanimously to withdraw their recommendation of Halligan. But the Marshal informed them that they were too late. They had voted for Halligan and were stuck with him.

Halligan was a short, stocky, squarly-built, impressive-looking Ulsterman of the Black-Irish type – with magnificent head and shoulders, and a beautiful thatch of thick black, wavy hair, which at the time he became Warden was already streaked with gray. He wore a closely-cropped iron-gray mustache which added a touch of severity to his stern features.

By almost any standard, he was an extremely handsome man, and he was said to be very fond of and attractive to the ladies. At the time he was eventually removed from office by President Wilson in 1920, one of the complaints made against him was that he was entirely too attractive and too attentive to the good-looking female relatives of his wards who visited the prison.

For a short man, he wore his clothes extremely well, and on more than one occasion the Writer has seen him dolled up like a Christmas tree to make a sudden and unexpected trip to town on the same boat upon which some good looking female visitor was going ashore. In fact, the Writer upon many occasions has, upon seeing good-looking women visitors arrive at the prison, made bets that The King would be going ashore on the 4 o'clock boat, and he never lost one of those bets. That was during the last year and a half of his sojourn at the Island.

No! It cannot be denied that the King had an eye for beauty, but whether or not he actually made passes at these women is something the Writer is unprepared to say, nor is it very important.

But there was one period of about five years duration when Halligan did not set foot on the mainland, and if he ever looked at a woman other than his wife, no convict or guard knew anything about it. In the beginning his wife visited him every weekend. Later, she quit her job at the Asylum, opened a millinery shop in Tacoma, and the visits dropped to once a month. Then they stopped entirely, and The King went for more than a year without leaving the prison for as much as an hour. This fact coupled with the observation that The King's eye for beauty was not confined only to the female sex, convinced many of the convicts that he was a wolf. He had as sharp an eye for a good looking kid as any old *yegg* in the prison. He usually had the two best looking boys in the prison for his personal runner and personal chambermaid – and it was a sure bet that any time a better looking boy came to the prison, the chambermaid would lose his job. But he would always be given a trusty job somewhere else that kept him out of the wolves' way.

Naturally, all the cons were jealous and accused The King of being too monopolistic, and they were forever trying to get the goods on him, but so far as the Writer knows, they never did. The odd thing was that not one of these boys ever admitted or denied the charge. The Writer saw several of them accused to their faces. They simply blushed, turned, and walked away.

Only two boys who were ever offered the job turned it down. One of them was Meed, and the other, Mitchell, was previously mentioned. Both of these boys were very frank about their own conduct; yet, neither would discuss The King. Meed would say nothing. When questioned, he would simply say, "I did not want the job."

"Did he proposition you?"

The boys face would turn blank and he would say, "You wouldn't be looking for a punch in the mouth, would you? If not, remember that whether he did or did not is his business."

Mitchell would say, "I'd liked to have had the job, all right, but I am not his kind of a boy."

Now there was no doubt about the kind of boy Mitch was, and in addition, he was sweet enough to hang on a Christmas tree. So it is much more likely that the King's interest in these good-looking boys was strictly fatherly. No doubt he wanted to keep them out of temptation's way, for a while at least, until they became adjusted to prison life and able to take care of themselves. In either case, it was his own business and not too important.

Like many of his countrymen who were denied self-government at home, The King had always been intensely interested in government. He had supplemented his little formal education by reading widely and well. He loved his adopted country with a passion felt by few native Americans, and he believed that it was the duty of every good citizen to carry on in the footsteps of the Founding Fathers and always strive, on no matter how small a scale, to make it a better place to live. He had thoroughly familiarized himself with American history, the principles upon which our laws and institutions were founded, and the biographies of the men who had brought forth those principles and made of them living realities, and he continually tried to make those principles a part of his own character.

The convicts had promptly named Halligan, "The King," and although few men had the temerity to call him that to his face, no nickname was ever more perfectly chosen or of greater satisfaction to the person upon whom it was bestowed.

As the disgruntled guards and convicts had soon learned, he was the absolute boss; his word was the ultimate law. He was a hard and stern man, saved from being a complete martinet only by a strict sense of justice, a fine judicial mind, a profound sense of noblesse oblige, and an Irish humor that enabled him to stand back and laugh at his own vanities while not taking things, including himself, too seriously.

He was Warden of only a small prison, but he was, nevertheless, one of the greatest of American Wardens. His word was law, but it was law first and foremost unto himself, for he was a man with a broad understanding of human frailties, including his own.

No hereditary monarch ever ruled his kingdom with a firmer hand or a stronger sense of public obligation. It is true that his printed rules, that is, those he retained, were word for word the same rules in force at Leavenworth and Atlanta, but their application was vastly different.

It was natural for men to talk. He saw no reason for stopping it unless it bothered others or interfered with the running of the institution. Talk might confuse the guards during count. Unnecessary talk at the table might cause trouble. Loud talk after lights-out might disturb some other inmate's sleep, but in each case it was the harm done or the possibility of harm that was responsible for the rule – and any failure to obey the rule that he chose to enforce brought swift, certain, and severe punishment. The Congress had ordered him to supply each prisoner who smoked with so much smoking tobacco per week. He bought a good grade of tobacco, Union Leader, and each smoker was issued just one ten-cent bag. For the men who chewed tobacco, he also bought a standard brand, Star, and each man received a ten-cent plug. But the man who did not smoke or chew did not receive any. He took a bag of tobacco and an average sized pipe. He found that there were just forty-eight pipefuls of tobacco in the weekly ration. There was no necessity for a man to let his pipe go out more than once. So he issued each smoker a block of exactly ninety-six Chinese sulphur matches each week, and there was never as much as one extra match. If a man dropped his block on the concrete and it exploded, that was just his hard luck. There would be no more matches until the next week; it would teach the inmate to be more careful next time.

He bought the Chinese matches because they were cheaper. He could have purchased cheaper grades of tobacco, as they did at Leavenworth, and given the men more of it, practically all they wanted, but Halligan would never do that. It was better in his eyes to give them less of the best. What they did get, they would enjoy and appreciate more, and they would miss it more when it was cut off.

Since Congress said that the men were permitted to smoke, they were permitted to smoke anywhere at any time, excepting where smoking might be obnoxious to others – at the table and when passing through the guard's dining room. Even in the latter case, all the rule said was that the man should take his pipe out of his mouth while passing through the room. In like manner, he should take his pipe out of his mouth while addressing a guard or official, but he did not have to stop smoking. He simply had to refrain from blowing the smoke in the guard or official's face.

There was no necessity for banning smoking or talking on the work. If a man could smoke or talk and still do his work, well and good. If he neglected his work, he could always be reported for loafing.

Halligan considered it his duty to society to prevent his wards from escaping and to punish them by rigidly enforcing their sentences to hard labor. He considered it his duty to his wards to do them the least amount of physical and mental damage possible during the process – his duty to the taxpayers was to to accomplish those desired ends with as little expense as possible.

He ran his little prison with an average of only one civil employee for each ten to fifteen inmates. When his count was one-hundred, as it was when the Writer went there, he had ten civilian employees, including himself and the Doctor. When the population was one-hundred and fifty, as it was when the Writer was made Laundryman a year later, he had only eleven civilian employees. When his count was two-hundred and fifty, as it was when the Writer left there, he had only twenty-one civilian employees.

Hard Labor

Halligan was too much of a realist to imagine that he could reform any man possessed of anti-social tendencies, but he could teach him that prison was no joke. Every man sentenced to prison by the courts, had an implied sentence to hard labor, and it was his duty to see that all of them performed labor within the limits of their capacities. To that end, every man who entered the prison, be he a reformatory punk or a multimillionaire, be he young or old, so long as the Doctor said that he was physically fit, went on the excavating gang.

Congress had made money available, upon the recommendation of Superintendent LaDow, for the building of a new cell house, dining room, kitchen, Deputy Warden's Office, and for modernizing the old cell house. Plans had been approved for constructing other buildings just as soon as the sites for them could be prepared. Consequently, the work of the excavating gang was pressed with all possible vigor, and organized in such a manner as to get the most out of the men with the least possible driving.

There was an embankment gang for which only experienced miners were chosen. The face of the bank was divided by horizontal ledges twenty-five or thirty feet high and about four feet wide. Beginning on the top ledge, the embankment men marked the face out into sections approximately twenty-feet wide, depending on the strength of the formation at any particular spot, and under cut this section to a depth of four feet. Then, six-inch upright channels were cut at the ends of the section, and a string of long steel bars were driven down behind the section from above until it was broken loose and fell in a single block, weighing several hundred tons. This block of earth would hit the ground so hard that most of it would be broken up into chunks small enough to handle with a shovel.

Being part of the embankment gang was considered a promotion from the car crews, but it was dangerous work and was only open to the huskiest men as well as men who were experienced miners.

The guard never drove the embankment gang or gave its members any orders. Actually, it was the other way around. The men on the embankment gang told the guard what dirt should be moved first so as not to interfere with their work or endanger the men below.

It was their duty to keep enough dirt down to keep ahead of the car crews. Two men were allotted to the embankment gang for each car crew, and these teams worked independently or together, as they chose. So long as there was plenty of dirt down, no one said anything to them. If they wished to spend an hour or an afternoon lying in the shade, that was their business.

Naturally, these men worked harder than anyone else because they wanted to keep enough dirt down so they could loaf when they felt like it.

The car crews consisted of eight to ten men each. There were six to eight shovelers, who loaded the dirt into one yard dump cars, and two pushers, who rode the dump cars down to the dump[116] where they dumped into a hopper which emptied the dirt into similar cars thirty feet below and outside of the wire fence. Then the pushers pushed the empty cars back.

The shovelers loaded the car as quickly as possible, for when it was loaded, they were permitted to sit in the shade and rest. No one bothered them. The guard never even spoke to them, so long as they were back at their place of work as soon as the car got back. If an individual man was shirking, the guard might urge him to *snap to it*. If a gang was running slowly, the guard might order them to *pop it up*, but this was usually unnecessary. More often, the guard was apt to tell a man doing more than his share of the work not to kill himself. A man's car mates might tell him the same thing, but every man wanted to see the car filled as quickly as possible, so each worked as hard as he could.

The pushers rested while the car was being filled. Their work was considered easier than shoveling, so they did not want to be put back on a shovel; they quickly dumped each car and brought it back as soon as they could.

There was the outside car crew, which consisted of six men: four pushers and two shovelers. These men were semi-trusties. They worked outside of the wire, and while they wore stripes and were in plain view of the tower guards, they had no guard directly over them. The problem they had was that they only were given two cars to take away the dirt that was brought down from the upper level in three or four cars, so it kept them humping to stay ahead. They were filling in a slough about two hundred yards across. On the short end of their run they had it easy, but on the long end, it kept them on the run. Any time there was a delay, the guard from the upper yard would walk down to the dump to find out the reason, and if he thought these men were not doing their best, he would put them back on the shovel and assign other men to the outside crew.

Of course, if a team on one of the outside cars got their car back before there was one ready to dump, they could lie on the grass and smoke while they were waiting for a car from the upper yard to arrive at the dump.

The outside shovelers kept the dirt leveled off and the track moved up to the edge of the fill. Naturally, they were compelled to keep their work up with the car crews, for if they did not, the dirt piled up and they had more shoveling to do.

Every new man was put on a shovel, and regardless of what the guard or his mates said about not having to kill himself the first few days, he realized at once that no shirker would long remain popular with the men who had to do his share of the work. So, if he had any character or pride at all, he would try his best to throw shovel-for-shovel of dirt with the rest of the crew.

That is the way it was with the Writer and most of the men. For several years before coming to prison he had done no hard manual work, and he had spent almost eight months in jail. His hands were as white and soft as a schoolgirl. Within an hour of shoveling, they were one mass of blisters, and long before noon the blisters had broken open, leaving them raw and bleeding so that they stuck to the shovel handle after each car was filled. His car mates kept telling him to take it easy, and even the guard told him a couple of times that he did not have to kill himself, but he could not give these strange, hard-faced men with whom he was going to be so closely associated, probably for many years, the idea the very first day that he was a shirker or a weakling. He just had to hold his end up, and he did.

What they had for supper that night, he never knew. Whatever it was, he probably gulped it down like the rest of the men, without even stopping to taste it.

When he reached his cell that night he sat down on his stool and started to take off his shoes. The next instant, it seemed, Mike was shaking him into consciousness. It was time for breakfast. He had fallen to the floor and slept while trying to take off his shoes. Mike and Tom had undressed him and put him to bed without waking him up. For thirteen hours he had slept like one drugged. He was so stiff and sore that he was unable to dress himself, and his cellmates had to help him into his clothes. The strictly rationed food seemed not half enough to fill his empty stomach, for every cell in his body was crying for fuel. When he reached the work, he found it almost impossible to grasp the shovel handle, but he did grasp it, and he threw shovel-for-shovel of dirt with his car mates.[117]

Monday morning Mr. Meyers ordered the Writer to stay in. There were four or five men who had stayed in for sick call. Fuzzy was completing the cleaning up of the cell house when one of the other men made a crack to the Writer, intended to embarrass the boy. Fuzzy's face flamed. But to the speaker's surprise, so did the Writer's. He thought it best to let everyone know exactly how he felt, as it might save trouble later.

Shortly thereafter, the King came to the wicket and called:

"Stroud."

---

117   At that time the men at McNiel Island worked a full eight hours every day. They went to work at seven-thirty and worked until noon. They were given an hour and a half for dinner, then they worked from one-thirty until five p.m.

When the Writer stood before him in the office, he growled:

"Know anything about calcimining?"

"Yes, Sir! I know all about it."

"Done it before?"

"Many times."

"Know how to mix it? How much to mix per room?"

"Certainly! It gives the covering power on the package. You simply figure how many square feet you have to cover. If the wall is in bad condition, it takes more."

"Hmm!" He led the way upstairs and into a room. "Two rooms like this, ten by twelve. How long will it take you to do them?"

"If the walls were in good condition, it would take me an hour for each room. However, this old calcimine will have to come off, and the wall will have to be resized with glue. I would say, four days."

"If you had someone to help you?"

"That would depend on how much help he was."

"Say it was _____." He called Fuzzy's name.

"I don't know him."

"Yes, you do! The boy you were talking to when I called you out. They call him Fuzzy. He has other work to do, but he could help you for about five hours per day."

"In that case, I can have them done in two days, providing I can get horses and some boards. It would take twice as long to do them from a ladder."

"Come on!" The King led the way to the storeroom. He handed the Writer a box of calcimine. "How many boxes will it take for both rooms?"

"Three boxes will do both rooms, but I will need a step ladder, two horses, two ten foot long planks, three pounds of glue, a five gallon bucket to mix the glue in, a bucket to mix this stuff in, a bucket for hot water, a brush, a tool to scrape the old calcimine off with, and also some rags."

He gave the Writer the three boxes of calcimine, the glue, and a new brush.

"Fuzzy will get the other stuff!" He led the way to the blacksmith shop, nodded toward the convict blacksmith. "Just tell him the kind of scraper you will need."

The walls were in terrible condition, and the work was going slower than the Writer had expected. There were cracks in the walls, caused by the roof leaking, where the plaster was damaged.

During the afternoon the Writer sent Fuzzy for some lime plaster and a trowel. While the boy was gone, The King came into the room.

The Writer put down his tool, climbed down from the staging, took the pipe Mike had given him from his pocket, filled it and lit it without speaking.

The King looked about the room.

"You seem to understand this work," he said pleasantly.

"I should! The best friend I had during my childhood was a painter and decorator by trade. I was always a curious kid, and he taught me all there was to know about it."

"I noticed at once that you seemed to have a good grasp of the problem."

"A habit my mother taught me. I always liked to build things. She would not permit me to start building even a box until I had figured out everything I would need, even to the last nail. Then when I started it, I had to finish it."

"Hmm! A smart woman!"

"That is what I think."

The conversation lasted for thirty minutes. Finally, smiling, The King said, "This has been interesting. I'll go on now and let you get on with your work."

"Thank you, Sir!"

The King's footstep had hardly died away when Fuzzy, all excited, came bursting into the room.

"Was the King here? Was the King here?"

"Sure. He just left. You know, the old bastard seems to be at least half human. He did not try to bite my head off once."

"I forgot to tell you! Did you do any work while he was here?"

"No! I don't like for anyone to stand and watch me work. It makes me nervous. So I stopped, lit my pipe and chewed the rag with him. He must have seen those snipes in the corner too, but he didn't say anything."

"Gee! That is swell! If you work when he is around, he will think you are just trying to impress him, and he will never trust you. He will know whether you have been working or not. You don't have to show off to him, for he does not miss anything. As for the snipe, that doesn't matter much; he knows we all smoke cigarettes. He won't say anything about it so long as he doesn't catch you in the act. Then he will try to make you tell where you got the paper."

"Well, he could see my hands, too. He knows that I was not loafing on that shovel. He also saw that I had a full bag of tobacco."

"That was a rotten trick, but if you go to him he might change that order."[118]

---

118   This referred to the remark The King had made about the Writer being too young to smoke. Pursuant to that opinion, he had ordered Mr. Meyers not to issue the Writer any tobacco.

"He will change it, all right! In the meantime he will never see me when I am not smoking."

What the Writer did not understand at that time was that The King had dug up the calcimining job just to give his hands a chance to heal.

He played no favorites on that shovel, however, and some of the cases were pitiful.

One of these was the banker, Parker, of United Wireless. He and DeForrest had been tried for mail fraud, and he had been convicted and given seven years on the Government's contention that their claim of being able to transmit the human voice without wires was too preposterous for consideration by intelligent persons.

DeForrest was acquitted and he went on to make that stock he was accused of selling fraudulently worth thousands of times what the public had paid for it. In fact, if you had a single share of that stock today, you would not have to work for a living, but all that did not help Parker.

He was a sixty-five year old millionaire banker, suffering from asthma, heart trouble, and arteriosclerosis. His attorney had argued that sending him to Atlanta or Leavenworth would be a death sentence to him. So he had been sent to the Island because it was thought that the mild climate would be better for his health. But had his attorneys known about that embankment, they would not have been so sure.

He had been a banker and financier all his adult life. He had never been given to physical exercise, and it is doubtful that he had done anything more strenuous than clip a coupon since his college days. In recent years he had spent many thousands of dollars on Doctor bills.

At the time he arrived at the Island, he was at least sixty pounds overweight, and his skin had the sickly yellow color associated with senile decay.

Parker was put on the same car crew with the Writer, who by that time, was as tough as whalebone.

The old man did not know how to lift or throw a shovelful of dirt. It was probably the first time that he had had a shovel in his hands in his entire life, and he hardly had strength enough to life the empty shovel.

His soft hands blistered, and the blisters broke. He staggered and almost fell, trying to keep up with the other men – everything was done on the run – but he did try, and he kept right on trying. The soft flesh melted from his body like snow under a summer sun, until his clothing hung on his gaunt frame like a circus tent on a scarecrow, and his flabby skin hung in great folds like that of a rhinoceros. But the old man stayed with it until the color flooded back into his skin, and he was able to turn out a good days work. When The King offered him an easy job, he said that he liked the one he had.

Every man got his taste of that hard work, but if he were serving a long sentence (three years or more was a long sentence in those days), he could be pretty certain to land a good job in due time, providing that he did his work and kept out of trouble. The short timer, or a man who showed that he was not trying to get along, was pretty apt to serve his whole sentence on a shovel, and every time he got out of line the least little bit, he would serve ten days in the hole; and it was a worse hole than the one in Leavenworth.

Because someone told The King that there was danger of a man digging out through the ventilators, the King had had the ventilators filled with gravel. With the ventilators plugged and the solid doors, the air in the hole became very bad. Also, at the Island, a man was cuffed to a ring set in the door, which is much more uncomfortable than being chained to the bars. He was chained up before the men went out to work in the morning and let down shortly before they came in at noon. He was put back up before they went out to work at one-thirty, and he did not come down again until after the evening count, which made him stand up a full nine hours, compared to seven and a half at Leavenworth.

Tobacco

As had been indicated, tobacco was always a problem at the Island, and taking a man's tobacco privilege was really the severest punishment the King could inflict upon a man who smoked, for no one received enough tobacco to satisfy his desire; and because non-smokers were not permitted to receive tobacco, no one had any to give away.

Now, what actually prompted the King to arbitrarily deprive the Writer of his tobacco, the Writer never knew, but in a way he did the Writer a favor, for he threw to the Writer the sympathy of every man in the prison.

As soon as Mr. Meyers turned the Writer away from the window that first Saturday afternoon, a dozen men flocked around him. They all wanted to know the score.

"I don't know! He made that crack about me being too young when I came in, but it is obvious that there are kids here much younger that I am."

"That is right," said one of the boys standing near the Writer. "I am only seventeen, but I told him that I was twenty-one. Most of the kids here told the court they were twenty-one to keep from being sent to some reformatory. Those joints are pure hell. So you are probably the youngest one on the books, Bob."

"You should tell him___ ___ ___ ___"

The Writer received much free advice about what he should tell the King, and this continued for weeks. Every time there was a group discussion in which the Writer was present, there were new suggestions for the argument he should put up to the King, but he was in no hurry. He wanted to get his arguments well formulated in his mind before going out to see the King. He had never forgotten the force of the argument of Status Quo as he had used it on his mother when he was eleven, when she had first caught him smoking. He had said in substance:

"All right, Mom! Now that you know I smoke, there is no use hiding it any longer. You might as well know that I have been smoking for two years. You also might as well know that there is only one kid in this whole neighborhood who don't smoke. He is the kid who just gave me these cigarettes. He bought them to prove to me that his parents would let him smoke, if he want to."

She had replied, "I know most parents punish their boys for smoking."

"Sure, Mom, parents are good at punishing kids for the things they do themselves, but they don't stop the kids from smoking. And you can't stop me from smoking. I have been doing it for two years, and I am going to continue. You did not catch me until I was ready for you to catch me. I can tell you the first time you smelled smoke on my breath. That was because I let you, because I was tired of hiding it. Now, it don't matter what you do to me. I am going to continue to smoke. If I can't get money for tobacco any other way, I can steal it like some of the kids do, or I can shoot snipes like others do. I ain't done those things yet, but I can do them, if I have to."

That had been an easy victory. The Writer wanted to have equally forceful arguments to present when he went before the King.

There had been other men who had not talked. One, an old *yegg* about fifty named Morton. He waited until he could catch the Writer alone. He slipped the Writer his unbroken bag of tobacco and a fine brier pipe.

"My heart has been bothering me for some time, and I've known that I was going to have to quit smoking. You can have my tobacco every week until you get yours; then I will give it to someone else who has lost his tobacco."

There was old Tom who said, "Here kid, is half a bag of tobacco. I draw smoking one week and chewing the next week, and I have been giving the smoking to my partner, as he is a heavy smoker. I talked it over with him, and from now on, I'll give you half a bag every other week."

"No! That is not fair. I am getting Morton's tobacco now. You better give it to Rosie."[119]

"No, you keep it! He wants you to! You won't have any more than you need anyway."

"O.K. Tom! But you got to give him a book of papers." The Writer had ordered the Jap, Frank, to spend that money for cigarette papers and to give him two books at a time."

A smuggler, name forgotten, called the Writer to one side and said, "I have been smoking too much. I will give you half a bag every week."

"No! I don't want to take your tobacco. I am getting tobacco from two other parties now, and as soon as I can get set, I will have plenty. I just got to get one visit from my wife."[120]

"Take it anyway. Blow smoke in that old penny-pinching buzzard's face every chance you get. That will give me more satisfaction than anything else."

"I have planned on doing that."

And that is what the Writer did. He made it a point to be smoking every time the King saw him. If he saw the King looking at him on the work, he stopped working at once and loaded his pipe and lit it. The men on the gang and the guard did not complain, for both knew that he always threw more than his share of the dirt.

The third week the Writer was at the prison, he had his first visit from Kate, and while kissing her whispered:

---

119   Tom's partner was a kid called Rosie because of his bright rosy cheeks. Under the King, fall partners were never permitted to cell together because of the danger of them planning escapes together, so Rosie celled with another *yegg*.
120   The Writer was not married, but he had claimed Kate, the woman he had been living with in Alaska, as his wife, and had arranged to have her move to Tacoma so she could visit him. He knew that Kate had known the convict boatman in Alaska.

"See the boat man!"

"I've already seen him, Honey, and everything is all right."

That evening the boatman came to the cell and asked, "Can I duck in here while they are setting the tables? I want to talk to Bob. We have mutual friends out to The Westward."[121]

"Sure! Come right on in," said Mike.

The boatman was a big Norwegian named Charles F. Johnson.

He slipped the Writer two bags of prison issue tobacco, two bags of Bull Durham, and a book of cigarette papers.

"I would not do this for anyone else. I knew Kate in Alaska. She told me how you copped a plea to turn her loose on a first-degree murder indictment. She game me five dollars for you. I will bring in what you want as you need it. I'll do something else. I will pick up money at your request from any visitor who comes here, and I will buy what you order with it. I do not want any cut for myself, and I do not want anyone but you to know how it is done or that I am involved."

"Gee! Johnson! That is swell! I really don't know what to say!"

"Just call me Charlie! Don't say anything, but remember, I am your friend."

"O.K. Charlie. Just bring in two books of papers and three bags of Durham at a time."

The Writer was elated. He had been in the prison less than a month. He had the best connection in the institution, and he would always have tobacco, much more than he could use himself, whether the King ever issued him any or not, and he had his arguments already. It was true that he had a terrific awe of authority, which he did not completely overcome for many years. It was almost impossible for him to resist a preemptory command, but there was always a point where he developed a cold, boiling anger deep within his being, where his halting, stuttering, stumbling voice became firm and steady, and his thoughts flowed off his tongue in a smooth placid stream that totally belied the burning passion just below the surface.

On his third Saturday in the prison he had reached that point in regard to the issue of the tobacco. As Mr. Meyers finished issuing the tobacco, the Writer saw the King step into the office. He stepped up to the window.

"Will you ask the Warden to step over here, please?"

"You want to speak to me?" The King said, stepping to the window.

"Yes, Sir! I think that I am being unfairly and unjustly punished, and I want a personal interview with you tomorrow forenoon upon the issue of my tobacco."

"Can't you say what you have in mind right now?"

"I can, but I don't want to."

---

121   The Gulf of Alaska and Aleutian Islands are always spoken of by Alaskans as The Westward.

"Very well! I will call you out tomorrow morning."

"Thank you, Sir!"

The next morning.

"Sit down, Stroud!" The King said pleasantly as the Writer stepped into the Deputy's office.

"I would prefer to remain standing, Sir. Maybe I will be able to express myself better on my feet." This time the Writer told himself, he is the one who is going to have to look up.

"Proceed!" The King's face became hard and expressionless.

"I wish to know just why I am being punished and in just what respect my conduct had been at fault."

"Why, you are not being punished."

"Oh! But I am! Didn't you order Mr. Meyers not to issue me any tobacco?"

"Yes, but that is because tobacco is not good for a boy of your age. I had no intention of punishing you."

"Then, why do it? Isn't loss of tobacco privilege a form of punishment here? Remember, if I am too young to smoke, I am too young to be sent here for three of the best years of my life."

"Yes, but…"

"I cannot see the but. I feel that so long as my conduct is good, I am entitled to the same treatment as any other prisoner – no better and no worse. As you know, I entered my plea of guilty on the distinct understanding that if I kept a good record for three years, both the United States Attorney and the Judge would recommend me for a pardon."

"I did not know that, although the Marshal did say something along that line."

"I came here with the firm determination to make that good record if possible. You are deliberately making it impossible."

"I'm sorry you feel that way Stroud. You are a young man just entering life. You don't realize it, but you will still be a young man with your best years in front of you when you go out, even if you serve every day of your sentence. You have been entrusted to my care. I am responsible for you, and I am only acting for your own good."

"That is what every parent says when he beats up his kid, but he is lying in his teeth when he says it. He beats up his child for one reason; because he has the power. If the child was big enough to defend himself, it wouldn't happen. You are taking my tobacco because you have the power."

"You should not feel that way."

"How should I feel? How would you feel?"

"I assure you that I have only your welfare in mind. The best medical authorities say that tobacco is harmful to a growing child. Nineteen years old! You are still only a child. A man does not complete his growth until he is thirty years old, and it is a well-known fact that smoking stunts growth."

"Who? What medical authorities say that?"

"Why, I don't know! I have read it."

"I have read some that say that isn't so. A study conducted by the Royal Society says that tobacco has no influence upon growth, but we don't have to go to any Doctors. Did you smoke when you were a kid?"

"Why, no!"

"Well, I did! Both my parents and grandparents are as short as you are. It is food and climate that influences growth, but I was through growing when I was thirteen. I was as tall as I am now and fifteen pounds heavier."

"I honestly think that quitting smoking would be good for you. Now, I will make you a proposition. Won't you honestly try to quit smoking for one month and see if you don't feel better? If you don't, then come to me and I will give you your tobacco."

"No! Not for one day! Smoking is the only recreation we have here. I do not intend to deprive myself of it. All those stories about it stunting your growth or dulling the mind are untrue, in my case at least, but that is not my main point."

"Have you ever seen me when I was not smoking?"

"No! You seem to always have a pipe in your mouth."

"You never will! Knowing that you are punishing me for nothing, the men here are all sorry for me, and there is not one of them who will not deprive himself to see that I have plenty of smoke. So I actually have more tobacco than anyone else in the prison. Really, you are punishing other men more than me. That is not fair to them. I want to get along and make a good record. I want to stand on my own two feet. Those are the things that are important to me, but you are not making it any easier for me by trying to do the impossible. Congress provides money to supply me with tobacco, but if you won't give it to me, you force me to supply myself any way I can, and you can't blame me for doing it."

The old King chuckled.

"I am sorry you feel as you do, but I must admit that you have the best of me on that argument. If you insist on smoking, I know that I can't stop you, and if you insist on your tobacco, I am morally and legally bound to give it to you."

"I do insist!"

"I'll tell Mr. Meyers to put you on the list for next Saturday."

"No! I am still robbed out of all I have missed. You owe me three bags."

"But no one is given three bags at one time. You don't need that much."

"It ain't what I need. Maybe I like to pay by debts."

~ 229 ~

The King laughed.

"You are a persistent young man. Will you compromise for two bags?"

"I guess I'll have to, if that is all I can get."

The King pulled some keys from his pocket and handed them to Mr. Meyers.

"You can get him two bags of tobacco," he said.

"You must have made a good impression on the Old Man," said Mr. Meyers while taking the Writer to the storeroom for the tobacco.

"I hope so. At least, I got my tobacco."

"If you hadn't, you wouldn't have gotten it. He is not a man whose mind, once he makes it up, is easily changed by argument."

PART I – CHAPTER XIV

McNiel Island, Continued

Noblesse Oblige

The King's word was law, but first, last, and always, it was law unto himself.

He once said to the Writer:

"The only way I can teach good character is by example. How can men be forced to respect the law if the man who enforces it is no better in his personal conduct than the man who is being punished for violating it? No man has any right to sit in judgment upon the conduct and characters of others until he is absolutely certain that his own conduct and character is above reproach. I feel that my conduct may have been partly responsible in this case.

"For that reason, I do not feel qualified to punish you; so I am submitting all the facts to the Attorney General. Whatever is done will be at his orders, and when I receive his instructions, I will call you out and read them to you. Until that time, you will remain in your cell."

These words were spoken on Friday, November 3, 1911, at a hearing on the matter of the Writer's stabbing of the Doctor's orderly, which occurred on November 1, 1911.

The Costly Kiss

When men go to prison, they do not leave any of their natural instincts on the outside, least of all, their sex instincts. Naturally, homosexuality is a common part of all prison life, as has been previously indicated on many occasions. That subject is thoroughly discussed in Part IV of this work, and the King's attitude and concern over it is made the subject of a complete chapter and discussed in some detail. It is only necessary to say here that his attitude was as completely realistic as were his attitudes on most subjects of prison management.

Never once while he was a guard did he write a report reflecting on any man's sex morality, and never once while he was Warden did he try to punish a man on such a report, or put such a charge on any man's record. He considered such conduct more the crime of society than of the individual, but he felt that the individual should have enough self-respect to conduct himself with a little circumspection. Those who did not were sure to pay for their carelessness. The King could turn his back on sexual offenses but not on sexual play in public.

The classic case of this kind involved little Mitch, the boy who had given Mike those first six cigarette papers, and a thirty year old *yegg* named William.

Little Mitch was a small, slender boy about five-feet-four-inches tall and not weighing over a hundred-and-ten pounds. He was nineteen or twenty years old, but looked much younger, was beautiful as an angel and as completely feminized as a boy can be. He was serving five years out of army for female impersonation, and actually, he did not need a dress. Even in striped pants, one had to look twice to be sure that he wasn't a girl. Mitch was in love with and married to Percy Huntington, his cellmate, who was William's partner. Both Percy and William worked on the embankment gang, while Mitch was on the Writer's car crew.

One day after a car had been filled, as the crew was walking over to sit down in the shade, William, who was already sitting against the building, lifted his arms in a spirit of play and said, "Come here, Mitch, and give me a kiss!"

"Okey dokey!" the boy cried, throwing himself into William's arms and kissing him as if he meant it.

The gang all laughed, and the tower guard, who otherwise might not have noticed, looked down and saw them.

That night they were called before The King.[122]

"You are charged with osculating in public." The King said gravely. Then he read the guard's report aloud. "What have you to say for yourselves?"

"We were only playing!" Mitchell pleaded. "You know there ain't nothing between us!" He knew that the Warden did know exactly where his affections laid.

"I knew! I know that it is very difficult for a boy your age to be cut off from the other sex and all the play and affection that naturally belongs to youth. I try to be as lenient as I can in such matters, but there is no excuse for making a show of yourself in public. I am not criticizing either of you for anything of that nature you may do or desire to do, but you should have enough self-respect not to misbehave in public. What do you have to say, William?"

"What can I say, Warden, more than Mitch has said? It was just done in a spirit of fun. Christ, life is drab enough here at best. We just want to have some fun and get a laugh out of the other boys. We cannot deny it, for we only did it as a joke, with no thought that we might be reported."

"That is not sufficient excuse. If I permit such demonstration in public, sooner or later it will give the prison a bad name, and I will be forced to clamp down on you fellows a lot harder than I do. Seven days in the hold and six months tobacco privilege. Examine them, Doctor!"[123]

"Just a minute, Warden!" said William. "Six months tobacco! Aren't you being pretty stiff? I don't mind going to the hole if you think we deserve punishment, but six months tobacco? I'll admit we acted thoughtlessly, but we intended no harm."

---

122   No trials were held during working hours, excepting on special occasions. They were usually held after supper.

123   Under The King no man could be put in the hole without a physical examination.

"Teach you to be more careful next time."

Six months tobacco, for a man who smoked, was just about the roughest sentence The King could pass out.

Now, if that were the end of the story, there would be no point in telling it at this place.

A few weeks later Rider and a man named Russell were reported for sexual play in public and received the same punishment.

The King was a son of Ireland, even if he did wear an orange colored ribbon on the Good Saint's Day, and sometimes, when things went wrong, he nipped the bottle a little too heavily. When he had a few drinks under his belt, his heart bubbled over with the milk of human kindness, and all the sorrows and sufferings of the world lay as a burden upon his soul. All the warm sentimentality which was his birthright, but which he ordinarily kept under such iron control, escaped from restraint and ran riot.

Every inmate knew that if he could catch the King when he was drinking he could get almost anything he asked for. But drunk or sober, The King was still King, and his word was still good. Everyone knew that, too.

About six weeks after he had taken Mitch and William's tobacco, his wife paid him what was supposed to be a weekend visit. She arrived at the prison about noon on Saturday. Normally, upon such visits, she did not leave the prison until Monday morning, but on this day the King's chambermaid reported that there had been a big fight. The waiter in the guard's dining room reported that she and the King were not speaking to each other at supper that night, and that neither did more than pretend to eat. Johnson, the boatman, was routed out after dark and ordered to put her on shore. The King did not go down to the boat with her, and she did not open her mouth during the trip.

No one knew for sure, but it was rumored around the prison that she had demanded that The King resign and take employment as a deputy Marshal in Tacoma, and The King refused to do so. In any case, it was the parting of the ways for them. She never came back to the prison, and for more than a year The King did not leave the Island.

The next morning a fellow named Fain came back from sick call and reported that the King was out in the yard drunk and had promised to give him his tobacco privilege back.

There was a rush for Mr. Meyer's window. Mr. Meyers was supposed to be Deputy Warden, but actually, his functions were those of a turnkey rather than Deputy Warden, since The King performed the Deputy's functions himself. Mr. Meyers put men in the hole when The King ordered it. He chained them up and let them down himself. He withheld the privileges the King had taken away. He censored the mail; granted extra letters; checked men in and out of the cell house, dressed in new men and he was responsible for the morning and evening counts. He sent men on sick call, arranged interviews with the Warden, but he could not change any man's cell, his place of work, excuse a man from work, or inflict punishment excepting when the King was not on the Island.

Every man in the prison who had lost privileges wanted to go on sick call. On week days, the Doctor came down to the cell house to hold sick call, but on Sundays the men were sent to the hospital, one or two at a time, and they crossed the yard unattended.

Mr. Meyers knew why these men were suddenly sick, but if they said they wanted to see the Doctor, it was his duty to either call the Doctor or send them on sick call, so he wrote down all of their names, and he let all but two of them go to the hospital. He informed the last two that the Doctor had been called away and could not see them.

As each man crossed the yard he approached The King and made his request. The King promised to grant the requests, but he always said, "Tell Mr. Meyers! Tell him to write it down! Otherwise, I might forget!"

Mr. Meyers dutifully wrote down everything the convicts told him The King had said.

Poor Mitch had not been able to see The King, but William, the last man out, being an older and bolder person, had searched the enclosure until he found the King down in the lower yard, back of the storeroom, vomiting into a garbage can. He had held The King's head, patted The King on the back, and helped The King up the hill. He reported that The King had said, "Sure, and you are good boys, the both of you. It breaks my old heart to have to punish you, but if I did not do it, someone else would and he might be worse than I am. He's a sweet kid, too. The good Lord knows I don't blame you for wanting to kiss him. If I were in your place, I'd probably want to kiss him myself. But I can't permit it in public. You don't understand, my boy, but if some busy body ever got hold of a thing like that, the preachers would all be on me like a pack of wolves. I would have every preacher in the world on my neck, and they would rip the hide off my back so quickly I wouldn't know how it happened. You must learn to be careful, my boy, learn to be careful, always be careful, or you'll get me in bad."

"We will be careful, Warden! I promise! I'll see that Mitch promises, too. If he don't behave I'll tell Percy to knock his ears off."

"That's a fine boy! Tell Mr. Meyers I said that both of you are to have your tobacco privileges restored. Tell him to write it down. I might forget."

The next afternoon, The King, still suffering from a hangover, came down to Mr. Meyer's office.

Mr. Meyers confronted him, a long list in his hand.

"Did you promise Fain that you would restore his tobacco privileges?"

"I don't know. Did he talk to me? I seem to have some recollection…."

"He talked to you on the yard coming back from sick call. He said that you told him you would restore his tobacco and that you told him to tell me to write it down."

"Well, if he told you that, I guess I did. Give it to him."

This formula was repeated time after time as Mr. Meyers worked down the long list, and each time The King ordered his Deputy to keep his drunken promise. It was his duty to punish others for their moral derelictions, but how could he expect them to accept that punishment without bitterness unless he himself was scrupulously honest in his dealings with them. At last Mr. Meyers came to the name of Williams.

"Did you promise William that you would restore both his and Mitchel's tobacco privileges?"

"Were they on sick cell, too?"

"Yes! Both of them. Mitchel was disappointed. I asked him if he saw you and he said, No, that he could not find you."

"You know, it's a pretty good boy Mr. Meyers, who wouldn't lie to get his privileges back."

"Yes, Mitch is all right, even if he would be happier in skirts. William found you down in the lower yard, back of the storehouse, and brought you up the hill. When I saw you, he had his arms around you to keep you from falling. He said that you told him you would restore both his and Mitchel's tobacco privilege and that you told him to tell me to write it down."

"Well Mr. Meyers, I know that I was pretty drunk, but I never had any idea that I could get that drunk, but if Williams told you that, give them their tobacco. I don't think he would lie about it."

"I don't either. I think every one of them told me the exact truth."

"You know, Mr. Meyers, we have a pretty good bunch of boys here. I would not want any of the guards to know this, but I had my pistol on me, and any one of them could have taken it."

"I know! Williams told me. That is why I did not let anyone else out. Russell and Rider were very much disappointed that they did not get to see you. To me it seems a little unfair to them, but I could not take the chance. Russell would have been all right, but Rider is a wild kid, and you never know what a kid might do on the spur of the moment."

"Hmm! That is right! You had just as well give them theirs, too. If they have made up their minds to be more circumspect, the punishment has accomplished its purpose. If they haven't, they won't have their tobacco long, anyway. Just as well give it to them this evening instead of making them wait until Saturday."

"By the way! Did you say Williams had his arm around me?"

"Yes! When he was helping you up the hill."

"You didn't see him kiss me, did you?"

"No!" said Meyer, laughing. "But he may have."

"You know, I'll always wonder about that," said The King with a chuckle.

The King's English

Another phase of the King's character was discovered by Fain.

Fain, a school teacher by profession, had served as Fourth-class Postmaster in some little town in Eastern Washington where he and his wife, also a teacher, had been running the school. There had been a shortage in his accounts, and he had been given two years. His story was that he had sold a money order and used the money to cover some immediate need for cash, fully intending to put the money back on pay day. Something he had done on many previous occasions, but this time, a postal inspector dropped in on him.

Shortly after arriving at the Island, Fain had been caught making a suit of clothing from blankets evidently with the intention of attempting to escape, for which offense he had lost all of his *goodtime*. None of the guards liked him, and they rode him pretty hard. He was reported almost every time he turned around, and every time he went before the King, he went to the hole.

One day he was reported for reading a book on the work. That night he was called before the King.

"You are reported for reading on the work. What have you to say for yourself?" The King asked.

On all previous reports, Fain, being an educated and intelligent man, had put up a logical defense to the charge of which he was accused, but even when he had been right he had never missed the hole. This time he was disgusted. He was sure he was going to the hole, so what was the use?

"Certainly! What of it? I cannot see anything ethically wrong with a man trying to use his spare time to improve himself. I am not accused of neglecting my work."

"Do you mind repeating that?"

"What is the use? I just plead guilty. I'm going to the hole anyway, so why argue about it?"

"I am the one to decide your guilt and your punishment, but only after I have heard and considered your side of the matter. I wish you would repeat that sentence, for I am certain that I understood you correctly.

Fain repeated the sentence and noticed muscles in the Kings lips and throat move as he came to the word ethically.

"Hmm! As you say, there may be nothing ethic-ic--"

"Ethically!"

"Exactly! – Ethically wrong with reading on the work, so long as you are not neglecting your work. It might create a bad example and cause others to neglect their work, however. Don't do it anymore! You are excused!"

The next day The King came out on the yard, called Fain over to him, and caused Fain to neglect his work for almost an hour while he engaged him in conversation about Herbert Spencer and one of his great books, Data of Ethics. He wondered if Fain had ever read it. Of course Fain had, and he was able to discuss it intelligently. During the conversation The King used the word Ethics in all of its modifications and in all parts of speech, and he used it correctly. In more than a year that Fain had been in the institution, this was the first time that The King had ever spoken to him like a human being.

That night Fain checked with the Librarian.

Yes, after he had delivered his books the night before, The King had come into the library and asked him if he had any book on ethics. He had given The King Spencer's Data of Ethics. The King had brought the book back in the morning and told the Librarian how much he had enjoyed it.

That was enough for the sharp-minded Fain. He passed the good word along.

"He turned me loose because he did not know the word Ethics, and he was smart enough to know that I suspected the reason. So he had to come out and try to convince me that he had known it all the time. During our conversation he used the word correctly in all its parts of speech. That is not all, he told me that he had read the book years ago, but he really read it the other night. I don't know how he did it. He must have set up all night, but even then, I don't know how he did it. I spent a month on that book when I was in college. He must have read it clear through though too, for he discussed enough of it to show me that he had. Now here is the way I figure it:

"Much as I hate him, I have to give him credit for being sincere. Also he takes himself and his job very seriously. Our Constitution, the whole spirit of our laws, is based upon a man's right to be heard. He takes that seriously. You all know that you can walk up to him any place and talk until you are blue in the face. He will never interrupt you, and he will never try to stop you. That is because he recognizes your right to be heard upon any subject at any time. On a report, he feels that it is his duty to hear and consider what you say before he has a right to punish you. If you use any word that he does not know, he has to either ask you to explain what you mean by it, and expose his ignorance, or he has to turn you loose. For in his eyes, he has no right to punish you without hearing, which means understanding and considering your defense. His pride won't permit him to expose his ignorance, while a better educated person would think nothing of it. He is evidently very sensitive about his lack of schooling."

Dictionaries became popular. Within a month a dozen or more men, including The King, ordered unabridged Webster's Dictionaries.

Every time a man was reported, his argument was couched in ten-dollar words, and every time a prisoner employed a word The King did not know, The King asked him to repeat it, then excused him. Every time that happened, just as sure as the sun shines, The King would engage that prisoner in conversation the next day, and he would use that word correctly in all its parts of speech. Certain short-sighted inmates were not above inventing words on their own, to be found in no dictionary, and sometimes they got by with it, but it was a dangerous process, for when The King discovered that he had been imposed upon, he was apt to return the compliment, with interest.

It was usually not too difficult to catch the man violating some rule, himself. In that case, the man was given his chance to be heard on the spot. Then The King fixed the punishment.

Even before he became Warden, The King had gained a reputation of being a well educated and very brilliant man by the simple process of knowing when to keep his mouth shut, and knowing not only exactly what he was talking about when he opened it, but also that every word he used was grammatically correct.

When he was unsure of himself, he said nothing. At the time he became Warden, he was usually unsure of himself. Adams had written his official letters for him and had often given him tips on bad pronunciation and misused words, but The King's forte was always that of a good listener.

When important personages came to the prison, he would show them around, but he would let them do the talking, while he put on his most impressive look and confined himself to such meaningless statements as:

"Hmm." "Well, well." "Interesting." "Tell me more about it." "I'll have to give that some thought." "Now just what is your opinion?" "Yes, yes." "Very interesting."

The speaker would you go away with the firm opinion that The King was one of the smartest men he had ever met, because The King had been intensely interested in everything he had to say and had not disagreed with him once.

In the beginning The King had been prevented from saying more by the fear of exposing his ignorance through his own bad grammar. But within a year of Fain's discovery, he had developed a really amazing vocabulary, every word of which he could use with complete confidence, and when he wanted to, he could hold a really brilliant conversation upon almost any subject. Listening was always his greatest accomplishment, however. It was only with the ladies that he loved to strut his stuff.

All went well until the Spaniard came to the institution. The Spaniard's name has long since been forgotten. He came to the prison on a stretcher and served much of his time in a wheel chair.

You see, the Spaniard had been an officer in one of the rebel armies during the Mexican revolution. He had been captured and stood before a firing squad, and five bullets had passed through his lungs. He had lain for hours in a pile of corpses, left unburied for the buzzards. Then he was rescued, smuggled into the United States, and later sent to prison for some violation of the neutrality laws.

An Indian boy had been assigned to take care of the Spaniard, and one day a guard caught the boy stealing a glass of cream from the guards' kitchen for his patient, and he told the boy that he was going to report him. The Spaniard lit in on that guard and told him his pedigree in half a dozen languages. So the guard reported them both.

That put the King in a bad spot. He could not punish the Spaniard, and in fairness, he could not punish the boy. The best he could do was reprimand them both. He lectured the Spaniard on doing his own time and not involving himself in the affairs of others.

Now this Spaniard was a brilliant and well educated man, but he pronounced in Spanish.

"You theenk that eet ees kee-o-keek that I defend the eendeeoo?" the Spaniard said. "But I weell have you to understand that eet ees the duty of those capable of doeeng so to defend the weak and oppressed who are not capable of defendeeng themselves, eef eet were not for defendeeng eendeeos, I would not be een thees chair, or een your preeson."

"Do you mind repeating that first sentence again? I am not sure that I understood you correctly."

"You theenk that eet ees kee-o-teek that I defend the eendeeo, ees what I said. I weel...."

'Ha! I see! Well, be careful hereafter! Try to contain yourself! I know that may be difficult in your condition, but try to do the best you can." The King turned on his heels and walked away.

He went up to his room where he kept the unabridged dictionary. He did not come down for supper. He did not come down for breakfast the next morning.

Twenty times he had gone through all the cs and ks in his dictionary without results before he remembered that some words beginning in Q have a K sound. A dozen times he went through the Qs without results. One word arrested his attention. Quixotic, but the pronunciation was all wrong. It was pronounced kwiks-ot-ik. Like or pertaining to Don Quixote.

The King had heard of Don Quixote. He was a Spaniard, and the first syllable was pronounced kee or quee. That was it. The Spaniard had employed the Spanish pronunciation. The King read the rest of the definition:

…the hero of a Spanish romance by Cervantes ridiculing knight-errantry; hence, ridiculously, chivalrous, or romantic.

That must be it. The King closed the big book with a resounding report, rose slowly and stiffly to his feet, unlocked his door and walked slowly and stiffly down the stairs.

In the meantime the story had spread throughout the prison. Every man in the institution knew the word that The King was looking for and many of them were placing bets on how long it would take him to find it.

The King forced his tired features into a smile as he turned into the library.

"Hmm! By the way did you ever hear of a book entitled Don Quixote by some Spaniard named Cervantes?"

"Oh, yes!" said the Librarian. "It is one of the classics. I had it in my literature course when I was in school."

"It exists in English?"

"Certainly!"

"Do we have a copy?"

"Yes!" The Librarian ran his eyes over the shelves. "Would you care to read it? It is considered one of the world's great books. Oh! There it is, right under your hand on the end of the counter; one of the boys must have just brought it in."

The Librarian reported that The King turned a little green around the gills as he picked up the thick volume and noticed the small print, but he forced a smile.

"Yes! I've heard a lot about this book. I believe I would like to read it," The King said as he tucked the book under his arms, went back upstairs to his room and locked the door.

Shortly before noon the next day the King appeared. He had bathed, shaved, dolled himself up in some of his best clothes, and placed a white hyacinth in the button hole on his left lapel.

He approached the Spaniard, who was sunning himself in his wheel chair on the front lawn and, after inquiring about the man's health, turned the conversation to the subject of the great, Spanish writer, Cervantes, and his wonderful book Don Quixote, and as he talked of and laughed over the old stories, which according to his statement he had read some years previously, the Spaniard laughed, too, but not over the stories The King mentioned, which demonstrated that he had actually read the book from cover to cover.

"I take my hat off to you," said the Spaniard, bowing as low as he could in the wheelchair. Now I know why all zeese men call you zee Keeng. You are zee keeng. I am zee very fast reader een Spanish, but I could not have so thoroughly digested zat book in one night to have saved my life."

The King's face flushed a deep scarlet.

"You know, Keeng, eet appears zat we are both a leettle kee-o-teek, or as you would say kwicks o tik."

"Hmm! You are probably right, General. But if you give me away, I am a ruined man."

"I could not give you away," said the Spaniard without a trace of accent. "Every man in the institution knows all about your deep interest in exact words. I was told of it on the day of my arrival. You are King to all these men because they also know that you are human…"

"And more than a little kee-o-teek," said The King with a chuckle. "You know, I got my biggest laughs out of the fool, San Chopansa, particularly that place where he sat as judge. The way he handled that rape case was worthy of Solomon. I am going to read that and several other parts again."

The King Philosophy of Imprisonment

Normally the King was a very pleasant man, but he felt that in his job he had to always be on his dignity, and keep both guards and convicts in their proper place – and in this he was probably right. But he could, on occasion, step down to the convict's level and joke with him without any loss of prestige. But no new man would ever guess that. The King would growl and snap at them as if he were going to fry them in oil and eat them for breakfast. One day the Writer had occasion to mention this, and The King expounded his philosophy substantially as follows:

"The prisoner must be made to realize at once that loss of liberty means something. Half of these youngsters sent here should never have been sent to prison in the first place. In Canada or England, they would have been spanked and sent home, and I think that policy is better than ours. If I could take them and give them all the hell the law would allow for about one month, then send them home, not one in fifty would ever come back. Once they become hardened or adjusted to prison life, it is not so easy. They know that life, even in prison, is bearable, and they no longer dread it. The greatest kindness one can do for them is to make things as disagreeable as possible, and teach them that prison is no joke. I can do that with men serving sentences of two years or less. I cannot do it with a boy with a sentence like yours without doing more harm than good. I have to find a soft spot for the long timer, if I do not want to ruin him completely."

"The second or third morning would have been enough for me."

"What happened?"

"That was the morning Devenpeck ran the Chili in for getting out of line."

"Oh! That! I guess it did look pretty rough to you, but I have never tolerated brutality."

"I know."

The Chili Affair

This was referred to in the prologue, when discussing the Writer's philosophy of serving time.

The second evening after the Writer's arrival at the prison, Chili was turned out of the hole. The next morning he was sent out on the Writer's car crew.

As previously mentioned, the men went to work at almost a dogtrot, and there were guards along the line hurrying them at every step. In going out to the excavating gang, the men passed between the end of the laundry and the new kitchen which was then under construction.

The Chili was about ten feet behind the Writer as he came out of this passageway. The man looked terrible after ten days on bread and water, and it was obvious that he was very weak.

"Close up, there! Close up! Close up!" shouted Guard Devenpeck several times.

"Aw, for Christ's sake! Keep your shirt on! I'm coming!" The Chili's voice was drab, weak, and listless. He staggered a little on his feet, and stepped sideways to let the man behind him pass.

Devenpeck sprang forward, grabbed the Chili by the throat, gave him a quick shove that sent him sprawling over some stones behind him and rolling in the dirt.

The Writer heard the snap of a rifle bolt, looked up and saw that two guards had the fallen man covered. Devenpeck approached the Chili as if he were going to kick the fallen man.

Chili scrambled to his feet and fled toward the office, his arms thrown over his head as if expecting to be struck from behind.

"What will they do to him?" The Writer, sick at his stomach at the sheer horror of the whole performance, asked the man beside him.

"Put him back in the hole."

"How long?"

"About ten more days."

"But they can't! He didn't do nothing! I saw the whole thing! The poor fellow was just weak! He just came out of the hole!"

"He will be charged with attempting to assault a guard. He knew better than to step out of line. There was a pile of shovels over there. The guard was counting his men as they came out. If he permitted Chili to step aside and went on counting the other men, the Chili could have snatched up a shovel and knocked his can off. He is very treacherous, and the guard knows it. In most joints he would get his brains beat out for a stunt like that. In Folsom, the tower guard would have shot him.

The utter callousness of his associates to human suffering was more horrifying to the Writer than what had happened to the unfortunate Chili. He wondered if prison would do that to him, too…so harden him that he could look upon suffering and injustice without emotion. If that is what prison did, if it killed all the good in a man, like sympathy for suffering and resentment of injustice, would not it be better to end the whole business at once? He wondered if those guards could and would kill him if he hit that wire? That would be one quick way out.

He voiced the question to one of the men beside him.

"No! They would not kill you, but they would cripple you, and you might lose an arm or leg. They are all trained marksmen, and any one of them can hit a dollar at that distance. They have been ordered to stop you, but not to kill you."

"Well, if what just happened to the Chili happened to me, I would kill someone or make them kill me."

"So long as you feel that way, it will never happen. A thirty-five year sentence in Folsom, twenty-one years flat, in one of the toughest joints in America, and I haven't a scar on my body. I have never had a hand put on me. These screws are not fools. They pick their marks, and they never pick on a man who has any character. I've seen hundreds of guys worked over, but like the Chili, they usually asked for it."

But the next Sunday, every man on the car crew and a lot of others abstained from eating their roast beef for dinner. They took a chance on being punished themselves in order to carry it away from the table and smuggle it to the Chili.

The men had the run of the corridor all day long on Sunday. The meat was cut into thin slices; each slice was placed in a tobacco sack and pulled through a quarter inch crack under the door. First a wire was slipped under the door, and the Chili pulled the sack in. Then he passed the wire out, and another piece of meat was put in the sack and sent in the same way. A bunch of men crowded around the hole door, arguing so that their bodies shielded the man doing the passing from the man in the window.

McGuire

The King recognized the fact that force was necessary in controlling men, but he really did not tolerate any form of brutality. Any force employed was to be the result of a cool and deliberate evaluation of necessity, a judgment formed without heat or passion. He considered any man who could not hold his temper under every form of provocation utterly unsuited for prison work. He was ably seconded in this view by Mr. Meyers. Both of them had had experience in handling insane persons.

Mr. Meyers was a big blond, pleasant-faced young man, with smooth, clear skin and very little beard. Actually, it is doubtful that there was as much as a year's difference in his and The King's ages, but on first contact, Mr. Meyers appeared to be at least fifteen years The King's junior, both in appearance and personality.

He was a big man, but it was a deceptive bigness that did not register on the minds of others at once. He stood a little under six-feet and weighed well over two hundred pounds. Years and good living had covered his well-knit body with an even layer of fat, none of which had gone to his abdomen or to double or triple chins.

He had played both football and baseball in college, and for some years after leaving college, he had played big league baseball. At one time, he had even been catcher on one of the Chicago teams, and if the Writer can trust his memory, Meyers had also been a catcher for one of the Boston teams. When an arm injury made it impossible for him to continue in baseball, he had taken employment at the Washington Asylum at Steilacoom and married a nurse.

It was at the Asylum that Meyers met Halligan, and the two men became firm friends. As soon as Halligan had become Warden, he had induced Meyers to become his deputy.

Mr. Meyers did not like the job, although it paid him more than the State. He was an extremely kind-hearted man, and it often hurt him to have to carry out orders that to him seemed harsh. Also, the job kept him separated from his wife, who had become a supervisor of one of the Women's buildings at the Asylum.

Everyone liked Mr. Meyers. He almost never reported an inmate, and he took no responsibility for enforcing the rules, excepting when The King was off of the Island. At such times he had to act as Warden. It is an odd fact that he was much less liked in that capacity than The King, for then he would see many things that he never saw as Deputy Warden, and was much quicker to inflict punishment that was The King. Although his punishments were always less severe, he lacked The King's judicial sense of fairness. And it must always be remembered that kindness, no matter how great, can never be a substitute for justice in the handling of human beings.

Meyers used to be fond of saying:

"Any person who loses his temper in dealing with a child, a prisoner, or an insane person, no matter what the provocation, is unfit to exercise authority over human beings. He does not belong in prison work. The prisoner is forced to live an abnormal life, so he cannot be expected to be normal. He is actually no more responsible for his conduct than the insane person. It may be necessary to inflict punishment in order to maintain good order, but it should never be done in anger or in a spirit of vengeance. Such conduct stamps the prison man as a worse social menace than the prisoners he rules."

Now, McGuire was a big hotheaded Irishman serving ten years. He loved to fight, and he would fight anybody at any time. As a consequence, he had been in constant trouble throughout his sentence and had served it flat.

McGuire looked upon a man without a temper as some sort of a sissy or freak. He could not imagine any red-blooded Irishman not seeing red under provocation; so he looked upon Meyer's statement and The King's policy as so much hogwash. He had deliberately tried to make both of them lose their tempers on many occasions, and he boasted that he would make them both blow their tops before he left the prison.

On the evening of his eleventh to last day in the prison, Mike McGuire[124] walked up to Meyers' window just before supper, threw the window up with enough force to almost shatter the glass, and cried to Halligan, who was standing in the office.

---

124   This man was also known as Big Mike, but he is to be distinguished from the Big Mike previously mentioned – Part I – Chapter XII.

"Hey Halligan! Do you want to know what I think of you?"

The entire population sensed that something was up and flocked around the window.

Halligan walked over to the window and said in a calm voice, "I don't think that is important, Mike, but it is my business to listen to anything you have to say, then take such action as to me seems justified by the facts."

"I sure wish you would, for if you did that, you would hang yourself. I think you are __ __ __." There followed a full fifteen minutes of the vilest invectives that ever flowed over a human tongue. There was not a low, mean, vile, or degrading act of which a human being is capable of which McGuire did not accuse the King. He wound up with these words:

"__ __ __ __ and if you could trace your ancestry back for six generations, you would find them swinging from tree to tree by their tails, you yellow-bellied, North of Ireland, ____ ____! God damn you!" Mike spat with disgust, turned, and started away from the window.

"Is that all?" asked The King in the same calm, unruffled tone of voice.

"Well, Jesus Christ! Ain't that enough?"

"Don't forget to close the window!"

That night they put Mike in the hole.

On the evening of his seventh day on bread and water, Mike informed the Doctor that he had not had a bowel movement in a week and secured a big dose of salts.

It was the rule for Mr. Meyers and a guard to come in directly after breakfast, but before the gangs went out for the day, and wash his face and hand, before chaining him to the door where he remained until noon.

Mr. Meyers always brought the handcuffs in with him, but because it took two hands to unlock the bull lock, he handed the cuffs to the guard to hold while he opened the dungeon. There was always a gun guard in the window of the Administration Building with a rifle.

On this particular occasion, the guard with Mr. Meyers was a new man who had arrived at the prison from Leavenworth only a few days before.

Mike's salts had worked well. He had emptied the surplus water from his drinking can into his night bucket and thoroughly mixed the mess. Only a person who had taken a dose of salts after a week on bread and water without a bowel movement can appreciate the result – others can take the Writer's word for it that it was something – definitely, not lilacs.

As Mr. Meyers opened the dungeon door, McGuire neatly and deftly hung that night bucket and its contents on his head, and stepped back into the cell, out of the range of the gun guard.

Mr. Meyers extricated himself from the bucket just in time to get a glimpse of that new guard charging into the cell, the hand holding the cuff drawn back in the act of striking at Mike's head.

Now there is not much chance that the new guard could have whipped Mike, even with those cuffs and the advantage of Mike's weakened condition, for the big Irishman was tough as wire nails, and he had a kick in either hand that would floor an ox. The guard had no chance to try, however.

"None of that," snapped Meyers, as he shot out a gnarled, crooked-fingered hand that had snagged many a tipped foul hot off the bat. He grabbed the new guard's arm and sent him spinning against the wall, ten feet away. "I don't know how they handle such things at Leavenworth, but just one more stunt like that here and you will be going ashore on the four o'clock boat" (meaning that the guard would be fired). Dropping his voice to its usual calm, pleasant, conversational level, Meyers continued, "All right, Mike! You had better pick up your bucket, go down and get your water and wash up." Just as if nothing had happened.

The payoff came two days later.

At that time no civilian clothing was made on the Island. When a man came in, it was the custom to wash and press his clothing and store it in moth balls against the day of his release. The day before discharge, the clothing was taken out of storage, aired, cleaned, and pressed, and the discharged inmate left the prison in the same suit he had arrived in.

Mothballs however, slowly evaporate, and ten years is a long time. When Mike's suit was taken from the bundle, it simply fell apart.

The Government gave each released prisoner a completely new outfit of clothing, but allowed only twelve dollars and fifty cents for that purpose. A Jew clothing store in Tacoma had taken a contract to furnish complete discharge outfits for that price. Naturally, the shoes had paper soles and the suit and hat did not amount to much. It was the practice for some guard to accompany the discharged prisoner to Tacoma, get his clothing and buy his railroad ticket for him, but a man had to have something to go to town in.

"I don't know what we are going to do with you, Mike," Mr. Meyers remarked as he turned Mike out of the hole that last morning. "When we got your clothes out yesterday to press them, they fell apart. It looks like we will have to send you to town in a gunny sack or in stripes."

"Good Christ! You can't do that. It's against the law to take a man into any public place dressed in stripes, and you can't turn a man out naked."

"I know! But what can we do? Even if some other prisoner was willing to loan you his clothes, there is not a man here whose suit would fit you."

"God damned if you ain't right. But say! You and me are about the same size. You ain't got some geed-up clothes you could let me wear to town, have you?"

"For Irish gall you certainly take the cake. I am glad you brought that up, though."

"Now, don't be like that! You know we have always been pals. I've always contended that for a Dutchman, you were not a bad guy, though how you could stoop to working for that Orangeman had always beat me. But you know that I've always liked you. I was not even mad at you the other morning. I just wanted to see how you would look if you blew your top and got good and mad once."

"Tell you what I'll do Mike. I won't loan you a suit, but I'll give you the one you threw shit on."

"By the holy mother of God, what in hell do you think I could do with that? They would put me off the streetcar."

"There is no shit on the suit now. It has been washed and pressed. It will just about fit you. Frank can let out the sleeves and legs a little and maybe take in the waist of the pants an inch or two, and it will be a perfect fit. The suit cost me forty dollars when it was new. It's a much better suit than anything you will get over town, and there is a lot of wear in it, yet. If you want the suit, it is yours on one condition. You can use your clothing money for a good shirt, hat, and shoes, and you will at least look like a gentleman."

"Now, I like that! What is your condition? I might have known that any time a Dutchman gives you anything there will be a string tied to it."

"This is not much of a string, Mike. At least it is one that you should enjoy. The only condition is that if I ever meet you over in Tacoma, you will take a walk around in an alley with me. I cannot hit you while I have a gun pointed at your head, but if I ever meet you over in town, I am going to beat your God-damned Irish block off or try to, and I think I can do it."

"Shake! It'll be a pleasure! I always knew you were a pretty good guy for a Dutchman, but I still can't understand how you can stomach that Orangeman. May the best man win."

They did meet, but instead of fighting they had a few drinks and dinner together, and laughed over their past differences.

The Burglar Alarm

There is nothing more characteristic of the good sportsmanship of prison men of that day than The King's burglar alarm.

Both Halligan and McCloughry would have been ashamed to put a Dictaphone or a stoolpigeon in any man's cell. If either suspected a man was doing anything inimical to the prison he would order the guards to watch that man, but not to spy on him, and he would never stoop to spying on any man himself.

Prison maintenance was cared for by about twenty trusties working directly under the King. Each of these men had done his hitch in the excavating gang. In each case The King had studied the man's character carefully over many months before making him a trusty, but once a man was made a trusty, no guard was justified in reporting that man for anything without first consulting with The King. Nor could any guard, or even the Deputy

Warden, give a trusty an order. Either could ask the man to do anything they thought he should do, but only The King could give an order.

There were also many men doing special work under The King, such as cleaning windows, painting and all of the many odd jobs around the prison. These men wore stripes. They worked under The King without guards, and they took orders only from The King.

Not being a complete fool, The King knew that these jobs were prized by the inmates only in proportion to the escape from constant surveillance they afforded. He was also psychologist enough to know that the only way that you can trust any man is to trust him fully and completely within the limits imposed upon him.

He knew that all these men violated the written rules of the prison every day: they connived for cigarette papers, smoked cigarettes, gambled, had their own private little romances, indulged in horse play that wasn't always very nice or polite in nature, sometimes made wine or beer and got a little drunk, frequently sought secluded spots to settle differences with their fists, often sneaked away to spend a few minutes with some congenial friend when their work was finished, and often connived for little treats from the guard's kitchen and the hospital. He also knew however, that most of these men and boys were hard and sincere workers, they worked longer hours than the men on the gangs, and they carried their share of responsibility for making the institution function. He knew that if one of these men told him a given piece of work would be done at a given time, it would be done at that time.

If he caught one of these men red-handedly violating a rule, he felt that he was compelled to take some notice of the fact, but that was something he had no desire to do. He felt in his heart that so long as things did not get too far out of line, these boys had a right to any little pleasure they could steal.

So the King kept a pair of beautiful, little, well-trained fox terriers that ran before him everywhere he went. The convicts called them the burglar alarm for they always turned every corner at least ten seconds before The King turned it. If one of his boys was caught doing anything he shouldn't have been doing, it was pure carelessness.

It was the same principle that made him require his night guard to carry a lighted lantern at all times. The guard's function was to see that the men did not fight, did not come out of their cells and try to escape; but he was not there to spy upon the prisoners or eavesdrop upon their private conversations, and the lantern made any such conduct on the part of the guard impossible. Occasionally, new guards who thought they were smart would put the lantern out, and try to sneak around the galleries, but they usually did not do it more than once.

As different as they were in many respects, both Halligan and McCloughry would have been utterly ashamed to employ the stoolpigeon systems or electronic devices in common use in Federal Prisons today. Each would have considered the use of such methods a confession of his own utter incompetence.

PART I – CHAPTER XV

McNiel Island, Continued
(Aspects of Management)

The Big Strike

The Doctor who was at the Island when the writer went there did not last long. He was soon replaced by a Doctor Boles, who was not much of a Doctor, although he was a kind and sincere man who was perfectly frank and honest about his shortcomings. He once said to the writer:

"I can remove an appendix, reduce a hernia, set a broken leg, deliver a baby, and that is about all."

"Well, Doc, I don't think you will have to deliver any babies, though that is not saying that some of the boys don't try hard enough."

"Now, do they, really? I've heard about such things, but I never believed them. Tell me, isn't it terribly painful to them?"

"Doc! Such questions are out of order. The only way a man could answer would be from personal experience, and nobody is going to cop out."

"I did not mean it that way. For that matter, I am frightfully curious, but I would never, what you call, snitch on anyone. The truth is, I have never had an orgasm in my life. When I worked in the hospital in St. Louis, I was assigned to the women's venereal ward. What I saw so sickened me that I made up my mind that I would never touch a woman until I married."

"How old are you, Doc?"

"Twenty-seven!"

"Well, all I can say is that before you do marry, you had better see a good Doctor. I would not call you a liar, but I just can't see it. I had my first orgasm when I was nine, and was chasing women when I was thirteen, so I just can't understand how a normal person could reach your age without sexual experience. Once you get a taste of it you will see what you have missed."

"Taste!"

"Sure, Doc, I was speaking figuratively, but kissing a clean one never killed anybody."

The Writer and Mitchel had gotten their heads together at once. They were both boys of the type that are never heavy muscled, eat enormous quantities of food, which they burn up with the greatest of ease, without ever putting on an ounce of fat. They were both probably suffering from hyperthyroidism, and both had tachycardia (rapid pulse), but there really wasn't a thing wrong with either of them.

The Writer had discovered that by slightly holding his breath and starving his system for oxygen, he could drive his heart beat to well over one-forty and that the beat would become violent and irregular, so that it would sound like the explosions of a missing gas engine: put, put, put….put….put, put, put…put, put, put. The beats separated by commas were very close together. All this meant was that the heart muscle was overworked, but poor Doctor Boles did not know that.

Mitch had been using a similar trick to speed his heart up. He would work himself up emotionally until he was very mad, while keeping himself calm in appearance. The adrenalin thrown into his blood would make his heart pound and race, but it would not miss beats. So he adopted the Writer's method, which was surer and produced more dramatic results.

Doctor Boles, who also had tachycardia, attacks of palpitation, probably the result of his abnormal sex life and who worried about them, took the boys' condition seriously. He would permit them to miss work whenever they asked him, and he would given them codeine and morphine whenever they asked for it, not just a tablet or two, but an envelope half full.

So once or twice per week the boys would stay in and have a little bender for themselves, which greatly eased the strain of imprisonment.

During the Spring of 1910 a great deal of work was being done on the new buildings, and when there was concrete to pour, the gangs were taken off the bank and put to mixing and pouring it. That was hard work, and it usually did not take long for the Writer and little Mitch to check in sick. The boys had become very good friends, but that was all there was between them.

Because he was staying in that day, the Writer did not become involved in the first strike or witness it, but the following account of the occurrence was obtained from his cellmate, Frank Ironsides, who was one of the first men to quit.

There was a construction foreman by the name of Gregor or McGregor, (the Writer has forgotten which, so we will call him Gregor) who was a medium sized man.

The men were pouring the upper gallery of the new cell house and Gregor was driving them, hoping to get the paving all done that day. Two gangs of mixers mixed the concrete on the floor of the new dining room, and a long line of men brought it up the long ramps in wheelbarrows. The work was so organized that these men did not have one minute's rest. They went up one side of the block and down the other, round and round and round.

By three o'clock in the afternoon everyone was nearing exhaustion, and tempers were very short. There was a little fellow on the wheelbarrow by the name of Anderson who was as pugnacious as a game cock, and a big fellow named Carmack, who weighed about two hundred twenty without any fat, whose job it was to scrape the last of the concrete out of each buggy as it was dumped.

As Anderson dumped his load, part of the concrete spilled over the side of the form.

"Hey! You son of a bitch!" cried Gregor. "Be careful!"

"Why, f___ you!" cried Anderson. "If you don't like the way I am doing it, do it yourself!" he yelled, dropping his wheelbarrow and attempting to square off to Gregor.

The staging was narrow, and allowed him poor footing. The wheelbarrow went tumbling over the side of the block. Gregor reached out and grabbed Anderson, crying as he did so!

"Why, you little C____ S_____, I'll throw you off the block."

Carmack, who was as much bigger than Gregor as Gregor was bigger than Anderson, reached out a long arm and grabbed the back of Gregor's neck.

"If there is any of that," said the big man calmly, "I'll take a hand."

The ground guard, a new man by the name of Conners, took Anderson and Carmack in.

Now, when a man was taken in from the work that way, he was just turned into the cell house until The King was ready to try him, usually that night after supper, but sometimes he would try them at once and put them in the hole.

All the gang thought that Anderson and Carmack were going to the hole unjustly, for Gregor had no business cursing Anderson in the first place and certainly no business threatening to throw him off the block. So the whole gang quit, lined up in an orderly manner, and went on it.

The ground guard with the gang had lost his head and called up on the tower guard to shoot them. The tower guard had thrown down his rifle all right, hut he had also told Conners that he was taking command and for Conners to keep his nose out of it. Then he told the men to march on in, in their regular manner.

Meyers opened the door and checked them into the cell house.

That night The King called each man out.

"You are charged with refusing to work. What have you to say for yourselves?"

"I do not refuse to work, but I do refuse to work under conditions where a man can be cursed and have his life threatened for what is a pure accident. Those cell-wall forms are only four inches wide. Any man dumping a wheelbarrow of concrete is apt to spill some over the side. I am not willing to work under these conditions or if even Anderson or Camack are punished unjustly. And I am not willing to work under Mr. Gregor until he apologizes to Anderson."

"I have always tried to never punish any man unjustly. Anderson and Carmack were the first men tried. They were acquitted and will not be punished. Both Mr. Gregor and Mr. Conners have also been tried. They have been reprimanded and they have both admitted that they were wrong and have apologized to me. Are you willing to work under Mr. Gregor under those conditions? That is, do you consider his apology to be sufficient? I can inform you that Anderson said that it was acceptable to him."

There was only one thing the prisoner could say.

"Well, in that case, it is acceptable to me."

"And you are willing to work under Mr. Gregor? I can assure you that nothing of that kind will occur in the future."

"Yes, sir!"

"That is all! You are excused!"

One thing that the old timers, Tom Allen, Old Man Morton, Shea Bockman, and even his cellmate, Ironsides, who was serving his first stretch in prison, had preached to the Writer from his first day in prison was, never join in any mass action, by strike, petition or anything of that kind, for the authorities can't let you win, no matter how just your cause. Go as an individual. Use your own head, and you may win if you have a good case, but the minute the officials give in to any mass action, the cons will take over the prison and the authorities will no longer be in control. They cannot permit that.

And that night the Writer's cellmate and Beckman, who had become librarian, again renewed their warnings to the Writer.

"There is sure to be another strike. The con won on this one, but they will not win the next one, so watch your step. Don't you get involved. Remember you have more *goodtime* than two thirds of these fellows have time, so be careful."

"Remember!" Morton said. "If the cons don't start this strike, the officials will. The cons won this time because Gregor and Conners were wrong and they were fools, but that old King is wise. He will take the strike idea out of them."

The new strike was not long in coming. About three weeks after the first strike, the concrete work on the new building was completed and the men went back on the excavating gang. Little Mitch was no longer on the Writer's car crew however, and The King held his car crew in for some other work.

As the men lined up on the job to be counted after dinner on this day, the guard, a fellow named O'Conners, made a little speech.

The Warden has issued orders that you men work continuously. There is an extra car. When you shovelers have filled one car, you will go to the extra car and fill it while the pushers are bringing the other car back. When the pushers bring a car back, there will always be a loaded car waiting for them. Do you understand that? These are not my orders. It is the Warden's idea, but I am going to have to enforce them, and I will. I want you all to understand that."

All of the men went to work grumbling, talking of strike. The Writer saw Doctor Boles come down the hill and head for the office. The King was all set to have someone buck, or the whole gang buck.

"Listen!" the Writer said to his fellows, "the King is set for another strike. You guys can strike if you want to. You don't have to if you don't want to, but I want you all to remember this. If you strike, you will lose, and I am not going in on it. I am going my own way. I have my own plans. I am going to beat this, and after I do, maybe some of you can follow my example. But whatever happens, I am warning you; I will be all right. I do not want anyone to quit work to back my hand. You won't help me, but you might hurt me and yourselves. If my plan works, others can use it, and I figure enough of us can beat this order one at a time so the King will abandon it."

"I think we should all strike right now," said Fain.

All of the others began slowing down on their shoveling, for it was obvious that no man could follow their usual pace all day long without rest, but the Writer tore into that work at a faster pace than usual.

"Slow down, Bob! Christ, you cannot keep that pace up all day," several men protested.

"You set your own pace and let me set mine. Only, do not try to back my play. You won't help me, and you may spoil it."

"You have a plan?"

"Sure I have a plan, and I think it will work. If it does, I will tell you all how it is done."

The Writer kept right on working as hard as he could for about half or three quarters of an hour. He swung his shovel until the buttons of his shirt worked loose, his shirt worked out of his pants, and his body was caked with dust and streaked with sweat. Then he started starving his body for oxygen – by holding his breath. It was not long until his heart started missing beats, and his head began to spin.

He dropped his shovel, walked over to a pile of sand, and threw himself to the ground and stretched out on his back.

The guard came running over.

"What is the matter, Stroud? You refuse to work?"

"No! I am all in!"

"Come on!"

The guard took the Writer to Mr. Meyers' office. There was The King sitting in the chair in which he always held court. Mr. Meyers was standing on one side of him and Doctor Boles on the other. The Writer had held his breath almost all the way into the office. He now suppressed his tendency to gasp for air and only took what little he needed to stay on his feet.

"I have Stroud here for refusing to work," O'Conners said.

"I beg your pardon, Sir! Did I refuse to work?"

"How about that, Mr. O'Conner?" The King said. "Just tell me what happened."

"I saw him drop his shovel, stagger over to a pile of sand and throw himself to the ground. I ran over there and asked him if he refused to work. He said, 'No! I am all in.' I brought him in as per your orders. I want to add that he has always been one of the best workers on the gang."

O'Conners was trying to keep the Writer out of the hole.

The King went into his prepared speech. "I have timed you men with a stop watch, and I find that out of each hour you have spent twenty-eight minutes…"

"I am not interested in that. I have not refused to work. The guard has told you that I am one of the best workers on the gang. I simply went over and threw myself on the ground and told the guard I was all in. I cannot do the impossible."

"Well, I don't want any man to kill himself, to do the impossible. Examine him."

Doctor Boles stepped forward and reached for the Writer's wrist. He dropped it and placed his hand on the Writer's chest. With every beat of the Writer's heart, he could see the Doctor's hand move.

"Come here!" Boles beckoned to Meyers. "Feel that!"

"Why it is like a motor boat, missing on two cylinders."

"Just so! It is skipping beats, which is characteristic of heart failure."

"I never saw anything like it," said Meyers.

"Warden," said Doctor Boles, "This man is telling you the truth, he is all in. I don't know how in the world he ever got in here under his own power. His heart is beating one hundred and forty per minute. There are skips in it of as much as five beats. Most men faint before they reach that stage. He must have a terrific amount of will power to have kept going as long as he did, and he should not be on his feet now." The Doctor grabbed a chair and forced the Writer into it.

"Well, I want to know just how much work he can do."

"I would say not much of anything. Surely no heavy work at all."

"What do you say?"

"I am naturally a hard worker. I can do as much in a day as any man in this prison, but I must be able to work as I please. I am suffering from a congenital myocardial insufficiency. When I overstrain, my heart starts acting as it is acting now. It races, and all of the fibers do not work together, so it misses beats. When that happens I have to stop and sit down. If I don't, I will fall down, and that is not so good."

"The condition is noted on his record," said Mr. Meyers. "Doctor _____ noticed it when he came in."

"He has complained to me occasionally and I have given him lay-ins and sedatives when he needed them, but I never saw him in as bad a condition as he is today."

"Do you think you could take a pick and break up lumps that come down from the bank, if allowed to work as you please?"

"Certainly, I have always held my end up."

"All right! You may return to your gang, and please ask Mr. O'Conners to step in here." As soon as The King had ordered the Doctor to examine the Writer, always a preliminary to putting a man in the hole, O'Conners had returned to the gang.

As soon as the men saw him returning alone they all thought the Writer had gone to the hole, and in spite of the Writer's warnings, they all threw down their tools and quit; and as the Writer returned to the gang, he met the gang coming in. In a way it made him feel like a traitor to his group. These men were striking over him, because they thought he had gone to the hole, but he had used their common situation to gain his own ends. He had won everything, and they could only lose.

He had accomplished what he had been planning on accomplishing since his first day in the prison, for as he had left the office, the Doctor had followed him as far as the porch and had whispered, "Any time they try to make you do any work you don't want to do, send for me."

When the gang reached the guard's dining room, Halligan had them all lined up facing him. Then he repeated the carefully composed little speech justifying his action, and this time, no one interrupted him, and told him that his theory did not fit the facts.

"Now," he concluded, "it is my orders that you work continuously for a full eight hours per day. Do you want to work?" he barked at the first man in the line, a *yegg* named Love who had only been in the prison for a few weeks.

"No!" said Love.

"Stand over there!" barked The King, indicating a spot near the door to the cell house. "Do you want to work?" he barked to the next man.

"Yes, Sir!" the man said.

He went right on down the line, and all of the men wanted to work.

"Now," he said to Love, "don't you think you want to work too? You see you are all alone. There is nothing to be gained by punishing yourself."

"All right! You win! I'll work too."

There were two men on a car crew, Wheeler and Jackson, who had been down at the dump when the gang went in.

Hastily the Writer explained to them what he had done. Wheeler asked a couple of quick questions about the breathing technique.

"Come on," he said to Jackson. "I'm going in, and I am quitting for good."

"So am I."

These two men went to the hole, but two days later, Wheeler was taken to the hospital with a heart attack. It developed that he really did have a leaky valve, and that breathing technique came very close to killing him.

A few days later, Jackson followed Wheeler to the hospital. He had been complaining of stomach trouble for months, and it developed that he actually had cancer of the stomach. These two men spent the rest of their time in the hospital.

For three months the Writer puttered around and did what work he pleased. He was careful to do good work, however, and a fair amount of it on any job he did at all. But when he was not feeling like doing any particular job, he just went in and told Mr. Meyers to call the Doctor.

After about two trips the Doctor would say, "Any time he says that he does not feel like working, he does not have to. I will sign the lay-in slip."

The King hated to see any man idle, and he was always digging up light odd jobs for the Writer to do. If the job was interesting, the Writer would do it and do it well. If it was not interesting, he would not be feeling good.

One day a middle-aged man, a convict trusty named Atwell called the Writer to one side.

I am going out in thirty days. The King has told me to break in someone for my job. It is yours, if you want it. I promised The King that I would find a good man. It is not a job for a moron, but I think you could hold it.

The Writer did not know Atwell, had only seen him a few times.

"I would have to see the work before I made up my mind."

"You can come out in the morning. Just tell Mr. Meyers, and he will turn you out."

The Writer went to his cellmate and Johnson.

"Why would this Atwell want to pick me?"

"He didn't," said Johnson. "I told The King you were the best man in the prison for the job. Go on out there and learn the work. Do it Atwell's way until he goes out, then do it your way. The King was a little skeptical about making you a trusty, but I told him, "You do not have to worry about that. If that boy had wanted to escape, he would not have stayed here a week. He is only interested in improving himself. He knows that all he has to do is to sit tight for two more years, and he will be free."

Two Sundays later The King called the Writer out before himself and the Doctor, and the Writer learned that he had oversold the Doctor on the bad heart idea.

"The Laundry is hard work. You will have to be on your feet for long hours. You will have to iron all the officers' clothing by hand. I am afraid that it will be too much for you."

You forget, Doctor that I have never complained of any job where I can be my own boss and work as I please. You know Warden, that I have often done bigger days work than men much huskier than I am who have nothing wrong with them."

"Yes, I know that you do, but I don't want to do anything to hurt you, or of which the Doctor disapproves."

The Writer had to argue for thirty minutes and kick that Doctor in the shins three times to get the job. When they were alone the Doctor said:

"Now, if it is too hard for you, don't forget to come and see me."

"Thanks, Doc! You are a swell guy, but don't worry about this heart of mine, between me and you, there isn't a damn thing wrong with it, and I want that job."

"You mean to say that you can make your heart act up that way?"

"Sure! By holding my breath while taking violent exercise until I am starved for air. I can do it until my face and hands turn blue."

"Well! I never would have guessed it. You have more will power than I have. Anyway, keep it to yourself because if you ever need my help, it will give me a good excuse to take jurisdiction."

"Thanks, Doc! You are a swell guy!"

That is the kind of man Boles was. He was not much of a doctor, but he would always help any man who would give him a shadow of an excuse upon which to act. A short time later, he made up his mind to quit, go back to school, and really learn his profession. The Writer heard many years later that he had become a top-notch doctor.

Boles was replaced by Dr. Bond. He was a tall young man in his early thirties and was a real doctor. After being hired for the job, he started to work at once.

Frank Burns

Burns, a man in his mid-thirties, was serving seven years for counterfeiting. He and his partner had previously served sentences in San Quentin and Folsom. They had tried to escape a short time before the Writer arrived at the Island. About six months before Bond came there, Burns had claimed that he was sick and unable to work. He complained of pain in his back and left side, ranging from his shoulder blade to the lower part of his chest cavity. Boles had been unable to find anything wrong with him, and The King had put him in the hole for seven days.

When Burns came out of the hole, he was so obviously sick that Boles excused him from all work. For months he laid around the cell house without treatment, becoming worse and worse. Then he began developing abscesses in different parts of his body, and he was in that condition when Bond arrived. Bond took one look at Burns, got one whiff of his breath and said, "I am going to operate on you this afternoon. You had pleurisy in the beginning. Being left untreated, you have developed empyema. Your pleura are full of pus, and it is poisoning your system. Two months ago I could have saved you. Now, I don't know. I will have to go in to see. Are you willing?"

"Sure!" But you must promise me one thing; if you can't save me, you will tell me the truth."

"I will do that, but you must promise me that in case the verdict is bad, you will not kill yourself."

"Well, Doc, that is just what I was thinking about. If I can't live, why suffer?"

"I'll see that you don't suffer too much. I'll give you all the narcotics you want."

"Okay Doc, it's a deal."

"You can't operate," said Dr. Boles. "All operations have to be approved by the Attorney General. The Warden will not approve."

"Will you assist me? Asked Dr. Bond.

"Gladly," said Dr. Boles.

"All right then. We will operate at two o'clock. Come on! We will tell the Warden."

"But you can't," said The King. "I have strict orders from the Attorney General that all major operations must be approved by his office. I will get him on the wire at once, but we can't have a reply by two o'clock."

"Read me the order!" said Dr. Bond.

The order read, "All operations except in emergencies…"

"That is enough," said Bond. "All operations are emergencies. If they do not need to be performed at once, they do not need to be performed at all. This man should have been operated on six months ago. The fact that he was punished instead of being treated makes the case plain murder. I am going to operate at two o'clock. If I had to, I would do it on a scow out in the bay. And it must be understood right now; if I am to be Doctor, I'll be Doctor."

"All right Doctor! If you say the situation is that serious, you are the boss!"

Burns died of generalized pyemia a year later, but Bond was Doctor.

Men on punishment could be kept in the hole and chained to the door in the day time, but they had to be taken out and given warm beds at night. All windows had to be kept open from nine-thirty p.m. until six a.m. regardless of the weather. If a man was cold, he had to be given more blankets.

There were a number of cases of active tuberculosis in the prison. Bond insisted that a number of small wooden cabins be built down on the beach, outside of the wire and each man be given an individual cabin. He was given special food, and his clothing was washed separately from the other clothes and vigorously boiled.

"But these men may escape!" argued The King.

"They can't get far! They are too sick! I would rather have them escape than have them endangering the health of the other men."

Men had to be assigned to clean up the cell house and to do nothing else, for the cell house had to be kept clean.

YES!! Bond was the Doctor!

The Laundry

The laundry was really something. The equipment of the wash room consisted of a furnace in the top of which were set two, twenty-gallon, cast-iron pots for boiling clothes and heating water, a big wooden trough, like a horse trough, in which water could be heated by a jet of live steam, and half a dozen big tubs made from cut-off syrup barrels. All the clothing had to be washed by hand in these big tubs. There was not even a wringer.

In the other room, which served as the office, there were a number of large shelves and a counter in front of them where the clothes could be folded and sorted in piles according to number before putting them on the shelves. There was a big ironing table about four or five feet wide and seven feet long, a stove for heating the irons, and a small steam dryer for starched goods and special items.

The convicts' clothes were dried in two dry houses, indicated on Diagram No. 1. The Writer does not remember whether those dryers were heated by steam or by wood-burning stoves.

The Writer's duty as head laundryman was to supervise the work of the laundry and see that it was done, and done right. He worked under the direct orders of The King, took no orders from anyone else, and he had five men working under him who took orders only from him. There were four in the washroom and one assistant who folded convicts' clothes. The Writer was responsible for getting the work out, and he could get rid of any man, or get new or additional help simply by asking The King.

Only he and an Aleute boy about his age, name Georgie Pesterkoff, who was serving a life sentence for a murder committed when he was sixteen, were trusties, and Georgie ran the washroom. As a practical matter, the only persons to whom the Writer gave orders were Georgie and his own assistants, unless Georgie complained that his assistants were not doing the work right. When that happened, the Writer called the offender in and said, "Now this job beats a shovel. If you want to keep it, you must do your end of the work. If you don't I'll have to get someone else, for the work must be done."

The system worked very well, and the Writer had to remove only one man in the almost two years he ran the laundry, which is pretty good considering that the washing was hard and disagreeable work.

In addition, the Writer had to iron by hand all white goods and starched goods, fold and deliver towels to all the departments every day, check all clothing into and out of the laundry, mark all unmarked clothing sent to the laundry, and make up all the bundles for both inmates and civilians, as well as a number of other duties. One of those other duties included inspecting all fire extinguishers in the prison and seeing that they were in good order at all times and recharged at least once a year.

The gangs worked five and one half days per week – forty-four and a half hours. On Saturday afternoon, they bathed and shaved.

They shaved themselves with straight razors in the cell house. Razors were handed out to men who were allowed to have their own, but after shaving they had to turn them back in to Mr. Meyers. If a man had no razor, there were about a dozen prison-owned razors that could be borrowed. The Writer often wondered what some of the officials of the present day would think of issuing straight razors to a hundred men all running around the cell house and going wherever they pleased, for all cells were open on Saturday afternoon.

Bathing was done in the washroom of the laundry, for that was the only place in the institution that could heat enough water. The men bathed in the same wooden tubs used for washing clothes, two men to a tub.

With the furnace and the steam jet going full blast to heat the water, and the hot water being dipped out into the tubs in buckets, the room was so full of steam that it was impossible for the guard who brought the men out to see what was going on in those tubs, and more than one couple used that opportunity to do more than wash each other's backs.

In lieu of these hot baths in the Laundry, men who wished to were allowed to go swim in the Sound for two hours. This salt water bathing was the nearest thing to recreation that these men enjoyed but because of the temperature of the water, not more than twenty percent of the population would take advantage of it. Yet, any time there were as many as ten, Mr. Meyers would let them go. One gun guard was sent down the beach about three hundred yards in each direction, and one guard accompanied the men. They were permitted to swim out a quarter of a mile, but as the Channel was five miles wide at this point, there was no danger of escape. Had any man refused to come back when told, it would have been an easy matter to have picked him up with a boat.

The Big Hit

Someone once remarked that the greatest general gives more thought to a blistered toe or a mosquito under his netting than to the fate of a battalion, or words to that effect.

And it just happened that the mosquito under The King's netting was a sore neck.

The first Sunday that the Writer was in charge of the Laundry, The King came out there.

"Stroud! I wish you would take a look at this shirt and see if you can figure out any way to keep it from cutting my head off. I have a short neck. I have to dress according to the accepted style, and wear starched shirts and collars, but even though I buy the lowest collars made, they still cut my head off. See how the shirt bulges up beneath my chin!"

"Yes! I did that shirt as Atwell told me you wanted them done, but I see no reason why they should be done that way." It was a pleated bosom shirt and was starched as hard as armor plate and polished until it shone like glass, in the same manner as the hard-boiled shirts of a previous decade, which many men still wore. "I really do not think these shirts were ever intended to be starched like that. I will do a little experimenting and see what I can work out. So long as the shirt is smooth and will hold its shape, that is all you want, isn't it? You would have no objection to it also being soft?"

"No! That is what I want! Can you do them so they are both smooth and soft?"

"Sure! I can starch them so they are as soft as pocked handkerchiefs, but they will have a dull finish. See how you like those you get next week."

The next Sunday, The King was all smiles when he came to the Laundry.

"You smoke, Stroud?"

"Yes, Sir!"

"My compliments." He handed the Writer two twenty-five cent La Vera cigars, the kind he smoked. "This shirt is perfect. It is the first starched shirt I've ever had on that did not cut my head off, and I like this dull finish. It seems to have more distinction than a high gloss. I want you to do all starched work like this in the future."

"You mean for the guards, too? Some of them might not like it."

"Yes they will! Anyway, they will look better and feel better, and if anyone complains, send him to me. If it will make you more work, I'll give you another man to help you out on something else. I would like to know how you do it. Atwell never could, and I have tried sending my shirts to Tacoma, with no better results."

"I have always been a curious person. When I was a kid, girls used to wear starched drawers and starched petticoats. I used to watch my mother starch them for my sisters. She always diluted the starch about one to ten with water. I simply took a bunch of handkerchiefs and tried out different dilutions until I found the thinnest one that would make the cloth hold its shape."

"That was wonderful. Can you do the same thing with collars? Starch them with that dull finish, so they hold their shape but are not really hard as glass."

"Sure! It will be easier than the other way."

It was not until ten years later that soft-starched, dull finished shirts and collars became the rage.

This laundry work was hard work, but it was interesting. It was nice to be boss and not have a guard looking down the back of one's neck all the time. The Writer went to work directly after breakfast, and he did not return to his cell until six or seven o'clock in the evening. It was seven days per week of about ninety-one hours, which was more than twice as much time as was put in by the men on the gangs – and for most of that time the Writer was kept on the jump.

But there were advantages. He could bathe in that horse-trough every evening before going to the cell. He could put on clean clothes every day. He was free to organize his work as he pleased. He ate in the kitchen, and he not only ate all he wanted, but he also scored a couple of glasses of pure cream and pieces of pie each morning – one in the kitchen and the other in the hospital.

Jackson! The fellow with cancer of the stomach was allowed to order anything that he thought he could eat, and each morning he would have a piece of pie, a glass of cream and several morphine tablets for the Writer. The latter were important. For the young man in prison, an occasional emotional release, obtained either from drink, drug, or sexual aberration is absolutely essential to continued sanity. In those days, it was opium or morphine; today, it is barbiturates. But it has to be something. That does not mean that those men became addicts, though probably a few did, but they went on a jag occasionally, which relieved their emotional tensions.

There were many other little treats and advantages connected with the job too, and one of the best was derived from pressing the guard's clothes.

There was a rule posted in the laundry which read:

> The Laundryman will do no special work for any guard or official of this institution without a written order from the Warden.
>
> O.P. Halligan, Warden

This rule was not intended to stop the Writer from pressing any man's clothes if he wanted to, but he did not have to do it unless he wanted to. So if any guard or official wanted his clothes cleaned or pressed, he had to pay for it by leaving something in the pocket to make it worthwhile.

At the time the Writer took charge of the Laundry, this little graft was divided between Frank Hiasheda and Atwell, and Atwell's customers fell to the Writer.

It was generally agreed that twenty-five cents was a fair price for the work, and many guards just left a quarter in the pocket. Others left candy, Bull Durham cigarettes, cigarette papers, chewing gum, or other items of that kind. The Doctor and Mr. Meyers always left cigarette papers, but they always sent their clothes to Frank. The King always left two of his twenty-five cent cigars in the pocket of any suit he sent to be pressed, and he always sent his clothes to the Writer. Some guards would come and ask the Writer what he wanted from town, and there were other cheap skates who would try to get their clothes pressed for nothing.

As soon as the Writer took over, he made a deal with the Jap that each would always tell the other what he got from any particular person and neither would steal the other's customers. It was also agreed that neither would press clothes for any man who failed to come across with either a quarter or that amount of desirable merchandise, and neither would press the clothes of any man that the other had turned down.

Patterson

Shortly after the Writer became Laundryman, Mr. Meyers was offered a job at the State Hospital that would pay him more than he was making at the Island, and since this would permit him to be with his wife, he jumped at it.

A young man named Woodrough took his place for a couple of months, but he could not make the grade, and The King made Guard Patterson Acting Deputy Warden until he could find a good man for the job. This Patterson was one of the cheap skates. He is the same man who is mentioned in *The Case of McCarthy*.

Now it happened that Frank had pressed Patterson's clothing a time or two and had received nothing, but he had not told the Writer about it. So when Patterson sent a suit to the Laundry to be pressed, the Writer pressed it, and he did a good job. When he took the suit back, he said, "How do you like this job Mr. Patterson?"

Patterson examined the suit critically. Then he smiled. "You certainly know your business! I like the way you do my shirts, too. I've never seen anyone else do shirts that way, but it makes them look better, and they are so comfortable. I have been intending to mention that before."

"Thank you, Mr. Patterson! Are you going to town?"

"Why yes. Why?"

"Buy four bits worth of wheat straw papers and accidentally on purpose forget and leave them in your pocket the next time you send your suit to the Laundry, and your clothes will always look nice."

"Yes, I will!" said Patterson with a sarcastic sneer.

"You will, all right, if you want your clothes pressed. If you don't, you need not send them to me, for it won't do any good."

"You'll press them if I tell you to!"

"I wonder!" The Writer turned and left the office.

He went to the tailor shop and told Frank what had happened.

About two weeks later Patterson again sent his suit out to the Laundry.

The orderly said, "Mr. Patterson says that he has to have this suit pressed by three o'clock as he is going to town.

The Writer took the suit and searched the pockets. They were all empty. "Take this suit back to Mr. Patterson and tell him that I said, 'There's a man in hell who wants ice water.' I am too busy to press it; I am always going to be too busy to do anything for him. The sooner he gets that through his head, the better."

About an hour later Frank came to the Laundry with Patterson's suit.

"What do I do?"

"Take it back to him. No! Just a minute. We had just as well teach these cheap skates something."

The Writer filled a glass with water and then added a few drops of sulphuric acid. He sponged the seat of the pants and the elbows of the coat lightly with the fluid.

"Now, take it back to him, Frank and tell him that you can't press it. The only way you can press anything is with my irons, and the order says that you can use them only at such times as I am not using the irons or table. Now when his suits come out to be pressed, I am always going to be using the irons or table, even if I have to sleep on it. The order doesn't say anything about what I am using it for."

In a few minutes Frank was back. "I told him Stroud say, 'no press, no can do.' I got no irons. Only Stroud has irons. He say, 'no use, I can't use.' More better you talk to Stroud!"

At noon Patterson brought the suit out himself and said, "I want this suit by three o'clock. That is an order!"

"Your orders are no good! Just read those two over there on the wall! I said this morning that I was busy. I am always going to be too busy to do anything for you, or any other cheap-skate, and Frank can use my irons only when I wish to let him do so."

"You will be sorry for this."

"I wonder."

The second order referred to was one that said the tailor could use the irons only for prison work and at such times as the Laundry man was not using the irons or table.

The day happened to be Wednesday, and the Writer had organized the work of the Laundry so that there was nothing to do on Wednesday and Sunday afternoons. Those were the only free times he had, and he had no intention of using his little free time to press the clothing of any cheap skate.

After dinner, he let his fire go out. He drew the blinds on the windows and locked the front door. That was a sign that he did not wish to be disturbed, and it was generally respected by everyone, even The King. If The King had business with him, he would knock and call his name, then wait for him to open the door.

He and Georgie, the Aleute boy, shaved and bathed during the noon hour. Then they put on clean clothes, placed a couple of big pillows on the end of the table and stretched out side by side, their arms under each other's necks. For a long time they lay there talking in low tones, slowly drawing on their cigarettes, telling each other of the few happy moments in their young lives, of their dreams for the future, and then, they would be wrapped in each other's arms, kissing each other passionately.

Someone tried the locked door, but they paid it no mind. A moment later Patterson burst in upon them through the washroom door, which they had not locked.

Patterson started to berate the Writer.

"Go tell your trouble to The King. This is my afternoon off, and I am trying to take a nap. I do not want to be disturbed."

"A likely story!"

"Well, go tell it to The King and see how he likes it. He is the boss around here. I am only following his written orders."

Patterson stormed into The King's office. Adams reported the conversation to the Writer.

"He told The King that you would not press his clothes because he would not bring you cigarette papers. He told The King that he saw you and Georgie kissing each other. He demanded that you be punished and that The King give him a written order for you to press his clothes. The King just let him talk until he had told the whole story, but when he demanded that you be punished, The King snapped, 'Just a minute, Mr. Patterson. Those boys are working for me. They are under my exclusive jurisdiction. I am the one to say when they will be punished. When I want you to go around spying on them, I will give you orders to that effect. They are good boys, both of them. They work harder and longer hours than anyone else in this prison. If they have their work done and want a few hours alone, that is their privilege. I don't think they would do anything wrong, at least nothing more than a little harmless play, but if they did, so long as they had the door locked and the blinds drawn, it would be none of your business. If I ever hear of you again mentioning what you saw, I will fire you for it.'

"'As to pressing your clothes, if Stroud does not want to do it, he does not have to. If I caught you bringing him cigarette papers, I would fire you for that, too. And if I ever learned of you promising to bring him anything in order to get him to use his little spare time to do work for you and then not keeping your promise, I would fire you.'

"'He always presses my suits, but I never send them out there without carelessly forgetting to remove from the pocket some treat of equal value to what it would cost me to have them pressed in town. If you had done that, I don't think that you would have had any trouble getting better service than you could get over in Tacoma. I will not order him to press your clothes. I would not order him to press mine. Any time he tells me that he is too busy to press my clothes, I will send them to town, and it is my order that you send all of your suits to town to be cleaned and pressed hereafter.' You should have seen Patterson's face, Bob. It was almost purple, but all he could say once The King lit into him was, 'Yes Sir!'"

The odd thing was that when the tailor over in Tacoma pressed that suit, the seat of the pants and the elbows of the coat just fell out under the hot iron.

The tailor contended that the damage had been caused by sitting on some newly-varnished seat, probably in a street car.

Another odd thing is that The King had been correct in his evaluation of the boys' conduct. They probably had as strong an attachment for each other as two boys can have, and stronger attachments do not exist. Even in the presence of others, it was hard for them to keep their hands off each other. When they were alone, it was impossible. But they were both serving long sentences, and such is the power of Mrs. Grundy in a restricted environment that their lovemaking never passed beyond the stage of harmless play, though looking back upon it from the vantage point of forty-two years, the Writer now knows that it would have been better for both of them if it had. Frankly, the Writer was restrained by only one thought. He did not want The King to block his release as he had Fuzzy's, but he now knows that fear was foolish.

There was no more trouble with Patterson, who did not last long anyway. There was no trouble getting cigarette papers either, or any other little things the Writer wanted, even if he had lost his friend Johnson through a pardon. All the guards knew that he was studying chemistry. They also knew that he did better work than they could get over in town.

That street car idea might be all right, but you never could tell, and there was no use taking chances.

PART I – CHAPTER XVI

McNiel Island, Continued

Stoolpigeons

The King did not like stoolpigeons. He was smart enough to know that the sycophant and stoolpigeon[125] are men hoping to advance themselves without merit at the expense of someone else. They are usually spineless individuals, as free from character as a jellyfish. But what The King, as most men, did not realize is that both the sycophant and the stoolpigeon always bitterly hates the man he serves, and is the last man in the world to be trusted.

Halligan realized that to encourage weaknesses of character in his wards was a poor way of discharging his duty to the society he served. Yet, running a small un-walled prison with only a skeleton force of guards, he felt that he was obliged to listen to all reports brought to him and to investigate them, even though he despised the men who brought them to him. So as a sort of compensation for what he considered an unavoidable evil in his own conduct, he appended to his rules the one quoted previously,[126] but which may be profitably repeated here.

It is the duty of each and every inmate to obey these rules at all times. No inmate should concern himself about the conduct of others until he is absolutely sure that his own conduct is above reproach.

It has been previously mentioned[127] that there was no rule against talking from cell to cell, or even calling from one end of the cell house to the other, but the difficulty of understanding each other made such conversations almost impossible. Those lattice doors broke up the sound, and the soft brick of which the block was constructed absorbed sound like a sponge. So the only times when men called from cell to cell were when they had something to say and this did not disturb the men back in their cells, for they did not even hear them.

But whistling was something else. It was absolutely forbidden in all buildings, as it should be in all places where human beings are crowded together. For there is no sound more distracting or more apt to make one want to commit murder.

---

125   With extremely few exceptions, the two words are synonymous. There are very rare cases where the sycophant is not a stoolpigeon and more, where the stoolpigeon is not a sycophant, but the psychology of both are the same, and is always completely criminal.
126   Part 1 – Chapter XII
127   Part I – Chapter XII

The new cell house, Deputy Warden's Office, and dining room were completed during the summer of 1911, and the men were moved out of the old block early in September.

The new block contained sixty-six modern, open-front cells, six feet wide and eight feet deep. Each one contained a toilet, washbasin, two iron bunks that folded up against the wall, a table, and two stools.

For the first time in American prison history convicts were furnished cotton-felt mattresses and feather pillows, as well as sheets, pillow cases, and all the thick, woolen, double blankets they wanted. Also for the first time, they were provided with chambermaids.

One man was assigned to each gallery, and it was his duty to take care of the cells on that gallery. No brooms or other cleaning equipment were allowed in the individual cell. All the cell occupant did when he got up in the morning was fold his bed up against the wall. When he came in at noon his bed had been neatly made up, his cell swept and mopped, his toilet and washbasin had been cleaned and their brass work polished. There was one man who did nothing but polish brass. During good weather, all blankets were carried out and spread on the lawn for a couple of hours of air and sunshine.

These measures were taken at the orders of Dr. Bond. He did not want the dust caused by individual bed-making and floor sweeping to circulate in the cell house when the men were in it, as he believed that dust was responsible for the spread of tuberculosis; his precautions did stop that spread.

Also, during the summer of 1911, a two-story Laundry and power house was constructed down on the flat, where the slough had been filled in, but this had not been completed at the time the Writer was locked up for cutting up the Doctor's orderly.

It is a strange quirk of human nature that the Writer and most of the other men who had been in the old cell house for some time felt dissatisfied in the new cell house. All the new comforts, the greatest of which were the good beds and cleanliness, could not compensate for the loss of the feeling of privacy afforded by those old dungeon-type cells. The thick brick walls had so effectively absorbed sound that the men in each cell seemed to be in a little world of their own, where distractions from without did not enter, while the new cells were like living in a bird cage, and conversations carried on in an ordinary tone of voice could be heard from one end of the building to another.

At this time there was a large influx of men convicted under the Mann Act, of a type not previously seen in Federal Prisons, and one of these men was a Greek pimp serving seven years.

The man was a good worker and a perfect sycophant, and as with all men serving long sentences, it was not too long before The King took him off the shovel and put him on special work as a semi-trusty. This Greek was not a fool, and he had little trouble convincing The King that he would not run off, and that he wanted to be cooperative in every way possible. He obtained a good job through ability, but he soon made himself the most obnoxious stoolpigeon in the prison. He snitched on everything he heard or saw, but he was too smart to snitch on anything without supporting evidence. It was his method to ingratiate himself into the confidence of both guards and convicts, and then run to The King with things The King would have otherwise overlooked.

Both guards and convicts hated this Greek, but the guards all figured that his job under

The King made him immune from petty reports, and guards who had a chance to report him for more serious rule infractions refrained from doing so for fear that they could not make their reports stick and would be accused of trying to ride the Greek.

These guards had failed to notice one thing, and the Greek had failed to notice it, too. Halligan had not put him in gray clothes. He was still wearing stripes, which meant that The King was not yet sure of the man's character.

The one thing The King feared more than anything else was adverse publicity. He was holding a normally political job strictly on merit, without political influence of any kind. Adverse publicity might force him out at any time, and he knew it. So the worst offenses any inmate could commit were those of having stationary or a postage stamp or attempting to smuggle a letter out of the prison. Having money, opium, morphine, whiskey, cigarettes, or cigarette papers were minor offenses. Postage stamps, which might mean uncomplimentary publicity, were very serious, for there are usually men in every prison who can turn such a connection to good account, if they want to.

A few days prior to the occurrence to be described presently, the Greek had tipped off a box of contraband that had arrived at the prison.

Then a storekeeper on the Island appeared at the prison and demanded that he be paid for a box of merchandise that had been assigned to him but unloaded on the recently built prison wharf by mistake and stolen by the inmates.

The King laughed as the merchant read his bill of lading.

"Candy, tobacco, cigarette papers – harmless items his boys would naturally crave – but the smile faded as the storekeeper read: one dozen tablets, twelve boxes of envelopes, and twelve books of stamps.

He had not laughed when the Greek had brought him a tip that it was not an accident at all, but a plot to ship contraband into the prison at his expense.

The storekeeper, threatened with prosecution, had cracked. Two guards had been fired, and eight convicts had gone to the hole. And the Greek, a very arrogant person, thought that he was on top of the world. He began running around the prison with a chip on each shoulder. There were both guards and convicts who would have like to knock them off, and the Greek's head with them, with a pick handle, but were afraid to.

With the opening up of the new block and completion of the power house, bathing was shifted from the Laundry to a row of bright new showers at the back of the block, and on Saturday afternoons, all men came into the new cell house to bathe.

On this particular Saturday, men were moving around in every direction. One guard was busy opening and locking doors, for the doors were no longer left open as they had been in the old cell house, and three barbers were shaving men at the front end of the cell house. The Greek was up on the second gallery whistling in an ear-splitting manner.

The Writer, who was then in solitary confinement in Cell No. 3, cried, "Dry up! You rotten, stoolpigeon!"

Several other men took up the cry. Some booed. The Greek whistled all the louder.

The guard, a pretty good fellow named Graham, who had also come from the State Asylum, said, "Take it easy, Bob! I'll dry him up!"

"I would like to, with a foot of steel. I'd dry him up permanently!"

"I'd pipe down on that whistling if I were you," Graham said, addressing the Greek.

"To hell with you! I'll whistle all I please and you or none of these other _____ can stop me. See!"

Graham turned to his orderly, a boy name Wilkinson.

"Do they have any report books around here? I've never seen one."

"Report me, you rotten s.o.b. and see what good it does you. Me and zee keeng are like zees." The Greek held up two fingers very close together.

That night The King read Graham's very conservative report for whistling to the Greek and asked him what he had to say.

"Eet ees lie. Zey all hate me because I am good prisoner and tell you everything."

"The first duty of a good prisoner is to learn to obey the rules. If you told me that any other guard in this prison had lied on you, I might have believed you, but not Mr. Graham. He has been here for two years, and you are the first man he has ever reported. I have known him for twenty-five years, and I have never known him to do one unkind act. He has charged you merely with whistling and not stopping when he told you to, but I know that if there were not more to it than that, he would not have reported you. Your sentence is, Third grade.[128] Ten days on bread and water. Excavating gang! Examine him Doctor!"

"I find him okay," the Doctor said after the examination.

"Then put him in the hole!"

The Greek served the rest of his sentence of over six years in third grade and in the excavating gang.

The King, unlike McCloughry, sometimes listened to stoolpigeons, but it was not a popular method of winning his favor, or a very safe one.

Escape

During The King's reign there were numerous plots to escape, and several men did get away from the prison proper, but there was not one case of a man getting off the Island, and the really odd part about this was that any man who wanted to go the rough way could have done so without any great difficulty.

Before the completion of the new cell house, the armory was a little cubbyhole under the stairs that was protected by a heavy, steel-barred door that was locked with an ordinary

---

128   Third grade involved loss of all privileges for three months.

padlock that could have been broken by a single blow of a pick or hammer.

The King carried a pistol, but Mr. Meyers never carried anything, and when The King was out roaming around the prison, any two men could have gotten themselves sent in on a pretext of being sick, or any men not working under a guard could have come in themselves, over-powered Mr. Meyers, and taken the armory. Then they could have waited for The King to return, stuck him up and forced him to call in his tower guards. Or the guards could have been called by telephone and told that they were covered with rifles from the windows and ordered to leave their guns where they were and come in unarmed. Or The King could have been taken out around the prison, unarmed and his pistol used to take the Deputy Warden. Then, the guards could have been brought in one at a time by telephone.

Then, in either case, it would have been a simple matter to cut the telephone cable to the mainland, wreck two of the prison boats and take off in the third one. By calling in all the convicts and locking up all those who did not want to leave, it would have been possible to get at least a twenty-four hour start.

Even after completion of the new Deputy Warden's Office, with its concrete walls over a foot thick and armor plated doors, it was not hard for almost any man to find a pretext to be admitted to that office, and with a knife, or nothing but his hands, overpower Patterson or Mr. Mewy, the man who finally became Deputy Warden. Then they could have accessed the armory which was upstairs.

All of the convicts knew just how simple this would be, but it did not occur, even though it was discussed many times, and here is why.

You may not know it, but every convict knows that there is no case on record where men who have shot their way out of a prison, got away with it. Most of them either died or were brought back within less than a week. The single exception is the Dillinger gang, and they were all dead in less than a year.

Knowing this, no sane convict, no matter how badly he wants to escape will go the hard way unless he has reached the stage of complete hopelessness, where he no longer cares whether he lives or dies. So long as men are not hopeless, they are not dangerous. The one exception to this rule is the green kid doing a short sentence. A wild youngster serving a year and a day is more dangerous than the same boy would be if he were serving a life sentence, for the long sentence would make him think, whereas the kid serving a short sentence is apt to do anything without thinking.

The Writer has pointed out such opportunities to fellow inmates wanting to escape on many occasions and heard them exclaim with horror.

"No! I don't want any part of it!"

"I thought you wanted out!"

"I do, but when you go out that way, you are just too damn hot to live long." And that is the truth. The fact that convicts realize it, is responsible for the infrequency of violent escapes, and not the lack of opportunity. Another factor is that convicts are individualists. It is impossible to organize them on anything but the smallest scale, and even then the organization is apt to crack under pressure.

Discipline

A great many differences between the discipline at Leavenworth and that at the Island have already been pointed out, and others are discussed in detail in another place, but there was a fundamental difference that has been so far referred to only indirectly.

Leavenworth was a rather large community under the strictest possible rule of law. There were only two acts not mentioned in the rule book for which a man might be punished: sodomy and smoking cigarettes. These were acts violative of State Law, and the proof required to convict the inmate had to be such as would stand up in a court of law. The Leavenworth guard in writing his report was required to allege a violation of a specific rule, then state facts that would constitute a violation of that rule – and where such was not done, the inmate could beat the report on technical grounds.

The Island was an absolute monarchy under the rule of a just and benevolent monarch. There were a minimum number of rules, and only a few of them were enforced; yet, any guard could report any conduct that he thought inimical to the institution, and The King would decide whether or not such conduct was violative of the rules in any particular case. If he thought that it was, then the trial would be conducted more as a hearing in equity than a suit of law. The conduct was punishable or blameless not because it violated the written rule, but because of bad results flowing or apt to flow from it, rather than the illegal act per se. In circumstances where harm, actual or potential could not be shown, there was no offense. Thus, it might be an offense to do a given thing under one set of circumstances, but no offense to do the same thing under different circumstances. It might be an offense for one inmate to do a given thing and no offense for another inmate to do the same thing.

The Writer, being a chain cigarette smoker, has often thoughtlessly walked into The King's presence with a cigarette in his mouth without a word being said. Yet, if some other convict was present, The King would jump all over him and demand to know where he got the papers.

"I found them."

"Where?"

"In a pocket."

"Whose pocket?"

"I don't remember."

"I demand that you tell me at once."

The Writer would drop his eyes from The King's glaring face to his shirtfront.

"I still don't remember."

And The King would flush to his ears, turn on his heels and walk away.

It was that way with everyone to some extent. For the first six or eight months The King studied each man's character carefully, and a misstep during that period was apt to color the treatment that particular inmate received throughout his sentence. A man who got off to a bad start was apt to spend his whole sentence in the excavating gang and a lot of it in the hole, for once a man got in bad, the guards would write him up every time he turned around.

On the other hand, once a man got off on the right foot and The King became convinced that he was trying his best to get along, the worst punishment that ever followed a minor report was a reprimand.

Serious offenses were escape, attempt to escape, smuggling letters, and having stationary or stamps. The punishment was ten or more days in the hole, loss of all privileges, and loss of all *goodtime*.

Refusing to work was the next most serious offense. There were only a few cases. The men were kept in the hole until the Doctor took them out, unfit to work. Two spent the rest of their sentence in the hospital; one had only a short time to serve, and his health was not recovered at the time he went out. One died within a few months of tuberculosis, and one died of pyemia.

These deaths caused the Dr. Bond to order all men on punishment to be fed two slices of bread three times per day and to be taken out of the dungeons and given warm beds to sleep in at night. This action coincided with the visit of the woman lecturer.

The next most serious offense was loafing on the work. This called for ten to fifteen days in the hole and loss of thirty to ninety days *goodtime*.

As a rule, fighting was not a serious offense if the two men were evenly matched, and either Halligan or Meyers were present (no guard would assume authority in the presence of either). They would be permitted to fight until one of them showed a definite advantage, and then they would be ordered to stop. If they stopped when commanded to do so, they would be told to go wash their faces, then come back. When they returned, they would be asked if they wanted to shake hands, and if they shook hands, that was the end of it. There was no report.

If the men failed to stop when ordered to do so, convicts known to be friendly to each man would be ordered to grab him. Then after a few minutes cooling off period, if the men were willing to shake hands, there might still be no report. But if either refused, both went to the hole for the same period.

If any inmate failed to obey a direct order to grab a man, he went to the hole for a week to ten days.

No guard was ever supposed to grab a fighting convict. Out on the gangs, the guard would order the men to cut it out, and if they failed to do so, he would throw up his hand to the nearest tower guard. The tower guard would rack his rifle bolt and order the men to cut it out. If that failed, he would drop a bullet too close to them for comfort, and that was always effective. Every convict knew that the guard's orders required him to knock down with his second shot the man who appeared to him to be the aggressor.

In all cases where men were reported for fighting, both men went to the hole. If one man walked up to another and knocked him down with his fist, and they were reported, both men went to the hole for the same length of time and received identical punishment in other respects.

The King would say, "It takes two men to make a fight. If you had not done something to him, he would not have hit you. Only a crazy man hits another person for nothing. The mere fact that I do not know why he hit you does not indicate that he did not have a good reason. You must have done something to him, and you are both guilty."

And Halligan had a lot more respect for men who would say nothing and take their punishment than for those who would try to put the blame on the other party. But even where he was thoroughly in sympathy with one man over the other, both were punished alike.

A classic case was Baldy Blake.

Shortly after the new dining room was completed, Dr. Moore, Professor of Music at the University of Puget Sound, brought a group of his advanced students to the prison to put on some entertainment for the inmates, many of whom had enjoyed nothing of that kind for many years. But there was one pimp who had been in the prison only a few months who could not enjoy the entertainment himself or let anyone else enjoy it, due to his criticism of the performances and his vile remarks about the performers.

Several prisoners around him had told him to dry up, but it had done no good. He persisted in spoiling their enjoyment of the entertainment by telling all how he would go about making three-way artists out of the girls if he met them on the outside. Every other convict near him was mad enough to murder him, but no one wanted to start trouble there.

The next day out on the gang, the loud-mouth began criticizing the performance and the performers again and repeated some of his vile remarks about the girls. Several men took it up. The loud-mouth, who happened to be thirty pounds heavier than any one of them, told them that if they did not like it, they could lump it, in much less polite language.

There was a large quiet young man on the gang known as Baldy Blake, because he was bald as an egg.

Baldy was sitting down by himself, saying nothing to anyone, as was his habit. He had been in the prison about a year at that time, and he had never been reported. He just did his work and attended strictly to his own business. He probably would have been off the gang before that time excepting for the fact that he was so self-contained that neither The King nor anyone else had been able to figure him out.

It had rained the night before, and there was a big mud puddle not far from where the loud-mouth was standing.

Baldy got up, walked over to the loud-mouth, and without a word, picked him up, carried him to the mud puddle, shoved his face down in the mud, and held it there until the pimp was nearly drowned.

Two guards and half a dozen convicts carried the whole story to The King in the hope of keeping Baldy out of the hole.

That night The King called Blake out, read the report to him, and asked him what he had to say.

"Nothing."

"You don't want to tell me about it? You know that you might have drowned him."

"That is what I intended, but I changed my mind."

"You are a strange character, Blake. I never know just how to take you."

"Don't! Just leave me alone."

"You know that I have to punish you, whether I want to or not?"

"That is all right. Make it as stiff as you want to. I'll enjoy every minute of it."

"I have the whole story from half a dozen different sources, so you won't be telling anything I don't know. But you were not involved in the argument, and I would like to know just why you took it up. Won't you tell me?"

"From the filth that was coming out of his face, I thought a little clean mud might do it some good. Those girls came over her to give us a little pleasure. The least we could do was try to act like gentlemen. If a man made such remarks about one of my sisters, I would kill him. Those girls had no brothers present, so it looked like it was up to me. If he ever opens his filthy mouth again in my presence, I will drown him just as I would any other rat."

"Ha! I see! How about twelve days in the hole, ninety days *goodtime*, and third grade."

"That will be fine, Warden."

So they both served twelve days in the hole, lost ninety days *goodtime*, and went in third grade.

When they came out of the hole, Baldy came to the cell where the Writer was in solitary confinement and told him what had occurred.

"The King sent me in here to see if you would tell me how you mixed the starch for those shirts. The fellow he has on that job now is doing them so they cut your head off, and he is going to give me that job."

"Gee! That is swell, Baldy! You do it this way...... Now about those screws' clothes. You do a good job the first time and when you deliver the clothes you say...... And remember, I need some cigarette papers."

"Oh, I almost forgot! Here is a book that was on The King's desk. I don't use them, but I stuck them in my pocket. I think he may have intended for me to give them to you."

That was The King. He had to punish Blake, but he found a way of making it up to him by putting him on the best job in the prison, and he did not forget that the Writer smoked cigarettes. Of course, Baldy's *goodtime* was restored for subsequent good conduct, which brings us to another of The King's habits.

Figuring Time

Most prisoners figure and refigure their *goodtime* allowance and the day of their discharge, using every conceivable method of calculation in order to convince themselves that the official figures are wrong, and then they run to the officials, demanding that their discharge date be corrected. Now when The King figured a man's time, he always made an error of two days in the inmate's favor, but any time the inmate asked to have his time recalculated, The King would do it for him, and he would take those two days away.

His handling of lost *goodtime* was on a similar basis.

He had a little black book which he carried on his person at all times. In that book there was a page or more for each man, on which he kept his private record of each prisoner and his conduct, and any promises he had made the prisoner, as well as a great many other things. Whenever he took *goodtime* from a man, he noted it in the little black book. He could transfer that item to the official record whenever he pleased, but so long as it was not transferred to the official record, the inmate never knew for sure whether or not The King was going to really take it. The King would never tell him, and it was not safe to ask, for The King might say, "Ha, let me see! I did take twenty-five days from you, didn't I? I'd forgotten all about it. I will have the notation made on your official record at once." Then that man would serve his twenty-five days. The smart man, who had made a good record after losing his *goodtime*, never said anything about it, but he never knew for sure just when he was going out, either. The suspense was part of his punishment.

Food

It is odd how time changes a man's point of view. Back at the Island under Halligan, food was the most important subject in every man's mind, yet, the Writer almost forgot to mention it except in passing.

The food was good. It was always of the very best grade. It was all cooked on a range, and it had to be well cooked, for The King sampled every item from every meal, and any complaints about the quality of the food were always taken seriously.

The diet was well balanced, and with the exception of pastries, which they just did not have, it was much more liberal than the diets existing in most Federal Prisons today. For instance, in most Federal Prisons today meat is rationed as strictly as it was back in the old days under The King, and when they serve frankfurters, the ration is two. Under The King, the ration was four or five, depending on the size. The King always rationed meat by weight and allowed one half pound to the man.

What is more, it was strictly a working man's diet, with a good substantial meal for breakfast, and none of this fancy breakfast food and dried fruit. On Monday morning the breakfast consisted of baked beans, and the ration was what the waiter could pick up in a pint dipper, approximately one quart. There was one pint of syrup for each six men, bread, black coffee without sugar or milk, and a side dish containing about two ounces of oatmeal mush, about two ounces of milk and one teaspoonful of sugar. That little side dish of oatmeal milk and sugar was served every work day morning, and was as much a part of the breakfast as the black coffee, syrup and bread.

Tuesday morning was beef steak. It was fried round steak, cut a little over a half inch thick, and cooked on a hot range, so that it was always a little rare inside. Served with it were potatoes and gravy in addition to the syrup, oatmeal, bread, and black coffee. The ration of steak was a piece not quite as large as a man's two hands placed side by side, a full half pound.

Wednesday, the main dish was red beans.

Thursday it was pork sausage, potatoes and gravy.

Friday was frankfurters.

Saturday was boiled navy beans.

Sunday's menu was four hotcakes, syrup and butter. That was the only butter served, but it was real butter, not oleo.

The Writer cannot remember all the noon meals.

At the time the Writer went to the Island, the Sunday dinner was always roast beef, brown gravy, and mashed potatoes. It was the poorest noon meal of the week since the meat was always overcooked. At the suggestion of the inmates it was later changed to fried halibut steaks. These were cut three-quarters of an inch thick, and the ration was one large cut or two smaller ones off a medium sized fish. With halibut there was cream gravy, mashed potatoes and lemon.

Tuesday and Thursday was beef stew, about a quart to the man, and it was good stew.

Wednesday was halibut again.

Friday was clam chowder.

The Writer has forgotten what was served for dinner on Monday and Saturday.

There was always a pint of good soup with the noon meal, and as many men did not eat their soup, a man who did not care for the main dish could always make a fair meal of soup and bread.

The main dishes for the evening meals, which were always the poorest meals of the day, were rice and curry, fried liver, boiled potatoes and gravy, macaroni and cheese, hash, creamed codfish, fried parsnips, and cold lunch meats, consisting of corn beef or headcheese, in the order named.

On each weekday evening there were always two side dishes of cooked vegetables: corn, green beans, boiled cabbage, lima beans, fried carrots, boiled cauliflower, boiled turnips, and some kind of cooked greens. The evening meal always included either stewed dried fruit or fresh fruit from the prison farm. On Sunday evening, in addition to lunch meat, there were two buns and two apples, and the men were permitted to carry all these items away from the table if they wished.

During the growing season, there was lettuce, radishes, fresh fruit and berries almost daily from April to October, and in some seasons the crop was so large that the inmates could not eat it all. Each of the five big cherry trees indicated on the drawing[129] yielded enough cherries to give every man in the prison two quarts, and the berry crops were equally large. On one occasion after the Writer was in the Laundry, he heard that some of the berries were rotting on the vines. He went to The King and said, "Why don't you have those berries picked and served? There is no sense in letting them go to waste."

---

129   Diagram No. 1, Part I – Chapter XI

"Sugar! We have already served so many berries that I've run over my sugar budget."

"Serve them without sugar!"

"Think the boys would eat them that way?"

"I know I would. I never put sugar on any berry right off the vine, and I've always eaten all I could get. I like them better off the vine than any other way."

"We might try it, if there are no complaints."

"There will be no complaints; I will see to that."

"How?"

"I'll ask them which they like best; fresh berries without sugar or stewed prunes without sugar." That year they had berries daily, often twice a day all the way up until November.

But as good and liberal as this diet was, these men were doing hard work and breathing lots of fresh, cool sea air, and they had appetites out of this world. They always left the table hungry. Practically all of them lost weight the first month, but at the end of six months, most men had gained in weight, even though they were always famished.

There was some tuberculosis, mostly among the Indians, but on the whole, those men and boys were so healthy it hurt.

The King's Favorite Joke

As hard as The King was, any man who did not feel like getting up could lie in bed in the morning, report sick when the Deputy counted, and his breakfast would be brought to his cell. He could always be excused from work for a half day or a day, if he did not do it too often. At nine or ten o'clock, he could get up and dress, have Mr. Meyers let him out of his cell, and he could loaf around the cell house until noon, or for the rest of the day.

The boys, for whom the work was really too hard, did this more often than the older men, and so long as they did not abuse it, The King did not mind too much. But he would often come to the window, call one or two of them over there and ask them if they felt able to do a little light work.

The first boy would usually be too sick. The King would smile and say, "That is too bad. I wanted a couple of you to pick cherries."

The boy would make the most rapid recovery on record. Sometimes The King would take him, and sometimes he would say, "No! I'm afraid you are too sick. You might fall out of the tree. I'll get someone else."

When he took the selected boy or boys out to the tree, he would scowl and say, "Now, don't you dare let me catch you eating any!"

Of course, telling any boy not to eat cherries was like telling a fish not to swim.

The boy knew that he was expected to pick enough cherries to feed the prison that night for supper, and he usually would, but if by two o'clock, it looked like he was not going to have enough, The King would send someone to help him.

That evening just before five o'clock, when the boy turned in his cherries to The King, his abdomen would be pooched out until he looked as if he were pregnant. The King would glare at the boy and say, "How many did you eat?"

"Oh, not many, Sir!"

"Let me see your tongue!"

"Ha! Well, I guess you didn't do too bad." The boy would relax a little, and then The King would say, "I hope you don't have cramps."

The next day some other boy would get the cherry-picking job, and the first one might worry because he thought he had gotten himself in bad with The King. Actually, The King passed the job around to give as many boys as possible a chance at it, and each night he would laugh as he told Mr. Meyers how the boy's face looked when he was ordered to stick out his tongue.

Vanity

The King was a vain man.

The ancient Hebrews considered vanity to be a deadly sin. This may have been due to generations spent in slavery, when they had little of which to be vain, and when they suffered because of the vanity of their masters. The Writer thinks that the suppression of vanity has been the greatest curse of the Jewish people. No people throughout the ages has, according to their numbers, contributed more to the human race, either in knowledge, service, or in plain humanity; yet, no people has been more severely persecuted, and the cause of this must lie in the Jew himself, since he has contributed to the betterment of every country that has given him asylum; yet, he has been persecuted to some extent in all of them.

Now, there are good and bad in all groups, but the Jew's misfortune has been that the good in his group have failed to tell the world how good they are or to boast of their accomplishments, while the bad elements have been advertised by others. Consequently, the Jew has come to be judged solely upon the faults of the worst members of his group rather than upon the virtues of the best.

The Irish have never been cursed with the fault of modesty, however, and have always been judged for their virtues, while their faults have been condensed or overlooked.

Actually, vanity is one of the most pleasing, important, and human traits, not only of man, but also of all animal life. We love the rooster for his crow, his strut and his well- preened feathers. But it is vanity that makes the rooster crow, the canary sing, and the peacock strut his stuff. It makes men and women go to untold trouble and expense to make themselves pleasing in appearance and attractive to others. The person who does not love his or her own face in the mirror is not apt to be a very lovely person. But vanity is a lot more than that.

It is vanity that makes the explorer sail the uncharted seas or climb the highest mountain.

It is vanity that makes the dreamer dream the impossible and then go out and make his dream come true, or die trying, simply because his vanity will not permit him to admit defeat.

Yes, The King was a vain man. Otherwise, he would have been far less human and much less worthy of his place in these pages. Being an honest man, he had no false modesty[130] about telling the world about it.

At the Island the men enjoyed their two hours of canned music every other Sunday afternoon. Prior to the completion of the new cell house, the machine was set up in Mr. Meyers' office, the horn facing the window opening into the cell house.

The convicts sat on the stairs and galleries and on the long benches at the tables on that side of the cell house to listen.

The King always dressed in his Sunday best with a white flower in the buttonhole of the left lapel of his well-tailored coat, placed the first cylinder on the old Edison machine, and it was always the same one, a popular song of that day; the The King's favorite.

As the first bars of music echoed through the corridors of the old dungeon-type cell house, all the convicts groaned. But The King expanded his chest and his smooth face wore a broad and satisfied grin as the singer's voice came scratchily from the big horn. And maybe he had a right to grin.

Even though they groaned, many of the convicts grinned too.

> "H-A, double R-I-G-A-N spells Harrigan.
> Proud of all the Irish blood that's in me.
> Divil the man kin say a word ag'in me.
> H-A double R-I-G-A-N-U-C.
> As a name that a shame never has been connected with.
> Harrigan! That's me!"

All of the convicts swore that The King was singing it as H-A- double L-I, as they watched his lips move with the music, and more than likely he was, but none of the convicts hated him for that. It was one of the things they like to laugh over because it told them that he too was of common clay, which made him a great Warden, stern and severe as he was.

On one occasion the Writer heard Deacon Marsh, an ex-member of the Soapy Smith gang, angrily exclaim, "You are the sixth Warden I have stood before, and you know less than any of them!"

But the Deacon was wrong, for The King knew enough to listen to him and to follow his suggestions when they were sound.

****

---

130   The Writer knows of only one other kind, and that is *pathological.*

This concludes our discussion of the early history of Federal Prisons. No attempt will be made to discuss the early history of Atlanta, which must have been very similar to that of Leavenworth, with differences due to geography and other physical factors.

The Writer has talked to men who were there during the building of the wall and the first cell houses, and conditions were harder, if anything, than at Leavenworth. The food was poorer, and there seems to have been much more brutality than at Leavenworth. This was due to the fact that most of the guards at the Southern institution were crackers drawn from the Southern prisons, to whom the average meal at Leavenworth would have seemed like a Christmas dinner.

These men had been used to brutality on the State farms and chain gangs, and they knew no other way. They were in all respects inferior to the soldier guards at Leavenworth.

There were three respects in which the men at Atlanta were better treated than those at Leavenworth. Atlanta never had the silent system. Due to the blazing Southern Sun, those big cell houses were like bake ovens during the late afternoon and early evening. So from the very first, the inmates of Atlanta were allowed to stay out on the yard after supper until sundown. And they were allowed to have stringed musical instruments, which they were permitted to play on the yard. That yard was much larger than the one at Leavenworth, which was another advantage.

PART II – The Band Wagon will deal with the development of the Prison Reform Movement and its influence upon the lot of Federal Prison inmates.

Diagram-1

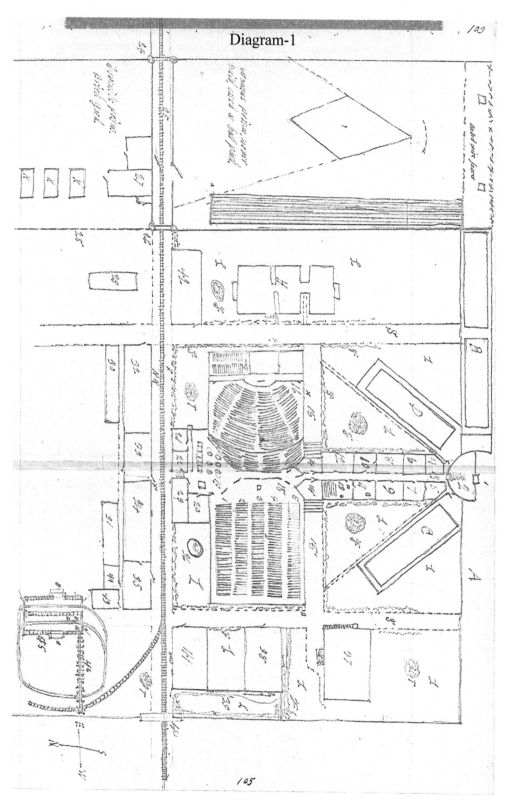

Diagram-2

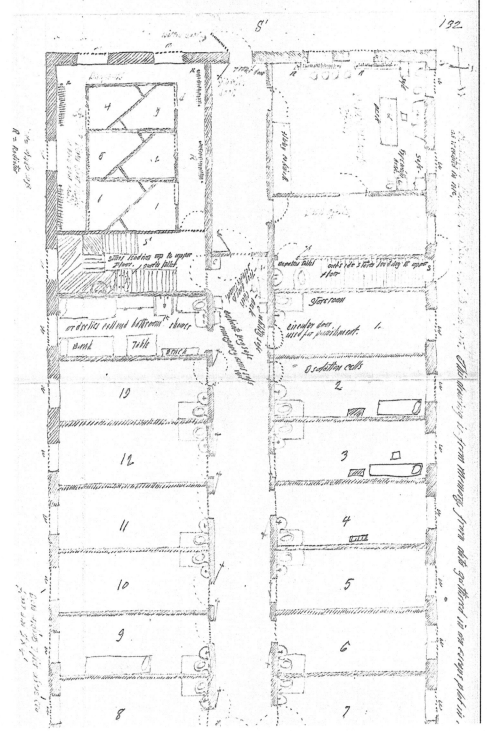

Diagram-3

170

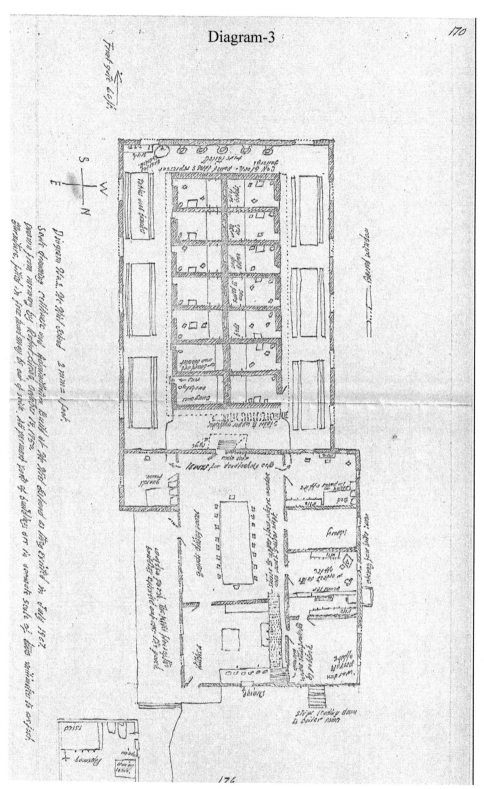

Diagram-4

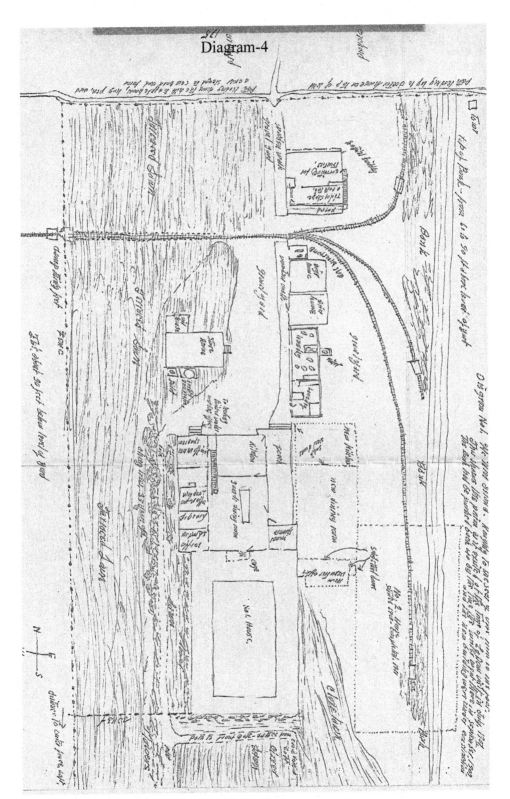

~ 285 ~

CPSIA information can be obtained
at www.ICGtesting.com
Printed in the USA
BVOW06s0217190517

484598BV00016B/119/P